The Lost Café Schindler

THE LOST CAFÉ SCHINDLER

One Family, Two Wars
and the Search for Truth

Meriel Schindler

HODDER &
STOUGHTON

First published in Great Britain in 2021 by Hodder & Stoughton
An Hachette UK company

1

A CIP catalogue record for this title is available from the British Library

Hardback ISBN 9781529332056
Trade Paperback ISBN 9781529332070
eBook ISBN 9781529332063

Typeset in Sabon MT by Hewer Text UK Ltd, Edinburgh
Printed and bound in Great Britain by Clays Ltd, Elcograf S.p.A.

Hodder & Stoughton policy is to use papers that are natural, renewable
and recyclable products and made from wood grown in sustainable
forests. The logging and manufacturing processes are expected to
conform to the environmental regulations of the country of origin.

Hodder & Stoughton Ltd
Carmelite House
50 Victoria Embankment
London EC4Y 0DZ

www.hodder.co.uk

To Jeremy Taylor and our three children, Sepha, Georgia and Zac; and

to the lost and unremembered of two world wars

Contents

Prologue

Growing Up with Kurt

Hampshire, England, Christmas 2016

I arrive at the small shabby cottage where my father lives. The twilight has drained the colour from the small garden, though I am glad not to be able to see it properly. Once beautifully tended by my mother Mary, it has become overgrown since her death eleven months earlier.

My father, Kurt Schindler, sits in near darkness, shuffling through papers on his lap. He is scribbling on various sheets – loopy, indecipherable scrawls. I turn on the lamp, but it sheds little light on what he is doing. His behaviour and character are obsessive; this scene an echo of so many others over the years when, in a less demented state, he showed me documents and sought my approval on this or that matter. He wanted discussion, but not dissent.

I stay little more than an hour. I cannot wait to get away; it is too painful. It is also the last time I see him.

I only remember Kurt holding down a job once, briefly in the early 1970s. He hated being told what to do, and so he preferred to work for himself. He set up and ran multiple commodity trading companies, importing nuts, herbs, vitamin C supplements, jam and alcohol, and then reselling them, often at a loss. He had scant regard for the basics of accounting or regular commerce. Frequently, he would fail to pay his suppliers, instead using whatever he earned from the resale to fend off – or pursue – litigation against those he believed had wronged him.

When Kurt's companies collapsed, as they inevitably did, engulfed in debt and litigation, he sought the help of lawyers and even psychiatrists to get himself out of the financial and legal mess in which he found himself. Like a compulsive gambler, he always promised never to trade again, but invariably he did, claiming he had no choice.

In one unusually perceptive moment, he admitted that he liked 'living on the edge'. For him, the fact that his wife and children had to live there with him was simply how it was. As a father, Kurt failed to provide even the most basic stability, and so we, his family, lurched between extremes. At times, we lived in expensive houses, rode in BMWs, attended upmarket private schools and stayed in fancy hotels; at others, we lived on our wits, dodging debt collectors, facing eviction, and in due course fleeing abroad. Often, those extremes coexisted. As a child, it was both exhilarating and bewildering.

In the early 1970s, my younger sister Sophie and I were often left alone for days at a time in our mews house in Kensington, while our parents drove around London visiting lawyers. We grew to fear the visits of the bailiff. I distinctly remember, when I was about ten, hiding in the house as someone banged away on our front door. We had strict instructions not to open it when we were alone, so Sophie and I lay quietly on the wooden floor upstairs, trying not to breathe too loudly.

I inched forward to the top of the spiral staircase and leaned my head over the edge of the first step so that I could see through the open tread of the steps down to the front door below. The metal flap on the letter box rattled impatiently. I held my breath. And then, in a moment of acute embarrassment, my eyes met another's eyes peering through. The figure outside was squatting down. He seemed as shocked to see a young girl's face hanging upside down above him as I was to see his, and he left hurriedly. On this occasion, he had failed in his mission to serve legal documents on my father. Bailiff o – Schindlers 1. Another delay in some never-ending case that I never fully grasped.

Then my father's luck ran out. It happened on the morning of 28 February 1973, when he was dropping us off at our Kensington primary school. I remember the moment as two plainclothes police officers stepped forward and asked Kurt to come with them. Sophie and I were hurried into school as he was led away, under arrest.

My godmother put up money for his bail, and Kurt was released shortly afterwards. Our lives were then defined by his predicament. When the fraud officers visited to search the house, I was ill in bed with flu. They insisted on looking under my dark red satin quilt to check if he had hidden any papers there. He had not, for planning of any sort was not his strong point. Instead, in the commotion, I bit on the thermometer I had in my mouth, and was struck by the beauty of the tiny silver beads of mercury as they chased each other down the seams of the quilt.

At school, I remained a quiet, unobtrusive child, albeit one slightly prone to crying. A concerned French teacher once asked if everything was all right at home. I assured her it was – and made sure never to cry again at school. Shame prevented me from confiding in her. I trusted no one.

Amongst Kurt's papers, as I later discovered, was his 1975 Bill of Indictment, which laid bare how he had used multiple companies to purchase commodities. The prosecutor commented that no supplier's asking price appeared too high for Kurt, but that the goods were invariably acquired on credit. The prosecutor's implication was clear: Kurt never *intended* to pay the suppliers. However, I don't believe that was the case. I think he just never got around to paying them, because some other crisis intervened, and the proceeds he made from sales were set against whichever was the most pressing debt. His fraud was not premeditated. It was a by-product of the chaos of his mind and possibly his history.

When my father's creditors were asked by the police why they had agreed to supply him with such large shipments of goods on credit, they explained that he had inspired complete confidence through a combination of the sheer size of the orders and his detailed grasp of the international commodity markets. It rang true. I remember him spending hours on the telephone, often sitting on the edge of my parents' double bed as he cajoled suppliers. He was handsome, charming and utterly persuasive.

The indictment recorded the fact that much of Kurt's business was also done by telex. I recall the telex machine well. As a small child, I used to sit in the dark grey metallic space underneath it, imagining that it was the opening of a tunnel to a different, magical world, where I could roam freely, away from the pressures at home. And I listened to it spew out long rolls of printed paper. It became my special job to destroy the punched telex tape by tearing it into tiny pieces, and I took my role as shredder very seriously. Kurt was always keen on preserving his confidentiality. Indeed, he assumed the house had been bugged by the Fraud Squad and would shush us in dramatic tones if we ever asked questions about what was happening.

After the arrest, Kurt spent two years delaying his trial through a combination of medical certificates and rapid switches of his legal team. It was an impressive performance in procrastination. Incredibly, during this time and right under the noses of the police, he began trading again. He incurred further large debts by importing 10,800 gallons of French and Spanish wine and, of course, failing to pay the supplier.

Inevitably, Kurt ran out of road. In July 1976, London's hottest summer in 350 years, he finally stood trial for fraud at the Old Bailey, where he was found guilty and sentenced to a five-year prison term for fraudulent trading in the sum of £370,000. The prosecution told the judge that Kurt had not paid any tax or national insurance since arriving in England as a teenager. The judge was clearly horrified and commented: 'What the heaven is he doing here without putting a stamp on a card or paying a penny in tax?'

One newspaper report gave the impression – mistakenly – that Kurt had come to London especially to commit fraud, taking the opportunity to make a weak joke about 'Schindler' rhyming with 'swindler'. The judge made a criminal bankruptcy order against Kurt and disqualified him from being a director for five years.

A very different world awaited my 51-year-old father as he was taken down from the dock at the Old Bailey. As for his family, we swapped the Kensington mews house, from which we had been evicted, for several months in a squat in Ealing, courtesy of my older sister Caroline. I remember the brown-baked parks and the smell of heat radiating off the tarmac as we packed a borrowed van and drove to the small, terraced house that Caroline and her friends had commandeered.

There, they led a gentle communal and artistic life. They seemed not to mind in the slightest that a single mother with two children had pitched up, with their furniture, and moved into an upstairs room. They were kind and fed us when we had no money whatsoever. I had recently started at my new secondary school, Godolphin and Latymer, but I never breathed a word about my unusual home set-up to any of my classmates. My mother was relieved that Godolphin was not a fee-paying school at the time. Two years after I joined, though, it became a private school.

After several months, we were back in Kensington, but now in a two-bedroom council house. To me, it was a beautiful, airy home. Unusually it was set around open-air gardens several floors up above a local council depot and offices. Above all, I remember the relief of permanence, of finally having a home from which we would not be evicted.

My mother was resourceful and had found work as a secretary in a packaging company. The American owner revelled in her perfect manners and exquisite Received Pronunciation when she answered the telephone. Thrust into single parenthood, Mary rose brilliantly to the challenge of looking after her two daughters. Her earthy sense of humour and love kept us going. But all the while she missed Kurt. For her, life was on hold until he was released from prison.

Every other week, we visited my father in prison. Sometimes we took Kurt's mother Edith with us. Edith lived in a nursing home in Harrow on the Hill. She spoke with a strong Germanic accent and her world revolved around her only son. Edith found it difficult and upsetting seeing Kurt incarcerated. Our prison visits were time-pressured and tense. Other families spent their time chatting and laughing; there was intimacy, even a hint of sexuality when warders turned a blind eye and girlfriends sat on their deprived boyfriends' knees. But Kurt always had an agenda and a long list of tasks for my mother. They were written in ballpoint pen on his arm.

We heard about prison life. Kurt's designated jobs included sewing children's hand-painted dolls and painting garden gnomes, tasks that irritated him and for which he was entirely unsuited. He told us that when he fell out with one fellow inmate, he painted the man's glasses black. The work paid him a small amount each week, which he was allowed to spend on phone calls, letters and chocolate. Occasionally, when we visited, he bought Kit Kats for me and Sophie. A rare treat.

Nothing about his prison time – served in Brixton, Wandsworth, Maidstone and finally Ford Open Prison – taught Kurt anything. I do not recall a single moment of reflection. Instead, he acquired more resentments. Unexpectedly, he emerged from Ford with a hatred of BBC Radio 4; it had been piped into the rooms of its white-collar inmates at 6 a.m. every day to wake them up. He did have a good stock of anecdotes, though, especially about the rakish, aristocratic inmates of Ford, with whom he had played Scrabble and chess. But there was no insight, no self-knowledge. My mother – kind, loving and optimistic – persisted in believing that once released from prison, Kurt would be able to provide stability for his family, despite all evidence to the contrary.

I was fourteen when Kurt was finally released. He disliked our new council house and looked down on our working-class neighbours. Perhaps in an attempt to prove he was special, better than those around him, he boasted endlessly about the famous people to whom he said we were related. He claimed kinship with the rich, the celebrated and the successful. His own failures as a man, a father and a businessman were refracted through the success and wealth of others.

Whenever he was brought face to face with his own problems, they were always someone else's fault; he was a child of the war and that accounted for everything that went wrong. He talked in dark terms of being 'pursued' by his creditors. Those that tried to help inevitably 'double-crossed' him.

On his release, Kurt made Mary give up her job and we lived on benefits. My father was restless and argued relentlessly with my mother. He hated the council house. He felt confined, trapped and angry – let down by an England that had rejected and incarcerated him. Even if he had wanted to get a job, it would not have been easy as a man in his mid-fifties with a prison record.

At night, I would lie in the top bunk in the bedroom I shared with Sophie and wrap my pillow around my ears to drown out the shouting. Things deteriorated. The doctor prescribed anti-depressants for Kurt, but they disagreed with him. He had psychotic episodes; occasionally, he was violent towards my mother. At other times, he thought he was a dog and took to barking in the hall.

After several miserable months in London, my father fled to Austria, his birthplace and the land of his early childhood. Kurt had a toehold there, in the shape of a half-built house in Trins, a remote Tyrolean village near the Austro–Italian border. He and Mary had commissioned the house when I was a toddler and they had experimented with living in Austria before the birth of my sister Sophie.

Leaving us with my mother in London, Kurt camped out there, hiring local builders to make the place habitable. I would visit in the school holidays, before returning to my real life in London. In the summer of 1979, I arrived in Trins as usual and Kurt announced, 'I have found a place for you at the best school in Innsbruck. You will start in September. Sophie will go to the local school for the moment.'

The author, aged three, walking up the road to the house in Trins

Kurt had grand plans. He wanted a fresh start back in his 'beautiful Tyrol', which for him was now less hostile than the England that had imprisoned him. 'But you will learn to ski,' he countered, when I protested at the sudden unheaval to my teenage life.

I was appalled. I loved my London school; I hadn't said good-bye to my friends. I drew up detailed plans to run away but abandoned them reluctantly, realising that a penniless fifteen-year-old who barely spoke the language would not get very far. Instead, grudgingly, I had no option but to try and adapt. Mornings began at 5.30 a.m., and proceeded with a two-hour trip to the convent school, arriving by 8 a.m. at the latest.

I would walk down the unmade lane to reach the bus stop. Sometimes it was magical, as when on a dark freezing morning I saw foxes padding across fresh snow in the moonlight. Mostly, it was so gruelling that I would fall asleep on the way home, sometimes miss my train stop and end up at the Brenner Pass about to enter Italy. I would have to beg the border guards to allow me to use their telephone and my mother would then mount a rescue operation to retrieve me.

Innsbruck felt small, provincial and very white after London. I was the only foreign student at my new school and immediately a source of interest to the other girls, some of whom had known each other since they were very young. They were kind and welcoming to this stranger. However, I spoke almost no German, and the lessons were exhausting and bewildering. A tongue that was, in London, merely one foreign language on the curriculum, was now the language of instruction for everything and my route to any social interaction outside my family. As the hurt and frustration of those first months began to fade, I became determined to learn German as fast as I could, and I discovered a patient side to my father, who now sat with me and translated my textbooks line by line so that I could do my homework.

Gradually, I acclimatised. Kurt seemed relaxed and happier. At weekends, we went walking in the mountains behind the house. Kurt would occasionally make *Kaiserschmarrn*, a classic Austrian dish of sweet pancakes, shredded into lightly caramelised fragments in the frying pan and dished out in untidy heaps, dusted with icing sugar, and served with a bowl of stewed apples or plums on the side. It is proper, filling peasant food, often doled out in mountain huts to hungry walkers and skiers. Locals sometimes eat it as a main meal in the Tyrol.

Kaiserschmarrn was the only dish I ever remember my father making. The name is colloquial and means 'Emperor's mess' or 'Emperor's nonsense'. Looking back, it was particularly apt that Kurt chose it as his signature dish. In most respects, he reverted to type in Austria, back to driving an expensive BMW, back to making deals and trading, back to the interminable litigation. There was a carapace of luxury, as we adapted to our surroundings: we skied in winter and spent summer weekends over the border, on the beach in Venice.

Whenever any of us queried whether he was trading again, Kurt waved away our concerns: 'It's fine, it's all under control.' He was as persuasive and charming as ever, and we so wanted to believe him . . . until we embarked on the now familiar pattern of irate creditors, bailiffs and looming bankruptcy.

We got to know the little blue car of the local bailiff well. Our house was out of the way, on the edge of Trins up a long, unmade road that forked, with a stream to one side. To reach the house, we had to take the right-hand fork, drive another 300 metres or so, then cross the stream via a narrow wooden bridge. However, our inquisitive bailiff often took the left-hand fork and parked his car where he could look across the field to check whether we were in. We could see him getting out and smoking his cigarette while he appraised our house.

If my sister and I were alone in the house, the sight of the bailiff's car was the cue for Operation Toaster. We had recently acquired a highly prized toaster that made very nice toasted cheese sandwiches. Once we spotted our antagonist, we would bundle the toaster into a plastic bag, climb out of the back window, and hide in the woods behind the house until the coast was clear. We kept a ladder permanently in the bathroom for the purpose. No one ever explained to us that bailiffs were not interested in toasters.

If my mother was also in the house, a different sort of subterfuge was necessary. We would creep down to the garage without turning on the lights, she would gun the car engine and, on her signal, I would fling open the garage doors and she would speed out. My job was to shut the garage doors, before hurling myself in through the passenger door as she accelerated hard over the narrow wooden bridge spanning the stream in front of our house, before executing a spectacular turn into the lane and speeding towards the junction.

As we flew down the rough road, the aim was to beat the bailiff to the fork in the lane. Laughing uproariously, we always won. My mother had been a rally driver in her twenties – with her at the wheel, the poor man did not stand a chance. Another writ foiled.

For two years that was my life, until, at age seventeen, I left home and moved to what, compared to Trins, was the big city:

Innsbruck. Ostensibly this was in order to reduce the travelling time to school when I was taking my final exams. But I never returned to live at home. It was too fraught there. My sister had to endure another three years before she, too, could make her escape.

Hampshire, England, June 2017

My sister Sophie and I, together with both our husbands, are at my father's cottage, sifting through papers and trying to work out what to keep and what to leave to the bailiffs. All over the house lie towering piles of loose documents; if there was ever a filing system, it failed long ago. The double garage – surprisingly large for the modest home it services – contains dozens and dozens of cobwebbed cardboard boxes, filled with yet more papers. Some have succumbed to damp and spilled their contents over the gritty cement floor; others have been chewed by mice, hoping for perhaps more nourishment than they found. Grappling with it all is filthy, exhausting work.

We start by trying to be systematic and by reading everything, until the scale of the task defeats us, and we give way to a hurried skimming. Kurt seemed to have kept every scrap of paper, from the most mundane – jottings of arrival times of our trains from London – to the most extraordinary. And now and then our sorting provokes cries of anguish, astonishment and anger.

We box up what we think is important and scoop up thirteen old photo albums. After two days we leave, abandoning the cottage to its fate. We never return.

Kurt Schindler had died on 6 May 2017, aged ninety-one. The death of a second parent is like arriving at the top of an escalator. Suddenly there is no one ahead of you. Everyone around me sent their condolences; I just felt numb. And angry.

Sophie and I were faced with the practical and legal tasks of sorting out probate. Yet as we looked at the piles of bills from the cottage, we knew for certain there was no point in taking out probate. The cottage was in my mother's name. Kurt's estate was insolvent, so we left it to the bank to repossess the cottage. There were so many charges on it that only a fraction of the creditors would ever be paid.

I had spent my entire adult life keeping my father at arm's length, telling him as little about myself as I could. I feared his intervention. I learned to be circumspect and vague, as I never knew what he would try to do next. He was always unpredictable, and even as Alzheimer's started to erode his considerable intellect, I could not bring myself to spend more time with him. I did not trust him.

It was not that he did not love his children. He did, to the point of obsession, as the documents from the cottage revealed. He had us both tailed by private detectives to find out what we were up to. When I was a university student in the 1980s and I set out to backpack on my own around South America, he tried to have me followed. It was not an easy task in the pre-internet era, and on this occasion it is clear that he had to give up. I left no traces. Travelling light, and communicating only through the odd *poste restante*, I proved impossible to track and slipped through the detective's fingers.

Kurt had more success with my younger sister. When she brought home a boyfriend he thought unsuitable, he commissioned a full stake-out of the boy's family and their business. The detective duly reported back. Kurt would then drop nuggets about the unsuitability of the boyfriend's family into heated conversations, without ever revealing his sources. We were horrified to find the detective's reports among his papers.

Why did he resort to this? What made him like this? My father was a man haunted by the past, by old traumas and by lost glories. When the litigation was not instigated by his creditors, he sought out the courts himself to try to right some injustice – in his eyes – done to him in earlier years. He would talk for hours about the businesses he had lost and the restitution claims he was pursuing. None of it made much sense to me, and when I asked questions, offered a view or suggested an alternative, he always responded, 'I have no choice.' As he plied me with a barrage of ever greater and more confusing detail, I became adept at staying silent and simply commenting, 'I don't see the world as you do.'

Growing up, the shadows of the past were all around us. Framed black-and-white photos of Austria were dotted around my parents' sitting room. My father slept with an old bottle of mocha liquor by his bed, a striking square-shaped thing from the 1930s. In raised glass letters a third of the way up was the brand name: *S Schindler*. I still have it. The cork has long since disintegrated. It floats uselessly in the sugary dark-brown liquid, which is now quite undrinkable; Kurt had inexpertly taped the top of the bottle to stop the contents escaping.

The letter 'S' for Schindler also adorned the china we ate off as children. I have some of that, too. Both bottle and china are artefacts of what was once a Schindler empire, Kurt assured us, whose most glittering expression had been an imposing café in Innsbruck where people danced and fell in love, and which made the finest apple strudel in all of Austria. The café had won a Gold Medal for its patisserie and Kurt had the framed certificate to prove it.

Kurt with his parents, Edith and Hugo, celebrating
25 years of the café

As well as glory days, if Kurt was to be believed, we also had illustrious connections. Oskar Schindler, who saved Jews from the Holocaust and is honoured at Yad Vashem? Oh yes, Kurt told us as children, of course, our families originated in the same part of Upper Silesia. The writer Franz Kafka? Yes, a relative too, as was Alma Schindler, the wife of Gustav Mahler and Walter Gropius. According to Kurt, the Viennese beauty Adele Bloch-Bauer, the subject of Klimt's painting *A Woman in Gold*, was also part of our extended family.

But there were more disconcerting and ambiguous tales, too, bringing my wider family into the orbit of some of the darkest figures of Europe's history. Exactly how we were related, remained elusive; Kurt was sparing with facts. He sweetened his anecdotes with sprinklings of detail and assertions that made them sound credible, but in truth, all was a mystery. There were so many stories swirling around in our childhood.

But even if he had still possessed the capacity to explain, he is no longer here. I look at the black-and-white photographs in the albums rescued from the cottage. Suddenly, I need to know who these people are. And I cannot ask him.

If I was going to understand this maddening man, and to separate fact from fiction, reliable from unreliable memories, I would have to immerse myself in his past and unravel a larger, longer family history. I would need to learn far more about Austria and what it meant to live in a turbulent country as it shifted from imperial grandeur, through the First World War and near collapse, to its absorption into the Third Reich. I would need to find out exactly what happened to the 'Schindler empire'.

I would also have to confront a cultural and racial heritage that inescapably framed my father's experience, and that of his father and grandfather, but which Kurt had always sought to bury. 'Never tell anyone you are Jewish,' he warned us as children.

My search began, though, not in Austria, but in Bohemia.

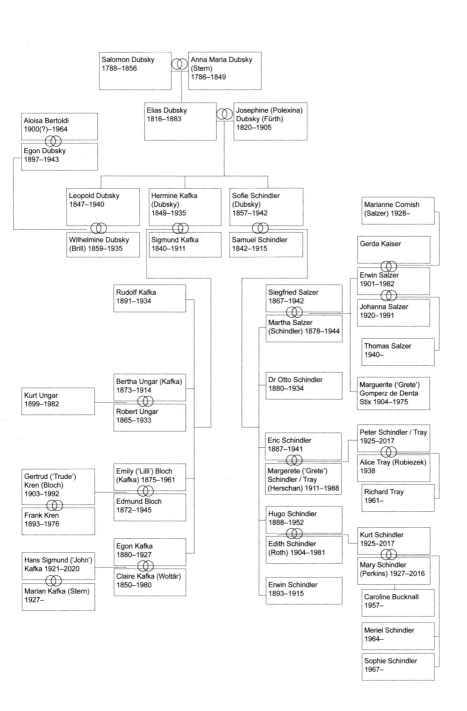

Part One

Part One

Sofie and Samuel

Innsbruck, Summer 2019

I gaze at a photograph, taken some time in the 1930s. In the fore-ground, a woman in her late seventies or early eighties, her hair combed close, sits on a bench quietly reading. She wears a long dark dress and sensible shoes, and a blanket is draped over the back of the bench, for her to use in case she is cold. Her hat and coat are beside her, too.

Behind her, the grassy clearing gives way to trees of straight, sturdy trunks, striped with sunlight. I am guessing it is summer-time because, in the middle distance to the right, there is a family picnicking on a rug and a boy wearing shorts.

The photograph does not appear posed; indeed, it looks as though the old woman is unaware of the photographer in front of her. Her face, looking down, is indistinct, absorbed in the thick book she holds with both hands. I would love to know what she is reading, but that secret remains hidden. However, I do know the identity of the woman on the bench: she is my great-grandmother, Sofie.

I remember this photograph from childhood, because my father always kept a framed copy near him, and occasionally he would refer to Sofie, always with a note of sadness in his voice. I never asked why and he never explained.

For a year after my father's death, I studied books, wrote and researched, working mainly at weekends. Digging into the past was my own form of bereavement counselling. But somehow, I

My great-grandmother, Sofie Schindler, at Igls, June 1938

could not quite bring myself to open the trunk where I had stowed the papers we had rescued from the cottage.

As the scale of what I had embarked on became apparent, I negotiated a three-month sabbatical from work so that I could travel, visit archives and spend time in the places I could see in the photograph albums. In 2016, shortly after the UK referendum on leaving the European Union, I had applied for an Austrian passport, and two years after my father's death I was ready to use it for the first time. I grabbed the top few inches of documents from the trunk, and set off for Innsbruck, arriving in early summer 2019.

From the plane I could see the green ribbon of the River Inn and the pastel buildings strung like beads along the water, all set against the mountains. It was undeniably beautiful, whatever ambivalence I felt about my teenage years there. As we dipped into the valley, I sifted my memories from childhood and what I was told by my father, and I started to make a list of what I needed to investigate. Top of that list was trying to cast light on my great-grandparents, Sofie and Samuel Schindler.

The next day I leafed through a slim, beige cardboard folder taken from the cache of documents we rescued from Kurt's cottage. The papers inside were fragile and tattered; some were stained, ripped and incomplete: they had passed through many hands. The mid-nineteenth-century dates revealed that they were probably the oldest original documents I had inherited. They were handwritten in beautiful but illegible script. I was not sure what they were, but I could at least decipher Sofie and Samuel's names. I was on their trail.

These documents were frustrating. Since those first halting teenage steps in German after my forced move to Austria, I now speak the language fluently, yet the words I looked at did not equate to any I knew. Many of the letters were formed differently – the letter 'S' resembling a 'P', the 'H' looking like an 'S'. Double consonants were denoted by a single letter topped off with a horizontal line to stand in for the second letter. I could barely make out one word in twenty. I turned to one of my Innsbruck historian friends, Michael Guggenberger, who helped me decipher the handwriting – known in German as *Kurrentschrift* – the stylised script taught for more than a hundred years in German and Austrian schools.

One Sunday afternoon, as if he were taking a primary school pupil through her reading homework, Michael pored patiently over the dog-eared papers with me. It was slow going, but over several weeks the words gradually became intelligible, and in time I even grew to like the black curlicues and strokes.

Along with the script, my great-grandparents came into focus. The birth of Sofie Schindler (née Dubsky) on 27 February 1857 was recorded, in a somewhat tattered 1890 certificate from the Roman Catholic Diocese of Budweis. The document declared itself to be a *matrik* – a register – for 'the Israelites in Gratzen'. Gratzen was the German name of a town on the Bohemian–Austrian border, known nowadays in Czech as Nové Hrady. Presumably, this certificate drew on details from the synagogue at which her birth was registered.

The curious, makeshift document described itself as a *Taufschein* – a christening certificate – quite inappropriate for a Jewish child. In order to customise it retrospectively, the word *Tauf*, 'christening', had been crossed out in six different places and replaced in the title with *Geburt*, 'birth'. This was not the only oddity. Bizarrely, given Sofie's gender, the word *Taufpathen*, 'godparents', was struck through and replaced with the words *Beschneidungs Zeugen*, or 'circumcision witnesses'. Surely a mistake made by some under-informed official who was repurposing the certificate? The *Beschneider* or mohel (circumciser) was recorded as the bookdealer 'Isak Dubsky'.

I sent a copy of the certificate to an archivist in the Czech Republic, who told me that this sort of paperwork, despite its oddness, was not uncommon and must have been needed by Sofie to get married or for some other official purpose. Importantly, it confirmed her birthplace: Niederthal, a municipality in the district of Kaplitz (Kaplice), hugging the Bohemian–Austrian border. Looking at these places on the map, I realised that my great-grandmother was a Bohemian, from the rolling, hilly country south of Prague.

Today, what was the Kingdom of Bohemia lies in the western half of the modern Czech Republic. At Sofie's birth, it was ruled from Vienna in the name of the Habsburg emperor, the *Kaiser*, its inhabitants only some of the many nationalities and minority groups comprising the Habsburg Empire's population of more than 36 million (according to the 1851 census). The monarchy's heartland was Austria, but the imperial writ stretched – in theory at least – over Hungary, over parts of modern Poland, Ukraine and the Balkans, and over much of northern Italy and down the Dalmatian coast towards Greece.

It was the middle two columns, though, of Sofie's certificate that excited me the most. It took me back a further two generations. Sofie's father was listed as Elias Dubsky, son of Salomon and Eva Dubsky. Elias Dubsky – my great-great-grandfather – was the landlord of a 'brandy house' at Niederthal No. 29. He was carrying on a family tradition as his father, Salomon Dubsky, was a landlord too, as well as a distiller of *Brandtwein* (brandy), in nearby Chlumetz. So, I came from a long line of distillers and tavern keepers, who had fanned out within the borders of Southern Bohemia in the first half of the nineteenth century, opening distilleries and taverns as they went.

My research told me that Jewish life in the Habsburg Empire was harsh and circumscribed. Jews were subjected to rules designed to curtail both their numbers and their commercial activities – they were excluded from guilds; among boys, only the eldest son was allowed to marry, and only then over a certain age; and they needed official permission before they could settle in a town.

I also discovered there was a special affinity between the Jews of central and eastern Europe and the trades of distilling and tavern-keeping. Before the 1860s, running a tavern was one of a small number of businesses open to Jews, and certainly the alcohol trade in Bohemia was dominated by Jews, its art passed down through the families. Recipes became closely guarded secrets – whether they were for varieties of vodka (made from starch-rich crops such as rye and potato), brandy (from grapes or other fruits), or the translucent fruit- or herb-flavoured spirits known as *Schnapps* in German.

Running a tavern also placed Jews at the core of their small communities. After all, inns and taverns were the places where people met and exchanged news, where tongues were loosened, where disputes broke out and friendships were made, where deals were done, and even where troops were mustered. As controllers of the production, supply and distribution of alcohol, these Jewish businesses therefore occupied an important place in society, though it was an ambiguous one, whose tensions are suggested in a traditional Yiddish folk song:

Shikker iz der Goy (The Goy is drunk)
Shikker iz er (A drunk is he)

Trinken miz er (He must drink)
Vayl er iz a Goy (Because he is a Goy)
Nikhter iz der Yid (The Jew is sober)
Nikhter iz er (Sober is he)
Davenen miz er (He must pray)
Vayl er iz a Yid (Because he is a Jew)[1]

Here is the cliché of the religious Jew and the drunken gentile (*Goy*), who lacks self-restraint when faced with the bottle. In some versions, *davenen* (pray) is replaced by *lernen* (learn), but the effect is the same: on the one side, abstemious seriousness, on the other, helpless abandon. Did the Jewish landlord look down on his gentile customer while pouring him yet another glass? Did the gentile resent the Jew for the irresistible power he had over him?

As I reflected on the information in Sofie's *Taufschein*, things started to fall into place. I remembered how as a child Kurt used to take me to food-and-drink trade shows in Austria and England; we would wander among the stands, as he sampled their wares and chatted to the stall holders about how he might help them break into new markets. He would often bring up our family's lineage as a conversation opener and a marker of credibility. At the time, I had no idea that I was part of a distilling dynasty through my great-grandmother stretching back well into the mid-eighteenth century.

Sofie was one of six children, whose staunchly Germanic names spoke volumes: Leopold, Hermine, Mathilde, Berta, Sofie and Heinrich. Such names typified the small-town Jewish mercantile class, who felt more aligned with Austria and Vienna than Bohemia and Prague. These Jews were inclined to abandon Yiddish, regarding it as the language of the East and of poverty, as they sought economic advancement and assimilation by embracing German language and culture. But this allegiance to the *Kaiser* was not without its own challenges in a Bohemia where Czech nationalists were trying to assert the Czech language and to loosen the authority of Vienna and the *Kaiser*.

Sofie's oldest siblings, Leopold and Hermine, were born in 1847 and 1849, their births bookending the 1848 revolutions that swept through Europe and were sparked by poor harvests and a thirst for greater freedoms. However, lasting constitutional reform was slow to arrive. When the eighteen-year-old Kaiser Franz Josef ascended the Habsburg throne in 1848, he was determined to tame his empire, by force if necessary; but by the 1860s, Franz Josef's views had mellowed. Among other things, he now understood the utility of educated Jews to his empire. By then, Jews had paid for constructing railways, financing wars, and building the textile, brewing, distilling and agricultural industries.

The watershed year was 1867. Following unrest in Hungary, the Austrian Empire was formally rebalanced as the 'Dual Monarchy' of the Austro-Hungarian Empire, and a new constitution was introduced. Along with other reforms, it finally granted the empire's Jews full and equal rights of citizenship. The effect was transformative and unleashed a wave of movement within the empire. My family was amongst the thousands of Jews to exploit this new freedom and relocate from the confines of southern Bohemia into Austria.

Vienna became the magnet for many of those Jews, who moved there in droves after 1867. But my family chose a different destination: the provincial cities of Linz in Upper Austria and Innsbruck in the Tyrol.

Innsbruck, Summer 2019

I set off on foot to find the Jewish Cemetery. Innsbruck is small and most places are within walking distance of one another. I soon locate the tiny Jewish graveyard next to the Catholic cemetery. I don't remember ever visiting this place as a child, so I am curious to know what might be waiting for me there.

I find it is a beautiful and well-tended, wedge-shaped cemetery, peaceful aside from the drone of traffic along the city's ring road on the other side of the wall. The mountains are visible beyond, peering over the wall. I find our family grave just inside, on the right. It is imposing and clearly designed to tell the world that the Schindlers have come to Innsbruck to stay. I note, though, that the marble is stained and looks rather sorry for itself, its gold lettering faded.

Then I feel foolish as I realise that it falls to me and to my sister to look after this grave and we have failed to do that. I look at the names. My great-grandfather Samuel Schindler is here, the first Schindler to die in Innsbruck. Others are listed below him, but oddly Sofie, his wife, is missing.

From records held by Innsbruck's Jewish community, I learned that Samuel Schindler was born in Sorrau, in Prussian Silesia. Initially, I assumed that he too came from a distilling family, but my sister reminded me that Kurt always said that Samuel was the son of a coal merchant.

Somehow, the fact that my great-grandfather was Prussian came as no surprise. Looking at the earliest picture I have of him, he comes across as upright and determined. His hair is precision-cut; every whisker of his handsome moustache is waxed perfectly into position.

The elongated region that was Prussian Silesia runs north-west to south-east either side of the River Oder and is now almost wholly in Poland, although small portions stretch into eastern Germany and the Czech Republic. Through history, it has been border territory, and for centuries it was bought and sold, and snatched back and forth, by competing states and rulers. After the grand diplomatic summit of the Congress of Vienna in 1814–15, Silesia passed to an increasingly powerful Prussia, already challenging the traditional Habsburg supremacy in the German-speaking world. In the nineteenth century, Silesia's coal and iron industries made the region essential in European industrialisation. Samuel's father presumably drew his supplies from these coal fields.

Samuel Schindler

In this borderland, Samuel Schindler was born in 1842. From the beige file of documents I took to Innsbruck, I learned that at the age of sixteen, in July 1858, Samuel became a *Handlungseleve* or commercial apprentice to a retailer, one Philipp Deutsch in Neustadt. Modern Germany has many Neustadts (meaning New Town), but I took this to be the Neustadt that is now Prudnik, very near the Polish–Czech border.

Four years later, Samuel was ready to move and on 1 January 1862, at the age of twenty, he travelled to Münsterberg, now Polish Ziębice. There he worked for a Simon Werner in a cloth and fashion business. Samuel stayed nearly two years, leaving in December 1863, I suspect to do his military service. Prussia was a kingdom that was acquiring a reputation for a militaristic culture; it had introduced obligatory military service in 1862, creating large standing and reserve armies – and in the years that followed, those armies were extensively deployed.

In 1866, a war broke out between Prussia and Habsburg Austria, in which other European nations and other German-speaking states took sides. Silesia itself was under threat of Habsburg invasion. In the event, the war lasted only seven weeks, and was fought mainly in Bohemia, the site of a decisive Habsburg defeat at the Battle of Königgrätz, one of the bloodiest battles yet fought on European soil.

I have no idea whether Samuel fought in that battle, but I do know that in the next year he escaped from further military service. According to a certificate from Berlin dated 22 April 1867, the Prussian military authorities released Samuel from active service at that point and instead slotted him into the reserve army, because of *schwacher Brust*, weak lungs.

Samuel returned to his previous employer Mr Werner and worked for him in his fashion business and bank until 1870, by which time he had risen to the position of 'book-keeper and manager of the business'. He left to pursue his own opportunities, with a glowing reference as being 'loyal, good and having led the business' to Mr Werner's 'greatest satisfaction'. Mr Werner added that Samuel left of his own accord 'to try his luck in distant lands'.

Samuel clearly wanted out of Silesia. The political landscape was changing. Prussia was solidifying its supremacy among German states. In 1871, an astonishing victory over France in the Franco–Prussian War presaged the creation of a new German Empire, as Prussia's leading statesman, Bismarck, managed to unify the mosaic of German duchies, principalities and free cities under Prussian control. Prussia's King Wilhelm I, of the House of Hohenzollern, now also became this new Germany's first *Kaiser*.

Prussian expansionism was not, though, necessarily to the benefit of Prussian Jews. Before 1871, Bismarck had tended to be liberal in his views on the Jews, by the standards of his time, and indeed his wars were financed by a prominent Jewish banker. But after 1871 and the creation of the German Empire, he allowed antisemitism to flourish around him. I suspect Samuel was conscious of an atmosphere of increasing insecurity and that this played a part in his decision, once he had completed his apprenticeship, to head over the border into Habsburg lands, where he believed he would find greater freedom following Kaiser Franz Josef's emancipation of the Jews in 1867.

Once Samuel arrived in the Habsburg empire, it seems he set about finding a bride. At some point, a match was arranged between young Samuel from Silesia, now a fully qualified businessman, and Sofie, the beautiful, blonde daughter of a Bohemian distilling dynasty. My father reported that Samuel and Sofie were married in a hotel in Prague. The first few years of their marriage appear to have been rather unsettled: their first two children, Martha and Otto, were born in 1878 and 1880, both in different Bohemian towns. Was Samuel now working for his father as a coal merchant? Had Sofie envisaged this itinerant lifestyle?

What is clear is that Samuel was ambitious and developing a plan: having married a distiller's daughter, he would become a distiller himself – and who better to teach Samuel the ropes than Leopold, Sofie's eldest brother, who was by now well-established in Innsbruck. So Samuel and Sofie moved to Innsbruck with their two small children. That way, they could be near Sofie's parents and some of her siblings, who had already followed Leopold there. Leopold was five years older than Samuel, and I believe that it was from him that Samuel learned the art of distilling. After the death of Elias Dubsky in 1883, Leopold became head of the Dubsky family.

In many ways Innsbruck – a tiny provincial city, out west in the Austrian Tyrol – was not an obvious choice of destination for young Jewish families. The city did not even possess a synagogue. Perhaps the Dubskys and Schindlers appreciated the scale of Innsbruck, because they came from small towns themselves; or maybe they were seduced by the sheer beauty of the alpine town, wedged between towering mountains. Perhaps too – and I fancy this was probably the most important reason – they saw opportunities to establish and extend the family distilling business there.

My father always told us that Samuel chose to open a distillery in Innsbruck because he spotted a gap in the market. Thousands of Italian workers were employed by the Habsburg monarchy to build the empire's railways and roads, and they liked to drink grappa – the strong spirit made relatively cheaply from grape skins, pips and vine stalks left over from wine-making.

According to a small display at Innsbruck railway station, from 1837 the imperial railway network was constructed from Vienna outwards in all directions. Its impact on the Tyrol was dramatic. Much of the work, particularly in the Alps, was difficult and dangerous; without mechanical diggers, labourers toiled for twelve hours a day, hacking their way through mountains using picks, shovels and dynamite. The workers lived in barracks, subsisting on mean rations. Many of the men died, and their graves can be seen in villages and towns all along the route.

When Innsbruck's main station opened in 1858, it was reputed to be one of the most beautiful in all the Austro-Hungarian Empire, and with the railway, suddenly this isolated backwater was connected to other parts of the empire, becoming a major north-to-south and east-to-west rail crossroads.

The earliest commercial trace of Samuel in Innsbruck is an announcement in 1881 in the local paper that he had set up a vinegar and liqueur factory at Bahnstrasse No. 2. The street no longer exists, but according to Niko Hofinger, a local historian, it was probably near the Westbahnhof – the Western Railway Station – which even now serves as a goods station to Innsbruck. From this address, he could easily receive supplies and then transport his grappa to the Italian labourers up and down the line.

As Samuel's business thrived, he extended it beyond grappa to the making of *Schnapps*, fruit juice and jam. This competition did not seem to bother Leopold, his brother-in-law, and there was clearly enough space in the market for both the Schindler and Dubsky businesses. In due course, they both opened retail shops near each other in the old part of town, and they sold each other's products in these outlets.

In 1887 the Schindler family moved to the Andreas-Hofer-Strasse to an imposing, newly constructed building, a stone's throw from the Westbahnhof, which remained integral to bringing in Samuel's supplies. I suspect both Sofie and Samuel were relieved to be moving into more spacious accommodation. The couple already had three children, and on 30 January 1888 Sofie gave birth to a fourth child, a boy they named Hugo. My grandfather.

On 2 May 1888, Samuel was ready to announce proudly in the local paper to 'his valued business friends' that he had moved his business to 'his house' at Andreas-Hofer-Strasse 1 (later renumbered 13). Niko Hofinger also supplied me with a fascinating 1905 photo of the street, which shows the road being dug up, and the workers – in white shirts and waistcoats – pausing to pose for the camera. The S. Schindler distillery is already a fixture on the street.

1905 photo of Andreas-Hofer-Strasse

Westminster Synagogue, London, 2019

I start to plan a trip to the Czech Republic to learn more about Sofie's Bohemian roots. But before doing that, I find a small museum down the road from my home at the Westminster Synagogue. Here I stand gazing at Bohemian Torah scrolls.

From Sofie's 'birth certificate', I know that her mother was called Polexina Fürth, and came from Horažďo'witz (or Horažď'ovice in standard Czech spelling). I also discovered that Sofie's older sister, Berta, settled in their mother's home town and married yet another local distiller, Eduard Münz, who with his brother ran the most famous business in Horažď'ovice, producers of the locally celebrated Münzkova Whisky. Berta was the only sibling to remain in Bohemia.

Here in London, I am astounded to find myself looking at a Torah scroll dated 1842, from Horažď'ovice – the same scroll that would have been used by my great-great-great-grandfather, Veit Fürth, when he attended the synagogue there. The Chairman of the Memorial Scrolls Trust, Jeffrey Ohrenstein, explains how this scroll travelled from that small Bohemian town to this grand building in Knightsbridge.

From September 1941, two and a half years after Germany occupied most of Czechoslovakia, Jews were prohibited from holding religious services. On 24 May 1942, and under Nazi instruction, Dr Augustine Stein, the leader of the Jewish Community in Prague, sent a letter to the Jewish communities in Bohemia and Moravia instructing them to ship all their historically valuable items to Prague, where the Jewish Museum had been kept open. Jeffrey believes that the Reich Protector of Prague was a bibliophile, who admired the learning of the Jews, even if he did not value their lives. The communities obeyed.

It is unclear why the Nazis issued the order. One possible explanation (though there is no concrete evidence) is that the Nazis were planning a vast 'Museum of an Extinct Race'. Given the Nazi compulsion to record their crimes, this does not seem far-fetched. The Jewish communities of Bohemia and Moravia accordingly packed up their Judaica in crates and sent them to Prague. Many of the items passed through Horažd'ovice as a staging post on their journey.

I see in the Westminster museum a grainy black-and-white picture of men surrounded by wood, carefully unpacking wrapped items from crates. One man has a Star of David stitched to his jacket. The items they received included Torah scrolls, books, wedding canopies, candlesticks and even combs and circumcision knives. Indeed, the response from the communities was extraordinary: more than 200,000 artefacts, including 1,800 Torah scrolls, arrived in Prague, requiring forty warehouses to house them all. Jewish experts were employed to catalogue the trove. Once their work was completed, most of them were sent to Nazi death camps.

As I stand in front of a dimly lit, temperature-controlled glass cabinet in Knightsbridge, I can see dozens of scrolls lying on racks. At first glance, they look like bales of cloth on shelves in a draper's store. As I look more closely, I can see the texture of the parchment and the way in which each scroll curls around its two wooden rollers. Every *Sefer Torah*, or Scroll of Law, has two of these rollers, each known in Hebrew as *Etz Chayim* or tree of life; they resemble giant rolling pins and enable the parchment to be progressively wound on each week, from one roller to the next, as the relevant passage is read out during the service.

A few of the rollers have beautifully carved ends; but most are simple wooden poles, from poor country communities. Small, brown card labels dangle from the ends of some scrolls, giving them the air of items in a lost luggage office. I am immensely moved by this sight, and unexpectedly my eyes well up. Jeffrey is not surprised: it is, he says, a common reaction to the scrolls.

I find it difficult to fathom why the communities surrendered up their Judaica so readily. Did the prohibition on Jewish services mean they simply had no use for them? Were they just obeying the instructions from Prague? Given that the first trains leaving

Opening crates of Judaica in Prague ca. 1942

Bohemia for Auschwitz had departed several months earlier, maybe it was a last desperate effort to salvage something before it was too late – a way of protecting at least their artefacts, even if they could not save their own lives.

Jeffrey explains how, within three years of the collapse of the German Reich, Czechoslovakia found itself with a communist government and behind the Iron Curtain. The scrolls so carefully collected by the Nazis were relegated to a disused synagogue, where they mouldered in plastic body bags within its damp walls for the next sixteen years. In 1963, finding itself short of foreign currency, the scrolls were finally offered for sale by the Czechoslovak authorities. After an inspection, a tricky negotiation and the help of a generous benefactor, the next year 1,564 scrolls were rescued and transferred to the Westminster Synagogue, representing the largest collection of Torah scrolls ever seen together.

The Westminster Synagogue hired a *Sofer Setam*, or scribe, to repair those scrolls deemed salvageable. His work was painstaking and took decades: Jeffrey tells me that there are more than 4,000 rules governing how you write and repair a scroll. The Synagogue then created the Memorial Scrolls Trust to looks after, maintain and lend out the scrolls to Jewish communities around the world.

Jeffrey tells me that once they had ten cabinets, but they have repaired and lent out so many scrolls that now they need only one cabinet. I examine the racked rolls of parchment again and see how some of these last remaining scrolls are ragged and grubby. Some were too badly damaged to be put back into circulation. Usually religious law dictates that a scroll that is damaged beyond repair has to be buried, but Westminster Synagogue has special dispensation to keep these last scrolls on display, the only relic of communities that have disappeared.

When my nineteenth-century ancestors lived in Horažd'ovice, it was a thriving community. According to Philippa Bernhard, who has written the history of the scrolls, in 1941 the Jewish population of German-occupied Czechoslovakia – the so-called 'Protectorate of Bohemia and Moravia' – was registered at 92,199 Jews. By 1945, the number was believed to be 7,884.

Today no Jews live in Horažd'ovice.

2

Imperial Gherkins

Linz, August 2019

It is a hot summer afternoon, and I am wandering in Austrian graveyards again, but this time in a different provincial city – Linz, in Upper Austria. It's taken me about twenty minutes to walk here, to the edge of the city. I now pass through several football-

The padlocked entrance to Linz's Jewish Cemetery
with the sign, 'Enter at your own risk'

field-sized plots of Catholic graves, bright with flowers, until I get to a dusty corner and a narrow, rusted gate in a wall. *Enter at your own risk*, the sign warns.

The contrast between the burial practices of Catholics and Jews is particularly stark when, as here, their dead lie side by side. Catholic cemeteries are lovingly tended, full of flowers, candles, pictures and poetry – and sometimes photographs. I notice that one of the graves here bears a photograph of a man in his SS uniform. Jewish cemeteries are more matter-of-fact affairs. The inscriptions include names, dates and sometimes a profession, with maybe a few words to sum the person up. Strictly no flowers, no pictures, no ornamentation. At most, there is a small round stone or two balanced on a ledge to mark that the grave has been visited.

Earlier that day, I obtained the key to the gate's padlock – a small silver key on a blue-and-white woven band – from the Jewish Community of Linz, along with some stern instructions: 'Make sure that you lock yourself into the cemetery while you are there. You don't want strangers wandering in. When you are finished, put the key back into the letterbox.' They only gave me the key after I showed them my passport. Now, with some trepidation, I open the padlock, push open the gate and walk for the first time into Linz's Jewish Cemetery. There is no one else here. I lock the gate behind me, as instructed. I am alone with the Jewish dead of Linz, in the city that Adolf Hitler called home.

Partly overgrown with nettles and weeds, Linz's Jewish grave-yard is sunny and peaceful, yet also deserted and forlorn. The central stones are tall and black, made of marble, a phalanx that seems to be marching, somewhat haphazardly, towards the gate. There in the middle is Sofie's favourite sister, my great-aunt Hermine Kafka. Next to her is her husband, Sigmund. *Justice, a love of peace, truth and belief in God were the lodestars of his life*, the gravestone says of Sigmund. For Hermine, a lover of music, hers states simply: *Death holds no fear, the end of one melody and the start of another.*

As I stand contemplating whether my ancestors would be

pleased to be receiving a visit from their great-niece, I am startled by a large, caramel-and-cream-coloured hare, which bounds away from behind their graves. I watch its long ears flapping and I smile; perhaps this is all the company they normally have.

Then I remember why I am really here. My father made a number of strangely boastful claims about the Kafkas. I am keen to understand whether they are true.

Hermine was short, had thick dark hair and grey-blue eyes, a high forehead and a big mouth. She doted on Sofie, her youngest sister, who was everything that she was not: tall, blonde and strikingly beautiful. But Hermine had her own qualities. She excelled at piano and loved reading; even if her childhood, like that of her sisters and brothers, involved hard work in the family liquor business and on their smallholding in Bohemia, leaving little time for music or literature.

'Yes,' my father would claim, 'we are related to *that* Kafka.' He meant, of course, the famous writer Franz, author of *Metamorphosis* and *The Trial*. According to the Kafka Museum in Prague, Franz Kafka and his parents lived in Prague, but his grandfather Jakob Kafka had been a kosher butcher in Osek, a village lying to the east of Horažd'ovice. A bit of genealogical detective work revealed that Franz Kafka was indeed very distantly related. He was the first cousin of the wife of my father's first cousin, twice removed. If Franz Kakfa counted as a relation, then so did most of the Jews of Southern Bohemia. While Kurt may have been right, this claim to 'fame' seems a very tenuous one for a Schindler to make. But this was not the only story Kurt told about his cousins in Linz.

In 1873, Hermine and Sigmund moved to Linz, taking advantage of the new freedom of movement granted to Jews. Sigmund joined his older brother, Ludwig Kafka, who had already established himself in the city – as a distiller. Their company was rebranded as:

Ludwig und Sigmund Kafka, Kaiserliche und Königliche Hoflieferanten. Brandtweine, Konserven, Essig, Senf, Gurken.

Mercifully, they also adopted an abbreviated name for their company created from the conjunction of their two names, LUSKA. The full name translated as 'Ludwig and Sigmund Kafka, Purveyors to the Imperial and Royal Court of Brandies, Conserves, Vinegar, Mustard and Gherkins'. So LUSKA had something akin to a royal warrant and they displayed it proudly as evidence of the quality of their products. I loved both the extravagance of their company name, and the implication that Emperor Franz Josef himself may have been partial to gherkins supplied by this branch of my family.

Their royal warrant was certainly a valuable endorsement for a business that could spell disaster in the wrong hands. Toni Nagiller, a distiller of craft *Schnapps* in Innsbruck, had shown me how alcohol production needs patience and experience. Methanol has to be eliminated from the final product, but confusing ethanol with methanol can have dire consequences: a shot of alcohol containing just ten millilitres of methanol transforms into formic acid in the body and attacks the optic nerve, causing blindness; thirty millilitres of methanol can kill.

I visited the Linz City Archives in a modern, soulless office building on the other side of the Danube from the Baroque old part of town and viewed the town's commercial registration records, which showed that Sigmund and Ludwig, both born in Southern Bohemia, were registered as liquor manufacturers in 1873/4. Their place of business was identified as Landstrasse 38–44. Later, I visited their trading address in a handsome, double-fronted building on Linz's main street, to find that it now housed one of the outlets of the Billa supermarket chain.

Overall, I found it disconcerting that these brothers, despite their royal warrant, seem to have left so little mark in Linz. More revealing, though, was my visit to see Hermine's grandson, John Kafka, in the United States. From him, I learned that Hermine and Sigmund had four children: Rudolf in 1871, Bertha in 1873, Emilie ('Lilli') in 1875, and Egon in 1880. John was Egon's son.

According to John, his aunt Bertha was shy and suffered from a squint. She was encouraged into an arranged and unhappy marriage with a Robert Ungar. Every summer she returned to Linz to stay with Hermine and Sigmund.

One year, Bertha's baby son Kurt fell ill while they were staying in Linz, and Hermine called out a young Czech doctor to attend to him. This visit sparked what would evolve into the most surprising and unsettling dimension in the story of my Linz relatives.

Linz, 14 January 1907

Every morning, before his surgery, Dr Eduard Bloch walked the short distance from his flat to the small synagogue in the Bethlehemstrasse. A conscientious man, he offered a prayer for his patients, whose numbers had swelled since he moved to larger premises in the beautiful Palais Weissenwolff on the Landstrasse, a few blocks from Hermine and Sigmund's house. That was five years ago. Now, he enjoyed being part of the Linz establishment, away from the tensions in his native Prague where, as a young Jewish doctor, he feared antisemitic attacks and armed himself with a pistol as he went about his daily business. In Linz, he prospered.

Today, he had a new patient, a frail-seeming widow of few means, who had come from her humble, cramped flat on the Humboldtstrasse. Dr Bloch would later remember her as a pale, handsome woman in her middle years, distinguished by luminous grey eyes. Solicitous as ever, he enquired gently how he could be of assistance. The story he heard was a lamentable one of terrible chest pains and sleepless nights. He could guess what ailed her, but first there were the formalities, beginning with the patient's name and age. In his medical notes he duly recorded them: Age, 47. First Name, Klara. Family Name – Hitler.

At the time of his earlier visit to the sick young Kurt Ungar, Dr Eduard Bloch had not long been settled in Linz, though he was starting to make a name for himself. It was his first encounter with the Kafka family, as he recorded in his unpublished autobiography, now lodged in Washington's Holocaust Museum.

He had studied in the Bohemian capital, Prague, but had become familiar with Linz since being stationed in Austria as part of his mandatory military training. It is little wonder that he came to prefer the Austrian city to the Czech one. In Prague, hostility towards the Jews had increased during his training, Jewish doctors were finding it difficult to find permanent positions at the local university, and there were rising tensions, too, between Bohemia's Czech- and German-speakers. Linz seemed altogether more congenial – although it was not free from antisemitism.

Dr Bloch's introduction to the Kafkas had a happy outcome, as, with his treatment, little Kurt recovered. However, shortly afterwards Bertha's youngest brother, Egon, fell seriously ill with typhus. Their sister Lilli described in her own memoirs (also in the Holocaust Museum) how she and the doctor nursed Egon back to health, working side by side and spending long, anxious nights by his bed. In those hours, Lilli remembered, nurse and doctor 'saw each other as they really were'. By the time Egon recovered, Lilli and Eduard had fallen in love.

The dashing young doctor with his big, dark eyes and floppy moustache was not, though, the type of man Hermine had in mind as her son-in-law; perhaps she would have preferred a businessman. But Lilli insisted on marrying Bloch; she did not want to repeat her older sister's unhappy mistake. Lilli sought out the support of her grandmother, Josefine Dubsky, who was visiting from Innsbruck. Now a widow, after the death of her husband Elias in 1883, she lived with Sofie and Samuel Schindler in the Andreas-Hofer-Strasse flat. Surprisingly, Josefine agreed with Lilli's wishes. According to John Kafka, Hermine was furious, falling out so badly with her mother that Josefine hurried back home to Innsbruck.

Lilli had her way. In 1902, she and Dr Eduard Bloch were married. Despite Hermine's reservations, the wedding was a large and joyous celebration, with relatives and guests coming from far and wide. A wedding photograph survives in Washington D.C.'s Holocaust Museum. The younger women wore white, the older women wore black, while the men look smart in their dinner jackets and top hats.

From the faces in other images pasted into the photo albums inherited from my father, I thought I could detect some of the younger Schindlers in this wedding photograph, too: was that my great-uncle Otto in the back row, third from the left? And perhaps my great-aunt Martha in the middle row, fourth from the left? Maddeningly, I could not be sure, even with the magnifying glass. But it was a reasonable assumption. I know from Martha's own diary that she was very close to her Linz relatives.

Lilli and Eduard Bloch's wedding photo. Hermine and
Sigmund sit to the left of the bride and groom.

It was shortly before the wedding that Eduard moved his medical practice to the bigger premises on the first floor of the Palais Weissenwolff, at 12 Landstrasse, where he also had his apartment. At this fine old building, originally constructed in 1715, the muscular and largely nude sculpted Atlantes still hold the weight of the first-floor balcony on their heads, from which Eduard and Lilli would have been able to survey the comings and goings below. A year later in 1903, Eduard and Lilli's only daughter, Trude, was born.

Meanwhile, the medical practice went from strength to strength. Eduard was a good and committed doctor, and he made it his mission to treat all comers, even those who could not afford his services. And so, according to Eduard's autobiography, when on 14 January 1907 a severely ill Klara Hitler presented herself at his surgery, complaining of chest pains, he was keen to help.

Eduard had completed specialist training in women's medicine in Dresden, and even before examining his patient, he had his suspicions. They were confirmed when he found cancerous lumps in one of her breasts. Such a diagnosis, as he later commented, was likely to be a death sentence. He decided not to tell his

Palais Weissenwolff, Dr Bloch's surgery

47-year-old patient immediately about her cancer, but advised Klara, 'You may need an operation.' He gave her painkillers. He also set up a meeting with her children, so that he could break the news to them at the same time.

Klara's husband, Alois Hitler, had died in 1903. Klara had then sold the family's small house on the outskirts of Linz and moved to a more central location, believing her children would have an easier life there, even though their new flat, on the Humboldt-strasse, was tiny: one room, a kitchen and a box room. Klara's son Adolf lived in that box room.

The block of flats in which they lived still stands today. I walked past it on my way to the cemetery: a down-at-heel building on a noisy, dusty road leading out of Linz, full of Turkish food shops, and accommodating not one, but two neon-emblazoned cinemas showing pornographic films.

Klara Hitler, approx. 1890

Klara's personality was a gentle one. By contrast, her husband had been a violent alcoholic who frequently beat his children, particularly Adolf. According to Adolf's sister Paula, Alois hit Adolf most evenings and one day became so violent that they thought Alois had killed his son. Meanwhile, Klara had done her best to comfort and protect her children.

A few days after that first medical consultation, Klara attended Eduard's surgery again. But this time she brought her family with her, including Adolf, and Eduard broke the bad news to them. As Eduard recorded in his autobiography, Klara accepted it courageously, but tears streamed down Adolf's long, pale face.

The teenager asked, 'Is there really no hope for my mother?'

Hitler, 1904, three years before he meets Dr Bloch. Portrait by a school colleague.

The doctor explained, 'There is a small chance that radical surgery might help.' This tiny shred of hope, Eduard recalled, seemed to comfort the son.

Eduard pulled out all the stops to have Klara operated on as soon as possible. Klara had a mastectomy on 18 January 1907 at the hospital of the Barmherzigen Schwestern (the Sisters of Mercy) and, at Klara's request, Eduard was present during the operation. Adolf insisted that his mother was not placed in the overcrowded general ward, but was treated in a less crowded and more expensive room.

A couple of hours after the operation, Eduard visited Klara's children, who were anxiously awaiting the outcome at home. Adolf's eyes were tired and red from crying. The young man listened carefully to Eduard's report of the operation, before asking in a muffled voice, 'Is she suffering?' Eduard later described the operation as a 'difficult' one and it was clear that it would have been hard for him to hide the seriousness of their mother's condition from them.

With his mother helpless, Adolf now became the head of the household. He paid both the hospital bill and the doctor's bill, while Eduard continued to look after Klara during her convalescence. That year, Eduard also treated Adolf for various minor ailments, in the course of which, as Eduard later wrote down, Adolf appeared to him like any normal seventeen-year-old. In Eduard's view, Adolf was his mother's favourite child; and Adolf, in turn, adored his mother. But the young man lacked direction in life. Adolf had been a poor student and had left school in 1905 without completing his education. His guardian, Josef Mayrhofer, urged him to get a job, but he rejected the advice. Klara, though, had encouraged her son in his ambitions to become an artist.

Klara appeared to recover fairly well after the operation and was soon able to walk short distances to the local market to buy groceries. However, she found the stairs up to their third-floor flat very difficult to manage, and so the family moved once again, in May 1907, to a larger and brighter first-floor flat at 9 Blütenstrasse. This street lay on the other side of the Danube, in Urfahr, a couple of streets away from the orchards and summer house that supplied fruit to the Kafka distillery. Dr Bloch visited and noted that the flat was clean and well-polished – and that Frau Hitler was an excellent housewife.

Several months after the operation, in the autumn of 1907, Adolf travelled to Vienna to sit the entrance exam for the painting school of the Vienna Academy of Fine Arts. He sent a postcard to Dr Bloch – a sign of his respect for his family doctor – with the words: 'From my Vienna trip, warm greetings, your eternally grateful patient, Adolf Hitler.'

However, the Vienna in which Adolf found himself was a challenging place, teeming with many new arrivals from an empire that was disintegrating. Its population had nearly trebled since 1880, reaching almost 2 million. There was deprivation and a severe shortage of housing. Social unrest was on the increase, and so too was antisemitism. Jews now formed around 10 per cent of the Viennese population and were by far the largest minority. Although some formed part of a well-off, powerful class of cultured intellectuals, the vast majority were poor, spoke Yiddish not German, and were refugees from rising hostility in other parts of the Austro-Hungarian Empire.

Vienna rejected Adolf. Of the 113 candidates applying for entry in 1907, the Academy took only twenty-eight. Hitler was not among them. According to his childhood friend, August Kubizek, the feedback on Hitler's artwork was that it was not good enough for the Academy, and though he had shown some promise as an architect, Adolf had ruled himself out of that line of work by failing to complete his schooling. He returned to Linz, but did not tell anyone about his failure.

By October 1907, Klara's health had deteriorated. She had developed metastatic breast cancer. Dr Bloch broke the news to the Hitler family that the situation was now hopeless. From 28 October, Klara was bedbound, and Adolf took over the household chores. Kubizek was surprised at how diligently Adolf carried out his new domestic duties:

I knew Adolf's low opinion of such monotonous chores, necessary though they were. And so, I was sceptical of his good intentions and imagined that they would not exceed a few well-meant gestures. But I was profoundly mistaken. I did not understand that side of Adolf sufficiently, and had not realised that his unbounded love for his mother would enable him to carry out this unaccustomed domestic work so efficiently that she could not praise him enough for it. Thus, one day I arrived at the Blütenstrasse, I found Adolf kneeling on the floor. He was wearing a blue apron and scrubbing out the kitchen, which had not been cleaned for a long time.[1]

From 6 November 1907, Eduard visited Klara Hitler daily. As the doctor later described in his biography, Adolf slept nearby, so that he could be on hand if his mother needed anything. The doctor administered Jodoform, a healing and antiseptic dressing, to Kara's chest wounds; he also gave her morphine to help her cope with the enormous pain. Klara Hitler died during the night of 21 December 1907. As they knew that Eduard could do nothing further for her, Klara's small family waited until the morning to tell Dr Bloch.

Eduard travelled out the next day to Urfahr to fill out Klara's death certificate. He arrived to find Adolf sitting next to his dead mother; the young man had clearly not slept. As his last memento, Adolf had made a sketch of her. Eduard sat with the family for a while to comfort them. He explained that in this case, 'death was a release'. He wrote later that he had never seen anyone so destroyed by grief as Adolf Hitler was on that day.

At Klara's wish, she was buried next to her husband on 23 December 1907. The next day, the family arrived at Dr Bloch's surgery to thank him for the care he had given to Klara. Adolf shook the Jewish doctor's hand and told him, 'I will be eternally grateful.'

Linz, August 2019

I am still in the graveyard. Three generations of Kafkas made their home in Linz; and three generations are buried here. In front of Sigmund and Hermine lie their daughter Bertha Ungar and their grandson, Kurt Ungar. Their graves are also of black marble, though not so high, more modest. But there are no descendants here after that. It is the end of the line in Linz. Later, I send a photograph of my graveyard visit to my Kafka relatives in the United States – to Sigmund and Hermine's grandson John and to their two great-grandsons. They are delighted, as it is unlikely that they will make the trip in person any time soon.

It was an odd source of pride to my father, almost a badge of honour, that his Jewish Uncle Eduard had treated both Adolf and Klara Hitler. I wonder whether any sort of prominence-by-association was better for my father than a feeling of obscurity. To us as children, it always seemed too far-fetched to be true. And yet, here it is, laid out in Eduard Bloch's writings. I see it too on a public information panel at John Kafka's old school: Dr Bloch, it says, had enjoyed the 'dubious honour' of being Hitler's doctor.

After his mother's death, Hitler attempted one more time to pass the art school entrance exam in 1908, but failed again, after which he drifted in Vienna, unemployed and increasingly short of money. In total, Adolf Hitler spent five years in Vienna. As he explained in *Mein Kampf*: 'I owe it to that period that I grew hard and am still capable of being hard.' At the same time, Hitler was honing his political views; he admired Vienna's antisemitic mayor, Karl Lueger, and in his words had 'ceased to be a weak-kneed cosmopolitan and become an antisemite.'

Yet Adolf still remembered his old Jewish doctor fondly. During this period in Vienna, he sent him a second postcard – this time hand-painted – with a New Year's greeting. Eduard later described it as having a monk on the front holding an overflowing glass of champagne and the words *Prosit Neu Jahr* – 'Cheers Happy New Year'. On the back, his grateful patient had written: 'The Hitler family sends you best wishes for a Happy New Year. Your eternally grateful Adolf Hitler'. Eduard liked this card very much. After painting it, Hitler had dried the card in front of an open fire, giving the picture 'a rather pleasing antique quality'. This token of affection was the young Hitler's last direct communication with my great-uncle.

The two men would never meet face-to-face again; but they never forgot each other.

3

Compote

13 Andreas-Hofer-Strasse, Innsbruck, 2019

I have never pole danced before. Yet here I am, at Innsbruck's premier studio for 'pole dance, aerial arts, acrobatics and floor work', which runs a sideline in exotic chair dancing. The English sign outside – *Pole Dance Playground* – hangs next to the entrance of this former headquarters of the Schindler empire. But I find curiosity has got the better of me. Having walked up the stone stairs to a beautiful light room, with views over the courtyard to the rear, I have committed myself to a 75-minute beginner lesson. Gyrating around a pole is not usually my thing: I like yoga, weights and running.

First, I am shown to the changing rooms, to be faced with some terrifying racks of platform boots in a choice of beige, red or pink suede. I am having second thoughts, until the instructor catches my look and reassures me that beginners start off in bare feet. Still, my plan is to hide at the back of a busy class, go through the motions, and soak up the atmosphere of the one-time flat in which my great-grandparents lived.

I am shown into a large wooden-floored room with evenly spaced, shiny steel poles, the whole thing reminding me of the inside of a London Underground carriage. I expected there to be windows looking onto the street below, but instead there is a purple wall strung with fairy lights. Incongruously, the studio shares this floor with a lawyer's office, so I assume they have acquired the street-facing rooms.

Hoping for anonymity and the teacher's neglect, I carefully pick a pole at the back, in a corner. Then I realise there is only one other student at this session. Like the audience at a thinly attended lecture, I am instead invited to the front. I contemplate fleeing again, and nearly do. But it seems rude to leave before the class has even begun.

Instead, I try to push my nerves to the back of my mind and focus on counting the fairy lights, stretched across the wall. The instructor starts the warm-up exercises and bends her body into peculiar origami poses, each one trickier than the last. I have no hope of emulating them. The lights are low, the music is heavy and thumping, with the insistent non-descript beat of a night club. It feels like the small hours, yet it is only 10 a.m.

Then, onto the first pole exercise. With as much elegance as I can muster, I try the 'fireman's spin'.

'It's easy!' the instructor proclaims. 'Left foot, right foot, step to the side of the pole, hook one leg around round the pole, simultaneously lifting the other leg out to the side to gather momentum and then twirl elegantly to the floor.'

I don't do this. Instead, I collapse in an embarrassed heap, sweat trickling down my back as the instructor makes encouraging noises at my hopeless efforts. I carry on swivelling, or trying to, as I watch the clock tick slowly towards the end of the lesson, hoping only to get through it.

To take my mind off my predicament, I let my thoughts wander, conjuring up turn-of-the-century images of Schindler children running around this space and the smell of jam being cooked, wafting up from the courtyard. I imagine Sofie calling them to order and telling them not to make too much noise as Samuel is working in the shop downstairs. I imagine the street sounds of horse-drawn carts, and later motorised trucks, delivering fruit and other supplies through the archway and into the courtyard at the back.

Then I have another image: one of incomprehension and then mirth spreading across my great-grandmother Sofie's face, as she sees a Schindler twirling in this paradise for pole dancing that her No. 13 Andreas-Hofer-Strasse home has become.

Having moved the Schindler business to the Andreas-Hofer-Strasse in 1887, Samuel decided to extend and expand the premises in 1908. At the Innsbruck City Archives, I found copies of the whole file, which included his application for permission to operate the new lift he had installed, as well as a letter objecting to an expansion of the business. I was surprised that Samuel was allowed to operate a distillery and jam factory in such a densely populated residential area of Innsbruck, where the additional traffic, distillery fumes and jam-making would very likely irritate his neighbours. Samuel had now clearly made his mark in his adopted city as a *Fabrikant* – a manufacturer – to use the description embellishing his tombstone.

It must have been the fashion to choose long company names, advertising the breadth of its range of products. Samuel's brother-in-law, Leopold Dubsky, called his business the 'Dubsky Brothers, First Tyrolean Vinegar Essence and Liquor factory as well as Brandy Distillery, Fruit Sorting Industry' (*Brüder Dubsky, Erste Tiroler Essigsprit und Likörfabrik sowie Branntweinbrennerei, Obstverwertungsindustrie*).

In naming his own enterprise, Samuel was equally audacious in appropriating the word 'First', with its connotations of both pre-eminence and pioneer status, calling it the 'First Tyrolean Fruit Juice Presser, Distillery for Agricultural Products and Liquor Factory, Samuel Schindler'. The German is impressive: *Erste Tiroler Fruchtsaftpresserei, Landesproduktenbrennerei und Liquörfabrik Samuel Schindler*. I used to love this tongue-twister as a child and practised it until I could get it to roll perfectly off my tongue at great speed.

For a company emblem, Samuel chose an eagle proudly emblazoned with his initials, 'SS'. The eagle harked back to his past, to the Silesian coat of arms; but it was also a nod to his present, to the red eagle of the Tyrolean flag. Forty years later, overwhelmed by history, the family quietly dropped the 'SS' logo.

It was also Samuel who designed the distinctive square bottle for the alcohol he produced – the type of bottle my father

Samuel Schindler's logo

treasured by his bedside – with the Schindler name in raised glass letters, running in tramlines a third of the way up from the base. At least one square Schindler bottle survived in Austria, now preserved in the archives of the Jewish Museum at Hohenems, on the western edge of the country. Unlike my father's heirloom, with its undrinkable coffee liquor, the Hohenems one is empty.

Samuel continued to expand his business beyond the Andreas-Hofer-Strasse, too. He opened a new jam factory at the Karmelitergasse, conveniently near the main railway station and a shop on the Kiebachgasse in the old part of town. Apricot, raspberry and redcurrant jams were manufactured, in both a sieved Austrian version and an unsieved version 'in the English manner'. The English range proved especially popular and besides orange – a classic marmalade – included redcurrant, plum and strawberry flavours. The range of soft fruits he was using confirmed Kurt's stories that Samuel relied heavily on the railway to bring his supplies up from the South Tyrol, in what is now Italy, but then was very much part of the Austro-Hungarian Empire.

Alongside jam, the Schindler factory produced *Kompott* (compote), that particularly Central European dish of stewed fruit, of which the best-selling lines turned out to be apricot, cherry and peach. It was a dish that was served frequently by Sofie to her children and it crops up in a dream that Sofie's daughter Martha later recorded in her diary: 'Today I dreamt that my mother was trying to serve me some compote, and I was laughing and trying to refuse, "Oh please let me be," and she begged, "But this is my only joy now."[1]

Being a talented distiller, Samuel experimented with formulating new liquors. One of his distinctive creations was a tricky sweet liquor made from Tyrolean full-cream milk, packaged in an elegant bottle and targeted specially at women. I suspect that blending the alcohol and cream to manufacture a drink with a decent shelf life was not easy. I like to think of it as an Austrian precursor to Bailey's Irish Cream.

Another of Samuel's inventions celebrated both his headquarters and the local Tyrolean hero whose name had inspired it: 'Andreas Hofer Herb Liquor'. Using alpine herbs and roots, Samuel created a drink that supposedly both 'encouraged the appetite' and 'strengthened the stomach'. At the International Cooking Exhibition in Vienna in 1908, this herbal concoction earned him a Gold Medal that, by 1910, was proudly cited at the top of the company letterhead.

That letterhead says much about the confidence of an expanding business empire. Anyone opening a letter from Samuel would be treated to a bird's-eye view of the frontage at the Andreas-Hofer-Strasse, set at right angles to the Nordkette, Innsbruck's most famous mountain backdrop. Behind was depicted an

S. Schindler letterhead, 1913

enormous multi-department factory, distilling *Schnapps* and brandy, pressing fruit juices and roasting coffee. In the middle distance, other factories belched out smoke, a sign of busy success. It was, of course, an exaggeration. In reality, the courtyard of 13 Andreas-Hofer-Strasse was nothing like as spacious as depicted, as I could glimpse from photos and during my pole dance.

13 Andreas-Hofer-Strasse, the S. Schindler HQ

In these years of growth and success, the Schindler family had considerably expanded too, in generations and geography. Bohemian-born Martha had married Siegfried Salzer in Vienna on 1 July 1900. I found the details of their marriage in the records held by the Jewish Community in Vienna. Their wedding took place at the main synagogue in Vienna in the Seitenstettengasse. Siegfried and his parents were newly arrived in Vienna, from Hungary, and stayed at the Hotel Central. Siegfried's profession is given as *Prokurist* or agent. From his business notepaper, I knew he was a cloth merchant, who dealt in silk and velvet.

I also have a studio portrait of the newlyweds, which was taken in Innsbruck. It is undated, but I guess that it was commissioned by Sofie and taken shortly after their wedding, perhaps when they were on honeymoon in Innsbruck. My great-aunt Martha is in a stunning cream dress with matching hat and parasol. She has linked her arm in Siegfried's. She is looking self-assured and directly at the camera; Siegfried by contrast is gazing absent-mindedly into the middle distance.

Martha and Siegfried had two children of their own, Erwin (born 1901) and Marguerite (born 1904), in whom Martha invested all her love and attention, during what was otherwise a less than happy marriage. Siegfried was, by all accounts, not an easy man. As Martha wrote to herself: 'Often I cannot bear Siegfried's booming voice for any length of time. It becomes

Martha and Siegfried Salzer, possibly a honeymoon photo
taken in Innsbruck after their wedding in Vienna in 1900

practically physically impossible, and then I become so irritable that it is distasteful even to myself.'² In Martha's view her husband was a cheapskate: 'I would love to see eye to eye with him in everything, but I can't . . . We also disagree on matters of instruction. In everything, Siegfried is guided by the principle of cheapness.'³

Martha was no lady of leisure: she worked in Siegfried's business looking after the accounts. Yet this activity caused her to fret constantly about her children and their education. She was a guilty working mother, worried that she did not spend enough time with them:

If I were of a more pedagogic bent, I would be better at raising my children, so that I could take pleasure in the short time of our being together and would not be grieved and angered by Erwin's neglectfulness and Grete's impatience. Don't let life go by without noticing. Look for beauty in every hour, try to discern its glory. See how the day and life rushes by, see how childhood is evanescent, the time of young adulthood around the corner. And at that time, when I would like to create in their souls the foundation for all that is good and beautiful, would like to awaken their understanding of what is elevating and pure, I am always rushing about, have no time to work on what is the most important work of all.⁴

Martha was grateful to her mother for allowing her children to stay with Sofie in Innsbruck during the summer and was particularly delighted that her daughter Marguerite could spend time with her cousin Trude, from Linz. Martha was very fond of her Linz cousins and hoped that the two girls would grow up to be good friends. 'Truderle is so loveable a child, [and] despite her loveable qualities so childlike and modest. I would be pleased if Gretl would find a friend for life in her.'⁵

I found several pictures in one of my albums of Martha's daughter Marguerite standing in the back courtyard of the Andreas-Hofer-Strasse building next to Samuel's enormous St

Bernard dog, Tasso. In them, Marguerite is about four years old and only slightly taller than the dog, around which she has draped her right arm. She is wearing a classic Austrian *Dirndl* – the dress, shirt-and-apron combination that Tyroleans call their national costume. By this age, Marguerite was already fluent in German and French; she was also growing into a voracious reader, who, as her later biographer wrote, 'read everything that she could lay her hands on in the house of a cultured family with intellectual interests'.[6]

Otto – Sofie and Samuel's eldest son – was still unmarried and working as a dermatologist, also in Vienna, where he had a large medical practice. I have photos in my father's albums showing him attending an autopsy and doing ward rounds. According to my father, he studied the treatment of skin conditions with Marie Curie in Paris and was the first to use radium therapy in Austria.

Sofie and Samuel's three youngest children, Erich, Hugo and Erwin were a tight-knit trio. Sofie and Samuel's flat on the first floor of 13 Andreas-Hofer-Strasse had six bedrooms but no garden, and the back courtyard was really no place for these three boys to play, as they would have got in the way of the carts and trucks, loading and unloading. So, in summer, the Schindlers decamped to a large rented villa in Igls, a beautiful village on a sunny plateau just above Innsbruck, at the foot of the Patscherko-fel mountain.

Siegfried Salzer owned a nearby villa, the Fichtenhof, which they visited frequently with their family. From Linz, Hermine's family came regularly too, to enjoy the Igls summers. Summer in Igls was a tradition that lasted through the generations. Martha's granddaughter Marianne told me recently of her own summers there; and when my parents first tried life together in Austria, when I was three, they chose to live in Igls too.

As Erich, Hugo and Erwin grew into young men, all three of them went to work with Samuel in the family business, travelling as their father's emissaries and visiting hotels, taverns and restaurants all over western Austria and Germany, selling the Schindler

Marguerite Salzer, daughter of Martha and Siegfried,
in the courtyard of 13 Andreas-Hofer-Strasse,
standing next to Samuel's dog Tasso

products. They probably also had to fit in some obligatory military service – in principle, all men in the empire had been required since 1868 to be trained to fight for their *Kaiser*. In practice, not all of them were called up. Hugo, however, volunteered to join an elite mountain regiment and between 1908 and 1912 served as a cadet in the army. I suspect his choice was very much driven by his love of the mountains.

For my Austrian ancestors, the Tyrolean mountains held a very special magic, as they came to do for me. I remember, aged thirteen, opening some wooden shutters in a hotel room one morning and suddenly seeing mountains up close. We had driven overnight from England, and in the darkness I had missed the foothills that preceded these enormous peaks. The brutes that I gazed at now were quite different to the abstract distant pyramids I drew in primary school. They were bold, irregular and leaned over the valley. I was overwhelmed.

In summer, the family hiked in the mountains, wearing long dresses, hats and tweeds; in winter, they went tobogganing. Looking at some of the earliest pictures I have inherited, I marvel at the women – including Martha – wearing long coats, hats strapped firmly to their heads, and gloves, as they prepare to hurtle down snowy slopes on hooped wooden toboggans. Although their boots look sturdy, in general I am struck by how inappropriate their clothing appears for what they were doing.

In their outdoor lives, I also see these Schindlers with their dogs and riding horses. In one extraordinary photograph, whose puzzle I was unable to solve, my grandfather Hugo appears to have acquired a leopard. It may not have been a successful pet, as it does not appear in any of the other photos.

Martha tobogganing with friends

Hugo loved the mountains and the outdoors. I have endless pictures of him on mountain hikes, usually accompanied by a dog. In these images, the adolescent Hugo invariably wears *Lederhosen*, the practical and virtually indestructible leather shorts with braces that are perfect for climbing trees and hiking, and as common in the region then as jeans are nowadays. In one photograph, an older Hugo does a headstand in the snow; in another, he has removed his shirt and he basks, spread-eagled, enjoying the contrast of the snowy cold on his back and the sun's rays on his front. He is a man at one with his mountain environment, comfortable in his skin.

It seems entirely fitting to me that my grandfather was, along with his brother Erich and his uncle Leopold, a member of the *Deutscher und Oesterreichischer Alpenverein* – the German and Austrian Alpine Club. 'Alpinism' – the serious pursuit of mountain challenges, whether walking, hiking or conquering peaks – really started in the 1860s. I don't think Samuel was an avid walker, or at least I've seen no evidence in the photos. However, Hugo's photos are full of men in tweed or leather knickerbockers and hats, crossing glaciers and bestriding peaks.

The joint Alpine Club was created in 1873–4, when the separate German and Austrian clubs merged. Leopold seems to have been the first family member to join. One of the most important figures in the former German Alpine Club was Johann Stüdl, a tradesman from Prague, and it is possible that Leopold had already joined the club through this Bohemian link, before he moved to Innsbruck in the 1870s. He was certainly a member of the amalgamated club by 1899, as I discovered through a visit to the handsome reading room of Innsbruck's *Ferdinandeum* – the Tyrolean State Museum. It holds the club's membership records, including the 1908 annual report with Leopold's details.

This slim grey-green volume, stamped with an edelweiss on the cover, bespoke the seriousness of the institution. The Alpine Club was responsible for maintaining mountain huts and pathways; it provided lists of guides, as well as maps and training to members, and it acted as a central information point for anything to do with mountains, hiking and climbing. It laid on events, too, such as winter balls and lectures.

Being a member of a club was, and is, a deeply ingrained German and Austrian cultural phenomenon, part of the fabric of social relations. Nearly half of all Germans nowadays are members of a club, often a sports club, and sometimes more than one. Not for nothing is Groucho Marx's famous quip – 'I don't care to belong to any club that will have me as a member' – greeted with some incomprehension whenever I have found myself dropping it into the conversation with Austrian friends. And if you look in a German dictionary for a translation of 'unclubbable', the nearest you get is *ungesellig*, which is closer to 'anti-social'.

The idea of not wanting to embrace membership of something generally regarded as fun and socially useful, of standing contentedly apart and individual, is not quite understood, much less valued. And for my ancestors – building new lives as newcomers to Innsbruck – fitting in was a driving force.

Connecticut, USA, 2018

'I remember your father. He was a crook and a shyster.'

These were Tom Salzer's first words to me when I met him. It is my teenage son who, after my father's death, suggests I take to the internet to try and track down missing family members. And that has led me here, to meet Tom, a tall, well-preserved, moustachioed man in his seventies. He is the grandson of Martha and Siegfried Salzer, and so, like me, a great-grandchild of Sofie and Samuel Schindler.

This visit has followed a few emails, and then a nervous phone call to a cautious Tom, who is wondering why I am in touch after all this time. I explain that I am trying to piece together my family's history. Tom says he has inherited lots of family photos from his father, which I might like to see. So I have flown to the United States to visit him and his wife, Betty.

I arrive at his house in Connecticut on a sunny October afternoon, only to be floored by Tom's opening remarks. I am barely across the threshold. It turns out that he only met my father once, in the 1950s, when Tom was a child and Kurt was visiting his father, Erwin. There was, Tom says, a violent quarrel between Erwin and Kurt. Erwin threw my father out – and refused to speak about him again. Tom does not know any details. So I promise to see what I can glean from Kurt's papers when I return to England. I have never heard anything about this argument. But then it was one of so many.

I sit down in Tom's sitting room and he hands me several photos that I have never seen before. One shows Martha in a beaded dress and sweeping hat. But it is the second one that captivates me. I have never seen a photograph of Sofie and Samuel's *whole* family together. As Tom and I gaze at our shared great-grandparents, a special moment replaces the awkwardness of our first few minutes. Sofie stands at the left edge of the picture behind Samuel, who is seated, half turned towards the camera. The three younger boys – Hugo, Erich and Erwin – are ranged to the right, while Tom's grandmother Martha stands next to Sofie and close to Otto. All are in their finery, the women in their best dresses, the men in starched wing-collars and evening dress.

Samuel appears somewhat stiff, somewhat awkward. But then the patriarch must be nearly seventy, for Tom and I guess the photograph was taken around 1912; Martha and Otto are well into their thirties, and the three younger brothers are young men. We are struck by the composition, which is the reverse of the usual family portrait in which the women are seated with the men standing behind them. This photograph lends Sofie an air of authority. I speculate that it is she who has arranged for it to be taken and has instructed Samuel to keep entirely still.

Sofie was reputed to be a real beauty. According to my cousin John Kafka, his grandmother Hermine described Sofie as the blonde and beautiful sister, and herself as an 'ugly duckling'. Here, Sofie's hair is swept back into a bun, showing off her high

Martha Schindler, c. 1912

Sofie Schindler with Martha, Otto, Hugo and Erich
(all standing) and Samuel and Erwin (seated), c. 1912

forehead and dark eyes. The beginnings of a smile play about her lips. I get a strong impression of what she must have looked like as a younger woman. At the same time, the woman I see now is in her middle-aged prime, confident and comfortable, the power behind the throne, radiating love and pride in her grown family.

I adore this photograph.

Membership of the Alpine Club seems to me to be only one marker of the Schindlers' successful integration into Tyrolean life and society. In a population of around 66,000 Innsbruckers by 1914, the Schindlers were among fewer than 500 Jews in the city, amounting to less than 1 per cent of the local people – a similar proportion as in Linz. Most of this Jewish community, like Samuel, Sofie and Leopold, were middle-class, well-to-do businesspeople. And with business going well, the family could enjoy their status as assimilated members of Innsbruck society.

I suspect they only participated in Jewish religious life on high holy days, if at all. The city's Jewish community still did not have its own synagogue, instead using various rooms in private houses, until eventually installing a prayer room in the annexe of a building on the Sillgasse.

The Schindlers' business and their address in the Andreas-Hofer-Strasse seemed to symbolise their embrace of traditional Innsbruck life, running to the very core of Tyrolean identity. In the early nineteenth century, the eponymous Andreas Hofer was a local innkeeper and distiller in South Tyrol. That fact alone made for an entirely appropriate consonance with my family's roots. But more than that, Hofer rose to become a freedom fighter and national hero.

It was Hofer who recruited a militia after Austria's defeat at the Battle of Austerlitz in 1805, and led Tyrolean resistance against rule by Napoleon's Bavarian allies. His greatest victory was over the Bavarians at the Second Battle of Bergisel in 1809. He was, though, abandoned by the Habsburg emperor, who agreed by treaty to French rule over the Tyrol; in so doing, the emperor in effect signed Hofer's death warrant. Hofer continued his armed struggle, but in the end was overwhelmed and on 20 February 1810, he was executed on Napoleon's orders.

Martyrdom solidified the legend. Although practically unknown outside Austria, Hofer acquired a special place in Tyrolean hearts, standing as a symbol of its independence and its people's bravery. Today, whether in the reading room of the County Archives or near the former Olympic ski jump, you cannot escape his image. His rallying cry in the local dialect, *Mander, s'isch Zeit!* – 'Men, it's time!' – echoed down the decades following; a defiant assertion of the preparedness of these mountain folk to defend themselves. For my family's business, this address must have seemed a powerful and helpful association.

The Schindlers fully bought into the Hofer legend and clearly considered it good for their business, and I have a photo to prove it. To mark the centenary of the Tyrolean uprising led by Hofer in 1809, they decorated their headquarters with garlands and bunting and an enormous red and white flag. They could not yet have imagined how Hofer's legacy, in the hands of others, would come to shape their futures.

Despite all the solid respectability the Schindlers had acquired, by the late 1880s there were worrying signs that the 1867 equality so cherished by the Jews of the Habsburg Empire was beginning to be questioned. Other names from history were also feeding the Tyroleans' sense of identity. In 1620, a physician, Hippolyt Guarinoni, published a story about the fifteenth-century murder of a little boy named Anderl, who lived in Rinn, a village ten kilometres south-east of Innsbruck.

Guarinoni encouraged the creation of a Catholic religious cult around Anderl, who was – so his allegations went – murdered by Jews. The stone on which the boy was supposedly sacrificed was named the *Judenstein* (Jew stone); it became a place of Catholic pilgrimage. A large church was built in Rinn. It contained paintings depicting two swarthy, bearded men, with tousled locks under turban-like headgear, holding down a white-robed small boy, his arms raised to them in supplication; a third man, equally menacing, sharpens his knife. At the museum in Rattenberg, there is a copy of wooden figures once placed in the church. One, also sharpening his knife, has his tongue hanging out in anticipation.

Anderl was beatified by Pope Benedict XIV in 1752, though he was never canonised. Among the people, though, he lived on. Plays based on the alleged ritual killing were regularly performed at village celebrations throughout the Tyrol. The Grimm brothers even wrote up his story in their book of German legends. Perhaps the oddest thing for me was that it was not until 1994 that the Bishop of Innsbruck forbade the cult, and the Catholic Church finally declared that the child's supposed murder by Jews had no basis in reality.

From the late 1880s, just as my family were acclimatising to their new lives in Innsbruck – and despite the tiny number of Jews in the Tyrol – Anderl's story, together with several similar blood libels, were being used to whip up antisemitic feeling. In the 1890s, a Viennese priest, Joseph Deckert, published several pamphlets, including one shrilly entitled *Four Tyrolean Children: Victims of Hassidic Fanaticism*. Despite protests from several rabbis that the so-called victims had absolutely no historical foundation, the Catholic Church generally took the view that it could not interfere with 'the living consciousness of the people'.

At the same time as the poison of this religious-based antisemitism was being spread, even more strident voices began attacking Jewish commercial interests. In October 1889, an anonymous four-page pamphlet was widely distributed in the Tyrol.[7] Entitled *!Vorsicht vor Juden!!* (Beware the Jews!!) and seeking the widest possible dissemination, it urged its readership *Lesen und weitergeben!*, 'To read and pass on!' Its first page warned readers to 'buy only from honest Christian German businesses' and avoid those owned by Jews. The pamphlet's readers were instructed not to vote Jews onto any representative bodies, nor to let Jews into their homes or holiday accommodation.

They were also warned, in stark terms, that Jews were moving to the Tyrol in 'terrifying' numbers, especially from Vienna, with new faces appearing every day. For as long as Innsbruck had Jewish shops, the pamphlet asserted, it would be *ein schmuziges Heim* – a dirty home. The pages describe the Jews as *gefährliche Schmarotzer*, 'dangerous parasites', who should be shown the door. It also gave advice on which newspapers to buy and which – the Jewish-owned ones – to avoid.

I gazed in shock at this unsigned, cowardly and vicious attack. On its first page was a list of all the Jewish shops in the Innsbruck area to be avoided. My great-grandfather Samuel appeared two-thirds of the way down as a manufacturer of vinegar in Wilten, at the time an independent parish of Innsbruck. My great-uncle Leopold was listed as a distiller of brandy.

With this pamphlet, as the Innsbruck historian Martin Achrainer has pointed out, the generalised antisemitism of the blood-libel fabrications was morphing into libels against individual living Jews, who were all well-known among the people of Innsbruck.[8] And shortly afterwards, the antisemites began to come out of the shadows and discard their cloaks of anonymity.

In 1906–7, a supplement to the newspaper *Deutsche Tiroler Stimmen* appeared, signed by two men: Dr Fritz Lantschner and Dr Friedrich Frank. They warned that Jews were gaining the upper hand in the Tyrol's commercial life. The authors asserted that it was still possible to stop the general *Verjudung* – meaning literally 'Jewification'; the prefix *ver* often denoting something negative in German. But, they wrote, the Tyrol needed to engage in 'self-help', specifically that Tyroleans should not bleed their national economy dry by putting money into the hands of the Jews, who would only exploit the people.

Lantschner and Frank saw themselves as Germans and called on other Germans to protect 'German Tyrol'. To achieve this, they urged Tyroleans to avoid Jewish shops 'like the plague', helpfully providing a complete list of them, along with their owners' names and addresses. Here again were Leopold Dubsky and Samuel Schindler, listed under sellers of 'brandy and liquor'. For good measure, the authors also listed Jews who had converted to Christianity.

Social and leisure institutions like the Alpine Club were not immune from this slide into antisemitism. The historian Gebhard Bendler has pointed out that there were many Jewish names among the early members of the Innsbruck branch of the Alpine Club, reflecting a relatively liberal period in which membership was one expression of the Jewish dream of emancipation. That is one reason why I suspect Leopold might have joined early.

That 'golden age' was brief. In 1894, the Gymnastics Club passed a resolution denying membership to Jews. The Alpine Club did not immediately follow suit, but its records noted which Jews had converted to Christianity, and Jewish membership ceased to be encouraged. Perhaps my grandfather Hugo and his elder brother Erich were among the last few of Innsbruck's Jews to gain entrance.

Innsbruck, 2019

For the moment, I am no longer gazing at photographs. Instead, I am in lawyer mode, though not in my comfort zone of English employment law. I am reading a piece of nineteenth-century legislation in German. Section 302 of the Imperial monarchy's 1857 *Strafgesetz* (Criminal Law), to be precise. It makes for interesting reading.

I note that Section 302 prohibits the 'incitement to hostilities against nationalities (tribes), religious or other societies, individual classes of civil society . . .' Section 303 of the same Act prohibits 'the publication or distribution of pictures or writings which seeks to mock or demean the teaching, customs or institutions of any in the state legally recognised church or religious community.'

It is clear that these sections protect not only Catholicism but also all other recognised religions, including, implicitly, Judaism. Breaching Section 302 carries a prison sentence of three to six months, while for violating Section 303 the sentence is up to six months. As I read the full text of the statute, I find myself astonished that such broad protection against what we now call 'hate crime' is in force so early, a full ten years before the reforms of 1867, and more than 100 years before the UK had any legislation quite as specific.

My surge of positive feeling at these enlightened provisions is tempered by the consciousness of two realities. That a statute is only as effective as the willingness of authorities to enforce it; and that history can, and does, go into reverse. I think of the cartoon I have seen, dated 1909, which originally appeared in the newspaper of the Innsbruck Choir. It imagines the *Zukunft*, the future, of the city's main street, Maria-Theresien-Strasse. In this vision, outsize Jewish businesses ('Saloman & Sohn', 'Levison', 'Zum billigen Jakob', etc.) are depicted as New York-style skyscrapers. They jostle for space, squeezing what are clearly meant to be taken as honest, Christian German businesses out of this premier location.

Striking a commanding pose in front of the vulgar edifices is a fat, rich capitalist with a top hat; just outside the frame, an impoverished-looking figure in more traditional Tyrolean dress, with a pig on a lead, pulls away out of the picture's border as if this new Innsbruck is no place for rural folk like him. In the top right-hand corner, there is an inset image of Innsbruck's university, collapsing into ruin. The message is clear. Jewish business threatens Tyrolean life and culture.

This drawing is reproduced in Martin Achrainer's chapter in the book *Jüdisches Leben im Historishen Tirol* (Jewish Life in Historic Tyrol), which is a fund of information. Although there were some voices who protested against propaganda like this, by now the authorities were taking no formal action. In the 1880s, as Achrainer points out, 'the state prosecutor officially seized antisemitic leaflets and launched proceedings' against publishers and distributers of these pamphlets. However, a decade later, such behaviour resulted in 'public applause'. Achrainer concludes: 'Jokes, ridicule and mockery about Jews had become part of everyday language in taverns, on the mountain tops, in clubs and finally in public administration.'[9]

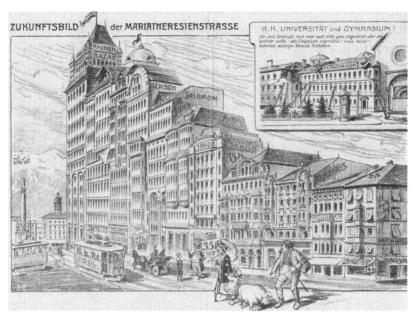

Cartoon showing the imaginary future of Maria-
Theresien-Strasse, overrun with Jewish enterprises

A puzzle remains. Why did hostility towards Jews arise when
there were so few Jews living in Innsbruck – and especially when
those were generally intent on assimilating to their environment?
Was it a case of their disproportionate business success spawning
resentment?

My family, like so many other highly motivated migrants the
world over, in all periods of history, approached their lives with
goals of self-improvement, integration and economic advancement. Perhaps a more established majority found them a threat to
the status quo, and they embodied a sense of change or moder-
nity, which conflicted with traditional Tyrolean values.

I don't know how Leopold and Samuel reacted to the pamphlets
and cartoons, or whether those attacks on Innsbruck's Jews had
any impact on their businesses or day-to-day lives. My guess is
that they assumed it was yet one more wave of antisemitism, similar to ones that generations of their families had experienced in

the past, in Bohemia and Prussia. They probably thought that like the other waves, this too would pass.

But I do wonder at the corrosive effects that these pamphlets might have had on the non-Jewish majority of Innsbruckers. What is shockingly controversial in the first instance, so easily becomes normalised through constant repetition. My father spent his entire life hiding the fact that he was Jewish. I am beginning to understand more of the paradox of a man who, though he constantly ruffled feathers, was also driven by a lifelong desire to assimilate, to fit in.

I am aware too that the clock was ticking here. Only two years after the family portrait that Tom Salzer and I admire so much, something happened in a different corner of the Austro-Hungarian Empire that threw everyone's life into disarray. A shot fired on 28 June 1914, in the Bosnian city of Sarajevo, meant that the ageing Emperor Franz Josef would need all his disparate subjects, Jew and antisemite alike, to rally to his defence.

My family answered that call.

Part Two

4

Rum on the Eastern Front

Sarajevo, Bosnia–Herzegovina, 28 June 1914

A motorcade rolls slowly along the Appel Quay. The route, tree-lined on one side and edged by the River Miljaka on the other, has been widely advertised, swept and beflagged. Locals have been encouraged to turn out to see the man who will one day be their *Kaiser* and his wife, Sophie. Even though it is shortly after 10 a.m., the sun is hot. Sophie wears a long white dress, with a matching white wide-brimmed hat, and carries a white parasol. She looks regal and the photos of that trip show her smiling broadly, at the side of her husband, who has just completed two days of troop inspections.

The province of Bosnia–Herzegovina is the Habsburg Empire's latest acquisition. It has only been 'officially' Austrian since its full annexation in 1908, though for thirty years Austria-Hungary has occupied and administered it after the Ottoman rulers were driven out.

Among its mixed population there are many ethnic Serbs and Bosnian nationalists, who have a bewildering array of visions for the future. Some want an independent Bosnia; others a union of southern Slav states; and some want to join neighbouring Serbia. The only thing they agree on is that they do not want to be ruled by Austria-Hungary or its Emperor Franz Josef. For a band of young, largely teenage revolutionaries trained up by the shadowy Black Hand society, today is their opportunity. And they have come prepared.

In one of the official open-topped cars sits the emperor's nephew and heir apparent, Archduke Franz Ferdinand. Seated on his right is his Bohemian-born wife – Sophie Maria Josephine Albina Gräfin Chotek von Chotkowa und Wognin – who, despite her magnificent name, has come from relatively minor Czech aristocrat stock and is therefore barred from performing duties at the Viennese court at the side of her husband. Instead, at court she has to give precedence to more senior royal figures.

Fourteen years earlier, after Franz Ferdinand resisted months of pressure to abandon Sophie in favour of a more suitable match, Kaiser Franz Josef had extracted a solemn oath from him renouncing any claim by Sophie, or any of their future children, to the throne or to royal privilege. The promise was made at a spiteful little ceremony on 28 June 1900, two days before their wedding, an event that Franz Josef and other royals refused to attend.

It is no wonder that Sophie and Franz Ferdinand spend as much time as they can away from the Viennese court and at their various castles and estates in Bohemia, where they can create a more relaxed family life for themselves and their three children. There, Franz Ferdinand can also indulge his passion for hunting. He pursues it too during visits to the Tyrol, where he dons traditional costume and shoots industrial quantities of chamois.

Today, a sunny one in Sarajevo, it can hardly have gone unnoticed by Sophie that it is fourteen years to the day since that oath of renunciation. However, here in this faraway province, she is at last allowed to play the part of royal consort.

Suddenly, from the crowds lining the route, a grenade is thrown. It bounces off the royal car and explodes under the car behind, causing alarm and fear, as well as injury to the occupants. The archduke – shaken and angry, but still with a sense of purpose – continues on to Sarajevo's city hall. There he interrupts the welcoming speech.

'Mr Mayor, what is the good of welcoming speeches? I came to Sarajevo on a friendly visit and someone throws a bomb at me. This is outrageous!'

Sophie leans in towards him and calms him down enough for

the formal proceedings to continue. From there they head off again, by car, to visit the wounded party in hospital.

Then, there is a mistake. The planned route is altered for extra security, but not all the chauffeurs receive the new directions. There is confusion. The royal couple's driver turns down what is now the wrong road, and he is shouted at to reverse back onto Appel Quay. He stalls the car. It is already too late.

A nineteen-year-old Bosnian radical, standing on the pavement in front of a café-delicatessen, draws a Browning 9mm pistol. He cannot believe his luck. Gavrilo Princip has dreamed for years of killing a Habsburg oppressor as a way of liberating and uniting the southern Slavs. He fires point-blank and hits Franz Ferdinand in the neck; Sophie, realising that something is wrong, stands up and is hit in the stomach by a second bullet. As the blood starts to seep onto her hitherto spotless white dress, Franz Ferdinand urges his 'Soferl' to stay alive for their children, but they both die within minutes.

More than a century later, I am in Vienna's Museum of Military History, standing in front of the vehicle in which the couple were travelling when they were attacked. I am struck by how exposed its occupants were in the open-topped car. Given how unpopular the Habsburgs were in the region, why didn't the organisers arrange a closed carriage as some measure of protection?

Immediately after the assassination, Princip is arrested, tried and then incarcerated in a southern Bohemian military prison in the old Habsburg fortress town of Theresienstadt, a place that will be repurposed for very different inmates a few decades later. He is too young for the death penalty. Before tuberculosis takes him in 1917, he expresses one regret: he did not mean to kill Sophie.

Austria-Hungary is aghast at what it believes is a state-sponsored assassination. Emperor Franz Josef – old, possibly senile and deeply superstitious – believes the atrocity is divine retribution for the morganatic marriage between Franz Ferdinand and Sophie. Throughout Europe, there is an appalled outcry at this act of terrorism. *The Times* reports the 'tragic news' in the same terms as the *Neue Freie Presse*. This assassination confirms the general view that the Balkans are a hotbed of instability and barbarity. The Habsburgs point the finger at Serbia. In Austria-Hungary, many of the *Kaiser*'s more hawkish politicians as well as the imperial army's chief-of-staff, Franz Conrad von Hötzendorf, have been itching to get at Serbia for years.

But many also fear, rightly, that any form of punishment could easily get out of hand. It takes one month for them to be proved correct. On 28 July 1914, Austria-Hungary, backed by Germany, declares war on Serbia; Serbia appeals for support to its Slav ally Russia, which has a mutual-defence alliance with France. Meanwhile Germany, already fearful of encirclement by the Franco–Russian alliance, has a strategy of pre-emptive action, and declares war on both.

When Germany promptly invades Belgium to get at France, Britain, a legal guarantor of Belgium's neutrality and inviolability, throws in its lot with France. In a week of war declarations, the hostilities between Austria-Hungary and Serbia have exploded into the biggest Great Power war ever in Europe.

One hundred and one years later, I am visiting Serbia's capital, Belgrade. It is a beautiful city, yet one still full of the detritus of more recent war. I see burnt-out ships on the River Sava, abandoned buildings and bullet-ravaged walls. Only twenty or so years previously, Serbia was again a pariah nation – bombed by NATO, its leaders complicit in ethnic cleansing, atrocities, and fomenting war. I come across a stallholder near Belgrade's castle selling T-shirts. They are adorned with a grainy black-and-white photograph of a face that is vaguely familiar. I stop and look for a while, without being able to place the face. The storeholder approaches me, sensing a sales opportunity.

'Gravrilo Princip!' she announces proudly. 'Freedom fighter!'

History is all about perspective.

In the summer of 1914, patriotic fervour erupted across the continent, including in the Schindlers' city of Innsbruck: Tyroleans, by
and large, were deeply loyal to Austria and the emperor, and few
doubted their cause was just. They would be victorious and they
would all be home by Christmas. Yet few – including my family
– would be immune to the war's consequences. My great-grandmother Sofie, with four sons, had more at stake than many.

Since 1867, the Austrian and Hungarian halves of the empire
had been allowed considerable autonomy in their day-to-day
affairs. However, foreign policy and military matters were still
under overarching imperial control, and since 1868 a policy of
universal three-year conscription had applied to men from all
social backgrounds, with the requirement to be available for call-
up for several years afterwards.

Many of the empire's military records are no more – casualties
themselves of war over the course of the twentieth century.
However, at the War Archives in Vienna, I was able to track down
some of my grandfather's records and build a picture of the handsome young man in uniform that I can see in my photos.

I learned that by the outbreak of war, Hugo Schindler was
already attached, after his period of training, to some of the most
illustrious of the emperor's elite mountain troops, the grandly
titled *Kaiserliche-Königliches Tiroler Landesschützenregiment
Nr. 1* – the Imperial-Royal Tyrolean State Rifles Regiment No. 1.
At the War Archives in Vienna I applied for, and received, a copy
of his training records, which were written in a beautiful script,
but were full of mystifying army abbreviations and difficult to
read.

Once I got them back to Innsbruck, I needed help in decipher-
ing them. The records revealed that my grandfather had initially
offered himself 'of his own free will', and moreover at his own
expense, for one year's training on 14 May 1909 as an *unterjäger*
– a would-be infantryman. The papers also noted that this was
effectively the beginning of a twelve-year obligation in the army
reserve forces, alongside civilian life.

Before the war, Hugo's regiment was assigned to the area from Lake Garda to the Dolomites. The idea was that the soldiers in the regiment would get to know every corner of the landscape. According to Heinz von Lichem, in his book *Spielhahnstoss und Edelweiss* ('Rooster Feather Hackle and Edelweiss' – a reference to the regiment's insignia), these troops were drawn predominantly from Tyrolean men who knew and understood the mountains and were recruited from the broadest section of the population. According to von Lichem, in the high mountains officers and soldiers climbed, hiked, skied and slept alongside each other, forging close friendships that crossed lines of class and background.

Hugo's progress, judging by the paperwork, was not entirely straightforward. He seems to have failed some of his first-year exams, but managed to pass the one that would allow him to be a reserve officer. He took part in manoeuvres in 1910. The records list those parts of the Alps with which he was particularly familiar: Vallarsa and the Lavarone Plateau. It was noted that he could swim and ride horses as well as bicycles, although quite how useful any of these skills would be in mountain combat was unclear.

After a transfer to a different unit, things started to improve. Nevertheless, in June 1910 his commander found both his diligence and his interest in military service to be low, although his behaviour was judged to be good. I imagine that Hugo was stung by these comments and pulled his socks up, as only three months later his company commandant described Hugo's 'lively' interest in military service, accompanied by good ambition and matching industriousness; the commandant's superior heaped more praise on the 'very good' trainee, pronouncing him 'suitable for mountain service'.

By January 1911, Hugo was a *Kadett* with the *Landesschützen-regiment*. He was based for much of his training in Bozen (Bolzano), in the South Tyrol, and appropriately for the area had acquired some Italian. I found, in these military records, a glimpse of the private man: in 1912, my grandfather was summed up as 'single, with private means, finances in order; a businessman with an income of 3,000 Kronen'.

He possessed a 'cheerful, good natured character' and was deemed 'honourable', as well as someone genuinely interested in military service, good at fighting and manoeuvring in a *Zug* (platoon), and a good shooting instructor to boot. Although he appears not have been judged to have the self-sufficiency and initiative to be military leadership material, he was affirmed as being capable of providing useful service under direction.

Working through these records, I felt an odd source of pride at this impression of a sociable, outgoing, practical and dependable man, who had channelled his love of mountains into becoming a decent alpine soldier. These reports chimed with the smiling man I saw in the photographs, a man I never met. They also helped, I admitted to myself, to balance the sense of shame I'd felt for much of my life about the choices his son – my father – had made.

In January 1914, six months before the outbreak of war, Hugo was an ensign with the *Landesschützen*. I presume his two older brothers Otto and Erich must also have undertaken some similar peacetime military training. As for the youngest brother, Erwin, his training appears to have been overtaken by the onset of actual war. I know that when mobilisation orders were issued in late July 1914, and the empire declared war on Serbia, Erwin was away in Hamburg on business and was about to embark on a business trip to the United States.

Abandoning those plans, he immediately turned round and returned to Innsbruck. He and Erich were both attached to the *1. Tiroler Kaiserjägerregiment* – literally the '1st Tyrolean Imperial Hunter Regiment'. It was one of four Tyrolean Rifle regiments in the regular infantry, whose origins dated back to the early eighteenth century, and which fought against Napoleon in the nineteenth century.

War inevitably raised issues of identity and allegiance. Erich and Erwin's regiment, and even more so Hugo's, were among the elite units of a large but very varied military force, as diverse as the empire itself. Operating with fifteen languages and embodying all the peoples and tensions of the patchwork empire, the army's willingness to fight and obey orders among its rank and file could never be taken for granted.

The German-speakers, forming just over a quarter of the empire, were regarded as dependably loyal, and they comprised the majority of the officer class; for a mixture of reasons, Croats and Poles also had a strong sense of allegiance to the emperor. But would Czech-speaking nationalists fight for Franz Josef? Would Bosnians take up arms against Serbs, or would Slavs in the east of the empire fight Russians?

There was little doubt, however, about the allegiance of the Tyrol's German-speakers, expressed in the close connection between the province's military units and the imperial dynasty. Emperor Franz Josef himself was honorary *Inhaber* – Colonel-in-Chief – of the *Kaiserjäger* regiments. In serving their emperor, German-speaking Jewish Austrians such as the Schindlers would also have an opportunity to demonstrate to the critics their worth to the empire, and strike a blow against the creeping antisemitism of recent years.

For the family's medical men, call-up took a different form, for war would need all its doctors. Otto Schindler became an 'Imperial and Royal Assistant Doctor'. Over in Linz, his cousin Lilli's husband, Dr Eduard Bloch, was asked to run one of Linz's 1,000-bed reserve hospitals, where Lilli would pitch in too, as an administrator. When Martha visited Linz from Vienna during the war, she commented that her 'darling, beloved Liliechen is looking very stressed; her grief and exhaustion readily apparent'.[1]

Eduard's former patient Adolf Hitler dodged his own military service for Kaiser Franz Josef, later claiming he abhorred the ethnic diversity of the imperial troops. With the outbreak of war, in August 1914, Hitler was granted permission to sign up with the Bavarian army. Ahead of him lay service on the Western Front, for a different *Kaiser*.

Back in Hitler's home town, Dr Bloch's hospital was soon over-flowing with wounded soldiers sent back by train from the front. As he later described, the medical staff worked extraordinarily hard as there was a shortage of doctors. When they ran out of beds, local schools and the larger houses had to be converted into makeshift hospitals.

Innsbruck, August 2019

I have farewell photographs in front of me. A family on the cusp of war.

In one, Samuel and Sofie are seated on hard-backed wooden chairs in the garden in Igls. It must be summer 1914. Behind them stand three of their boys in beautifully cut uniforms and kepis: Erwin in the centre, his arms around the shoulders of his big brothers Hugo and Erich. Erich and Erwin wear the same style of uniform, being in the same regiment. They are proud that the Emperor Franz Josef himself wears the same buttoned grey tunics.

I assume that Otto is charged with taking the photograph, as he is absent from the photo. Samuel looks stoically into the camera, every inch the smartly turned-out Prussian businessman, his bowler hat shading his eyes from the bright sunshine. His waxed moustache shines silvery white.

Sofie is facing forwards, but slightly turns towards her sons. Erich's right hand is casually inserted in his pocket, belying the formality of his uniform; but his left hand rests protectively on Sofie's shoulder, and he is clearly calming an anxious mother. Her face betrays fear. She looks older now and less well-dressed than in the family portrait of two years before – but then this is not a formal studio photograph.

The boys, by contrast, look relaxed. Hugo is standing directly behind Samuel. His *Landesschützen* uniform is a little more ostentatious than his brothers': the regiment's silver edelweiss is clearly visible on his pointed collar patch, and a rooster's shiny plume, the *Spielhahnstoss*, protrudes from his cap. These ornamentations have only been introduced in the last decade. All of the young men exude a pride in what their uniforms represent; they are serving their country and their emperor.

Another photograph, much more informal, shows Hugo and Erich larking around on the grass, playing at soldiers. Erich lies down against his brother's chest, grinning and wielding his standard-issue sword. His jacket is unbuttoned and he is hot. I imagine Erich racing up the grassy slope, exuberantly practising his swordsmanship, counting how many of Franz Josef's enemies he is going to impale. He has collapsed against Hugo's side, exhausted and laughing. Looking at the photo, I have a powerful impression of the close bond between these two brothers; and with Erich, a sense of the invulnerable confidence of youth. He can have little conception of the degree to which it is bullets and artillery shells that will decide the battles to come, not swords.

I have only one son, and the thought of sending him off to war is unimaginably awful. I look at Sofie and contemplate what must have raced through her mind. Does she calculate her odds? It can be some comfort that Erich and Erwin are in the same regiment, so they can look out for each other, but they might also be in the same danger. Is it better to spread the risk and hope that her four sons end up in different places?

A fourth photograph shows what I assume is Hugo's regiment packing up and leaving with their horses, ropes and backpacks, swarming over a meadow as if they are setting out on a large-scale summer picnic. As it ended up in Hugo's album, I assume that Hugo took this photograph.

I know that Hugo's cousin, Egon Dubsky, is also serving with the *Landesschützen*, and wonder whether he might be among this group. I imagine that Egon's father, Leopold, asked Hugo to keep an eye on his son, whose health was always considered frail by the family. As far as I can tell, Egon was never one for the outdoors. He certainly did not follow his father and cousins into the Alpine Club.

Erich, Erwin and Hugo Schindler with Sofie
and Samuel Schindler, 1914

Erich and Hugo Schindler play soldiers, 1914

Andreas Hofer bids farewell to the *Kaiserschützen*,
from *Tiroler Alltagsleben Im Ersten Weltkrieg*

Then I find a reproduction of one of the propaganda posters of the time. Here are the *Landesschützen* heading heroically into battle, the imperial eagle raised aloft, bugles blaring, and caps doffed to an outsize figure of Andreas Hofer, who looms, godlike, in the mist above them, bidding them farewell. The old hero has been wheeled out to embolden Tyroleans – once more, 'Men, it's time.' His right arm is raised in blessing. His left arm is wrapped around an Austrian flag.

Facing enemies to the east and west, Conrad von Hötzendorf sent much of the imperial army to the borders with Serbia, hoping for a swift defeat of the upstart kingdom, and to the north-eastern province of Galicia, beyond the Carpathian Mountains, facing the Russian border.

When the Austro-Hungarian First, Third and Fourth armies went into action, attacking into Russian Poland and Ukraine in late August 1914, they discovered to their cost that Russia had mobilised far quicker, and in far greater numbers, than was thought possible.

Within three weeks, those Austro-Hungarian armies were in a headlong retreat back towards the Carpathians, having lost hundreds of thousands of men and leaving the fortress of Przemysl – the largest stronghold of the Hapsburg Empire in the East – as a besieged island. As Austria-Hungary was being invaded, German Silesia – Samuel Schindler's homeland – now found itself under threat should Krakow fall. Germany knew it could not ignore this wider Russian Front. Soon German troops were pouring into Russian Poland as a winter of atrocious weather and inconclusive stalemate beckoned.

I cannot pinpoint exactly where all the Schindler brothers were at this time. I know, from her diary, that their sister Martha was permanently terrified for them. On 25 November 1915, she indicated that Otto was 'in a horrid little hole where cholera is raging. I crave his letters, awash with unbearable fear.'

I discovered that Hugo's regiment – though trained for mountain combat – was sent by train in early August to the plains and forests of the Galician Front. There, the 1st *Landesschützen* Regiment, part of the Third Army, was involved in the battles of Lemberg (August), Grodek (September) and Przemysl (October), and in fighting in the Carpathian Mountains, where all the *Landesschützen* regiments suffered high losses. Erich and Erwin's regiment was on the Eastern Front too, and certainly in action at Grodek; for them, 11 September 1914 seems to have witnessed particularly fierce fighting, judging from records of the wounded and lost in Erwin's own battalion.

The war on the Eastern Front that the brothers faced was developing its own characteristics, different in some respects to the trench-based war of mud and attrition on the Western Front. Trenches did spring up in the east, especially as winter approached, when all sides were keen to consolidate their positions. But on the Polish and Galician plains, these were not the fixed phenomena taking shape on the Western Front, where, between the Swiss border and the English Channel, a more-or-less continuous series of complex trenchlines would bog the war down for years of violence. On the Eastern Front, apart from such natural obstacles as lakes, mountains and forests, the fighting was less constrained. As a result, hundreds of miles of territory could, and did, change hands, as fortunes varied.

The scale of human tragedy in the east was no less than what has often been called the 'mincing machine' of the Western Front, something that the Schindler boys would have appreciated very quickly. The statistics tell their own story: estimates of Austro-Hungarian casualties by the end of the first year have been put at around 1 million, sometimes more. Out of those, the military historian John Keegan has written of the *Kaiserjäger* and *Landesschützen* that 'no less than 40,000 had become casualties, a loss that deprived the Austrian army of its best and bravest elements, never to be replaced.'[2]

As one generation of Schindlers and Dubskys went off to war, another had to acclimatise to both loss and absence: Sofie was widowed on 2 March 1915, when Samuel died at the age of seventy-three. It must have been a lonely bereavement for Sofie, given that her five children were all away from Innsbruck. Certainly, Martha in Vienna dreamt often of her dead father.

In a host of ways, women's lives were profoundly affected by the war. As their menfolk were progressively pulled out of agriculture, manufacturing, business and transport, the women of Innsbruck emerged from their homes and became more visible in public life. In photographs, I see them for the first time as ticket inspectors on the trams, toiling in workshops, taking on business roles.

With her four sons away in army service, and Samuel dead, Sofie needed to step up and run the family business. Martha remained in Vienna to help with Siegfried's business and dispatched her daughter, Marguerite, to Innsbruck to sit out the war with her grandmother.[3] It must have been a frightening time for the now seven-year-old girl, arriving to find her uncles had all left to fight in the war.

By the spring of 1915, the war was going badly for the Austro-Hungarians, who needed rescuing. Germany agreed to a joint offensive in Russian Poland and Galicia – help that was offered through slightly gritted teeth. Austria-Hungary was by now the junior partner in an unbalanced relationship. In the words popularly attributed to German general Erich Luden-dorff, Germany was 'shackled to the corpse' of the dying Hapsburg Empire. Nevertheless, an Austro-Hungarian exit from the war, or from fighting the Russians, would be a disaster for Germany.

The new operation, known as the Gorlice–Tarnów Offensive, took place between these two towns in Austro-Hungarian Galicia, south-east of Krakow. German and Austro-Hungarian forces converged secretly on the area, vastly outnumbering the Russians. A short but blistering bombardment heralded the attack on 2 May 1915. Although the volume of artillery was modest by the standards of large Western Front offensives, nothing like it had been seen or heard on the Eastern Front to date.

The shocked Russian defenders were sent reeling from their trenches by the rapid attack, their forces fragmented, streaming back over the rolling Galician plains. The shattering effect of the subsequent breakthrough rippled all the way along the frontlines, as demoralised Russians surrendered in their tens of thousands, or raced to get out of the way, abandoning their weapons and supplies.

By the end of Russia's 'Great Retreat' in September 1915, all of Russian Poland had fallen, and the Russians were almost entirely expelled from Galicia. More than a million Russian prisoners had to be stashed somewhere, ending up in odd corners of the empire. Some of them wound up in the tiny Tyrolean village of Steinach, near where I lived in Trins, where they worked in the local leather factory.[4] Others fetched up in Igls and in Innsbruck, perhaps grateful to escape the Russian Tsar's disappointment at such an ignominious defeat.

Austria-Hungary erupted in celebrations. This victory went a long way in erasing earlier humiliations. Erich's, Erwin's and Hugo's regiments were part of the Third Army, punching through south-east of Gorlice, at the northern end of the Carpathians. Hugo's regiment seems to have returned to the Tyrol in June, to face new challenges, but Erich and Erwin remained on the Eastern Front.

When I saw Tom Salzer in the United States, he gave me two photographs of my great-uncle Erwin and his army comrades – ones I had never seen before. In one of them a group of solemn, exhausted soldiers crowd at night-time around a small barrel of what looks like rum. It took me a while to work out which one of them was Erwin – he appeared so different to the laughing boyish figure in the 1914 photos in Igls.

The Erwin I saw here now sat on the ground, his boots muddy, clutching a tin cup; all smiles gone and gazing into the middle distance, over the right shoulder of the photographer. For a moment, I wondered whether the alcohol in his cup reminded him of his father and the family distillery. But he looked keener on drowning his sorrows than on reminiscing.

Erich and Erwin, both lieutenants by now, survived the first brutal days of the Gorlice–Tarnów campaign. However, Erwin was killed on 9 July 1915, aged twenty-two, and during what was supposed to be a ceasefire. His unit was positioned north-east of Krakow, in Krasnik, Russian Poland. When Erwin stood up to salute a senior officer, he was hit in the head by a bullet. Steel helmets were beginning to be introduced, but only on the Western Front. All Erwin or his fellow soldiers had was his *Feldkappe*, a cloth cap and no impediment to bullets.

It fell to his big brother Otto to retrieve his body for burial in Innsbruck. As Martha recorded: 'Poor Otto had to look on the destroyed fragments of this once blooming person. He brought him home from his temporary resting place in foreign soil.'[5]

Erwin Schindler (fourth in from the right, sitting
on the ground).

In the local press, a family announcement appeared, lamenting the loss of their 'most beloved and proud' Erwin. It registered that in his year of service, he had earned both the Bronze and Silver Medal of Bravery. But now, 'A life of blossoming hope sinks with him into the grave.' The family names appeared below as signatories, first Sofie's, then Otto's, Erich's, Hugo's, Martha's and her husband Siegfried's.

In the space of four months, Sofie had lost both her husband and her youngest son. The war had come home.

The Jewish Cemetery, Innsbruck, 2018
Erwin's name appears on my family's grave directly below Samuel's. I see that Erwin also receives a mention on the nearby memorial to the Jewish soldiers who died in the First World War.

Death notice for Erwin Schindler

Some of these soldiers have their own gravestones. They march in an identical line down the right-hand edge of the Jewish cemetery. Given the small number of Jews in Innsbruck at the time, I am surprised at this noticeably high number of casualties, including not only local Jewish boys, but also those casualties who arrived in Innsbruck and never recovered from their injuries.

I presume that it was Sofie who ordered Erwin's name to be chiselled into the stone panel. She may well have been grateful that Samuel did not live long enough to know that his youngest son had been killed in action.

Martha was devastated by the loss of her little brother. In her diary entry for 16 August 1915 she wrote: 'Practically all my thoughts are concerned with him. It fills me with pain that we had so little time together.' She fretted that she dreamt about her dead father, but questioned: 'Why did I never see darling Erwin in my dreams? The sunny lad, dressed in Tyrolean costume when he went about with us in Igls to look for mushrooms, or when he was wearing his tennis clothes, with the crown of curls falling into his face.'

I imagine Sofie trying to comfort herself that losing Erwin had not been in vain and he died a hero's death; and that in the meantime she prayed for the safe return of her other three sons. But the enemies had multiplied. Now the South Tyrol itself was part of a new frontline – against Italy. And it was already calling back those loyal Tyroleans like Hugo and Erich to defend it.

5

Schnapps on the Southern Front

London, Austria, and Slovenia, 2018

For two years I become obsessed with Austrian First World War military history. I buy books, visit museums and drag my family on long walks up mountains. I want to understand what it was like for the young men who lived, fought and died from 1915 to 1918 on the Austrian–Italian border, a theatre of war that receives little attention in the histories of the First World War written in English. I want to look behind the photographs that I have inherited of my grandfather's service there.

My father was inordinately proud of Hugo's military service – though, when the opportunity arose, he did not choose that path for himself. Kurt described how as a child he loved hearing about his father's exploits on the front. But beyond that he was vague and never passed on any details, and sadly I never asked. The photos Kurt kept near him of long-dead men in uniform seemed too remote to be interesting. But now I find myself scouring these same photos with a magnifying glass, searching for clues as to rank and regiment, location and date. I have to work outwards from the photographs and the memorabilia, and inwards from the books and museums, and hope that I can pinpoint where my grandfather fought on this bigger canvas of history.

I have three pictures of Hugo taken during this war of the mountains. The first shows him with two other soldiers and a German shepherd dog. The dog is wearing an elaborate harness, both as a restraint and also as protection in case it falls into a crevasse. The leather straps are sturdy enough to hold the dog's weight if it has to be lifted out of difficulty. Hugo has his arm around his dog and in a moment of humour, he has put his hat on the dog's head. His gun lies carelessly on the ground to the side. Hugo and his companions wear white overalls over their tunics, as used by their regiment in winter, making them practically invisible in the snow.

A second photo, taken in spring or early summer, shows Hugo and two other soldiers, set against a high alpine background. There is still a fair amount of snow on the ground, but some has melted leaving patches of alpine grass. Hugo is seated on a rock, his pike-grey jacket unbuttoned, doubtless from the heat of the climb up. He looks directly into the camera and a lock of hair falls into his eyes. He is squinting slightly in the bright light, as the photographer asks Hugo to look at him and into the sun. Hugo looks older and more careworn than the 1914 photos in the back garden in Igls.

A younger soldier sits to his right, blank-faced: his emotions are difficult to read. He looks uneasy, maybe he is uncomfortable with being photographed; maybe he is simply scared. Behind them both stands the third soldier, complete with a monocle, holding a squat round-bellied bottle of *Schnapps* in his right hand, a cigar in his left. He would not be out of place at a regimental dinner. All three soldiers are clearly posing. This is more than a quick swig of *Schnapps* from a metal flask to fortify themselves before the next climb.

The photograph is perfectly composed: Hugo and his companions form a triangle, which is set against the steep and misty mountain backdrop. Again, a dog – perhaps the same dog – lies at their feet. The picture is printed in large format and pasted onto card. I wish I could make out the label on the *Schnapps*, for the whole scene could almost be an advertisement for S. Schindler products. Did Hugo order it to be taken so he had something to send back to his mother in Innsbruck?

Winter campaign, Hugo Schindler

Spring campaign

Try as I might, I cannot identify the precise location; all I know is that this picture, in a scratched frame, was always with Kurt, perched on a table wherever he was.

The third picture is a studio portrait of Hugo as a decorated officer, his chest bursting with pride, adorned with the medal he has just earned. It is a *Tapferkeitsmedaille*, a Bravery Medal, of the type Erwin had also been awarded – but I cannot tell whether it is Bronze, Silver or Gold class. It is not the only decoration he was awarded. I also have Hugo's Golden Cross of Merit. In 18-karat gold, with red and white enamel, it bears the initials 'FJ' for Franz Josef, who introduced it for exceptional service to the crown and country in 1849 – the date embossed on the reverse.

In the studio photograph, Hugo's uniform is clean and pressed, and his silver buttons gleam, showing off the figure one, referring

Hugo Schindler, decorated *Kaiserschützen* officer

to the number of his regiment. But most noticeable of all is the silver edelweiss on his collar, the symbol that truly marks him out as belonging to the *Landesschützen*, which literally translates as 'Defenders of the land'.

I spend time in the tiny regimental museum in Innsbruck and learn that the origins of Hugo's regiment stretch back to the time when the Tyrol had its own military constitution, granted to it by Emperor Maximilian I in 1511. In return for the obligation to muster a certain number of troops in case of war, the Tyroleans were given special military rights, including the freedom to bear arms and a release from the duty to fight outside the Tyrol. In addition, the emperor agreed not to conduct warfare within the Tyrol without the Tyroleans' consent. It was a big concession and helped forge a sense of unity and independence for the mountain people of the Tyrol.

These voluntary rifle companies evolved into the *Landes-schützen*, and then became the world's second-oldest specialist mountain warfare troops, after the Italian *Alpini*. They were renamed the *Kaiserschützen* in 1917. Their training was extensive with a curriculum comprising rock and ice climbing, skiing, abseiling, alpine battle tactics, movement in steep terrain and across glaciers, as well as geology and meteorology. One of the aims was to identify those men who could undertake special operations and reconnaissance missions in high alpine patrols, which would require high levels of mountain-craft, resilience and independent action. I cannot be sure, but I suspect Hugo was engaged in some sort of patrol in the two pictures I have of him in the mountains.

With his arms folded, Hugo, in the studio photograph, exudes relaxed confidence. He is handsome, and he knows it. A slight smile hovers around his lips as he looks directly at the photographer; the flash from the camera dances in his eyes. I read into this picture a deep sense of pride and belonging. This was what so many young Jews of the Habsburg Empire craved. Hugo's military success – perhaps in reality fairly modest – is for him the pinnacle of assimilated achievement.

This photo stands in contradiction to all the antisemitic jibes his family faced in Innsbruck, the unpleasant leaflets with their allegations of rootlessness, internationalism, self-interest and disloyalty. It demonstrates that Hugo is first and foremost a brave and patriotic citizen of the Austro-Hungarian Empire, then a Tyrolean, and lastly a Jew.

Armed with these three photos, I set out to discover what I can about what Austrians called their Southern Front. Somewhere along the line, I hope to find out what part Hugo played there, and understand what he and his comrades endured. But first I have to understand why it was happening at all. Why did Italy pick a fight in the mountains?

On 23 May 1915, Italy declared war on the Austro-Hungarian Empire. In theory, Italy should have been an ally of Germany and Austria-Hungary, following their Triple Alliance, signed in 1882. The Alliance formally recognised the borders of the young Italian kingdom, whose unity and independence was established only in 1870. But in some respects, cracks had been papered over. Italian patriots lamented the 'loss', as they saw it, of *Italia irredenta* in the north-east – those lands with large numbers of Italian-speakers that were still under Habsburg rule, but in times past had been part of the great Italian empires of Rome or Venice.

By 1915, nationalists in Italy not only coveted the eastern Adriatic coast, including the Austro-Hungarian port of Trieste, but aspired to become a power in the Balkans. This expansionist dream also included the South Tyrol, with its many Italian-speakers, who called the region 'Trentino'.

Italy was pulled in different directions. Germany pressed Italy to join them; however, Italy's price for cooperation included the South Tyrol, which the Austrians flatly refused to hand over in the spring of 1915. After all, the South Tyrol was one of the empire's most valuable and productive provinces. Austria-Hungary was fighting this war to consolidate its empire, not to relinquish parts of it.

Ultimately, the British and the French successfully bribed the Italians with the promise of land and money that they did not possess. It was not hard to convince the Italian Prime Minister Salandro or the Italian king that the collapse of the Austro-Hungarian Empire would benefit them – and in early 1915, that collapse seemed ever closer, as the Austro-Hungarian armies were bloodied on the Eastern and Serbian fronts.

Salandro coined the phrase *sacro egoismo*, 'sacred egotism', adding a religious dimension and a sense of national duty to Italy's claims on *Italia irredenta*, even though some of the territory they coveted had been under Habsburg rule since the Middle Ages. The one-time anti-war socialist Benito Mussolini now spoke fervently in favour of war and 'the return' of those lands in the north and east. In an Italy only recently unified, some saw in an imperialist war the possibility to bind the nation together and create a new, collective memory.

Secretly, on 26 April 1915, Italy committed to declare war, in the Treaty of London. Britain and France promised Italy chunks of the Austro-Hungarian Empire, including South Tyrol from Lake Garda up to the Brenner Pass, in return for a speedy offensive against the Austro-Hungarians. They considered Italy's demands a price worth paying for bringing a million Italian bayonets into the war on their side. At the same time, they scorned their new ally's craven behaviour. Prime Minister Herbert Asquith called Italy 'greedy and slippery'; his First Lord of the Admiralty, Winston Churchill, regarded Italy as the 'harlot of Europe'.

Many Tyroleans were appalled at Italy's declaration of war, feeling betrayed, incensed and threatened. This was a war in their backyard, which would pit neighbours against each other. Emperor Franz Josef issued a wounded rebuke: 'After an alliance lasting for more than thirty years, during which Italy's land was able to flourish in previously unforeseen ways, Italy has abandoned us in our hour of danger and has run with its streaming flags to our enemy's camp.'

War with Italy could have spelled disaster for a hopelessly overstretched Austria-Hungary. Hoping for an easy 'walk to Vienna', the uncompromising Italian chief-of-staff, Luigi Cadorna, had spent the months since 1914 preparing the Italian army – increasing its size, improving its equipment, and recruiting many young officers, from whom he demanded unquestioning obedience. Cadorna assumed that Italy's numerical superiority would win the day.

However, compared to its new allies, Italy was still under-prepared and under-equipped for a modern war. Moreover, by the time Italy joined the war, in May 1915, events had changed to Italy's disadvantage. The successful Gorlice–Tarnów offensive rescued Austria-Hungary's Russian Front from collapse, and released troops that could move south – in particular the highly trained mountain troops like Hugo, who knew and understood the Alps.

Hugo's *Landesschützen* arrived back in the Tyrol in June 1915. Exhausted, and having already lost a third of their men on the Eastern Front, the *Landesschützen* were transferred straight up into the mountains and distributed along its steep, treacherous terrain. This new Southern Front snaked in a 450-mile (600-km) S-shape, from the Swiss border through the Alps and around the mountainous 'U' of the South Tyrolean bulge, before curling south for the remaining 45 miles (60 km) along rocky plateaux to the Adriatic coast. The Italians were attacking up from the plains into the defended mountains.

The bulk of the fighting occurred along the easternmost 70-mile (120-km) stretch of the front, as the Italians attempted to break into Istria and capture Trieste. For two years, they were met with fierce resistance along a front that would sink into its own form of deadly attrition, every bit as greedy for human life as the Western Front. In the first six months, Italian losses amounted to around 160,000 men, traded for just a few miles of territory.

Most of the heaviest fighting occurred along the steep-sided Isonzo (now Soca) River. The Austrians numbered these battles, and the Italians adopted that numbering. In the first eleven Battles of the Isonzo, Italian forces advanced, at the very maximum, around 18 miles (30 km).

The Italians, attempting conquest, embraced the idea of constant advance. In consequence, they did not create the same sort of infrastructure as the more defensively minded Austrian forces. A pattern soon emerged in the fighting. General Cadorna enjoyed a numerical superiority of roughly two-to-one, but he consistently underestimated the strength of the Austrian positions.

In the first year of the war, Italian tactics were always the same: bombardment, in theory to destroy the barbed wire, followed by an infantry assault advancing in lines over difficult uphill ground, often to find the wire still intact; at which point, the Austrian defenders began picking them off. On those occasions when the Italians managed to capture a first-line trench, the Austrians retreated to their second or third lines of defence, above their original position, and behind further impregnable rows of barbed wire. From there, they could launch counter-attacks, using Austrian artillery from higher vantage points, which often drove the Italians back out of their newly gained ground.

Moreover, the Italian army was of varying quality and commitment, reflecting the divisions in the country at large. The infantry's rank and file tended to be filled disproportionately by poor, uneducated conscripts from the south, who began to weary of being used as cannon fodder in these frontal assaults. Cadorna ruled through a culture of fear, frequently fired his senior officers, and imposed rigid and punitive discipline to force his soldiers to do his bidding. He wasn't the only one. Vincenzo Garioni, an Italian corps commander on the Isonzo, described the massacre of his Italian infantry as 'a necessary holocaust'.

Morale began to plummet, as did any belief that this was a just war to liberate ancestral lands from the grip of the Habsburg Empire.

Martha managed to catch up with Hugo, on 23 August 1915. Clearly, the war hung heavy for them both:

Yesterday we were in Linz. I had so very much looked forward to seeing Hugo again. But I found him to be very pale, and even though he did not say anything about it, I felt that he was oppressed by the prospect of soon returning to the front. He claims that it makes no difference, the idea does not frighten him, but . . .

For me, this thought is appalling. Suffering from an open, bleeding wound [i.e., Erwin's death] as I am, it is horrifying. The sacrifices on the Southern Front are supposed to be horrendous, and hopes for peace at an immeasurable distance.

Vienna, 2019

I can see that the Southern Front draws in my ancestors – not only Hugo, but his brothers Erich and Otto, and also their cousins Egon Dubsky from Innsbruck and Egon Kafka from Linz. I know from Erwin's 1915 death announcement that both Erich and Hugo were promoted from *Leutnant* to the rank of *Oberleutnant*, and that they were both decorated for bravery. However, after much frustrating digging, I conclude that I will probably never learn how they earned their medals. None of the Austrian War Archives reveal where, why or when they were decorated. At the end of the First World War, all the Austro-Hungarian records were sent back for safekeeping to the empire's nations, with no inkling that a second war would cause the destruction of many of them.

I also spend several weeks trying to work out exactly where Hugo fought. It is not an easy task. In the various museums and archives that I visit, I scour the available accounts of the war for mentions of his regiment, and scrutinise all the photographs for his face. The archivist at the Vienna War Archives looks utterly baffled when I ask him if there are records for each individual company. Slightly condescendingly, he reminds me that millions fought on the Southern Front. Chastened, I realise the naivety of the question. My chances of pinpointing where my grandfather fought are worse than finding a needle in a haystack. At least haystacks are stationary; in war, troops were constantly on the move.

The Southern Front ground on. Exhaustion and the depths of winter dampened down hostilities in 1915–16, but during 1916, there were five more battles of the Isonzo, to add to the four of the previous year. In August 1916, the Italians finally captured the town of Gorizia, on the Isonzo, and another three miles of territory; but the next three battles that year barely scratched any more land on a front that – metre for metre – was still costing more lives than the Western Front.

Then, for the first time on the Southern Front, Austria-Hungary took the offensive, switching tactics from its successful but frustrating defensive war. This attack, generally called the Asiago Campaign, burst forth from the middle of May 1916. It had a nickname – the *Strafexpedition*, 'punishment expedition' – intended to teach Italy a lesson for launching war, and a name that reflected Austro-Hungarian fury at Italy's impertinence. But Italian defenders, showing considerable bravery and tenacity, managed to regroup and contain the breakthrough. Was Hugo there? It seems very likely. Certainly, many units of his *Landesschützen* regiment were involved in actions, advances and retreats in these valleys, passes and mountains.

In June 1916, the *Strafexpedition* was called off, in part because of a renewed Russian attack in the east, which again threatened an Austro-Hungarian collapse until the Germans intervened. German (and Bulgarian) help also ensured, in 1916, that Serbia was finally subdued, after a multi-pronged invasion forced its king and the battered remnants of its army into a large-scale retreat.

From the evidence of one photograph I received from Tom Salzer, I know that my great-uncle Otto, the army doctor, was in Belgrade at some point. The photograph is undated: Otto stands, in uniform, in what appears to be a pharmacy. A long sword dangles from his waist, and it looks to me as though he is picking up supplies to treat patients.

Germany and Austria ended 1916 with the conquest of both Serbia and Romania, while Russia was exhausted on the Eastern Front. It was just as well for Austria-Hungary, as more and more divisions were needed to cope with the Southern Front; it would suck in almost half of the emperor's army.

That year also represented the end of a very long era, for Kaiser Franz Josef died at the age of eighty-six in November 1916, plunging the empire into mourning. Almost no one alive could remember a time before him. His successor was his

Otto Schindler in Belgrade

great-nephew, Karl. In 1917 the new emperor renamed the three *Landesschützen* regiments the *Kaiserschützen* – 'Imperial Rifles'. All the troops in Hugo's regiment swore an oath of loyalty to their new emperor.

Kolovrat, Slovenia, 2019

Frustrated by the gaps and lack of detail about Hugo's war, I find consolation in places and atmosphere. I gradually conclude that in some ways it does not matter where Hugo fought *exactly*. What matters is to absorb the environment and build a picture of what it must have been like, not only for him but for all those who fought in this landscape. And so, I take my family on several trips into the mountains in 2018 and 2019, to places that would have been killing zones a hundred years before. We travel to Slovenia, because the old Isonzo Front now lies largely within its borders.

One hot August day in 2019, we walk sections of the former Italian trenches at Kolovrat, above the town of Kobarid, known previously as Caporetto in Italian and Karfreit in German – its multiple names encapsulating its multi-ethnic identity. Here lived German-speakers alongside Italians, Slavs and Friulians. The trenches are maintained by the local First World War museum. From afar, they appear as pebbled ripples, extending up and down the steep hills. On closer inspection, they are narrow lines cut into the hillside. Barely waist-high, they would have offered no protection against accurate mortar shells.

The raw Italian recruits received little training. Frequently, they were not even warned to keep their heads down, and they died in their thousands here and elsewhere. I can see how artillery shells punched large round holes in the hillside, which nettles and scrubby trees have tried to fill. I avoid them, worried about what I might find buried there. In these fertile areas, farmers still dig up bones from the war as they plough their fields.

Looking out, I can see far into the Isonzo Valley – now called the Soca Valley – and across to the mountains on the other side. The day is hot and hazy. The river is just visible below us, its turquoise contrasting with the white-grey rocks and verdant green space between, as it winds its way through the valley floor. Halfway up, clouds wreathe the mountains opposite, sliding occasionally off the shoulders of the hills as the sun hits them.

More discoveries. Clambering over the rough ground inside the trenches, we find a two-storey cave linked by a spiral staircase, hacked out of the rock. It is cool in the cavern, a relief from the heat outside. It feels almost cosy. Outside I can hear summer thunder approaching, its sound disorientating as it reverberates between the rocks on the hillside. Suddenly, it is easy to imagine how terrifying it must be to hear artillery fire and to be overrun by Austrian soldiers wielding a flamethrower. There is nowhere to escape. What has been built to protect becomes a death trap.

Walking in the footsteps of soldiers who had gone before, it was not hard to feel the horror of this most vicious of mountain campaigns. I knew that engineers constructed long and precarious cable-car lines in order to transport artillery, shells and other supplies up the mountain. The Army Museum in Vienna has shaky black-and-white film footage of artillery being dragged in pieces up steep snowy slopes. To get to their assigned positions, soldiers trudged up these narrow, stony paths, carrying 35 kg packs. It was nearly impossible to move quietly. In the forest, the dry leaves crunched underfoot and gave you away; on the bare slopes, hobnailed boots clanged against the rocks.

The weather was, and is, highly changeable. In summer, the soldiers' climb would have been sweltering: each of them wore a thick woollen uniform, which quickly became sodden with sweat.

Yet in summer, too, the temperatures plunged into minus figures at night; their sweat-drenched uniforms would have frozen against the skin. In autumn and winter, the fog, hail and snow would have made movement nearly impossible.

But there was worse. Soldiers were regularly swept off paths by avalanches or fell into crevasses. According to Heinz von Lichem's account of the *Kaiserschützen* – and despite their expertise in this environment – an astonishing 60,000 soldiers from Hugo's regiment died under avalanches. Numerous others froze or starved to death, or died of normally treatable conditions (such as tonsillitis, tooth infections or broken bones) because they were stranded; connections to the valley below were disrupted for weeks at a time. Frequent fog and rain left soldiers isolated and disorientated.

When possible, the wounded had to be transported down by stretcher and cable car, but there was also a high mortality rate among the medical orderlies. As for the dead, there was often nowhere to bury them. Some corpses were simply weighed down with stones and left to rot; in summer the flies and smell were intolerable. The only other option was to roll corpses down the mountainside.

As we walked the Front, I visualised Hugo squatting behind one of the makeshift stone walls, or in a shallow trench on these near-vertical slopes, terrified that he would be overrun by Italian troops. In my head I heard artillery fire pounding the sheer limestone or granite slopes, shattering the rock and sending their shrapnel and deadly rock splinters flying. Neither side on the Austrian–Italian border received metal helmets until months into the Southern campaign.

Amid the smoke of artillery, there was also the fear of gas. When the weather conditions were right, both sides launched gas attacks, killing swathes of choking soldiers often before they could put on their gas masks. Many of the survivors returned to their homes with damaged lungs.

My grandfather's Linz cousin Kurt Ungar, the little boy who had been treated by Dr Bloch, was among the war's gas victims.

In 1917, as soon as he was old enough, he joined up. A month later, he fell victim to a gas attack in the Dolomites and was sent to recuperate in Innsbruck, where the family rallied round him. He was spoilt rotten by his two aunts, Sofie and Wilhelmine (Leopold Dubsky's wife) and his uncle, Leopold. I know this because he left a diary.[1]

[At] 1.30, kind Aunt Sofie arrived with a large parcel (big piece of veal in two slices of bread, two large pieces of strudel, 1 kg apples, two jars of apricot jam, etc.). I of course had to eat immediately and tell my story. My kind aunt stayed almost an hour with me. At 3 p.m. Aunt Dubksy (Wilhelmine) arrived (with biscuits, cheese, white bread with ham and cigarettes for my colleagues), I had to eat these immediately as well. My aunt stayed half an hour with me [. . .]. At 4 p.m. there was coffee and bread. At 5.30, Aunt Sofie's maid brought brought me 3 beautiful books to read and a box of apples (2 kg) to distribute. (Everyone was happy), at 6.30 was tea (soup with meat: very good). My stomach is overfilled today. At 7.30 uncle Dubsky (Leopold) dropped by and distributed a packet of cigarettes to my colleagues and brought with him a large slice of white cake as well as nuts, chestnuts and apples. He went quickly as we were already in bed. At 8 p.m. went to sleep. On 20 November 8 o'clock getting up and coffee (Diarrhoea from too much eating).

I was struck by the fact that the Schindlers and Dubskys could lay their hands on such generous amounts of rich food in a period of wartime privations, and also that Wilhelmine thought nothing of giving ham to her nephew. Plainly these were not Jews who kept kosher. As soon as he was well enough, Kurt was transferred back to Linz – and once again he was under the medical supervision of the man who had looked after him as a small child all those years ago, Dr Bloch.

The Eleventh Battle of the Isonzo, the biggest yet, was launched in August 1917 by fifty-two Italian divisions. They threw in their own shock troops, the *Arditi* – literally 'those who dare' – who helped push the Italian line across the Bainsizza Plateau north of Gorizia as well as winning further gains in the south. Austria-Hungary's endangered position now finally earned the German intervention on the Southern Front that had been requested for so long.

The result was a combined German and Austro-Hungarian counter-offensive that goes by many names. It was the Twelfth (and last) Battle of the Isonzo; but it is better known to many as the Battle of Caporetto, fought in the shadow of Mount Krn and made famous by Hemingway's novel *A Farewell to Arms*.

In the morning mist of 24 October, thinly held Italian lines of weary and demoralised soldiers collapsed under heavy and unexpected bombardments, gas, and the shock and awe of stormtroopers. Quickly, the Italians were surrendering in droves, including to a young German officer named Erwin Rommel, whose dash and daring in capturing Mount Montajur, south of Caporetto, laid the basis for a dazzling military career.

In November, Austro-Hungarian forces attacked too from the South Tyrol, catching the Italians in a comprehensive pincer. In only a few days, every metre the Italians had won on the Isonzo was lost; within three weeks, hundreds of thousands of Italian soldiers had surrendered or deserted, and the Italian line had receded all the way back to the River Piave, barely twenty miles north of Venice.

Mark Thompson, in his book *The White War*, has judged Caporetto 'the biggest territorial reversal of any battle during the war and the gravest threat to the Kingdom of Italy since unification'. According to him, the Italians lost 14,000 square kilometres of territory and 1,150,000 people.[2] The British and French were appalled at the ease of the Italian collapse. For Italians, it was a catastrophe such that 'suffering a Caporetto' entered the Italian language as the equivalent of 'meeting his Waterloo'. Their salvation was that their new line held, in part because the Italian retreat had been so fast that the German and Austro-Hungarian forces could not possibly keep up.

Hugo's *Kaiserschützen* regiment had travelled by train to Villach, north of the Isonzo Front, and was then involved in a breakthrough at Flitsch (now Bovec in Slovenia) on 24 October, followed by weeks of intense activity. We visited Bovec in August 2018, a pretty cream-and-pale-pink town set against mountains. It is now a centre for white water rafting and canyoning.

The Battle of Caporetto was Austria-Hungary's high point of the whole Southern Front campaign. I am in no doubt that Hugo would have rejoiced at this dazzling victory and I suspect he believed that it would herald the end of his war. Despite that, in 2017 its centenary passed unnoticed in Austria.

Mount Krn, Slovenia, Summer 2018

The easiest approach to the mountain is from the south-western side. Nevertheless, as my family discovers, walking it with a light pack in late August is a hard four- to five-hour climb up its 7,410 feet. This mountain, which Italians call Monte Nero, has a distinctive shark's fin shape. It is densely wooded until about halfway up and then gives way to bare, near vertical slopes on all sides except the southern side: that, though manageable, is still steep.

From two-thirds of the way up, we can see all the way down to the Adriatic; from the summit, we can take in the stunning view down into the National Park and across to Triglav, the highest mountain in Slovenia. Below is the town of Caporetto, now Kobarid. Now, dozens of multicoloured hang gliders fill the air as we refuel with bean soup in the hut at the top. It is peaceful and beautiful. It occurs to me that this place and this area, fought over tooth and nail between Italy and Austria, now belongs to neither.

Near the top of Mt Krn, World War One fortification in the foreground

I check my history. The Italians managed to snatch Mount Krn on 16 June 1915 in an early and isolated victory in the area. The 3rd Regiment of the *Alpini*, wrapping their boots in sacks of straw to reduce their noise, climbed the mountain in the dark. They over-whelmed the Austrians in hand-to-hand combat on the narrow top, where there was scarcely enough room to pass a fellow hiker, let alone fight. For two years they held their Monte Nero, but without being able to exploit the peak fully to dislodge the Austrian enemy from the neighbouring ridges. And then came Caporetto . . .

Climbing above the hut on Mount Krn, I find a cave that backs onto a small system of tunnels. Walking through them, it is clear from the rusted debris of tin cans that soldiers have slept and eaten up here and taken whatever shelter they could find inside its dank and mossy walls. Just short of the summit, I find my own war souvenir: a bullet casing, its rusted metal covered in a green-ish patina. It measures about 5 centimetres.

One end is blown off, the result of the bullet being fired, so the cylinder is warped and twisted by the heat of the explosion; it resembles a spent paint tube. The other end is still intact and stamped with '1914' and 'VIII' and 'IBM'. Later, the museum in Kobarid identifies it as Austro-Hungarian. It is one of the millions that littered the slopes after the war, and which hikers are finding even today.

In the museum, too, I find an extraordinary relief map of Mount Krn showing the Italian and Austro-Hungarian fronts in red and blue dotted lines. At the back of the mountain, and on the spines that radiate away from Krn, the two sides are only metres apart. This war could be very intimate. As I wander through the rooms, looking at striking black-and-white photographs, I hear a boy of about seven turn to his mother and say in German, *Aber Mutti, Krieg ist schrecklich!* 'But Mum, war is horrible!'

6

Food Riots

Innsbruck, Summer 2019

I have spent a lot of time in Innsbruck this year, and as I research, I realise I have arrived exactly a hundred years after a pivotal moment in Austria's story, when my family suddenly found itself no longer citizens of an empire. It was another anniversary that went unnoticed in Innsbruck.

I trace the key moments. At first, there is a prospect of triumph. The heady victory at Caporetto is accompanied in November 1917 by an early Christmas present in the form of Russia's exit from the war. In a coup, Lenin's and Trotsky's Bolsheviks – who have always opposed the war – grab power and negotiate an armistice at the Treaty of Brest-Litovsk on 3 March 1918. Austria-Hungary can now concentrate its war effort on the Southern Front.

Just over two weeks later, Germany launches its massive *Kaiserschlacht* – the Emperor's Battle – on the Western Front, hoping to snatch victory before the arrival of American troops. A triumph for the German and Austro-Hungarian *Kaisers* seems on the horizon.

It never comes. Despite Caporetto, Austria-Hungary is falling apart. Army morale plummets and soldiers desert. There is resentment that victory over Russia, bought with so much blood, has brought derisory gain. There are strikes, food riots, and angry demands for an end to war. I track the escalating food crisis in articles in the *Innsbrucker Nachrichten* (Innsbruck News) in 1917 and 1918, which report on potato shortages, on the need to overcome any aversion to eating horsemeat, and on a prohibition on coffeehouses serving sugar with their drinks – since that could allow guests to circumvent sugar rationing.

In June 1918, Austria-Hungary's final offensive to subdue Italy fails. Italy has recovered from the disaster of Caporetto, thanks to the swift dispatch of French and British forces to bolster the front on the River Piave – and to the sacking of the stubborn General Cadorna as Italian chief-of-staff. Come 23 October 1918, it is Austria-Hungary's turn to suffer its own version of Caporetto in the Battle of Vittorio Veneto: with this battle – Italy's only decisive victory in two and a half years of fighting – the Italian shame of the previous year can be expunged.

A chaotic Austro-Hungarian retreat follows, as hundreds of thousands of prisoners fall to the Italians. Soldiers in the imperial army, many now going hungry, lose the will to fight – not only Slavs, Czechs and Hungarians, but Austrians, too. Amid this chaos, Hugo and Erich have to make their way back to Innsbruck, ragged and exhausted, but relieved to be surrounded by their own familiar peaks.

Austria-Hungary signs an armistice with Italy on 3 November 1918 at the Villa Giusti, near Padua, but it is too late to save a disintegrating empire. Already, Austria-Hungary's individual nations are pulling away, asserting their independence. In Vienna and Budapest, protesters demand radical change: some want Bolshevism, some want new liberal regimes, others want something else; many want a republic.

On 11 November 1918, Kaiser Karl accepts the inevitable and abdicates – though he avoids using that word. That same day, in a train carriage in a French forest, Germany admits defeat in a separate armistice; Germany's own *Kaiser* has already fled. The empire has fallen. The First World War is over.

Somewhat prematurely, in Vienna a Provisional National Assembly announces the foundation of the 'Republic of German-Austria' and that this new republic is part of the new German Republic. The vast majority of people of all political persuasions are in favour of Austria being part of Germany. After all, they have fought and died side by side. In the vacuum of the lost empire, joining up with the Germans seems an appropriate consolidation of German-speaking peoples. But they are to be thwarted.

Hugo is such a proud, first-generation Habsburg citizen that I believe he is deeply saddened by the collapse of the empire for which he has fought with distinction. Suddenly, his medals are obsolete, bearing likenesses and initials of now defunct monarchs. From 12 November 1918, like other Austrians, he is a citizen of a fragile, newly born little republic. In right-wing and conservative circles, some voices are already casting around for scapegoats for defeat, blaming not the enemies without, but looking for enemies within.

However, Hugo is alive. It is nothing short of a miracle that three of Sofie's four sons have survived the war. I have discovered in the Washington Holocaust Archives a copy of a letter written to my cousin John Kafka, after the Second World War, describing Sofie as having 'the qualities of a reigning, absolute matriarch', who ruled the Schindler family as 'the Queen Mother'. Her sons' return to civilian life means that, at the age of sixty-two, she can finally take more of a back seat in running the family business.

While Sofie remains involved in all important decisions, it is time for Hugo and Erich to try and make a success of things in the new economic environment, in which few have money to spend on anything but the basics.

I come across several 1918 photos by the Innsbruck photographer Richard Müller, which show groups of women and children queueing for milk. They are beautifully lit and have an almost staged quality. The subjects all look obediently towards the photographer, but their pinched, unsmiling faces betray the poverty and lack of food of the previous four years.

The end of war did not mean an end to Austria's privations. An armistice was not yet a peace, and Austria was still blockaded.

The treaty that did emerge, on 10 September 1919, was called the Treaty of Saint-Germain-en-Laye; like the Treaty of Versailles with Germany, its terms were thrashed out by the war's victors, and they amounted to an emasculation of Austria. It confirmed the loss of empire, as an independent Czechoslovakia, Yugoslavia ('Kingdom of the Slovenes, Croats and Serbs') and Poland emerged. Austria lost 60 per cent of its own territory, while Hungary – dealt with in the Treaty of Trianon the following year – lost a staggering 72 per cent to neighbouring countries.

The one-time Habsburg Dual Monarchy, presiding over the third-largest population in Europe, was reduced to a rump of two impoverished, landlocked states. And Austria was expressly forbidden from joining Germany, ending that dream – for now. I was struck by a phrase in Eric Hobsbawm's autobiography, *Interesting Times: A Twentieth-Century Life*. The social historian, who lived in Vienna as a child, summed up the Austria he knew at this time as a 'smallish provincial republic of great beauty, which did not believe that it ought to exist'.[1]

With its mineral and agricultural resources greatly reduced, Austria struggled to feed its people. In Vienna, hundreds of children begged for food in the streets. In the summer of 1919, food shortages became so severe that the local governments of Upper Austria and Salzburg decreed that anyone on holiday in the area should leave immediately. In Linz, holidaymakers were given eight days to pack up and get out, otherwise they would face a fine. Even what should have been the joyous return of the 80,000 Austrian prisoners of war from Italy, in September 1919, increased anxiety: more mouths to feed.

In Linz, the local Jewish population was already struggling to feed 20,000 Jewish refugees, internees and prisoners of war – people who had arrived there after 1914 and were unable to return home. They continued to live in poverty in barracks on the edge of the city. Lilli and Eduard Bloch sensed an upsurge in anti-semitism and became worried about pogroms and violence breaking out.

Matters were different for Innsbruck's much smaller Jewish community, but here there was the trauma of land loss to add to the lives lost in the previous four years. In the treaty, Italy had laid successful claim to the South Tyrol, and its impending forfeiture was resented bitterly. The North Tyrol campaigned hard not to lose the South, but the complaints fell on deaf ears. Most Tyroleans felt duped. How, they asked, could splitting neighbours, families and communities from each other across an international border be consistent with Point 10 in US President Woodrow Wilson's much-trumpeted 'Fourteen Points' for a just peace? That 'the peoples of Austria-Hungary, whose place among the nations we wish to see safeguarded and assured, should be accorded the freest opportunity of autonomous development.'

The South Tyrol was definitively ripped from the North in October 1920. The old local hero, Andreas Hofer, was revived again in a cartoon, demanding that Wilson look him in the face and answer the question: 'Am I German or Italian?' Wilson looks puzzled. He has clearly given the matter little thought. Woodrow Wilson did not have long to live, but according to one historian, long enough to regret this particular decision.

The Italians wasted no time, sealing the new Tyrolean border with Austria and forbidding post or goods to cross from Italy into Austria. This was not only a humiliating loss of land, but also a sudden breach in the supply of raw materials, which for decades had flowed from the fertile southern parts of the country to Innsbruck. Partition was a human tragedy too, witnessed in the chaotic scenes at railway stations as South Tyroleans crowded onto trains, trying to leave before they were trapped; some died, swept off the train roofs on which they were balanced.

In the South Tyrol, a process of Italianisation began. From 1922, it was forbidden to speak German in schools and in public offices, while incentives lured migrants from Italy's south to settle there. Increasingly, ethnic cleansing drove out much of the German-speaking population, who fled to the North Tyrol.[2] As for the North, it suffered the indignity of occupation by 15,000

Cartoon depicting an imaginary encounter between Woodrow
Wilson and Andreas Hofer in which Hofer asks him, 'Look
me in the face, Mr Wilson and then tell me: am I German
or *Walsch* [an Italian-speaking South Tyrolean]?'

Italian troops. The local newspapers reported snidely that it was a
good thing that the troops would be bringing their own supplies, as
these 'spoilt Italians' would not find much to eat in North Tyrol.[3]
One reaction to the loss of the South Tyrol was to deepen a
yearning to be properly German. A popular image from 1920
shows the Tyroleans crowded on one side of a broken bridge with
a German flag-bearer waving at them from the other side, enticing
them across.[4] A Herculean man in *Lederhosen* lifts the missing
section of the bridge (labelled *Anschluss*, 'Union') into place, to
allow the crowd to cross and meld into Germany. That desire was
expressly denied by the treaties of Saint-Germain and Versailles,
but the yearning remained strong.

Propaganda postcard published by Goeth Vienna and
Munich, 1921, from a watercolour by Alfred Pirkkert

A plebiscite of 1921 asked the people of the Tyrol and Salzburg:
'Is Union with the German Reich required?' The result was a 98.5
per cent vote in favour. Such feelings reflected a lack of confidence
in the new Austrian state and even in the rump Tyrol's ability to
feed itself without the beautiful South Tyrolean vineyards and
orchards.

For the Schindlers, the rupture with the South Tyrol must have
played havoc with their supplies of fruit for their *Schnapps*,
compote and jam. Yet I suspect their involvement in the food and
drink business resulted in them being better off than most
Tyroleans. Certainly, the foodstuffs that they and the Dubskys
were able to deliver to the wounded Egon Kafka in hospital, in
1917, is one small piece of evidence suggesting that even in the
middle of the war they did not go hungry. But in turn, I wonder if

it also nurtured resentment from those less well off, less able to obtain food.

I began to get a glimmer, too, of how others began to interpret that very survival and the continuance of the business. Something dark and ugly, largely held in abeyance during the war, was resurgent now that war had ended in defeat, humiliation and hunger.

The Tyrol, 1918–19

On 2 August 1918, in the face of antisemitic gatherings and groundless accusations, the Jewish communities of Austria feel compelled to publish a declaration, claiming that the Jews 'in this war, sacrificed their wealth and blood unconditionally and unreservedly. In respect of war provision and the needs of the state, they contributed far more than others.' These communities make claims – perhaps unwise, in hindsight – 'to have suffered more materially than the rest of the population' and that:

> their psychological suffering was greater as unscrupulous antisemitic party leaders of the interior, not without success sought to transplant the hatred of Jews to the army, even at the Front. Successes have been ascribed disproportionately to non-Jews rather than Jews, while mistakes have been laid at the door of Jews, out of all proportion to the number of such mistakes made by non-Jews.

The declaration warns that if the authorities do not step in to protect Jews from pogroms, Austrian Jews will have to 'organise their self-help'.[5]

This is not the only such complaint; other notices and articles appear in the press, pointing out that 12,000 Jewish soldiers have fallen on the field of honour next to their Christian comrades, and begging German Christian mothers not to tolerate the mockery of bereaved Jewish mothers. Reading these articles a hundred years later, I feel discomfort and foreboding; competitive victim-hood is no way to make friends. At the same time, I know that a narrative is developing around Austria's Jews in the war, whose plotline they will struggle to influence.

As the terms of the Treaty of Saint-Germain become clear to Austrians in the autumn of 1919, their anger grows and is skil-fully channelled by antisemitic political factions. Added to the pre-war blood libels and resentment over Jewish commercial interests are new charges: Jews have been instrumental in Austria's defeat, and Jewish banks and businesses have profited, while patriotic Austrians have suffered and gone hungry. In this well of hatred, Jews somehow manage to be seen as both grasping capi-talists *and* Bolsheviks.

The antisemites are uninterested in the fact that the tiny Jewish population of Innsbruck is nearly broke. They invested their savings heavily in war loans to support their erstwhile emperor's war effort. Now, there is no chance of repayment. Innsbruck's Jews have to relinquish their dream of building a new synagogue.[6]

Meanwhile, in the June 1919 council and federal elections, the Tyrolean People's Party campaigns under the banner: 'The Tyrol for the Tyroleans'. According to their rhetoric, if people do not vote for them, the Tyrol will end up being run by Viennese Jews and socialists, who will trample on what remains of Tyrolean customs. In August 1919, five councillors from the Tyrolean People's Party demand that any non-Aryans be banished from Innsbruck.[7]

Rioting and looting break out in Innsbruck. On 4 December 1919, a large crowd of hungry people, mostly women, gather in front of the local government building and agitate to be seen by the county governor, named Schraffl. The demonstrators show signs of 'hardship and deprivation'. Several hundred women get in and demand better supplies of key foods such as bread, flour and potatoes, and better supplies of wood for heating. According to the next day's *Innsbrucker Nachrichten*, they also want an end to the black market, closure of the Café Lehner (a well-known black-market café) and – particularly relevant for the Schindlers – a prohibition on the display of luxury food in shop windows.

The food riots make the front page of the next edition of the *Innsbrucker Nachrichten* on 6 December 1919, which describes in detail the destruction wrought by the demonstrators in Innsbruck. One crowd heads for the Schindler jam factory in the Karmelitergasse and strips it of its supplies. A further crowd heads for the Schindler headquarters in the Andreas-Hofer-Strasse, where Hugo and Erich just manage to prevent them from destroying the shop:

A boy started to pull down the protective shutter from the display window to break the glass, when the owners appeared . . . and begged the crowd to cease their destruction, and this was partially successful as the owners themselves took jam and other tins of food from the interior of the shop and threw them into the crowd. This strange show attracted a large number of curious onlookers, who quickly divided up the food and left. The Italian military appeared and the crowd dispersed.[8]

Although cafés, inns and shops all over Innsbruck are looted and have their windows smashed, the politicians agree that nothing much can be done, as the perpetrators are women and young people. The businesses are left to clear up the mess and continue as best they can.

Newspapers such as the *Tiroler Anzeiger* are quick to identify enormous injustice in the provision of food supplies and point the finger at smugglers and black marketeers, whom they declare to be *die wahren Wegbereiter des Bolschevismus* – 'the true precursors of Bolshevism', which finds its nourishment where 'the consciousness of the people has been poisoned by the contrasts between need and luxury'.[9]

Other newspapers such as the *Deutsche Zeitung* of the

Nationaldemokratische Partei declare more generally that its readers have suffered not only a collapse of the monarchy, and a military, economic and financial breakdown, but also a moral disintegration.[10] The author identifies the origin of these issues in Hungary, Galicia and Poland: 'The Jews in these areas used the war immediately as an opportunity to make a profit.'

The mood is clear. The Schindlers can no longer wrap themselves in the blanket of assimilation. The trope of Jews profiting from the misfortunes of others is gaining currency.

Following the riots of December 1919, if Hugo and Erich were expecting sympathy from their fellow Jews, they were to be disappointed. Hugo Ornstein, a Zionist member of Innsbruck's Jewish community, opined in the *Jüdische Nachrichten* (Jewish News) that supposedly assimilated Jews, loved by the Christian population for their charitable deeds, could not expect to be protected from such looting by their assimilation. The Schindlers were not named, but Ornstein's reference to the plundering of the jam factory leaves no ambiguity.

His article was effectively an open plea to Hugo and Erich that there was nothing to be gained by assimilating and turning their backs on their religion; they should put themselves at the head of the Jewish community in Innsbruck. They ought not to be ashamed of their Jewish roots.

I found myself fascinated by the exposure of these tensions, between Zionism and assimilation, within such a tiny Jewish community. Pride in assimilation was one thing that my father inherited from Hugo. Clearly, in 1919 such views upset other Innsbruck Jews. I had assumed that the family at least celebrated the big Jewish holidays. Ornstein's criticism made me wonder whether they did even that. I scoured the photographs of various celebrations held by the Jewish community, and could spot Leopold Dubsky's wife Wilhelmine – but never the Schindlers.

I concluded that my family could not have been active members of the local Jewish community and perhaps barely even saw themselves as Jewish. And yet, as Ornstein warned, would that make any difference to how others saw them? Ornstein acknowledged that the riots were not *specifically* anti-semitic, as there was an attack the same day on a Jesuit convent. It was primarily the Schindlers' stock of food and drink that made them a tempting target. But how far was there something else involved?

I spent a lot of time puzzling over the particular strain of anti-semitism that infected Innsbruck, trying not to fall into the trap of reading history backwards – as if everything slotted into a causal chain of events defined by a conclusion we all know. The more I read, the more I realised that there was not one reason but many overlapping ones. I also understood that many of the explanations put forward elsewhere simply do not fit Innsbruck.

In one article on 'Anti-Semitism in Europe before the Holocaust', the authors identify 'four strains of anti-Semitism (religious, racial, economic, and political), which were ignited by the effects of declining economic well-being, increased Jewish immigration, growth of leftist support, and identification of Jews with the leadership of the political left.'[11]

However, of the four critical factors that sparked antisemitism elsewhere in Europe, only one struck me as relevant to the Tyrol and to the Innsbruck food riots of 1919 – poverty – and, of course, my family were business people who imported, produced and sold food and drink. For a hungry, improverished and angry crowd, I suspect this made them a target without much thought as to my family's roots – at least at that point.

As for 'increasing Jewish immigration', it was barely discernible in Innsbruck. Unlike in Vienna or even Linz, there was practically no immigration of Eastern European Jews to Innsbruck before and after the First World War. However, I concluded that the Tyrol would not be the first place where the fear of immigration existed even without the reality of it. Perhaps topography played its part. There is barely a street in Innsbruck from which you cannot see the mountains rearing up all around you. They are stunning, protective and a tangible barrier to the outside world. They could also, it seemed to me, create a fear of being overrun in what feels like a limited space.

As to the other two factors: the growth of popular support for the Left and the prominence of Jewish leaders within it, which contributed to antisemitism in Vienna; again these didn't seem to fit. Politically, the Tyrol – conservative, agrarian, provincial and deeply Catholic – saw itself as very different from the radicalism of 'Red Vienna'. The Tyrol was always proud of its identity and its independent mindset, emphasising its differences from Vienna.

However, political turmoil was rampant across Europe in the aftermath of war, as competing visions battled to reshape the old, collapsed empires. In such a climate, perhaps some Tyroleans began to fear the Jews among them as potential Trojan horses for the Left. Perhaps too, the loss of the South Tyrol so threatened the identity of the North Tyrol that the slightest whisper of difference in its ranks was enough to breed hostility against the Jews.

That certainly seemed to be the case for the *Tiroler Antisemitenbund* (Tyrolean Antisemites' Federation), which was founded in October 1919. I read its programme and found that it drew together, and amplified, disparate strands of antisemitism whether or not they had any basis in the Tyrol.

According to their manifesto, Jews were – unsurprisingly – held responsible for the loss of the war and for the poor economic situation in the Tyrol; in addition, 'Jewish-Bolshevik' elements had allegedly taken over public offices and now dominated commerce, universities, the theatre, the arts and the press. Even the German people had given up their political leadership to the Jews and thereby lost their self-determination.

Their demands included a Tyrol for Tyroleans, and specifically that any land or houses sold to Jews since 1914 should be expropriated – though compensation was allowed. The Federation set out criteria for determining who was properly Aryan, and – in a stricter definition than even the Nazis' later Nuremberg race laws – advocated that if only one grandparent were Jewish, that would define a grandson or granddaughter as Jewish too (irrespective of any actual religious preference).[12]

Innsbruck, Austria, 1920

This provincial city – capital of a reduced Tyrol, in a reduced Austria – becomes home to the first Austrian branch of a new German political party, which has changed its name to the *Nationalsozialistische Deutsche Arbeiterpartei* (NSDAP): the National Socialist German Workers' Party. This nationalist, anti-capitalist and antisemitc party is only one manifestation of a new, far-right populism that is trading on economic dislocation and post-war anger. Its adherents, at present few in number, hate both the democratic governments that have emerged in Germany and Austria, and any whiff of Bolshevism.

In the same year, the Tyrol is the first region of Austria in which a new right-wing volunteer militia begins to operate, the *Heimwehr*, inspired by the *Freikorps* paramilitaries springing up in Germany.

In September 1920, Adolf Hitler arrives in Innsbruck to speak on behalf of the NSDAP. Distraught at Germany's surrender, which he hears about in hospital while recovering from the effects of gas, he quickly espouses the belief that an undefeated Germany has been sold down the river by home-grown Jews, Bolsheviks and the 'November criminals' – the politicians who signed the armistice and then agreed the Treaty of Versailles.

He is not yet leader of his fringe party. This is his first public appearance in Innsbruck, and it is poorly attended. Austria's new government is run by Social Democrats, and on 2 October 1920, their newspaper in Innsbruck, the *Volkszeitung*, issues a mocking report. It manages, too, to misspell his name:

So yesterday, there was really a mass meeting. The big town hall was full – of empty chairs . . . the first person to speak was a certain Hittler, from Munich, who was supposed to be something like a leader. It was typical for the National Socialist: as long as he spoke factually, there was pretty much an icy silence, only here and there someone occasionally yawned loudly and gave the 'honoured guest' to understand that he should stop his boring nonsense. The speaker appeared not to understand this, it was only as a heckler shouted 'dirty Jews' every two minutes, that he understood and picked up speed . . . so that those who had happily drifted off woke with a start and yelled 'out, out, Jew, Jew!' While the speaker began factually, he ended by being bizarrely senseless. But one thing we can envy him for, the good man certainly does not have lung disease or suffer from asthma. His excessively powerful lungs cannot however make up for his lack of brain power.[13]

Do my grandfather, or Erich or the Dubskys even notice this event in their midst? The Schindlers and the Dubskys are business people. They have adroitly navigated the riots in the previous year, and I feel sure that they calculate they can safely ignore this particular tiny, internally splintered group. They are right – for the moment.

For Hugo, there are always his beloved mountains to which he can retreat. Alpinism flourishes as the men who survive 'the war to end all wars' test their mettle in climbing, hiking and conquering. For some, it is a relief, a way to escape the everyday; for others, it is an expurgation of survivors' guilt: they are here, their companions are not. Yet even these refuges, where minds, bodies and souls can be cleansed and find solace, are beginning to be denied to some.

As many as 8 per cent of Innsbruckers are members of its Alpine Club: it is one of the bigger branches, wielding considerable influence. At its 50th annual general meeting, on 15 March 1921, a change to the rules of the membership is voted through, by which, as Gebhard Bendler later notes, 'any person of good character and of Aryan descent and German or Latin origin and exceptionally other peoples of Aryan descent [can] join as ordinary members.' Until this time, the only criterion for membership has been that the applicant has to be of good character.

In the discussion over the introduction of this new membership rule, it is noted that in contrast to earlier years, the main committee of the Alpine Club as a whole is no longer against such an 'Aryan paragraph'. It is also noted that, in any event, the Innsbruck club has not actually admitted any Jew as a new member in recent years. As Bendler points out, exactly how long such unofficial exclusion has been going on is unclear.

For now, Hugo remains a member and continues to climb the mountains he loves. But on every summit he finds a cross, marking the point where a Christian mountaineer has come closer to his God. Even the peaks are political. In one photograph he takes, Hugo inks in the cross after sticking the photo in the album – deep pen scores on the crucifix. Perhaps he has had an unpleasant encounter on that peak, or there was an eruption of anger. How far do the mountains still remain his sanctuary?

A century later, there's much that I have to infer about how my grandfather tried to reach equilibrium in the aftermath of war. I believe that he looked back on the war on the Southern Front as a just war, which was lost. I suspect that in December 1919 he sympathised with the food rioters: he was, by all accounts, a kind and generous man who gave freely to local charities. As for the growing antisemitism, I suspect he chose to ignore it. After all, antisemitism had always come in waves, and surely this one would recede, too.

Above all, Innsbruck was his home. Where else was he to go? He was a born and bred Tyrolean, and there was no guarantee that anywhere else would be better.

Moreover, Hugo had a new idea that would thrust him into the centre of local life as never before. He wanted to open a grand new café.

Part Three

Apfelstrudel

Innsbruck, Summer 2018

I am in the City Archives, this time tracking down images of the Innsbruck institution that my grandfather Hugo and great-uncle Erich created. I type into the computer's search engine: 'Café Schindler'. Forty hits. Surprised at the wealth of pictures that pop up, I enjoy spending the next hour or so opening one after the other. Some are familiar from my father's photo albums, but many are entirely new to me.

My attention is caught by the earliest photograph of all, which has a clean, film-set quality to it. Men stroll, chatting, newspapers in hand, down the middle of a sharply sunlit street. A cyclist meanders across the road: there are no road markings to keep him in check. Horses and carriages await passengers opposite the café. A sole car sits outside the café's neighbour, the Hotel Maria Theresia; no doubt it awaits a rich guest, as it is clear that cars are still a rare sight in Innsbruck.

At the top right-hand corner of the photograph, the Patscher-kofel mountain is visible, a smooth, reassuring and symmetrical presence. In most of the other photographs, taken from a different angle, it is the craggy Nordkette that looms, visible at the opposite end of the Maria-Theresien-Strasse.

My mind wanders back to scenes from childhood, where we eat off remnants of Café Schindler crockery: robust creamy-white plates, saucers and cups, each with red-yellow-red tramline lines running around them, stamped with a spatchcocked eagle, and with a large 'S' on their middle. We wash and dry them carefully for we recognise, even at a very early age, that they are special and mean a lot to my father. Despite the care we take, over the years the odd item breaks. Sometimes I am responsible, and I feel guilty each time.

These ceramic memories become the props for the stories that Kurt tells us about the café. The details are vague, but the impression of a treasured possession somehow lost is sharp in my mind. I come to understand that the ghost of this place haunts my father, its crockery an enduring reminder of everything he no longer has – and the person of importance that he no longer is.

Looking at these early photographs of the Café Schindler, I imagine Erich and Hugo first broaching the idea of the café with their mother. What would she think? Sofie remained a partner in the S. Schindler business and retained an influence over it. I suspect she was cautious. Possibly she questioned the wisdom of going into competition with their existing wholesale customers by, in effect,

The Café Schindler, 1920s

selling S. Schindler liquors and *Schnapps* direct to the public. But Hugo and Erich had something different, and much bigger, in mind.

Their idea was not for a tavern or *Gasthaus*, but instead a Viennese-style coffeehouse and patisserie. At the time, there was only one such coffee house in Innsbruck: the venerable Café Central, which was founded in 1877. Hugo and Erich wanted something similar but much grander, which would have live music, dancing, and even billiards and cards.

It was not only an enterprising idea; it was an audacious one. The overall economic situation remained dire, with Austria's economy on life support through the early 1920s. In 1922, the new republic had to rely on help from a recently formed international body, the League of Nations, to try and bring its spiralling inflation under control. In return, the League insisted on a scheme of reconstruction that saw the introduction of a new currency – the Austrian Schilling – as well as a set of austerity measures, declared necessary to stabilise the economy.

There were unpleasant side effects, as the measures contributed to both high unemployment and social and political discord. It would not be until the second half of the decade before Austria really began to recover, helped in part by tourists who were attracted to the Tyrol by the beauty of its mountains and lakes.

In 1922, against this still fragile economic backdrop, Hugo and Erich took over the commercial licence of the 'Zum Sandwirt' tavern on none other than Innsbruck's main street, the Maria-Theresien-Strasse. I imagine they felt the name of the previous enterprise was auspicious as 'Zum Sandwirt' was the name of Andreas Hofer's original tavern in the South Tyrol.

Hugo and Erich planned to launch something intended to become an oasis of luxury and enjoyment, two qualities that were in short supply in post-war Innsbruck. This prime location made good business sense, and I can see from the early photographs why they chose this address. The building was a stunning, triple-fronted edifice at No. 29; along the road from Bauer & Schwarz, western Austria's first department store, owned jointly by two other Jewish families. This is the shop that revolutionised shopping in the Tyrol, the place where all purchases could be made under one roof for the first time.

In fact, Hugo and Erich – whose names I could not find in the local land registry – must have leased No. 29 from Bauer & Schwarz, who owned the building. I realised also that, in the eyes of antisemites, the arrival of the Café Schindler on the main street would have taken Innsbruck's main street one step closer to the 1909 vision of towering Jewish businesses pushing out smaller Christian, German ones.

It was an imposing, unmissable site. In front of the café was one of Innsbruck's most famous statues, the *Anna-Säule* (St Anna's Column), a landmark that celebrated the 1703 battle in which Bavarian troops were driven from the Tyrol. The street outside led straight into Innsbruck's old medieval town. Beneath the windows of No. 29, the whole of Innsbruck's civic life flowed. Whether a success or a failure, the fate of the new Café Schindler would be very public.

In opening a coffee house, Hugo and Erich were tapping into a tradition going back to the late seventeenth century, when the first coffee house opened in Vienna. Coffee had already diffused through Europe: London, for example, saw its first coffee houses in the 1650s, and as time went on they became well-established hubs for the latest news, debate and gossip.

According to local legend, Vienna owed the introduction of coffee to the aftermath of the Second Siege of Vienna in July 1683. The story goes that when the city was relieved by the King of Poland, forcing the besieging Turks to flee, among their abandoned camels, horses and weapons were about 500 sacks of unfamiliar green-coloured beans. A Polish nobleman, Georg Franz Kulczycki, who had been instrumental in Vienna's salvation, recognised the coffee beans, claimed them as part of his

The Café Schindler, 1930s

Photo by well-known Innsbruck photographer,
Richard Müller, of the Café Schindler

reward, and was soon trying to peddle his bitter, black and gritty brew from door to door.

Unsurprisingly, Kulczycki's enterprise was a flop. But others saw its potential. An Armenian spy at the imperial court by the name of Diodato opened Vienna's first coffee house. Others followed and experimented with the recipe, adding honey, sugar and eventually milk and cream. Viennese coffee was born, and Kulczycki (or 'Kolschitzky' in German) was anointed the patron of coffee brewers, earning a statue on the Viennese street named after him. Naturally, he has a coffee pot in one hand.

I love coffee houses. Most of this book has been written in the latter-day coffee houses of Innsbruck, Linz, Vienna and London; I can concentrate well with a gentle flow of noise all around me.

When I read about their history, I realised the importance of coffee houses to society: they allowed men – and it was only men, to begin with – to meet on neutral territory, to discuss the issues of the day, to transact business, and above all to think, away from rowdy, beer-soused taverns. Coffee was transformative. One historian, William H. Ukers, even asserted that 'everywhere coffee is introduced, revolutions have happened. It is a radical drink and its function was always to make people think. And when people begin to think, it is dangerous for tyranny and those who oppose liberty.'[1] Cafés are inherently liberal affairs.

In the Innsbruck City Archives, I obtained the old planning department's file for the Café Schindler. The folder contained beautiful A2-sized hand-drawn plans for a café and various associated kitchens and offices. Being an employment lawyer, I was delighted to see far-reaching health and safety measures – for those times – and legal protection for the café's employees, including stipulations that surfaces had to be washable, there had to be adequate ventilation, and employees should have access to bathrooms with soap and towels.

There were other provisions, too. All machines had to have guards on them and signage to ensure they could be used safely. I was relieved to see that employees were officially prohibited from spitting on the floor, instead being provided with spittoons, which had to be kept clean. Tuberculosis was still rife in Innsbruck, given that it was another two decades before a vaccine became widely available.

In the Tyrol County Museum, I scoured the large bound books of local newspapers to see if I could find the very first advertisement for the café. I had almost given up on the 1922 volumes, when I turned a page and finally found an announcement squeezed into the end of that year, on 23 December. Hugo Schindler was offering his guests 'the finest Viennese baked goods and specialities'. He was leaving nothing to chance for the success of the café. I saw that Hugo had headhunted Karl Santol, a top pastry chef from Vienna, who was the author of the patissiers' bible *Der Praktische Zuckerbäcker*, 'The Practical Confectioner'.

I found a copy of this recipe book available from an antiquarian bookseller in Germany and could not resist ordering it. It arrived a few days later, and it has been delighting me ever since with its tips on how to create the crispest pastry and most unctuous cake and pie fillings, and its seven different cheesecake recipes.

Hugo was aiming high and it was a real coup to hire Santol. He had been pastry chef at Demel & Sons, Vienna's most famous coffeehouse. Named after Christoph Demel, the café was founded in 1786. Even today, a century after the end of the Habsburg dynasty, it describes itself glowingly as *Hofzuckerbäcker* (Confectioners to the Court). Demel's is famous for its beautiful marzipan and sugar sculptures as well as the fact that it has the legal right to make *Sachertorte*, the rich Austrian chocolate cake with an apricot jam filling and a dark-chocolate mirror glaze.

Austria's best-known chocolate cake turns out to be its most legally disputed one, too. According to legend, the eponymous *Sachertorte* was invented in 1832 by the sixteen-year-old apprentice chef Franz Sacher, who had been tasked to come up with a novel cake that would be a credit at parties hosted by his employer, Prince Metternich, the most famous diplomat of his day. The cake was a success and Franz's eldest son, Eduard, perfected the recipe while working at Demel; but later, in 1876, he opened the Hotel Sacher, which was to become one of the most famous hotels in Vienna, where he baked *Sachertorte* using a slightly different recipe.

For a while I found myself distracted by the surprisingly litigious history of this cake, of which I had such clear childhood memories. Whenever my father visited Vienna, he stayed at the Hotel Sacher. He would not have dreamt of staying anywhere cheaper. I remember visits there with him as a teenager and my delight at the mini *Sachertorten* that always appeared in our room each evening.

For many decades, the two purveyors of *Sachertorte* co-existed. However, in 1934 the Hotel Sacher went bankrupt and Eduard's son – carrying on the family tradition – went to work at Demel's. In 1938 the new owners of the Hotel Sacher took to boasting of selling 'the Original *Sacher-Torte*'. In the complex and bitter dispute that followed, the Hotel Sacher and Demel's each asserted that they had the exclusive right to call their cake the 'original'.

In years of litigation, the minutiae of the recipe were hotly debated: whether there should be one layer of apricot jam under the mirror glaze, or a second layer in the middle, and the percentage of cocoa solids the chocolate should contain. How dense should the crumb of the cake be? Could the chef use margarine? It must have been enormous fun for the lawyers to debate these very Viennese concerns. Each party called famous clients as witnesses, to testify to the superiority of their respective versions of the cake.

After decades of intermittent cake wars – interrupted by a real war – the parties finally reached a pragmatic out-of-court settlement in 1963, in which it was agreed that the Hotel Sacher could call its cake the '*Original Sacher-Torte*' and had the right to pipe this epithet on a round chocolate medal placed at the edge of the cake. Demel's could call its version the *Eduard-Sacher-Torte*, using a triangular chocolate label. The Hotel Sacher's cake has two layers of jam, and the Demel's version just one. The original recipe, handwritten by Eduard Sacher for his version of the cake, is kept in a safe by the Hotel Sacher. Any pastry chef joining the hotel team has to sign a confidentiality agreement before being allowed to see it.

I do not know how far Karl Santol tweaked the recipe for the *Sachertorte* he baked at the Café Schindler; however, I do know that on opening in 1922, the café with its cakes was an instant success. Hugo and Erich's gamble was correct – Innsbruck craved enjoyment and relief from the horrors and dislocations of war and, for many, the miseries that had followed the end of the war. It was one of the only venues in Innsbruck that had live music and where guests could dance. The Café Schindler became the focal point of Innsbruck's cultural and social life.

Innsbruck, 2018

Even today, I have conversations with misty-eyed Innsbruckers who remember tales told by their parents, or grandparents, of courtship and dancing at the Café Schindler. Frequently, I return to a cloth-covered album I have, which is devoted to photographs of the café. I have looked at it so often that I feel I can, quite easily, insert myself into that time and place . . .

First, I wander from the Maria-Theresien-Strasse into the retail shop on the ground floor, where they sell handmade chocolates and candied fruit in hinged wooden boxes branded with the S. Schindler name. I go up the broad, polished wooden staircase in the corner, which leads up to the first floor: that's where the café is. Perhaps Hugo Schindler himself is there to greet customers, a proud and congenial patron. A tail-coated waiter takes my coat and ushers me to a banquette, at right angles to the window. I have a view of the street below me, the *Anna-Säule* statue, and above all the mountains, which rise up dredged in snow, to the right of my field of vision.

I order coffee and contemplate the cakes that sit behind a curved glass vitrine: *Apfelstrudel* (apple strudel), *Topfenstrudel* (cream cheese strudel), *Mohnkuchen* (poppyseed cake), *Linzertorte* (hazelnut and redcurrant jam cake), *Topfentorte* (baked cheesecake) and

Gugelhupf. This last is a plain or chocolate-marbled sponge cake with distinctive ridges and a hole in the middle. And of course, there is *Sachertorte* – an unauthorised version. Far away from the capital, Santol knows he can serve it, as long as he does not call it 'the original'.

The coffee arrives, served on a metal tray. It is placed discreetly on the starched linen tablecloth in front of me, accompanied by a glass of water to counteract its dehydrating effect. Sugar cubes are piled into small bowls to be extracted with small tongs. Tiny handle-less white jugs hold the cream.

Slices of cake are lifted gently with a triangular cake slice and placed on a plate with care. The stakes are high: if they topple over, it is, according to Austrian folklore, certain that an evil mother-in-law awaits. Assuming the customer has escaped this fate, the cake is decorated with whipped, slightly sweetened cream, or *Schlag*. But I have chosen not a high-rise cake but the café's signature dish, *Apfelstrudel*, with its exquisitely thin layers of crisp pastry, holding, in their middle, slices of apple, nuts, breadcrumbs and cinnamon. The acidity of the apples is offset by the buttery pastry, lightly dusted with icing sugar.

I take in my surroundings. The café hums with conversation; the atmosphere is relaxed and understated. As a guest on my own, I am free to while away several hours over a single cup of coffee, if I wish, perhaps reading the newspapers, which are stretched each day onto special wooden batons and hung up near the door. No one dreams of trying to hurry me on.

If it is the afternoon, the pianist in the corner plays Mozart, Schubert and Chopin. But by the evening, it is time for a change of atmosphere and pace. Once the quieter, more conservative daytime guests have departed, a band upstairs on the second floor plays modern, more daring music.

Jazz has already made its debut in the Tyrol, in 1922 at the Hotel Sonne.[2] The Café Schindler is quick to pick up on the latest trends. On 10 March 1923, Hugo Schindler announces the opening of his dance café: 'A Café-Salon. 5 o'clock tea with music'.

This is so successful that by January 1925, as the *Innsbrucker Nachrichten* announces, music is on the menu every day until 2 a.m.[3] The newspaper also reveals that 'Mr Konstant from the Schwott Dance School will lead the dancing', and that, from 15 January onwards, the jazz band Sar-Seidle will play. This new music is a hit and Hugo ensures there is always plenty of jazz to be heard at the café.

Young couples hold hands over the tables and whirl on the dance floors of the second and, later, the third storeys of the building. Tango, Foxtrot, Swing and American big band music stream from the open windows on summer evenings. Soon, Innsbruck's younger women start appearing at the café in daring knee-length dresses and with bobbed hair. Sometimes they dance with each other; after all, in these post-war years there is a deficit of young men. Occasionally, there is also an all-female orchestra.

It is not New York or Paris. It is not even Vienna. But from the detritus of war, the Café Schindler is creating for Tyroleans, in miniature, their very own Jazz Age.

In the City Archives I found a beautiful gouache sketch done for the Café Schindler, in bright blue and cream. In the background there is a jazz trio, consisting of a pianist, a lively drummer raising his sticks, and a sax player. To their right is a dancing couple, the woman in a long dress, arching her back slightly to change direction, the ruffle at the bottom of her dress flicking up as she swirls with the tempo of the music. In the foreground is another couple: a woman with a short, modern haircut in front of a square-jawed man. It looks like they have just arrived and the woman is taking off her coat. Everything is elegant, stylish and modern.

I asked for the original drawing to be brought to me out of storage. It arrived half an hour later, wrapped in tissue paper. I unwrapped it carefully, feeling an intense pleasure as I held it in my hands. I love the ability of artefacts to communicate so much without words. I could see the artist's pencil marks still visible around the pianist and in the lettering on the thick, cream-coloured card. I could imagine my grandfather commissioning the picture and then holding it up to the light to admire its simple lines and clean bright colours: the blue, modern and fresh, a clear move away from the red, gold and black previously used by the S. Schindler brand. The date was 1932. The café, by now a decade old, was looking to the present and the future, not harking back to empire.

The City Archives also contained an original menu from the Café Schindler, with the prices for '3.30 in the afternoon' given in Kronen: from those details, it was clear that the menu was printed before December 1924, the date on which the currency was switched from Kronen into Schillings. On one side is a range of liqueurs and *Schnapps*, with pride of place given to the Schindlers' trademark 'Andreas-Hofer German Liqueur', pronounced the 'speciality'. But my eye was drawn to the five different coffees on offer.

Original gouache on paper, 1932

In these years, coffee was an expensive luxury. During wartime, as with so many foodstuffs, coffee in Austria became *ersatz*, its coffee-bean content reduced or removed entirely, replaced by cheaper alternatives. The post-war newspapers that I scanned in the local museum were full of advertisements for *Feigenkaffee*, fig coffee, one of the more common substitutes; roasted barley was another fall-back. Santol's 1914 cookbook gives stern warnings about serving adulterated coffee, commenting that if you buy ready-ground coffee, there is a likelihood that it has been cut with ground cereal, acorns or root vegetables. I think I can safely assume that the Café Schindler was offering the real stuff.

Innsbruck, 2019

I know from the Schindler letterhead of 1910 that my family had a long tradition of roasting their own coffee at the back of the Andreas-Hofer-Strasse headquarters. I am curious about where they sourced their supplies from in the 1920s. I seek out the advice of a modern-day coffee expert, Julian Schöpf of Brennpunkt, an artisan coffee roastery in Innsbruck. Julian confirms that the Schindlers probably imported their coffee beans from Italy. Amused by my last-century coffee credentials, Julian shows me around his business and explains how he mixes different beans to create special blends, each with their own particular acidity, which is critical for the final flavour in the cup.

As to roasting the beans, Julian uses much the same methodology as Hugo and Erich and Samuel before them would have done. I watch as Julian pours raw green Santos beans from Brazil into the metal funnel of the machine, from where they slide into a hot rotating drum. The turning of the drum ensures an even roast. The machine burns gas to create the right temperature and the hot air mixes with the room-temperature air as it is fed into the rotating drum.

The temperature inside it is between 200 and 250 degrees centigrade, depending on the roast. Julian's machine is computer-controlled, but it still needs human oversight to ensure that the beans are not over-roasted; the exact temperatures used at different points in the roast process and the exact mix of beans remain Julian's trade secrets.

Within a few minutes, a glass window in the hot drum shows that the beans have turned golden yellow. Slowly, they lose most of their remaining moisture and crack open along their seam; a few minutes later, they are heading towards a glossy brown roast and the room is full of their aroma. After sixteen and a half minutes exactly, this particular roast is complete, and the beans pour down a chute into a crate to cool.

In the next-door café, the beans are ground to order for customers: 1–3 mm for filter coffee, 0.3 mm for espresso and 0.1 mm for Turkish coffee. I show Julian an old 1920s menu from the café with its five varieties of coffee. He explains that 'Mocha Milk' is a traditional Austrian mocha, similar to today's espresso with the addition of cold milk or cream. The 'Turkish Espresso' involves boiling up the coffee grounds with water and sometimes with sugar. The 'Melange' was a mix of coffee and steamed hot milk, similar to a cappuccino but stronger.

Whatever variety Hugo and Erich's guests chose to drink in the 1920s, as they looked out over the Marie-Theresien-Strasse, it is clear to me that the Café Schindler offered hope, a taste of better times ahead, and affirmation that life could still be elegant and civilised.

8

The Matchmaker's Daughter

Innsbruck, New Year 1930

I am winding back ninety years. The last evening of December 1930. Tonight, the Café Schindler is hosting the New Year's Eve party, which in the intervening years has become a much-loved fixture in Innsbruck's social calendar. This year, the Fox Band will entertain the guests.

I know this because I hold in my hand the special invitation that Hugo and Erich commissioned for the event. It is a square 13 cm by 13 cm booklet and it says a great deal about their aspirations for the café and the clientele they would like to attract. Its cover drawing features one couple chatting and drinking champagne in the foreground, while in the background another couple dance, wrapped in each other's arms, forming one merged and silhouetted figure. They are framed, on the left, by elegant wisps of cigarette smoke and on the right by celebratory ribbons and a rosette.

The colours of the invitation – pink, purple and olive – are not obvious bedfellows, yet they work together beautifully. I feel the pink evokes the dawn of a new year, while the purple with mauve accents gives the figures substance, and the olive forms a near-golden background for the invitation's fresh white lettering. The designer has indulged in some artistic licence, adopting the letter 'C' for both the words *Café* and *Conditorei*. The latter is unusual, because the German word *Konditorei* – meaning cake shop – should really be spelt with a 'K'. It is noticeable, too, that the designer's font is less Germanic-looking, with rather more of an international – French or English – flavour. There is nothing traditionally Tyrolean here. The image oozes confidence, sophistication and cosmopolitanism.

Inside the booklet, there is a list of twenty-one events over two months to celebrate the carnival season. It kicks off on 31 December 1929 with its big new year's party, followed every Wednesday and Saturday night all the way through to the final Ash Wednesday celebration on 5 March. There is also the promise of additional events, as yet unspecified, which will be announced in due course. Guests are asked to appear in evening dress or fancy dress.

Invite to the New Year's Party (1929/30)

It must have been exhausting to be entertaining two or more times a week, but something tells me Hugo rather enjoyed being at the centre of Innsbruck's social life. The Schindlers took the business of partying very seriously and exhorted their guests to attend their upmarket and artistically decked-out rooms to greet the new year with *Übermut und voller Lebenslust* – 'high spirits and zest for life'.

I return to this invitation, from my father's albums, time and time again. I love the colours and the ambience. My eye is drawn to the young woman sitting in the foreground, depicted in profile. Her shoulder-less dress reveals bare, muscular arms. With one hand she toys with her champagne glass – a coupe, rather than a flute – and in her other raised hand, she holds a lit cigarette. A curlicue of smoke drifts upwards. Her male companion is half turned away, with one eye on the dancing couple behind, and so we see mainly his back. It is not him, but rather it is she who animates and dominates the scene, at ease with herself and her environment, in control.

It occurs to me, looking at her, how much has changed in women's lives in the aftermath of a war that thrust them from the home into offices and factories; a war that in Austria – as elsewhere – helped women win the right to vote and therefore have a public voice in defining their lives. Her neatly bobbed hair and cocktail dress make it clear that she is a modern woman, talking on equal terms with her partner.

But I also register this particular date, 1930: the start of a decade in which the gap between society's winners and losers is being magnified again. Many will look back nostalgically to the later 1920s as a time of comparative freedom and security, when Austria finally emerged from the hardship of the First World War.

From my research in the newspaper archives at Innsbruck, I could see that the Café Schindler continued to thrive. Occasionally, Hugo secured the appearance of international stars, including one summer, Richard Tauber, the most famous tenor of his generation. Erich even drew up plans to open a second café in the nearby Hofgarten (Imperial Park). He commissioned the well-known architect Clemens Holzmeister and left the running of the Maria-Theresien-Strasse café to my grandfather. I have visited the park and it would have been an idyllic setting. But as far as I can tell, Erich never realised the dream of opening a second café; I suspect because his health was starting to fail.

As the Café Schindler secured its position in Innsbruck's commercial and social life, so Hugo and Erich's domestic lives too entered new phases. I know from a letter sent by Eduard Bloch's daughter Trude to John Kafka that Sofie was determined to secure the Schindler dynasty. Her eldest child Martha was, of course, already long married, producing Sofie's first grandchildren, Erwin and Marguerite. Sofie's eldest son Otto still showed no signs of marrying. He was too busy with his large medical practice in Vienna.

However, Hugo and Erich were both single and eligible, so Sofie turned her attention to finding them brides. Trude later described how Sofie 'picked both her daughters-in-law according to the physical standards that she had decreed for the propagation of the Schindler tribe'.[1]

I think Sofie was spurred on by the fact that in 1920 her Linz nephew, Egon Kafka, had married a beautiful young Swiss Jewish widow named Claire Woltär. Claire's sister owned a hotel in Igls, at which Lilli and Eduard Bloch had been staying when Claire was helping out there, with her daughter Gretl. Having met Claire, whom they liked enormously, Lilli and Eduard had acted as informal matchmakers by encouraging Egon to join them on holiday, with the desired result that Egon and Claire fell in love. In 1921, Claire gave birth to my cousin John, then known by his Austrian moniker, Hans Sigmund.

For the Schindlers, Sofie now swung into action. The Jewish population of Innsbruck was too small to yield a suitable bride, and so it seems that she had to widen her search. I could not find any pre-existing links between the Schindler boys and their future brides, so I suspect that Sofie used the services of a Jewish matchmaker, a *shadchan*. In the end, the woman whom she chose for Hugo reflected Sofie's own background.

My grandmother Edith Roth was born in Budweis, Bohemia, on 9 September 1904, to parents Albert and Hermine Roth. I imagine that Sofie was highly satisfied with the match, not only for the Bohemian lineage – the Roths spoke both German and Czech at home – but also because Edith's family were successful, wealthy and cosmopolitan. Albert had even spent several years in London as a young man.

The Roths had a villa in Vienna, and split their time between Vienna and Plauen, a small town in eastern Germany, where Albert owned a match factory called Roth & Goldman, inherited from his father. Once this business was merged with several others, Albert Roth became managing director of the combined company, Solo AG, which he ran from Vienna.

I took delight, both in the fact that my grandmother managed to match-make with a matchmaker's daughter, and in discovering that some of the little matchboxes churned out by Albert's factories – the most humble and ephemeral of items – are still available to buy online. They are apparently collectors' items for those whom I was delighted to find call themselves phillumenists – 'lovers of light'.

On 6 July 1924, Hugo and Edith were married in Vienna, at Edith's home. I have one studio photo of Edith as a young woman. She has neatly crimped and bobbed dark hair and is wearing a white dress; she has something that looks like a large veil or possibly a scarf, which she holds modestly with her left hand at her throat before it cascades, in diaphanous folds, down her arms and gathers at the back of her neck.

This may have been the first image that Hugo saw of his future bride, via the *shadchan*, or – more likely – was taken shortly before the wedding. The pose is natural, as if Edith's name has just been called and she has glanced across towards the photographer. I assumed that, in reality, the photograph must have been carefully crafted, though its approach was a world away from the stiffer formal portrait of the Schindlers in 1912.

I looked at the photo carefully for clues as to its date and spotted the black-ink signature at the bottom: *d'Ora*. Something about the style of the photo tugged in my memory. I researched the signature and realised that Edith had chosen the most famous Viennese fashion and portrait photographer of her day, Dora Kallmus, for this image of her on the threshold of her new life.

Kallmus was a pioneer and in 1907 became one of the first women in Vienna to open a photographic studio. Her Atelier d'Ora quickly established itself as *the* place for artistic portraits. She shot portraits of Gustav Klimt in 1908 and Alma Mahler in 1916. I guessed that the photo of my grandmother must have been taken in 1924, before Edith's wedding and before Madame D'Ora's move to Paris in 1925, where she continued to shoot extraordinary society portraits of the likes of Coco Chanel, Marc Chagall, Maurice Chevalier and Pablo Picasso.

Edith Schindler (née Roth) (shot at
Atelier D'Ora in Vienna)

To my great surprise, I could not find any photographs of the wedding itself. I thought this strange for a man like Hugo, who liked photography so much, and who managed to preserve photos of so much else. I concluded that there was probably a whole wedding album at the time, but it simply did not survive.

Eleven months later, on 9 June 1925, my father Kurt was born. To be precise, he was born on the kitchen table, on the first floor of the S. Schindler headquarters at 13 Andreas-Hofer-Strasse, in the space now devoted to pole dancing. It should have been a joyous occasion for all, but Edith declared the experience so traumatic that she would never have any other children. For Hugo, Edith's decision was no doubt a disappointment: he had grown up in that very flat in a big, noisy family with four siblings, and I think he would have wanted a large family.

Sofie had arranged a highly respectable match for Hugo, but it was not necessarily a love-match or even a very happy marriage. I remember my grandmother clearly, and she was not an easy woman. Despite living decades in England, she retained her strong Central European accent – as well as a sweet tooth that was rarely satisfied by English cakes. Nevertheless, Hugo and Edith managed a *modus vivendi* in their new life together, getting on tolerably well while leading rather separate lives.

Edith chose to travel widely. Looking at her photograph albums, I detect a restlessness – she was constantly on the move, visiting Czechoslovakia, Greece, Italy, Yugoslavia, Albania and France. It is no wonder that, in later life, my father complained that he was left largely in the care of French nannies, and that his first words were in French rather than German. Hugo mostly stayed home and minded the business; he was rooted in the Tyrol and its mountains, only occasionally accompanying Edith on one of her grand tours.

Despite their apparent divergences, my favourite photograph of their small family shows a close trio. It is a studio photo-portrait: Hugo stands behind a sitting Edith, with Kurt dressed in a sailor's uniform, leaning protectively in towards his mother so that they are cheek-to-cheek. Edith gazes out, her large eyes alive and vital, while Hugo looks every bit the proud family man. It is a beautiful portrait and I read in it some warmth between the couple and, above all, pride in their young son. I know that despite her absentee parenting, Edith doted on her only son, and in years to come would speak nostalgically to me of her husband.

Marriage and family, combined with the burgeoning success of the Schindler businesses, spelled growth in other ways for Hugo and Edith, as I found out from files kept in the Innsbruck City and County Archives. In 1925, Hugo and Erich purchased adjoining plots of land on Innsbruck's Rennweg, next to the city's Imperial Park. It came with a pedigree. This was the same road on which lay Innsbruck's baroque Imperial Palace, complete with its large Habsburg eagle, at the edge of the old part of town; and several successful industrialists already owned villas nearby. Clearly, the Schindlers' land was intended to provide grand new addresses for Hugo and Erich, befitting their status as successful businessmen.

It would be a dramatic change for Hugo, who so far had lived all his life in the flat above the shop in the Andreas-Hofer-Strasse. The addresses were also convenient for the brothers – only a ten-minute stroll to the Café Schindler, while Erich would be less than five minutes from the second café he was planning in the Imperial Park. My father bragged that his was the most impressive address in the whole of Innsbruck.

With the land bought, Hugo commissioned one of Germany's most famous architects, Hermann Muthesius, to design and build a villa for him. Muthesius happened also to be a diplomat, and during his time in London as German cultural attaché he had fallen in love with the English Arts and Crafts movement. He remained fascinated by the English love of home and countryside, extolling the virtues of English middle-class domestic life in his three-volume *Das Englische Haus* (The English House); but he was also credited with influencing the Bauhaus movement and other pioneers of German architectural modernism.

Kurt Schindler in a clown costume

Hugo, Edith and Kurt Schindler, c. 1931

In the City Archives, I examined Hugo's application for permission to build the villa, and I could see that he was obviously trying to create his dream house. It was to have a cellar, a ground floor with a large terrace, a first floor and a habitable attic. The entertaining space was to consist of a large hall, two sizeable drawing rooms and a kitchen; upstairs on the first floor there were to be three bedrooms and assorted other rooms, while the attic would contain the staff accommodation. The floorplan was typical of Muthesius: an L-shaped footprint and different-sized windows.

It was a beautiful modern, light design for a house that was clearly built for partying; and from the villa there would be views across the road to the fast-flowing River Inn and then straight up the mountains of the Nordkette.

According to the archive file, Hugo handed in the final plans on 25 February 1928. They were approved, and the Villa Schindler was finished in 1929/30, providing spacious accommodation for its small family of three. Even three years later, it looked new and somewhat raw in a photograph I have of Edith and Kurt out riding. They had plenty of outdoor space, because Erich, not being ready to proceed with his own building project, had agreed to let Hugo use his plot of land as extra garden for the villa.

Unfortunately, Muthesius would never live to see his last project completed; he was knocked over and killed by a Berlin tram in 1927. That year too, a different death cruelly interrupted my family's procession of marriages and births: Sofie's nephew Egon Kafka died in Linz, at the age of just forty-nine.

On the evening before Yom Kippur, Egon had returned from a business trip, eaten a meal, and was walking to the synagogue. Six-year-old John Kafka (Hans Sigmund, as he then was) had been sent on ahead to the synagogue with his fifteen-year-old half-sister Gretl. Egon had a heart attack and collapsed a few blocks away from Eduard Bloch's surgery. Eduard was called immediately and warned that a second heart attack would be fatal – it soon came, and Egon died a few days later.

Villa Schindler at 10 Rennweg. Edith, Kurt and Hugo, 1933.

John, as he told me himself, did not learn of his father's death until two weeks later, when Gretl broke the news to him. He was utterly devastated; as an adult, he would still dream occasionally about his father. I learned that his Aunt Lilli and Eduard Bloch took him in protectively, and Eduard became his guardian, in order to help the widowed Claire bring him up. The action seems to be typically generous on the part of the doctor. John later wrote about it in his essay 'Worlds In-Between', while also explaining why his new guardian 'never quite became a father figure for me':

He was good-hearted and friendly and he had very pronounced ideas about the importance for me of a classical, humanistic education. Maybe he was, or I perceived him as too good-natured *generally* – he had the reputation of being 'a poor people's doctor' – to be close to *me* especially.[2]

As the 1920s drew to a close, Sofie turned her attention to Erich's future. She bullied her 43-year-old son, despite his heart condition and other health issues, into a late marriage with the 19-year-old Margarete Herschan. 'Grete' had striking, blonde, film-star looks, which attracted much attention in Innsbruck. They married in Vienna on 16 November 1930, and three years later Grete gave birth to their only son, Peter.

I was lucky enough to meet one of Grete's post-war Innsbruck friends. Gerti Mayer, a sprightly 94-year-old, told me in 2019 that Grete's marriage to Erich was not a happy one. This view echoed an interview Peter gave to the historian Gerda Hofreiter on the eve of his eightieth birthday, when he described his parents' marriage as a 'hateful' one, in which he always felt 'unwanted'. He, too, was largely brought up by a nanny; he recalled that at home he was never allowed to upset his father or make any noise.

I don't know whether Sofie detected these strains. As the Café Schindler celebrated New Year's Eve on 31 December 1930, Sofie might well have felt she could draw satisfaction not only from the success of her sons' business gamble, but also from Hugo's and Erich's domestically settled status and an expanding younger generation. In ten years, following the extreme uncertainties that followed the war, the Schindlers had found an equilibrium and were now able to look to the future.

The same could not be said for the Kafkas' company in Linz. LUSKA was in decline. Egon had done much of the hard work, and now his death left his elder brother Rudolf in sole charge – a man with syphilis, who required ever longer and more intense treatments in hospital. Rudolf had been responsible for expanding LUSKA, on the back of multiple army contracts during the First World War, but greater turnover was not matched by greater profit.

Looking back from today, the Café Schindler's New Year's Eve party of 1930 seems a last hurrah for a disappearing age of hard-won stability. The aftershocks of New York's stock market crash of October 1929 had now rocked Europe too, and they would plunge Austria back into political and economic crisis. These shocks proved the final straw for Rudolf's business. He began selling assets in order to try and keep afloat; when he ran out of those, he took up expensive loans. Then he was approached by a competitor wanting to buy the business, but Rudolf's mother Hermine insisted they would not sell. LUSKA teetered on the verge of collapse.

The re-emergence of hard times also put Austria's fragile democracy under renewed pressure, from the Left, but also from the Right, including its antisemites. Could Hugo keep his head down and focus on serving the perfect strudel to his guests in the café, while running the S. Schindler business with Erich? Their lives were dedicated to providing food, drink and entertainment, about creating conviviality and good feeling in others.

Who could object to that?

Washington, USA, 2018

I have numerous photos of the young Schindler cousins together, a new generation, playing in the snow or on summer outings. There is an eight-year age difference between Kurt and Peter, but it does not seem to be an impediment.

I know that they spent every summer in Igls, at their Uncle Siegfried's house. There, they were always joined by Martha and Siegfried's granddaughter Marianne. Her own parents were absent. Her mother had left, declaring herself not to be the maternal type; her father Erwin now worked as a patent lawyer in Frankfurt-am-Main and, unable to look after Marianne himself, he had lodged her with her grandparents at their home in Vienna. Technically, Kurt and Peter were Marianne's uncles, even though she was roughly the same age as Kurt. But they shared one thing: they all knew what it was like to be only children of unhappy marriages.

I see in the photographs the three of them playing happily in the garden. In one 1934 image, Kurt sits at the wheel of Hugo's large German car and plays chauffeur, while Peter and Marianne sit in the back. When I meet Marianne in the United States in 2018, I take with me a framed copy of this photo of the three of them as a gift. It evokes beautifully the grandeur and riches of a secure and moneyed time.

Marianne is a slight, wiry lady in her nineties, still in excellent health and mentally sharp. She is kind, and I warm to her. She remembers well not only the garden in Igls, but also the cream pastries produced in the café and how occasionally, to her delight, they were shipped to her in Vienna. She tells me how very fond of my father she was, and how she saw him now and then in later years, but was always careful to steer clear of any business matters with him. She does not know any details of the feud that would rage between the adult Peter and Kurt; but she thinks there may be truth in my theory that it revolved around the Café Schindler.

Kurt playing chauffeur to Marianne Salzer
and Peter Schindler in Igls in 1934

I also visit John Kafka in Washington, D.C. He bowls me over with his energy, charm and intelligence. At the age of ninety-seven, he shows me around not one but two art exhibitions, while we explore our shared roots. He remembers, as a young boy, the thrill of being allowed to stay up late and hear Richard Tauber sing at the glamorous Café Schindler. John reminds me that Tauber was a local lad, growing up in Urfahr, a short distance from Hermine and Sigmund Kafka's business in Linz.

I ask John whether he remembers my father, and whether they also played together as children in Igls. I know that over the years there were many visitors from Linz – Hermine and Sigmund with their family, their daughter Lilli, and John's guardian Eduard Bloch, who combined his visits with further study at Innsbruck's medical faculty. It seems logical to me that Kurt and John should have been friends. They were, after all, born only four years apart. But for some reason, I don't see him playing with Kurt in the photographs.

John smiles sadly. 'I am afraid I do not really remember Kurt – maybe I was just the poor half-orphan from Linz and we were not encouraged to play together.'

I am surprised to hear this, given how close their grandmothers Hermine and Sofie were. I conclude it is possible that Edith had discouraged Kurt's friendship with his Linz cousin.

I hope that some eighty years later, with this rekindled connection, I am making up in a small way for this slight.

9

Murder in the Mountains

Innsbruck, 1 January 1931

As another new year begins, the employees of the S. Schindler business throw yet another party, this time to celebrate the fiftieth anniversary of the company's founding. They give the Schindlers a large hand-drawn poster to mark the occasion.

The poster is bordered by extravagant, gold-coloured scrolls. At the top is a tinted photograph of the headquarters of the Schindler business in the Andreas-Hofer-Strasse. Beneath it, in a reddish ink, there are head-and-shoulder drawings of the founders, Samuel on the left, Sofie on the right. Samuel – dead for sixteen years now – has a faint ghostly appearance, being drawn in lighter, less emphatic strokes; it seems that the artist has been inspired by the group portrait photo taken in 1912, as the expression on Samuel's face is identical to that in the photograph.

Sofie, though, is etched in deeper red, looking older than her 1912 photo, but more vibrant than her husband. If ever proof were needed of her significance, not solely to the family but to the company, this is it. She and her two sons Erich and Hugo are described as *hochwohlgeboren*, 'noble'.

It is a mark of the Schindlers' social advance: in one generation they have moved from immigrants to 'nobles' – at least in the eyes of their affectionate and loyal staff, who praise them for being good and caring employers and for the fact that through their *Tatkraft und Umsicht* – 'energy and prudence' – they have managed to create such a large enterprise *aus kleinen Anfängen*, 'from small beginnings'. Thanks to the Schindlers' *Wohlwollen*

148

50th anniversary celebration poster

und Fürsorge – 'benevolence and care' – their employees have pledged themselves to the family in gratitude.

Below this effusive dedication sits the company logo, a red eagle bearing the black letters 'SS' for Samuel Schindler. The typescript in which the logo is written is known to English-speakers as Blackletter, and to German-speakers as *Fraktur*, from the Latin for 'broken'. Its origin is innocent enough; it was first developed by medieval monks who were concerned with creating even lettering for copying out manuscripts, and its revival now harks back to this heritage. Neither the Schindlers nor their employees can yet know how popular the same font will become in the officialdom of the Third Reich, forever to be tarnished by that association.

At the bottom of the poster, thirty-two employees, including Hugo's top patissier, Karl Santol, have signed it. It is a gesture of thanks and appreciation. Perhaps it is also an expression of hope that this large family business will endure. The relatively prosperous years of the later 1920s are already feeling a long time ago.

In 1931, beyond the warmth, music, cakes and conviviality of the Café Schindler, Austria's economy was nosediving. The government even had to intervene to try and save the country's largest bank, the Credit-Anstalt.

This venerable company, founded in 1855 by the Rothschild family, was – in modern parlance – 'too big to fail'. It was Austria's most prestigious financial institution and a major player in Europe and beyond, quoted on several international stock exchanges. But it lost liquidity and its problems became public in May 1931, prompting a run on the bank. Although the Austrian government tried to underwrite the bank's liabilities abroad, foreign investors fled. So significant was the Credit-Anstalt internationally, that within weeks the contagion spread to other banks in Austria, Germany and beyond, and in this way Austria accelerated all of Europe's descent into economic depression.

A year later, in May 1932, the diminutive Engelbert Dollfuss of the Christian Social Party became Austria's chancellor. His background was very different to my family's. He grew up in a humble, strictly Catholic family from Lower Austria before training as a lawyer, and his politics demonstrated a firm commitment to the farmers in Austria's agrarian economy. He did share something with my grandfather, though, for he had also served in the *Kaiserschützen* and fought, like Hugo and Erich, with distinction on the Southern Front.

Now, Dollfuss's task was to try and rescue the economy and create stability in Austria's increasingly fractious First Republic. On all sides, he was beset by strident voices; on the Left by those wanting Red revolution, and on the extreme Right by Austria's National Socialists, whose allegiance was to their ultimate leader in Germany, Adolf Hitler, and who cared little for Austria's independent existence.

The Austrian Nazis represented only the most sharply defined of the country's antisemites; but the return of economic and rural hardship seemed to reinvigorate past strains of antisemitism in the Tyrol. In a footnote to an article I was reading for my research, I stumbled across a high-profile unsolved murder case that I had never come across before, despite my living in the Tyrol for five years. The case appeared to shed light on contemporary attitudes to Jews.

It took place on Hugo's doorstep, in the local mountains and valleys; it even permeated the Café Schindler itself. Unsolved legal riddles appeal to my instincts as a lawyer, and so I read everything I could lay my hands on about the case.

The essence was simple. In 1928, a 49-year-old Jewish dentist from Latvia named Morduch Max Halsman and his son Philipp – both tourists in the Tyrol – set off on a hiking trip in the Ziller Valley, east of Innsbruck. Only one of them returned alive.

Innsbruck was instantly convulsed by news of this local murder – and immediately blame was laid on Philipp, the Jewish outsider, rather than on any local Tyrolean. Debate raged in the newspapers about what had impelled him to commit patricide: perhaps he had a poor relationship with his father, and they had argued. Did Max have valuable life insurance? Had he prevented Philipp from getting involved with a girl he had just met?

Keen to understand more, I called up the voluminous files on the case at the Tyrol's County Archives in Innsbruck. The archivist handed them to me with a degree of reluctance, questioning why I needed them, given (as he knew) that I was researching the Schindler family history. I also bought Martin Pollack's book *Anklage Vatermord*, 'An Accusation of Patricide', which has the best and most coherent description of the myriad twists and turns of the case. Reading the various accounts of that day, it was not easy to piece together what had actually happened, but the basic facts went something like this.

Max was besotted with mountains. He was an enthusiastic hiker and liked to project an image of fitness; but in reality, he had suffered from fainting episodes, headaches, and a couple of dizzy spells in the Dolomites where they had been holidaying before the trip to the Ziller Valley, and his family were very worried about his health.

Having left his wife, Itta Halsman, behind to rest, Max and Philipp spent the two days of 8 and 9 September hiking in the mountains and glaciers to the south, in the Zillertal. Overnight, they stayed in the Alpenrose Hut – one of the alpine huts that then, as now, provided food and shelter to hikers. There, guests remember the garrulous Max making poorly judged quips that Philipp would 'be happy if I fell, as he is waiting to inherit.'

Philipp appeared less keen that Max use the services of a guide, and the other guests found Philipp taciturn, even surly, compared to his father. At the Alpenrose Hut, Max unwittingly conformed to the trope of the rich, foreign Jew by insisting on separate rooms for himself and Philipp, a somewhat unusual extravagance in a cramped hut, where it was not uncommon to share bunk rooms, even with strangers.

According to Philipp, after a dawn start and having hiked up one peak that morning, Max told Philipp to go on ahead so he could 'relieve himself'. Philipp did as requested, then suddenly heard a cry. He turned round to see Max fall backwards from the path into the river below. Philipp later said the image was fixed in his mind like a photograph. He was convinced his father had had a heart attack. Philipp scrambled down to find Max face down in the water; the rucksack he was wearing had slipped up to his head. As he pulled his father's head out of the water and turned it to one side, he could see his father was still breathing and able to move his hand slightly.

Max had multiple head injuries, which were bleeding profusely. Philipp managed to pull Max clear of the water, resting his head on a stone, before running to get help. I saw in the later court testimony that two women walking past on the path above noticed Max lying at right angles to the river, with his arms by his side. Starting out for the nearest hut, a distraught Philipp encountered one Marianne Hofer, who immediately took Philipp to her brother, Alois Riederer. Marianne then went to get help from the Breitlahner Hut, while Alois returned with Philipp to the scene of the accident.

I found a hand-drawn diagram dated 11 September 1928 in the files at the County Archives, which showed that the path was about fifteen metres above the river. The steepness of the slope is not recorded in the sketch. However, a photograph taken during a later judicial site visit showed a narrow path and a rocky slope that was not particularly steep. Max's body is depicted in the hand-drawn sketch lying at right angles to the river. However, Alois later reported that when he first saw Max, he was lying more or less parallel to the river, face down with his head in the water.

Clambering down to Max, Alois could see that he was dead. Philipp and Alois pulled Max's body from the water and saw that his forehead had a gaping 7-centimetre-long gash. There were other wounds on the back of his head. In Max's wallet they found just 2.80 Schillings. The rest of his money and Max's gold-rimmed glasses were missing. Alois left in search of a stretcher, leaving Philipp sitting on a stone with his dead father at his feet.

Josef Eder, the landlord of the Dominikus Hut, then arrived

with his dog. Eder described how his dog made two discoveries on the path above the river: a fist-sized stone with hair, bone fragments and blood on it; and a 4-metre-long track of flattened blood-specked undergrowth caused by something heavy 'like a butchered pig' being dragged towards the water.

No one told Philipp about the rock or the drag marks, and the others present quickly formed their own conclusions that this was no accident. They claimed that the path (which Eder was supposed to maintain) was not dangerous. Perhaps to deflect responsibility from himself, Eder was the first to point the finger at Philipp, ordering him to be taken to the Breitlahner Hut and held there. One of the guests in the hut, a Munich police officer, examined Philipp for traces of blood, finding none on his upper body or on his light grey trousers.

On Tuesday, 11 September 1928, the parties walked back along the path to the scene of the incident. Philipp, still ignorant of the bloodstained rock or the drag marks, identified the point where he thought his father had fallen. During the night, it had rained. Nothing had been done to photograph the crime scene or secure it for evidence, and Philipp was upset that his father's body was still out in the open. In accordance with Jewish religious law, funerals usually take place within a day or so of death, and Philipp was therefore anxious to bury his father; he also wanted to inform his mother. The speed with which Philipp wanted to arrange the burial aroused further suspicion among the Catholic locals, who were used to funerals taking weeks to organise.

On Wednesday, 12 September, in a makeshift room adjacent to the Breitlahner Hut, two doctors from Innsbruck performed an autopsy. I found the report among the files at the County Archives, and it made for grim reading, describing external and internal injuries. It concluded that Max did not drown, but rather had received fatal head wounds that could not have been caused by his fall. Someone had bludgeoned him to death.

From the Breitlahner Hut, Max's body was transported down to the next village, Ginzling, and put in a hastily adapted chapel, which served as a makeshift mortuary. The locals removed the cross that normally sat by the altar. Itta Halsman arrived and begged the local police to open the coffin so that she could see her husband one last time. They refused. The reason would later become clear: during the autopsy, Max's head had been removed from his body and placed in formaldehyde, in a large mason jar. Dr Meixner, in charge of the Forensic Medicine faculty, was a bit of a 'headhunter' – according to one commentator – with a fondness for pickling the heads of murder victims.

Philipp was arrested, accused of murdering his father with a rock and throwing him into the Zamser River. He was taken to Innsbruck and to solitary confinement in the remand prison in the Schmerlingstrasse, less than five minutes from the Schindler headquarters in the Andreas-Hofer-Strasse. Fourteen days after Max's death, part of the missing money turned up under a rock near the crime scene, with bloodstains on one of the notes. No one seemed to know whether they were missed in the first examination of the crime scene or placed there afterwards.

The trial in Innsbruck, beginning on 13 December 1928, attracted so much attention that the court decided to issue tickets to those who wanted to attend. Places were soon oversubscribed and tickets would change hands for large sums on the black market. The streets outside the prison and the nearby court thronged with onlookers and journalists. It occurred to me that Hugo would have passed them as he hurried between the Andreas-Hofer-Strasse and the café in the Marie-Theresien- Strasse.

Innsbruck was divided by the case. As it made its way through the courts, journalists arrived from all over the world to report on it. Newspaper articles, letters, church sermons, even songs and limericks were written. This was more than simply prurient interest in a gruesome murder case set in idyllic mountains; rather, the case became the screen onto which both pro- and antisemites projected their views and ideas, often with scant regard for the underlying facts. For Hugo, these events played out not only in the streets near his flat, but in the café itself.

Innsbruck, 2019

I listen to a 2008 radio programme called *Mord im Zillertal*, 'Murder in the Ziller Valley'. It is an award-winning reconstruction of events by Eva Roither, and I realise how the Halsman case intruded into the very life of the Café Schindler. One interviewee, in gleeful anecdotal mood, performs a song that he recalls being sung in the café at the time:

> *Young Halsman, ah, poor Halsman oh,*
> *Don't think any more of the time,*
> *in the Ziller Valley*
> *there was a scandal*
> *The dad was found dead*
> *(. . .)*
> *When judgement*
> *is given to you*
> *show them a smiling face*
> *You too will be free again*

The sly implication is that Philipp will get away with his crime. The interviewee says the words were made up by his brother and set to the tune of a popular song of the day. After it was sung in the café, he recalls that it spread quickly around Innsbruck. He notes that the song was performed in the café 'despite the Schindlers being Jewish', but adds that when 'the Jews' heard it, they wanted to know who had composed it in order to drag his brother 'before the courts'.

He clearly revels in the song and his brother's notoriety. For him, the whole incident is a bit of a joke; he seems unconcerned by Philipp's predicament and untroubled by what the song suggests about Innsbruck's attitude towards 'the Jews'.

Then I wonder: by 'the Jews', does he mean the Schindlers in particular or the wider community in Innsbruck? I don't know. The song is gently mocking, subliminally rather than blatantly antisemitic. I can imagine Hugo feeling defensive and perhaps upset, but it seems unlikely that he would have considered chasing down his own guests and bringing them before a court. That would not have been in keeping with Hugo's image as a welcoming and generous host.

I can't know for certain what Hugo thought of this case happening around him, but I imagine that he explained away the palpable hostility towards Philipp Halsman in Innsbruck as something to do with Philipp's foreign-ness. Philipp was not an Austrian; rather, he was an *Ostjude*, an Eastern Jew, an interloper. I suspect it irked Hugo greatly as a longstanding member of the Alpine Club – and as an experienced mountaineer – that Max and Philipp took the Tyrol for granted, going hiking without adequate equipment or food, in mountains they did not know or understand. Hugo loved those mountains; but he also respected them.

Looking at the case files, I could see that the prosecution led with the evidence from various witnesses, who all found Philipp's behaviour deeply suspicious. The circumstantial evidence piled up. Dr Pressburger, a top Viennese Jewish lawyer, led the defence, bringing in numerous character witnesses who all attested to Philipp's good character, to the loving relationship between son and father, and to the lack of motive.

Nevertheless, as a lawyer I could tell that Philipp was a nightmare client. He interrupted Pressburger, deviated from the agreed trial strategy, and addressed the jury himself. He stuck obstinately to his story that his father must have died from a heart attack, even though the physical evidence pointed to a brutal attack. Philipp was clumsy and condescending, telling the jury, who were a mix of local farmers, bartenders and commercial people, 'You have to understand, members of the jury, even if you find it difficult . . .', doing little to endear himself to the court or the judge.

Pressburger conceded at the end of the trial that he was worried every time Philipp opened his mouth. But still, he insisted Philipp was the most honest of people, incapable of lying, and that he had been at pains to answer each question completely, truthfully and logically.

Although Philipp stuck doggedly to his version of events, the weight of expert evidence was against him, and it pointed to an attack with a rock. Philipp, precise to the point of pedantry, consistently contradicted that view, insisting, 'I was the only one there.' It was to no avail. After four days, the jury took only twenty-five minutes to find him guilty of murder, by nine votes to three. He was sentenced to ten years in prison with hard labour. That evening in his cell, Philipp tried to commit suicide using the blade of a pencil sharpener. He was stopped by an observant guard.

The saga still had a long way to run. Pressburger appealed the case and announced in a newspaper article of December 1928 that doubts had arisen about the most serious circumstantial evidence against his client: the bloody stone and the tracks from the path above the river. If the tracks were created after the accident, then suspicion would fall on the two men that claimed to have discovered them – the hut landlord, Josef Eder, and a climber who had joined him at the scene. It was a very serious allegation. On appeal, Austria's Supreme Court sent the case back to be re-tried in Innsbruck, having concluded that the original trial lacked proof of Philipp's guilt.

The second murder trial turned into even more of a media circus than the first, as the left- and right-wing press both weighed in. At all levels – local, national and international – journalists took up pens to do battle for their versions of the story. The case seemed to embody all the fractures in Austrian society; pitching Jew against Aryan, urban against rural, local against foreign, city against provincial, socially progressive against Catholic conservative, professional against working class.

The independent-spirited Tyroleans were deeply insulted at the international and critical interest taken in this case, considering the case to be a local matter to be settled by them. Antisemitic views fanned those flames. Some papers, both local and from further afield, detected a conspiracy of interference from international world Jewry in the Tyrol's domestic affairs. Others, occasionally local but often Viennese-owned or international, were simply appalled by the case.

Innsbruck, 9 September 1929

A whole year after the original incident, Philipp Halsman's second trial got underway at the *Landesgericht* (County Court House). Now, he was represented by two local lawyers. Dr Pressburger had made it clear that he did not want to return to Innsbruck; but it was also suspected that the hiring of a top Viennese Jewish lawyer, to defend a foreign and Jewish accused, might have been a mistake for the original defence case; possibly stoking prejudice and contributing to the first conviction.

One of his new lawyers was at pains to point out that Philipp and his family did not believe the Tyrol generally to be antisemitic, but rather that any small groups in Innsbruck holding such views were mostly incomers rather than locals. Given the local press and the demonstrations on the street, it sounded like a desperate statement of appeasement.

This time, in the face of the autopsy evidence, the defence switched strategy, moving from asserting that Max died from his fall to asserting he was robbed and killed by a third party. The defence pointed to Philipp's short-sightedness and invoked psychological evidence that Philipp may have had a false memory of seeing the fall. Given Philipp's prior insistence that he *did* see the fall, this was a difficult swerve. It is never attractive for the defence to have to change strategy, let alone go against the defendant's own testimony.

During the trial, the prosecution insisted on a gruesome and emotive exhibit: the jury was taken into the judge's room to view Max's severed head, in its jar. They could see for themselves a large wound, plainly visible in the centre of the forehead, as well as others at the back of the head.

As the testimony and evidence concluded, the judge summed up, covering all points *except* the most crucial one: that the jury needed to be certain beyond all reasonable doubt that Philipp was guilty before they convicted, and that if they had doubts, they must acquit. Without this vital warning, it is too easy for a jury to misunderstand its role and to become confused by the loose ends in the case, of which there were many. Did Max have a heart attack and fall? When was he attacked – before or after he slipped off the path? If Philipp did bludgeon Max to death, why were there no blood splashes on Philipp? Who, or what, created the bloody drag marks near the path? What about the missing money, and why did some of it reappear under a rock at the scene?

The jury retired for two hours and returned two split verdicts. On the charge of murder, the jury concluded, by seven votes to five, that Philipp was guilty. On the charge of manslaughter, they decided by eight votes to four that he was guilty.

The courtroom was in uproar. Philipp was distraught. He yelled that he was innocent and being denied justice in this country, but he was re-sentenced – this time to four years' imprisonment for manslaughter, rather than the previous ten years for murder. Having lost the appeal, his lawyers now prepared an application to the highest court in Vienna, and started to consider an application for clemency to the President of Austria, Wilhelm Miklas.

A further court appeal was rejected, and Philipp's sentence was confirmed. But the outrage about the case did not die down. Philipp's mother and sister campaigned relentlessly for his release and President Miklas was bombarded with letters of protest. The case became known as the 'Austrian Dreyfus Affair', recalling the scandal of Jewish scapegoating that racked France at the turn of the century. International luminaries including Albert Einstein, Sigmund Freud and Thomas Mann continued to press Philipp's case.

Eventually, on 30 September 1930, Philipp Halsman was pardoned by the president, but with a caveat: he must leave Austria within twenty-four hours. A pardon, though, was not the same thing as a not-guilty verdict.

The Halsman case split Innsbruckers, and it shone an unwelcome light on some of the region's darker recesses. The case was also damaging to the Tyrol's nascent tourist industry, more so because Max Halsman was not the only tourist to die violently in the Alps. I read an excellent article by the historian Niko Hofinger ('We don't like to talk about the trial, there are still too many foreigners here'), who noted that most local politicians tried to steer the safest course and stay out of the affair; however, their non-committal approach also had the effect of creating a vacuum, which was filled by the National Socialists.

In 1929, the Austrian NSDAP was still tiny, as its electoral haul in that year's local elections confirmed: a mere 202 votes (0.4 per cent of those cast). But they made plenty of noise and were outspoken about Philipp's trial, exploiting it for their own ends. Hugo would have seen the shrill NSDAP posters all over Innsbruck, summoning people to a 'lecture':

Innsbruckers! Innsbruckers!
The Halsman trial
Shows all those who want to see it,
the extraordinary influence of the Jews
The Jew is the master of the German People.
Ernst Grimm will give a talk on this theme on
Saturday 12 October
in the small room of the town hall.
Antisemites, come and help us in the fight against
the Jewish oppressors
of the German people and for a free German people!

> *Jews will be denied entry – entrance fee 40 Groschen*
> **National Socialist German Workers' Party**

The lecture was banned twice, but then it went ahead under a slightly modified title. Later, as Hofinger points out, the National Socialists looked back with pride at how they had managed to polarise opinion, even though it did not transform their performance at the polls. In 1931, they still only garnered 1,196 votes; on the other hand, at 4 per cent of the electorate, their trajectory was upwards.

In exploiting the Halsman case, Nazis fuelled the fear and resentment in the Tyrol caused by the very deep economic crisis overtaking Austria. The party was gaining members. And over the border, in 1932, something unexpected happened. The German Nazis stormed to electoral victory on the coattails of the Depression, becoming the largest party in the *Reichstag*.

The Ziller Valley, Tyrol, Summer 2019

I want to retrace part of the walk of Philipp and Max Halsman, so I set off with my husband for the Ziller Valley. On modern fast roads, it is a two-hour drive from Innsbruck. Kind friends, Claudia and Josef, have agreed to go hiking with us. The valley starts out wide, fertile and flat-bottomed, with very steep mountainous sides. As we head south, towards the glacier at the end of the valley, the landscape becomes narrower and wilder. The glacier itself has the ancient weather-beaten face of an old farmer; its granite-like surfaces pockmarked with snow and vertically gouged by white rivulets of 'glacier milk' – the name given by Austrians to a glacier's foaming, creamy meltwaters.

We find that it is no longer possible to follow Philipp and Max's exact steps. The point at which Max died is now covered by a reservoir, whose turquoise-green waters, gathered from several adjoining valleys, are held in by the spectacular, curved double wall of the Schlegeis Dam. On a summer's day, though, the area is perfect hiking territory.

We set off on a trek up to one of the many huts that dot the mountains. It is one of the hottest days of the year in 2019, but we are deceived. On our way down from the hut, it begins to rain in heavy drops, which turn to hail within minutes and then to buckets of icy water. Quickly, what have been minor streams tumbling merrily into the reservoir become muddy torrents that threaten to suck off our boots and send us sliding into the water below. Jagged boulders from a landslide block the previously clear path.

Utterly drenched, we arrive back at the car, glad not to have been caught under the rocks. I have learnt a lesson about the valley's unpredictability. Suddenly, it is easy to imagine how, even in dry weather, Max Halsman might have fallen into one of the fast-flowing streams that course through the valley. It is equally easy to imagine that the gushing sound of water might have obscured the sound of an attack on Max, either on the path itself or down by the river.

Researching the Halsman case has left me with an unpleasant aftertaste and a fear that justice was not done; more than that, a feeling that Philipp being a foreigner and a Jew, justice never *could* be done in Innsbruck at that time. My reading of the court files leads me to the conclusion that it was highly unlikely that Philipp killed Max. Philipp may at times have been a truculent, bad-tempered son, irritated and embarrassed by the way his father flashed his money around in the hut; Max may have joked, in poor taste, with strangers; but that was a long way short of a motive for murder.

I am relieved when I discover how Philipp Halsman's subsequent story took an unexpected turn. After fleeing Austria, he moved to Paris with his mother and sister and retrained as a photographer. He also changed his name to something more French: Philippe Halsman. From there, he tried but failed to reopen the case. In 1940, as war enveloped France, he followed his family to New York. Two years later, he shot his first cover photo-graph for the celebrated photo-journalism magazine, *Life*, begin-ning an association that would make him one of the magazine's most prolific and best-loved photographers.

He created striking photo-portraits of celebrities and aristoc-racy, including Edward VIII and Wallis Simpson, Marilyn Monroe, Grace Kelly and Salvador Dalí; a couple of Philippe's photographs even made it onto US postage stamps. Perhaps uniquely, he made his subjects jump in the air, believing that in those fractions of a second while airborne, their true characters revealed themselves. I ponder whether in those airborne seconds of his subjects, he was continuously re-examining that moment in his past when his father fell.

Philippe Halsman died in 1979, having rarely mentioned his traumatic trip to the Tyrol over the previous forty years.

Even Max's story did not conclude in 1928. Sixty-three years after Max Halsman's death, in 1991 an observant journalist spot-ted that none of the original reports mentioned the fate of Max's severed head. He made enquiries and found that it was still sit-ting in a jar of formaldehyde in Innsbruck's Institute of Legal Medicine.

Intrigued, I go to the offices of the Jewish community in Innsbruck, where I read the slim file of letters containing the deli-cate negotiations that preceded the release of the dentist's head for burial in August 1991. I find that even this last rite did not run smoothly.

First, Max's head could not be reunited with his body: his grave no longer existed in Innsbruck's Jewish cemetery. In the 1970s, the graveyard had been reduced in size and some of the graves relocated, to accommodate roadworks outside the ceme-tery wall. Then there was a further last-minute hitch: after burial, Max's head had to be dug up immediately, because the supremo of the Institute of Legal Medicine appeared in the cemetery, demanding that he should identify it personally before it was buried.

It was only this second burial that closed this dark and difficult chapter in Innsbruck's Jewish history. And the Schindlers? They would soon discover that it was not only foreign Jews who faced difficulties in Innsbruck. They would need every ounce of that 'energy and prudence' for which they were praised in 1931 by their grateful staff.

10

Anschluss

Innsbruck, New Year 1933

Winter and the Depression were biting deeply into Austrian life. In Innsbruck, it was the job of Hugo and the Café Schindler to spirit people away from their everyday cares. For the start of the year, Hugo printed an advertising flyer that proclaimed: *Zwei frohe Monate! Silvester und Fasching 1933* – 'Two Happy Months! New Year and Carnival Time 1933'.

But this invitation did not have specially commissioned art work, and the tone had changed. Hugo could not ignore what was happening outside his café, so he told the world that these celebrations would take place 'despite the terrible times'. Was there a hint of desperation?

Hugo's proposed antidote was to offer his guests no less than *die schönsten und gemütlichsten Faschingsfeste*, 'the most beautiful and relaxed carnival celebration'. *Gemütlich* does not translate easily into English. In Austria, it conveys a mixture of cosiness, comfort, conviviality, and a touch of slapdash laziness. *Gemütlichkeit*, the feeling associated with being *gemütlich*, has been elevated to an expression of a lifestyle: the polar opposite of stress, discomfort and hard work.

Hugo invited his guests to his newly refurbished rooms, where, 'in spite of the difficult times', the café would do its best to provide *frohe Stunden*, 'happy hours'. The advertisement reassured the reader that because of the café's well-known reasonable prices, it was possible for everyone to come and enjoy the Fox Band. Once in the café's convivial company, it was hoped

ZWEI FROHE MONATE!
SILVESTER UND FASCHING 1933
sollen in unseren Räumen in diesem Zeichen stehen!
Trotz der Ungunst der Zeit werden daher auch
in diesem Winter die schönsten und gemütlichsten

FASCHINGSFESTE

in den vollkommen neu ausgestatteten Räumen der
KONDITOREI SCHINDLER gefeiert werden.

So wie in den letzten Jahren werden wir bestrebt sein, allen unseren Gästen
trotz aller Schwere der Zeit frohe Stunden zu bereiten. Bei den bekannt
mäßigen Preisen in unserem Betriebe wird dafür gesorgt sein, daß jedermann
Gelegenheit hat, bei den packenden Weisen der

KUNSTLERKAPELLE „FOX"
in fröhlicher Gesellschaft die Sorgen des Alltags für einige Stunden zu ver-
gessen. Der erfolgreiche deutsche Meistertänzer Hans Lohr wird dabei die
tänzerische Leitung aller unserer Feste besorgen.

Zunächst laden wir Sie zu unserer großen, in allen Räumen stattfindenden

SILVESTERFEIER

höflichst ein und hoffen, daß wir Sie bestimmt bei uns begrüßen dürfen.
Gleichzeitig aber entbieten wir Ihnen zum Jahreswechsel die besten Wünsche
und bitten Sie, auch im kommenden Jahre recht häufig unser Gast zu sein.

Hochachtungsvoll

KONDITOREI SCHINDLER & CO.

Flyer for the café's New Year and carnival celebrations

that guests would be able to 'forget their everyday worries for a
few hours'. To help them, Hugo promised that the *Meistertänzer*
– 'dance master' – Hans Lohr would be on hand to lead the dancing at all their parties.

Hugo signed off with an invitation for the *Silvesterfeier*, the
New Year's Eve party – and the aspiration that people would
frequently still choose to be his guests at the Café Schindler.

I found Hugo's flyer at Innsbruck's City Archives. In other files I
could see how, over the years, Hugo applied for permission to
enlarge and improve the café, including the addition of a stunning
glass roof over the main dance floor, on the top storey of the
building. Even in the debilitating Depression years, some improve-
ments continued. In 1936, Hugo applied to add a small, illumi-
nated cube-shaped clock to the café's exterior, with clock faces on

167

two sides and, facing the street, the words *Tanz Café* lit up. The café was the only place to go dancing in Innsbruck, and Hugo wanted to be sure that people found their way easily to his front door.

Judging by the Schindler family's continuing investments in the fabric of their flagship business, they were doing well financially; they had become prominent, rich and fully assimilated members of Innsbruck society, as well as generous benefactors of local charities. The same could not be said of their cousins in Linz.

The Kafka family business, now under Rudolf after Egon's death, remained in trouble: his ever more frequent stays in hospital to treat his syphilis meant that he was an absentee manager, and, given the times, those with the means to buy high-quality *Schnapps*, fruit juice and jam were dwindling. On his mother Hermine's advice, he turned down a decent offer to purchase the company; Hermine simply could not bear the idea of losing control of it. Despite loans from Eduard Bloch, the business would sink into liquidation in the summer of 1934. Rudolf died a few months later, after which a now penniless Hermine moved in with the Blochs. Sofie's elder sister would die shortly afterwards, in 1935, unable to get over the loss of her branch of the family empire.

Despite their own wealth, and despite their rootedness in the Tyrol, the Schindlers could not ignore a world pressing in on them. Hugo had promised 'Two happy months' at the start of 1933. By the end of January, Adolf Hitler – once a speaker at an ill-attended rally in Innsbruck some thirteen years previously – had become Germany's chancellor. The popularity of National Socialism now surged in Austria. In April 1933, the Austrian NSDAP achieved more than 41 per cent of the vote in Innsbruck's local elections and became the third-strongest party in the local Tyrolean government.[1]

For an exhausted population, the Nazis were starting to sound like a viable alternative to the existing politicians. To celebrate their success, in May 1933 local Nazis paraded along the

Parade in the Maria-Theresien-Strasse, May 1933. Franz Hofer appears in the middle of the photo (from a 1938 book).

Maria-Theresien-Strasse, passing directly under the windows of the Café Schindler. I have seen a picture of them, crammed together, their arms raised in stiff, awkward-looking salutes. Recognisable in the centre of the throng is Franz Hofer, a key local Nazi, whose future path would cross several times with that of my family.

Hitler made no secret of the fact that he considered Austria's future as part of a greater Germany. As Austrian Nazis agitated, Chancellor Dollfuss took decisive action, banning first the Communist Party in May 1933 and a month later, the Austrian Nazis. Many Nazis fled to Germany, while others went underground, infiltrating local government, the police and academia. As tensions rose, German Nazis supported and trained the illegal Austrian Nazis, even assisting with terrorist attacks in Austria.

Dollfuss recognised the fragility of his regime and Austria's independence; he needed a protector, and he found one in

Europe's senior dictator, Benito Mussolini, already in power for a decade and similarly concerned about Hitler's expansionism. Photographs in August 1933 show Dollfuss, cap in hand but tie still in place, walking with *il Duce* along the beach of the Italian resort of Riccione, where Mussolini had a villa: Mussolini, bare-chested, flaunts his bronzed virility; Dollfuss is the desperate supplicant. Mussolini poured warm words into Dollfuss's ears about guaranteeing Austrian independence against any German encroachments. Thereafter, Dollfuss modelled himself on the Italian.

Following a dispute about parliamentary voting irregularities, Dollfuss seized his chance to dissolve parliament, instead ruling by emergency decree. It came to be known by opponents as 'Austrofascism', and the term stuck: it was Austria's very own brand of authoritarian rule. My family had seen their country pass from a royal empire to a quasi-dictatorship via just fifteen years of turbulent democracy.

In February 1934, several Austrian cities erupted into violence, this time as the army and the *Heimwehr* paramilitary cracked down on socialists, communists and their paramilitary groups. Vienna, where Hugo's siblings Martha and Otto lived, saw the worst of it, and the violence was significant enough for some to call it an 'Austrian civil war'. After that was over, a further crisis struck. On 25 July 1934, the Austrian chancellor paid the price for banning the Austrian Nazis, when a gang of ten of them forced their way into the Chancellery building and murdered him.

An outraged Mussolini broke the news personally to Dollfuss's wife and children, who were staying with him at his villa in Riccione: he considered the assassination in such circumstances a personal insult to him. Mussolini announced he would defend Austria's borders and he sent troops to the Italian side. Hitler denied complicity, blaming rogue elements, and closed the German–Austrian border to Dollfuss's assassins. In Vienna, 500,000 people turned out for Dollfuss's funeral cortege; while in Innsbruck, a funeral parade to mourn Dollfuss also wound its way slowly along the Maria-Theresien-Strasse, past the Café Schindler.

At this moment of national crisis, the Schindlers faced their own problems. Otto had tried to take his life by jumping from the fourth-floor window of his flat in Vienna. He was foiled in this attempt by his young niece, who happened to be passing by and forcibly prevented his jump. It had been a close call, and the family agreed that some time convalescing in the Tyrol was needed. Otto was brought across Austria to stay with his mother Sofie, in Igls. One day in July 1934, while alone and out for a walk in a narrow wooded gorge nearby, he took out his penknife and ended his life. It was a violent, lonely and desperate death for this talented doctor.

Sofie had now lost her eldest and youngest sons, and neither of them to natural causes. John Kafka, when I met him in 2018, remembered as a child visiting Sofie with his mother to offer his condolences. The family was deeply traumatised, its grief finding expression in the death notice that appeared in Vienna on 9 July 1934. No one mentioned suicide:

> By a dreadful blow of fate, our most affectionate and loyal son, brother, brother-in-law and uncle, Herr Doctor Otto Schindler, was suddenly taken from us during a stay in a health spa in Igls. The best and most noble person has now left us. We have given him a quiet burial in accordance with his wishes.

Under the announcement, Sofie was listed first as his mother, followed by Otto's siblings: Martha Salzer, Erich Schindler and Hugo Schindler, and then his brother- and sisters-in-law Siegfried Salzer, Edith Schindler and Grete Schindler. Otto's nephews and nieces, Margarethe, Erwin, Kurt and Peter were listed last.

I don't know what propelled Otto to kill himself. According to one historian, the Dollfuss regime – antisemitic, even if it wasn't Nazi – had unjustly accused Otto of 'overtreating' patients and exploiting their medical insurance by giving them therapies that were too expensive; and the authorities had even closed down his medical practice.[2]

Otto was the family's academic high-achiever. None of his siblings had gone to university, but he had graduated *summa cum laude* from his medical studies in Vienna; he had been a pioneer, the first to use radium therapy in Vienna. That form of treatment was unavoidably expensive, so perhaps that brought the accusations and then conflict with the authorities. I wondered whether the allegations would have been made if he had not been Jewish. Did Otto, under stress and feeling shamed and ever more exposed in Vienna, lapse into despair?

Then again, at the core of his hopelessness there may have been something more personal, to do with the Schindler family itself. Both his nephew Peter – as he told the historian Gerda Hofreiter – and my father Kurt believed that their Uncle Otto was hopelessly in love with Erich's wife, Grete; that he could not bear to hurt his brother, and eventually he saw no way out other than to take his own life. I will never know the truth, but what is clear is that he was deeply unhappy and desperate.

Meanwhile, in the aftermath of Chancellor Dollfuss's death, Austria's very independence was increasingly under threat. Dollfuss's assassins were rounded up and executed, and another lawyer, this time a South Tyrolean, inherited the office of chancellor. Kurt von Schuschnigg continued the policies of Austrofascism as the means to keep Austria independent. But within eighteen months, the rock upon which that policy depended – Mussolini's support – began to crack.

With the death of President Hindenburg in August 1934, Hitler solidified control of Germany as *der Führer*, 'the Leader', at the head of a Nazi dictatorship that was speedily rearming the country. Tempted by Hitler's offer of political backing for his deeply controversial colonial campaign to conquer Abyssinia, in 1935 Mussolini began to pivot towards Germany, and his support for Austrian independence melted away.

A desperate Schuschnigg scrambled to adjust. He tried appeasing Hitler. In July 1936, Schuschnigg signed a German–Austrian 'Friendship and Normalisation Agreement', in which he aligned Austrian politics generally (in particular its foreign policy) with Germany, in recognition of the fact that Austria was a 'German' state.

In return, Hitler lifted a 1,000-Mark levy that he had applied to all Germans who wanted to travel to Austria: it had been crippling the economy and in particular its tourist industry, on which the Tyrol, and indeed the Café Schindler, were so reliant. Schuschnigg was able to keep his ban on the Austrian Nazis, but accepted an amnesty for some imprisoned Nazis and a secret clause that paved the way for some Nazis, in the future, to enter government.

In the Tyrol there was rejoicing at the release of the Nazis. The German–Austrian agreement simply strengthened the Nazis' grip on the levers of power there, helped by those politicians and academics who already sat in senior official positions and were secret members of the Nazi Party.

Berchtesgaden, Bavaria, 12 February 1938

Eighteen months after the 'Friendship and Normalisation Agreement', relations between Austria and Germany had steadily worsened, as Kurt von Schuschnigg struggled to keep control of his country's fate. The Austrian chancellor now travelled into the *Führer*'s lair, Hitler's spectacular mountain-top retreat in the Bavarian Alps near Berchtesgaden, known in English as the 'Eagle's Nest'. From there, Hitler could gaze longingly and possessively into his native Austria.

Schuschnigg's reward for making this trip was to be harangued. The *Führer* mocked the very idea of Austrian independence, pointing out correctly that Italy was no longer an ally of Austria and that neither France nor England would lift a finger on Austria's behalf if the German army rolled in.

The mild-mannered Schuschnigg was shocked and cowed. Surrounded by German generals in a room with stunning and poignant views over Austria, Schuschnigg signed an ultimatum that would relinquish Austria's fragile independence. He agreed to lift the ban on the Austrian Nazi Party, to grant an amnesty to all imprisoned Nazis, and to appoint a Catholic pro-Nazi Viennese lawyer, Dr Seyss-Inquart, as his Minister of the Interior, with authority over the police and home security. Schuschnigg also agreed that the Austrian and German armies would establish closer relations. The Austrian chancellor was ordered to prepare his country for absorption into Germany. He left, humiliated and defeated.

Immediately after news of Schuschnigg's concessions leaked into the public domain, Austrian Nazis rejoiced and sought to consolidate their support. In Innsbruck, on 20 February 1938, 3,000 ebullient Nazi supporters paraded down the Maria-Theresien-Strasse, past the Café Schindler, to honour Seyss-Inquart. Most of them wore the knickerbockers and white socks that had been the covert symbol of the previously illegal Nazi Party; some of them sported the Nazi uniforms they had acquired whilst training illicitly in Germany. Elsewhere, all around the Tyrol, groups of Nazis marched through villages, sporting Nazi armbands and lapel pins, and singing once outlawed Nazi songs. Their moment had come.

When I look through the local newspapers for spring 1938, I am surprised at how quickly in February the advertisements appear for the sale of swastika flags and badges. It seems that local shop-keepers had been stockpiling them for some time. Again, I imagine Hugo watching the flags unfurl around him from the café and shop windows, wondering what this latest chapter will mean for his family and his business.

If Hugo was still inclined to wish for the best or wait and see, his wife had other ideas. Edith had been an inveterate traveller, and she had acquired a more international view. By the time that Schuschnigg was being browbeaten by Hitler, my grandmother had lost faith in the Tyrol as a place of security, despite the Schindlers' presence there for three generations. Edith wanted to leave the Tyrol; but she would need to persuade Hugo.

However, if they took the momentous decision to pack up and leave, where could they go? The southern Europe Edith had visited in the 1920s and early 1930s with Hugo (and sometimes with other friends) was clearly not an option, as fascism's influence was spreading through Greece and the Balkans. Instead, they looked north.

Thus it was that in the depths of winter, in February 1938, leaving Kurt in the care of Sofie, my grandparents set off on what appeared to be a sudden winter holiday, taking in Paris, Amsterdam and London. Looking uncomfortable and bundled up in their thick overcoats, Hugo and Edith took photographs of the Eiffel Tower, of Dutch canals and of Tower Bridge. I know this, because these photos were later stuck in one of their albums. Of course, tourism was a secondary concern, for their real mission was to scope out these destinations for a possible full-scale relocation of their lives and their business. Britain and France, Hugo's one-time foes in the First World War, were still functioning democracies, as was the Netherlands.

Hugo and Edith might have been influenced by their friends, the Stiassny family, who had already moved to London, bringing their women's clothes business there in the process. Edith also liked the idea of London, because her father, the match mogul, had worked there as a young man. On Hugo's side of the family, there was no connection with Britain. I know from Kurt that Hugo dragged his feet and was reluctant to accept this dislocation, which was being forced on them by circumstance. What would happen to the Schindler employees, and how about all the practicalities of winding up a business in Innsbruck?

However, they made a fundamental decision: Edith remained in London, while Hugo hurried back to Innsbruck to try and organise what inevitably would be a complex and difficult process – not least psychologically – of extracting the family and its business from the only place it had ever called home.

It was in Innsbruck that Kurt von Schuschnigg launched a last-ditch attempt to rescue Austria's independence. At the City Hall, on 9 March 1938, he announced a surprise plebiscite over Austrian independence, to take place on Sunday, 13 March 1938. I assume that Hugo must have been delighted, sensing a possible reprieve. Hugo's identity embraced that strain of Tyrolean independent-mindedness and a refusal to be cowed by outsiders, which perhaps Schuschnigg hoped to exploit.

Once again, it was Andreas Hofer's rallying cry of 'Men, it's time', invoked this time by Schuschnigg to inspire patriots to rise up and protect Austria.[3] He had a few other tricks up his sleeve: he raised the voting age to twenty-four, so as to disenfranchise large sections of the pro-Nazi youth; he refused to make the poll secret; and he had printed thousands of sheets of 'yes' votes, which could be handed in multiple times.

The plebiscite was too important to be left to chance, so the ballot paper did not even present a choice, instead calling for a 'Free and German, independent and social, a Christian and United Austria. For peace and work and equality for everyone who belongs to the People and Fatherland'. With a fiery speech, he rallied supporters by invoking the Austrian flag to proclaim that the country would remain *rot-weiss-rot* – 'red, white, red' – until death.

Belatedly, Schuschnigg also turned to his previously banned opponents – the unions, the Social Democrats and the communists – promising them increased participation in Austrian politics. The Catholic and Lutheran churches agreed to mobilise the faithful, and several prominent Jews lent money to get the plebiscite off the ground.

Hitler was livid, not least because a defeat in the plebiscite would be a humiliation for him. What he had in mind was a hero's return to his homeland rather than having to force his way back in; and, despite his bluster, he was still nervous about any intervention by France or Britain, especially if a land grab on Austria went in the face of a plebiscite. He demanded Schuschnigg's resignation in favour of Seyss-Inquart, as well as the abandoning of the plebiscite. For good measure Hitler's generals marshalled troops, munitions and arms at the Austrian border, ready to march into Austria 'in order to maintain peace and order'.

There followed a nail-biting two days, in which Austria's fate hung in the balance, and at which my grandfather had an unwelcome ringside seat.

Innsbruck, 11 March 1938

In the early hours of 11 March, local members of NSDAP mobilise to demonstrate against the hated Chancellor Schuschnigg and his imminent plebiscite.

9.00 a.m. The Nazis make their presence felt by striding energetically around town. The local authorities are utterly unprepared. Austrian Nazis block off the Maria-Theresien-Strasse and gather directly below the Café Schindler, where they unroll their large banner, which reads: *Alles für Österreich ohne Schuschnigg* ('Everything for an Austria without Schuschnigg'). Nazis mill around. Thugs in knickerbockers with knee-length white socks set up machine guns against the Saint Anna Column under the windows of the café.

As the morning goes on, the police are still nowhere to be seen. The authorities seem to be paralysed. The crowd grows more courageous and starts yelling Nazi slogans, such as *ein Volk, ein Reich, ein Führer!* ('one People, one Empire, one Leader!') and *diese Wahl, ein Skandal!* ('This plebiscite, a scandal!'). One banner proclaims: *Wir kämpfen für Freiheit* ('We're fighting for freedom'). It is not only men. A group of women on the Maria-Theresien-Strasse bring their own, memorable banner: 'No respectable man will vote on Sunday'.

Women demonstrate against Schuschnigg's
referendum on the Maria-Theresien-Strasse

Across the street, opposite the café, Hugo can see a long red
flag with a swastika unfurled from a top-floor window. The building he is looking at contains one of his competitors, the Café
Alt-Innsprugg – 'Old Innsbruck'. Inside it, a representative of the
local Nazi leader, the *Gauleiter*, has stationed himself; with a
loudspeaker, he gives directions to men of the Austrian Nazi SA
(*Sturmabteilung*) and SS (*Schutzstaffel*) paramilitary units to
march all over Innsbruck. This loudspeaker also relays news from
Vienna.

The Nazis are determined to make the biggest impact possible.
They want, with this show of force, to convince any waverers
among the general population to come over to them. The police
finally make a half-hearted attempt to clear the street, but already
their authority is seeping away, as they are warned off by the
Gauleiter's representative.

2.00 p.m. The Tyrol's Nazi *Gauleiter*, Edmund Christoph,
arrives from Vienna. The Nazis do not have an organised plan for
a coup, so he improvises. He tells the assembled demonstrators

and supporters to maintain order and that the Nazis are to act as an auxiliary police force. The SS and SA men don white armbands and are ordered to keep the peace. Hugo looks up and down the street, as other windows on the Maria-Theresien-Strasse begin to sprout red and black swastikas. The Café Schindler now begins to stand out as an exception. No flags fly there.

2.45 p.m. Dr Seyss-Inquart informs Berlin that Schuschnigg has caved in, will cancel the referendum and is going to resign. It is Schuschnigg's effort to avert, if not Austria's loss of independence, then bloodshed.

4.00 p.m. By now, the crowd of Nazi supporters is marching through the middle of Innsbruck, accompanied by the SA and SS men 'keeping order'.

6.00 p.m. Kurt von Schuschnigg resigns the chancellorship. One hour later, it is announced on the radio that the Austrian Cabinet has resigned too, except for Seyss-Inquart and the other Nazis. Rejoicing erupts on the streets around the Café Schindler.

8.00 p.m. Schuschnigg goes on air and tells Austrians not to resist Germany's assumption of power.

8.45 p.m. Once it is clear that there will be no resistance, Hitler gives the order to German troops to march into Austria. Kurt Schindler, ill in bed that evening, hears the cheering and the rumble of heavy traffic and marching feet outside the family's house on the Rennweg, sounds that he will not forget. By 9 p.m., the Innsbruck Nazis have hoisted a large swastika flag on Innsbruck's City Hall.

11.00 p.m. As this day draws to an end, one in which the dreams of Austrian Nazis have been realised, *Gauleiter* Edmund Christoph makes a speech, which is relayed over the loudspeakers to the people gathered outside the City Hall: 'We are proud and happy that we are allowed to lay our homeland, the Tyrol, that most beautiful pearl of the German garden, at our beloved leader's feet.'[4] The boast is that Innsbruck is the first county capital in Austria to be taken over by the Nazis. To ram home the point, on that day and the next, SA men block the Tyrol's international borders. The consequences for Austrian Jews are immediate: any trying to leave are stopped and required to hand in their passports.

As Hitler has correctly gambled, British and French politicians do not want to step in and risk war with Germany, not over little Austria. After all, some of those politicians feel that Austria should have been given to Germany after the First World War. When German troops now flood over the border into Austria, they are received everywhere by ecstatic, cheering, Heil-Hitlering crowds of all ages.

Nazi propaganda goes into overdrive and produces a postcard mocking Schuschnigg after his Innsbruck speech. It shows the startled ex-chancellor fleeing the country, whereas in reality, he is already under house arrest. Accompanying him on the postcard are a Catholic priest and a hook-nosed Jew carrying a *Kasse*, a

National Socialist propaganda postcard

money-box. Schuschnigg and a loyal young activist wear the Austrian red-white-red colours; but chasing and threatening to overwhelm them is an avalanche of swastikas. Predictably, Andreas Hofer's rallying cry of 'Men, it's time' is thrown back at Schuschnigg in the postcard's caption, to emphasise his humiliation.

By contrast to the 'fleeing' Schuschnigg, Adolf Hitler is already on his way home. And Hugo must be wondering whether he has made a terrible mistake: are he and his twelve-year-old son now trapped in Innsbruck?

Part Four

11

Postcards

Linz, Summer 2019

I stand in the archway of the building where Dr Eduard Bloch had his home and surgery: the Palais Weissenwolff at No. 12 Landstrasse. Embedded in the wall is a beautiful, wrought-iron disc bearing the words *Haus Glocke*, 'House Bell', running in raised letters round the outside. The bell-button itself, in the middle, is chipped and yellow like a nicotine-stained fingernail; a crack arches its way over the surface – evidence, perhaps, of the desperation with which the bell was rung repeatedly by the many people seeking Dr Bloch's services.

I know that the well-liked doctor took his calling very seriously. In all weathers, at all hours, he would put on his big black felt hat and drive his small horse-drawn carriage out to visit his patients at home.

'I never made the slightest distinction between the treatment of rich and poor,' he asserted in his later handwritten memoir. 'I answered the call of every sick person, even in the coldest of nights, so that my constant readiness to help became almost proverbial.' No wonder that in its heyday, Eduard's medical practice was one of the most successful in Linz.

Yet I know too, from reading his account that his success was evaporating even before the German Reich swallowed Austria in March 1938. The kindness, care and expertise that Eduard showered on his patients was no antidote to the poison coursing through the lifeblood of Austria. Older patients no longer dared visit him, as many of the youth of Linz were already enthusiastic followers of Hitler. Eduard later wrote of the city being a hotbed of antisemitic 'illegals' – as the Nazis described themselves when they were banned – who called for a 'return to the homeland'.

In his view, it was the intelligentsia who first advocated this *Deutschnationale* politics, and the working classes were then attracted to it as a response to what Eduard called the 'previously unknown phenomenon of unemployment'. In such conditions, 'poverty and hunger were the greatest enemies of morality'.

I turn my attention to the two large marble figures of Atlantes at the Palais Weissenwolff. The stonework is grubby, and the figures look careworn, slightly slumped, as they struggle to bear the weight of the first-floor balcony on the back of their heads and necks. Looking up at the balcony itself, I try to imagine what it would have been like for Eduard to witness Hitler's triumphant return to the town where he grew up. The photographs and Eduard Bloch's own account bring the scene vividly to life.

It is 12 March 1938. The crowds pack, seven or eight deep, along the pavement in front of the Palais, waiting excitedly for the arrival of the *Führer*. The early morning spring sunshine has helped tempt people out of their apartments and houses without heavy overcoats. Everywhere, there are now red, black and white flags emblazoned with the *Hakenkreuz* – the hooked cross of the swastika. Church bells are ringing, planes drone overhead, and loudspeakers relay the slow progress of Hitler's convoy, travelling east from Braunau on the Austrian border – a border that no longer has any international relevance.

As Hitler's large, open-top Mercedes finally noses its way along the Landstrasse, the crowds erupt, and there is an orgy of flag-waving and straight-armed salutes. For one thing, they are expressing their delight that Hitler has chosen Linz, his favourite Austrian city, as the first stop on his victory lap of Austria.

The city's population has been ordered to turn on all the lights in the buildings facing the parade route and to close the windows. The Nazis are nervous about assassination attempts on the *Führer*. Despite this, some still stand on balconies, unable to contain their

joy indoors. Eduard Bloch, though, is obedient. He stands inside
by his first-floor window to watch Hitler's motorcade roll by
below him. It is a moment he will never forget:

> I stood for a short time at my window full of anxious anticipa-
> tion at the arrival. Standing up in his slow-moving car, Hitler
> saluted in all directions, including up at my window; I assumed
> that the salute was not meant for me but for one of my neigh-
> bours who was an enthusiastic Hitler-supporter. I was informed
> the next day that this 'honour' was meant for me. Straight after
> his arrival at City Hall, the *Führer* asked after me.

Eduard's daughter Trude later remembers that the following day
a town councillor, Adolf Eigl, recounted Hitler's very words to
her: 'Tell me, is my good old house doctor, Dr Bloch still alive?
Yes, if all Jews were like him, then there would be no antisemitism.'[1] Trude can, she says, 'swear to it'.

In truth, this is not a new revelation. Eduard has already heard
messages about Hitler's continued fondness for him, from his
patients who were Nazi 'illegals' and who made the short journey
from Linz to visit Hitler at his Alpine retreat of Berchtesgaden.
He knows, therefore, that Hitler thinks him an 'exception', an
Edeljude – a noble Jew. He has already been told verbatim what
Hitler said about him: 'If all Jews were like him, there would be
no Jewish Question.'

The doctor admits later to thinking that 'Hitler could at least
see something good in one member of my race.'[2] Standing at his
window, it is clear that Eduard has very mixed feelings and cannot
help being a little proud at seeing the 'frail boy' he treated so
often, and whom he has not encountered for thirty years. Yet, he
is not naïve. As Eduard peers at Hitler, over the heads of the crowd
below him, he asks himself: What will he now do to the people I
love?[3]

For the rest of Linz's Jewish population – those not considered *edel* – life changed almost immediately after the *Anschluss*. Eduard later described how all the Jews in Linz were immediately required to surrender their passports in order to prevent flight. Then, the Gestapo set about stripping them of their assets:

> . . . they began the feared house searches, which normally took place at night or in the early morning hours. Naturally, nothing 'incriminating' was found, but with virtuosic cleverness, a Gestapo officer knew how to slip 'a communist leaflet' into a book on a shelf. Triumphantly, he would 'discover' it and show it to the unhappy and appalled flat owner, as clear proof of membership of an organisation which is hostile to the state. In this way, people who had nothing whatsoever to do with politics were labelled as dangerous enemies of the state; with that their fate was already sealed. Other members of the community were accused of tax evasion. In short, the Jews were arrested on the most unbelievable charges: after a few days all police cells were overfilled with Jewish inmates . . . National Socialist party people were posted outside shops and barred the entrance to shoppers; so soon the Jews were without the means of earning their living and the ruthless expropriations soon rendered them penniless.

Eight desperate members of the tiny Jewish community took their lives, terrified at what Hitler had in store for the Jews of Linz.

Even the Blochs were not immune to Gestapo attention, though for other and quite specific reasons. Sixteen days after the *Anschluss*, on 28 March 1938, some officers paid them a visit, while Eduard was out visiting a patient. 'I am informed that you have some souvenirs of the *Führer*,' one officer explained to Lilli. 'I should like to see them.'

He was referring to an article in a local newspaper, which mentioned that Bloch had two postcards and a landscape painting given to him by Hitler. That same article also described how Bloch had treated Klara Hitler 'extremely conscientiously and compassionately despite her poverty'.[4] Their interest piqued, the Gestapo now demanded the items be handed over.

Lilli located the two old postcards, which a grateful young Hitler had sent Eduard from Vienna before the First World War. As Eduard later described, one was a 'penny postcard' view of Vienna inscribed with the words: 'From Vienna, I send you my greetings. Yours always faithfully, Adolf Hitler'. The second was the one with Hitler's own artwork inscribed: 'Cheers Happy New Year'. A few years later, Eduard reflected that the Vienna period was 'the one time in his life that Hitler was able to make successful use of his talent' – even though, in reality, Hitler had been barely getting by; sleeping in a working men's hostel and scraping a living by painting such postcards.

Lilli told the Gestapo that they did not have the painting mentioned in the article. Later, Eduard conceded that he might have been given one by Hitler at some point, but had not retained it, because he was often given keepsakes. But Lilli did reluctantly hand over the two postcards, knowing – as did her husband – that in the current climate so much could depend on these little tokens of affection from an adolescent boy to his Jewish doctor. She could hardly resist; the officers would have torn apart the flat to search for them.

The Gestapo told Lilli they were 'confiscating' the cards and gave her a receipt, a worn copy of which would survive, eventually to be lodged by my cousin John at the Holocaust Museum in Washington, D.C. It read: 'Certificate for the safekeeping of two post cards (one of them painted by the hand of Adolf Hitler) confiscated in the house of Dr Eduard Bloch.'

All did not seem lost, though, for Lilli was told to pick up the cards the next day at the Linz Gestapo headquarters. However, on her arrival, the Gestapo told her that they dared not return them until they had received word from Berlin about what to do. Eduard fretted. In his opinion, 'the matter of the "safekeeping" of the cards was sufficient reason to request an interview with the Chief of the Gestapo in Linz (which was only rarely granted)', with a view to forwarding 'a general petition and a personal letter' from Eduard to Hitler.

As he entered the Gestapo building a few days later, Eduard was spared the customary formalities and ushered into the presence of the most senior Gestapo officer in Linz, the *Regierungsrat* (Governing Counsellor), Dr Rasch. This man, a German, had only arrived in the city that year and was still finding his feet. Bloch wrote a detailed account of their meeting.

Gestapo Headquarters, Linz

Dr Rasch receives his visitor warmly, extending both hands in greeting and invites him to take a seat. He knows little about this local man, other than he was once Hitler's doctor, but he is naturally curious about everything to do with his *Führer*'s youth in Linz. They chat animatedly, and the atmosphere appears 'favourable' to Dr Bloch. So Eduard summons up the courage to ask about the return of his postcards, which he describes as his 'ethical property', because they were freely given – he did not purchase them with money and therefore feels he has the right to ask for them back.

'Of course,' Rasch replies, 'that goes without saying, I do not understand at all how they could have been taken from you, Herr *Obermedizinalrat*.' He addresses Eduard by the honorary title of Higher Medical Counsellor, granted him for his services to medicine during the First World War. On hearing this highly obliging and courteous reply, Eduard knows immediately that Dr Rasch knows nothing about the postcards; but neither does he know much about Dr Bloch.

A puzzled Rasch asks some questions.

'Are you, perhaps, politically somehow suspicious?'

'I have until now entirely dedicated myself to my work, without engaging politically in any way.'

'Or have you had issues with the courts or with the Party?'

'Neither of those.'

Rasch falls silent, examining Bloch closely. Finally, Rasch stumbles on the answer.

'Or are you perhaps not Aryan?'

'I am,' responds Dr Bloch, 'a *Volljude, Herr Regierungsrat*.'

Bloch could just have said he was of Jewish faith (*Mosaische Glaube*), but instead he chooses to emphasise that he is 'wholly Jewish'. He is invoking the German Reich's own racial vocabulary, drawn from the 1935 Nuremberg Laws with their precise nomenclature. He does not mince his words, much less attempt any subterfuge behind the Nazis' 'lesser' categories of Jewish identity, such *Mischling Ersten Grades* (having two Jewish grandparents) or *Mischling Zweiten Grades* (one Jewish grandparent).

Bloch later describes the effect of his revelation on the Nazi official:

My response had the effect of creating an instant wall of ice between the two of us, which would freeze any friendly word. Indeed the well-meaning and accommodating tone completely vanished from the voice of the *Regierungsrat*.

Nevertheless, Rasch promises to look into the postcard issue personally and to pass on Dr Bloch's request that the cards be returned to him. Eduard suspects he will do no such thing. As Eduard leaves the room, Dr Rasch hesitates to shake his hand. Bloch reassures him: 'Herr *Regierungsrat*, you are allowed to shake my hand, as your *Führer* has repeatedly shaken my hand in gratitude.' Somewhat shamefacedly, Rasch does so. Another small victory.

After his meeting with Dr Rasch, Eduard took matters into his own hands, writing letters and petitioning for the return of his postcards. No response arrived from Berlin. He even asked his daughter Trude, who was studying in Vienna, to seek out Hitler's sister, Frau Paula Wolf, and ask her to convey a letter to her brother. Trude was unable to speak to her personally – at Hitler's insistence, Frau Wolf lived a reclusive life – but Trude did get word, via a neighbour, that Frau Wolf would try to pass on the letter to her brother. Eduard heard that a few days later, when Hitler was in Vienna attending the opera, he had received his letter. Whether Hitler ignored it, or the letter really reached Hitler's eyes, remained unclear. Eduard's quest ground on.

In any case, the *Führer* already had weightier and grander matters on his mind, and some of them concerned Linz. Eduard remembered the elation written over Hitler's face on 12 March 1938, when he returned to his boyhood city. Hitler had not been able to visit for years, and now that the town was his, it would become a minor obsession with him.

He envisaged an ambitious rebuilding programme for Linz, focused on the banks of the Danube, which included plans for an enormous museum to house art works personally selected by him. He would keep a model of the city in the bunker of the Reich Chancellery in Berlin. Albert Speer, Hitler's favourite architect, later described his *Führer* as having a small-town mentality and so preferring the 'manageable proportions of a town like Linz'.[5]

In the end, most of the buildings Hitler planned were never built. Instead, rather than art galleries and architectural gems, Linz would attract the 'Reichswerke Hermann Göring', an enormous steel and armaments conglomerate, built on the outskirts. This was a significant enough military and industrial asset to attract the keen attention of Allied bomber aircraft in the conflict to come, in raids that also flattened many of Hitler's favourite baroque buildings in the city.

Linz's Jewish community, slightly larger than Innsbruck's, was gutted much more quickly, through arrests, deportations and their own desperate efforts to get out. On 25 June 1938, Kurt Ungar, the young man whose treatment as a baby had first brought Eduard and Lilli together, was arrested and taken to the nearest concentration camp, Dachau, near Munich – the first opened by the Nazis. He remained there for several months, but luckier than many, he was then released unharmed. I wondered if Eduard Bloch had interceded on his behalf. Eduard does not claim responsibility for this; however, there were no other Jews in Linz who wielded any influence, so I suspect he had a hand in Kurt's release, as he did in a number of others.

Later, Eduard conceded that 'favours were granted me which I feel sure were accorded no other Jew in all Germany or Austria.'[6] He and Lilli were allowed to keep their apartment. They also retained their telephone and passports. But even these favours had their limits, as demonstrated when his son-in-law, Franz Kren, went to the Gestapo to try and take up the matter of the postcards yet again on Eduard's behalf. Shortly afterwards, the Gestapo arrived at the Krens' flat and turned it upside down, in front of Bloch's grandchildren, Johanna and Georg.

Having learnt from the terrified children that their father was visiting neighbours, the Gestapo then arrested Franz, after which the family heard nothing and feared the worst. Finally, Bloch's connections paid off when Trude went to the Gestapo and asked them whether 'the *Führer* will be pleased to hear that the son-in-law of his old doctor has been thrown into gaol?' After three weeks in prison, Franz was finally released, unharmed. But for Franz and Trude, this was the last straw: being the daughter of a 'noble Jew' was no guarantee of their safety. They were clear that they had emigrate.

In the meantime, Hitler, having effected Austria's annexation in a bloodless coup, was anxious to secure at least the impression of legitimacy. He also had another Austrian city on his itinerary: Innsbruck.

Innsbruck, Summer 2019

I am visiting the *Kaiserjäger* Museum of military history, which is situated near to Innsbruck's Olympic ski jump. The endless tableaux of uniformed men and the glorification of war leave me slightly cold. But in the basement I spot a cabinet of 1938 artefacts. Inside it is a cartoon-like voting paper. On it, a large circle is labelled 'yes', while a small circle is marked 'no'. The name 'Hitler' is prominent. The question on the paper is whether it is right for Austria to become part of the German Reich, and there is no mystery about what the new regime intends as the correct response.

This was the plebiscite by which Hitler hoped to apply a veneer of legitimacy to the *Anschluss*. Hitler's Austrian supporters who had cried foul at Schuschnigg's referendum on Austrian independence, the previous month, had no complaints about this new plebiscite despite all its irregularities.

Hugo Schindler has no need to agonise over which way to vote – nor does Sofie nor Erich, nor indeed any of the Schindlers or Kafkas or Dubskys. Austrian Jews have all been disenfranchised. However, Hugo cannot escape the propaganda campaign that ensues. In Innsbruck, it draws heavily on Tyrol-specific issues and belief systems, about the Tyrol as homeland and about the Tyrol's heroic history. The Nazis are presented as fulfilling the people's wish to join Germany, whereas the Jews are blackened as enemies of the people. The propaganda is aimed at attracting the support in particular of the working class and the conservative rural farming populations.

One enterprising publisher of postcards of Innsbruck reprints the classic view of the Maria-Theresien-Strasse with the Café Schindler on the right-hand side and the stunning Nordkette Mountains in the background. Presumably, the target market is the influx of the newly arrived Germans and returning Austrian soldiers, who are flooding into the city to take up military and administrative posts. This time, so there is no mistake as to his

Postcard of Marie-Theresien-Strasse with a rising swastika 'sun'

allegiance, the printer has placed a bright-white shining swastika, rising triumphantly over Innsbruck's most famous mountain chain. It is a card that manages to be both utterly incongruous and chilling at the same time.

The Nazis leave nothing to chance. As has already happened in the German economy, they announce large-scale investment and big infrastructure projects, particularly to benefit the agrarian economy, as well as initiatives to reduce unemployment and poverty in Tyrolean towns. There are some immediate successes: unemployment does come down, while unemployment benefits are paid again, and certain sections of the population are given free travel in order to visit Germany. The changes are welcome among those who have suffered years of poverty during and after the First World War.

By 13 March 1938, troops are pouring into Innsbruck. Tellingly, one photo of a senior Nazi official shows him saluting supporters opposite the Café Schindler. He cannot be seen acknowledging a

A senior Nazi drives past the Café, March 1938

Jewish business. To crown it all, Hitler visits Innsbruck on 5 April 1938. It is very different to his low-key visit in 1920, when sections of the press mocked his speech. This time, crowds throng the Maria-Theresien-Strasse, spilling off the pavement and into the street so that there is barely room for his car: it has to crawl through the chanting, saluting mass of people, some of whom have been bussed in from surrounding areas.

To add to the welcome, a square just outside the old part of town has been hastily renamed 'Adolf-Hitler-Platz' in the *Führer*'s honour. Ten thousand people listen to the speech Hitler makes in the nearby exhibition hall, which is transmitted by loudspeaker to other parts of town, before more crowds of Innsbruckers accompany Hitler on foot, back to his hotel, in a triumphal procession.

By the evening, enormous glowing swastikas are alight on the Nordkette, and the words *ein Volk, ein Reich, ein Führer* are emblazoned in 100-metre-high flaming letters in the snow. Hugo's beloved mountains have become the screen onto which the Nazis

Auf der Nordkette: Schrift im Neuschnee, die nachts leuchtete
(Lichtbild: Richard Müller.)

'On the Nordkette: words in the fresh snow,
that glow at night'

project their propaganda. Richard Müller, Innsbruck's best-known mountain photographer, captures the image and it appears the next day in the *Neueste Zeitung*.

Five days after Hitler's visit, on 10 April 1938, Tyroleans come out in their thousands to vote. In Innsbruck, the turnout is 98.73 per cent; and 99.37 per cent of those vote 'yes' to the annexation. Perhaps more surprising is that there are 288 brave 'no' voters. However, now that the Innsbruck Nazis wield local power, they seek to exact revenge for the time they spent in the wilderness. Sixty-three Tyroleans who had opposed them are shipped off quickly to Dachau.[7]

After the *Anschluss*, life became increasingly difficult for Jews throughout Austria, and the small Jewish population of Innsbruck was no exception. In the 1934 census, there had been only 365 people in the Tyrol who identified themselves as Jewish. But with Austria's absorption into the Reich came the full weight of German antisemitic legislation, which had progressively removed German Jews' civil and legal rights and pushed them into the margins of society – and sometimes beyond it. As well as insisting on a series of racial classifications for Jews, the Nuremberg Race Laws removed Jewish rights of citizenship and banned marriage between Jews and partners of 'German' descent.

These laws came into effect on 20 May 1938 in the 'Ostmark' – Austria's new Nazi name.

The application of the laws increased the 'Jewish' population of Austria, with a direct effect on my family. I found a police report in the Innsbruck City Archives, dated 1938, which listed my great-uncle Erich and his son Peter as having 'left the Jewish community' in 1933. I wasn't really surprised – my family were hardly observant, and after all, the Café Schindler had been happy to open on Friday evening and the Sabbath day, Saturday. But by virtue of the new laws, conversion to Christianity could not override the designation as 'Jewish', and converts like Erich and Peter were added back into the figures. So too was any Jewish Austrian who had married a 'non-Jew'. In this way, the Nazis identified 585 'full Jews' and 176 'half Jews' in the Tyrol.[8]

As Austria underwent its Nazi transformation, Hugo and Erich faced the struggle to wind up the Schindler family business in as orderly a manner as possible before their planned move to London. For the Café Schindler, the writing was on the wall – literally so in the same month as the plebiscite.

One morning in April 1938, Hugo arrived at the café to find it defaced with Nazi graffiti. On the ground floor, the word *Jud* appeared multiple times, scrawled in black paint, together with a poor caricature of Hugo with the obligatory large nose and a Star of David. On the first floor, someone had written in red capitals

Café defaced with Nazi graffiti

JUDE on the top half of the left-hand window and added another Star of David. On the next window, they had daubed *Gute Reise nach Palästina* – 'Happy travels to Palestine' – and that perennial slogan, 'Men, it's time.'

Andreas Hofer's words were, by now, twisted into a well-understood shorthand for locals to rise up against the Jews. The cube-shaped clock, still advertising the happy escape of a *Tanz Café*, looked absurdly out of place in the midst of this vitriol.

Looking at the three photographs of this racist attack on the Café Schindler, I imagine that Hugo must have been both livid and deeply anxious. The words exude hatred. I was surprised at the neat and even script of the graffiti. Whoever had wielded the paint brush had taken his time, and had evidently had access to a long ladder: there are no smears, no drips. Just perfectly crafted insults.

I was struck, too, by the nonchalance of pedestrians passing by in one photograph, seemingly oblivious to the graffiti, and even more so by the well-dressed people posing and smiling outside the café in the other photos, as if they had discovered a new tourist attraction. In two of the photographs, there is a uniformed soldier on duty, posted outside the café, barring entry to Hugo's customers. I was shocked that such crude antisemitism appeared to have become normal and acceptable, even on the frontage of Innsbruck's best-loved café.

Now too, as in Germany, Jews faced increasing harassment on the streets of Innsbruck, and a progressive exclusion from public life as their rights were stripped away. Seventy years after the Jewish emancipation that had given my ancestors new horizons and new security, everything they had gained was in rapid reverse. The goal was to drive them out. Groups of Nazis drank and marched past the homes of Jewish residents singing, 'SA Comrades, hang the Jews . . .' In a small town like Innsbruck, it was difficult to disappear. Unlike in the big cities such as Vienna and Berlin, it was not possible to slip into the shadows, certainly not for a prominent business family like the Schindlers.

The new rules came thick and fast, and my family was directly affected. Hugo had to hand in his precious car. Kurt, like all other Jewish children in Innsbruck, was no longer allowed to attend his school at the Adolf-Pichler-Platz, in the centre of town. There was an 8 p.m. curfew and a prohibition on Jews walking in the Hofgarten park or going to the cinema.

From July 1938, Tyrolean Jews were no longer allowed to wear the regional *Tracht* or Tyrolean traditional costume. I have dozens of photos of Hugo in lederhosen and of Edith wearing dirndls. These cherished costumes varied from valley to valley; they were, and are, woven history, creating a sense of belonging in the mountain communities. By denying Hugo the right to wear *Tracht*, the Nazi authorities were denying him even his alpine heritage in order to cast him as an outsider. By contrast, when a new Nazi *Gauleiter*, Franz Hofer, took up the reins in the Tyrol, he liked to be seen wearing *Tracht* to demonstrate that he was a man of the people.

In Linz, meanwhile, the net began to close around that city's Jewish population. Eduard and Lilli Bloch remained protected, suffering no Gestapo ill-treatment, and so they used their privileged position to try and help others. Their flat in the Landstrasse became a sanctuary, where frightened Jews could gather to exchange news on the progress of their exit applications. When friends and acquaintances were arrested or deported, it was usually Dr Bloch who visited the local Gestapo to plead for their release. He did this with some success; some of those that were incarcerated survived, when perhaps they might have perished. But Eduard could not work miracles, and all around him the lives of friends, families, patients and colleagues were thrown into disarray.

Certainly, Hitler's indulgence did not extend to Eduard's friend, the surgeon Karl Urban – the man who, at Bloch's urgent request, had operated on Klara Hitler in 1907. Being a Jew, he was dismissed from his university post. For several years already, Nazi laws in Germany had banned Jews from the professions and academia.

For the local Gestapo, Dr Bloch remained the exception and an uncomfortable puzzle. They repeatedly asked him whether he did not, after all, have some Aryan blood. But his answer was always the same: 'no', he was through-and-through Jewish.

The doctor would go on to record numerous ways in which he was treated better than his fellow Jews. When two men appeared at his flat one day, accusing Lilli of being rude about Hitler and demanding 4,000 Reichsmark as 'atonement money', Eduard showed them the newspaper article about him: they left, chastened and empty-handed. When the Gestapo ordered all landlords to cancel their rental contracts with Jewish tenants, the officers, as Eduard wrote, 'instructed my extremely anxious landlord to treat me in that respect like an "Aryan".'

In due course, Eduard and Lilli's ration cards were not stamped with a 'J' like other Jews', which meant that they could shop at any time and not only during the restricted shopping hours allocated to Jews. Eduard retained his own telephone line, received clothing coupons, kept his passport, and was even allowed to send telegrams to the United States when he wished – all 'privileges' denied to his Jewish friends.

Increasingly, Dr Bloch was visibly marked out from the rest of Linz's Jewish population. When Jewish-owned businesses were ordered to identify themselves with yellow stickers on their doors and the word *Jud* in black lettering, Eduard duly complied. As he later wrote, a few days afterwards the Gestapo paid him a visit to tell him that 'orders from Berlin' meant he could remove the sticker. Eduard refused to do it himself, for fear that he might subsequently be tripped up and accused of breaking the law. The Gestapo officer had to remove it.

The doctor also found himself exploited for propaganda purposes. The Nazi Party was keen to memorialise anything and everything to do with its leader's youth. Hitler's private secretary, Martin Bormann, arranged for a photograph to be taken of Bloch in his surgery, intending to use it as part of a documentary film of Hitler's early life. It seems hardly an experience that the doctor enjoyed. He appears glum and disconsolate, sitting alone in an otherwise empty consulting room, facing the chair in which he questioned so many of his patients about their ailments.

The planned inscription for the photo was: 'The *Führer* often sat on the chair beside the desk.' But the picture spoke more truth about Eduard's practice than perhaps was intended. Few sat in that chair now. As Eduard later wrote, 'By decree, my active practice was limited to Jewish patients. This was another way of saying that I was to cease work altogether. For plans were in the making for ridding the town of all Jews.'[9]

It was a different Austrian Nazi, Adolf Eichmann, who established the Central Office of Jewish Emigration in August 1938, in Vienna's old Rothschild Palace. Its purpose was to deal with the systematic stripping of assets from Jews before they were allowed to leave. Long queues of desperate Jews formed every day outside the palace as they waited in line for their papers, and

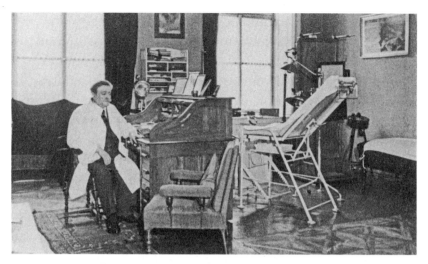

Photo of Dr Bloch in his surgery, taken on
the orders of Martin Bormann

as they did so, they became targets for harassment by Nazi
thugs.

Yet the Linz Jews had one advantage over the Jews elsewhere in
Austria, for Eichmann grew up in the city, and indeed his family
was well known to the Jewish community. Some years previously,
Eichmann's father had attended a celebration at the Linz
Synagogue, to mark the fact that one leader of the community
had been given a medal. Another community leader, Rudolf
Schiller, later told his daughter how on one of his many visits to
Vienna, to sort out emigration papers for members of the community, Eichmann 'had treated him very humanely and even offered
him, a Jew, a chair.'[10] A once-common courtesy had become
something that these browbeaten Jews fastened on to try and give
themselves hope.

Jewish community leaders now took the lead in navigating the
bureaucratic process for the many Linz Jews anxious to emigrate,
obtaining the numerous visas and affidavits required, as well as
making the necessary payments. Richer members of the community were persuaded to assist the poorer ones.

As Eduard's few remaining patients in Linz disappeared , so also business at the Café Schindler in Innsbruck dried up entirely. No one now dared visit a Jewish-owned café, and Hugo could hardly blame them – it would be foolhardy to do so in this new climate. There was little choice but to redouble his efforts to sell the Schindler businesses, notwithstanding the difficulties.

The problem would not be in finding buyers – after all, it was a valuable venue and opportunists now circled around many Jewish businesses, knowing it was a buyer's market; rather, the difficulty lay in ensuring that his staff were well looked after and in trying to get a decent price so the Schindlers could have some chance of restarting their commercial life in London. It would be a path strewn with obstacles.

Linz and Vienna, summer 2019

The Linz City Archives hold the original 1938 lists of the city's Jewish inhabitants, which the archivist hands me in a slim cardboard folder. The pages are from a ledger, bearing thin blue lines to mark out columns. The typist has used the first two columns for the details of each entrant: the address appears first, and slightly indented below are the name, title and year of birth. In a neighbouring column is a number so that the bureaucrats can keep an accurate tally of the remaining Jews.

Across the typed pages are various pencil amendments. Eduard and Emilie (Lilli) have big blue ticks next to their names. As time goes on, and as the information is updated by the Gestapo, the list acquires blue and red pencil corrections. Some names are removed as they turn out not to be Jews after all – even after the Nazi expansion of the definition. Other names are crossed through: a sign that they have gone away, whether that means emigration or deportation. It is a chilling document, marking the destruction of a community. I feel slightly nauseous as I leaf through the pages.

I hand the file back to the archivist and go and wash my hands thoroughly.

What shocks me most about the Linz record-keeping is the dry, methodical, actuarial nature of it. In Vienna's Jewish Museum, that impression deepens when I see a poster described as the 'bureaucratic obstacle course', which Eichmann set up for Austrian Jews wanting to emigrate. I stand in front of it for a good twenty minutes, trying to reconstruct the path my relatives had to negotiate. The poster has a detailed flowchart, which sets out the multiple ways in which Jews were fleeced and their assets expropriated.

It is later than 1938 – in fact, it is dated 1941 – and it says to me that by this time, in Austria, Eichmann had honed much that would be applied throughout Nazi Europe. Except, of course, for a 'final solution' that Eichmann would play such a role in arranging the following year.

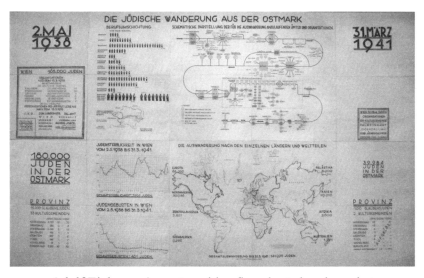

Adolf Eichmann's poster with a flowchart showing what Jews needed to do to emigrate, as well as an interim balance of precisely how many Jews were in each Austrian province in 1938 and how many are left as at March 1941

I remain astonished at the central contradiction of all this bureaucratic apparatus. It is remarkably counterintuitive for the Nazis to make the escape of Jews so difficult, given that ridding Austria of its Jewish citizens is one of their primary goals. My grandfather came to appreciate that paradox only too well.

12

Two Coffee Cups

Innsbruck, Summer 2019

Even today, the building in which I find myself is known in local guidebooks as the 'Villa Schindler'. The house that my grandfather built now houses a research institute that studies cell growth and ageing. It is part of the University of Innsbruck.

I applied to the head of the institute, Dr Pidder Jansen-Duerr, for permission to look around, and now I am here, on a hot August day. I find that the inside has largely been divided up into small offices, while the cellar has been enlarged substantially in order to create temperature-controlled labs for growing cell cultures. Dr Jansen-Duerr explains that 'the house is basically too small for the institute now, and we are looking to move back to be with the rest of the Natural Sciences Department of the university, on the other side of Innsbruck.'

The main problem with using the building as a scientific centre is the heat. Two green-glass wings were added in the 1990s to create extra space, and these are fully air-conditioned; but it is a constant struggle to keep the rest of the building cool enough in summer, particularly as the summers in Innsbruck are getting hotter.

Pidder's work is fascinating and he wants to explain it in detail to me. However, what I am really here for is to try to get a feel for what it would have been like to live in my family's villa. I want to match scenes in the photo albums to these rooms. Sadly, there are very few original features left on the inside of the house. One reception room has survived and it does have its original parquet floor and bookcases, as well as a built-in drinks cabinet with its wooden marquetry still intact. If I close my eyes, I can hear the clink of cocktails and the hum of voices. The enormous sunny terrace feels very familiar to me. I have numerous photographs of people playing ping-pong on it and of Edith and Hugo holding court there.

My mind recalls other photographs, of the lawn outside: I see my father as a small child, in summer playing in the grass with a dog, in winter building a snowman. He is on his own. It was a lonely childhood, surrounded by adults.

Back in the present, I chat to one of the employees of the institute, who was involved in the renovation works. 'When we were extending the cellar,' he tells me, 'we discovered a secret escape tunnel, which led from the cellar into the nearby Imperial Park.' He recounted how they gingerly crept along it, before reaching a point where it had fallen in and been boarded up because it was evidently too dangerous to go further.

This was not some desperate insurance measure on my family's part, as the Nazis approached Innsbruck. Rather – I am amused to note – it was constructed by the man who came after them, who evidently had such an insufficient faith in his own cause (or an all-too-clear understanding of his own guilt) that he thought it necessary to dig out his own escape route from the villa.

I say goodbye to the present occupants, wondering who will move in when they move out. Will it return to being a family house? I toy briefly with the idea of whether I would want to live there, before concluding that it is not for me. Yet, I would love someone to take it on, someone who is prepared to restore it to its original 1930s glory. My father was not alone in thinking it the best address in Innsbruck. It attracted envy high up in the ranks of the new Nazi elite.

Kurt told us as children that when the Nazis rolled into Innsbruck, he could hear the cheering of the crowds in the packed, beflagged road outside the Villa Schindler. When I think about it now, it must have been hard, even for this young Jewish boy, not to be caught up in the excitement that swept through the town. It was not long before he had his first encounter with the new regime.

It was late spring 1938 when the doorbell rang. The twelve-year-old Kurt had just got home from school and was now alone in the house. His mother Edith was still in London; his father was at work. Opening the door, Kurt encountered a tall, good-looking man in uniform, who smiled at the boy and enquired politely whether he could come in. 'Would you be so kind as to show me around?' he asked.

Kurt hesitated, but good manners overwhelmed him, and he allowed the stranger into his home. Kurt then proceeded to walk him through the two reception rooms and kitchen on the ground floor, pointed out the large and sunny terrace, and then showed him the three bedrooms upstairs. The man, satisfied with his tour, thanked the boy, tousled Kurt's hair, and left. It did not occur to the young Kurt to ask the stranger's name.

If he had, the guest would have replied, '*Gauleiter* Franz Hofer'. It was only later that Kurt realised he'd had his first encounter with the most powerful Nazi official in all of western Austria – a man who, as one of the enlarged Reich's forty-two *Gauleiter*, was a regional leader reporting directly to the *Führer* himself.

Hofer was born near Salzburg, but went to school in Innsbruck and saw himself as a local man. Indeed, he was once a business neighbour of Hugo and Erich, for he had owned a shop selling radios in the Maximillianstrasse, round the corner from the Andreas-Hofer-Strasse. Hofer later asserted that he was forced to give up this business two months after the *Anschluss*, when Hitler appointed him to run the new *Gau*, or administrative area, of the Tyrol and Vorarlberg.

In the intervening years, Hofer had proven his Nazi credentials, joining the party in 1931, and rising quickly through its ranks to become the most senior party official in the Tyrol before being arrested and sentenced to two years in prison in 1933, when the Nazis were declared illegal. He escaped from prison, fleeing to Italy and then Germany, where he was put in charge of helping other Austrian Nazi refugees who had escaped to Germany.

In the photographs I saw in the Innsbruck City Archives, *Gauleiter* Hofer was always very much the host whenever Hitler visited Innsbruck – standing next to him, sharing a joke, or walking a step or two behind him. The best photographs were all taken by Richard Müller, the brilliant pre-war, high-alpine landscape photographer, who then went to work for the *Gau*'s official press office. The most memorable photo is a flattering composite portrait of Hitler and Hofer standing together, which I fancy was commissioned by Hofer, probably to adorn his office.

Müller, too, was a local man; indeed, his studio was next door to the Dubsky family vinegar and spirits business. Unlike Vienna with its concentration of Jews in Leopoldstadt, in Innsbruck the Jews lived among their Aryan neighbours. Müller also shot

Hitler, with Hofer standing on his left, sharing a joke

a beautiful photo of the Heiliggeiststrasse showing his studio next to my great-uncle's *Essig-Sprit-Fabrik* – vinegar-spirits-factory.

Following his house call at the Villa Schindler, Hofer turned his attention to Innsbruck's small Jewish business community. By the early summer of 1938, he was becoming impatient that Jewish property was not being transferred quickly enough into Aryan ownership. With the fawning support of the local press, Hofer ratcheted up the pressure on my family and ensured that Hugo was arrested.

I knew that the Nazis liked to have an official reason for arresting Jews, and I wondered what their pretext was for Hugo's arrest. I visited the County Archives in search of files for a criminal case against him. In the state prosecutor's handwritten list of names of people charged in 1938 with crimes in the Tyrol, I found an entry for both Hugo and my great-uncle Erich: *Bestechung* – 'bribery'. I wondered whom they were supposed to have bribed, but no details were given and there were no other files available. It was strange to see my relatives' names among those had up for other crimes like assault, theft and even murder.

Kurt used to recall visiting his father in prison. It was July 1938, and Hugo had been held for several months at the Gestapo prison in the former Gasthaus Sonne, near the central station. He had missed celebrating his son's thirteenth birthday on 9 June.

Kurt told us, as children, that he visited his father in prison every day, bringing him a special tea for a bladder condition that Hugo had acquired during the First World War. As my father remembered, Hugo always made light of his predicament. He joked that he was among friends in prison, indeed in great company, for the *Bürgermeister* (Mayor) of Innsbruck and the Tyrol's *Landeshauptmann* (County Representative) were also locked up with him. He told Kurt that they were having terrific fun competing with each other as to who could kill the most bedbugs each night. Hugo boasted about his scores to Kurt.

Hugo also reassured his son that his batman from the First

World War happened to be one of the warders, and so he was well looked after, being permitted – as an ex-officer – to have some special privileges not extended to other prisoners, including these daily visits from Kurt. In making light of his predicament, I detected in Hugo a touching effort to reassure his son; a frightened boy now effectively orphaned in the outside world, with his mother far away in London and his father locked up.

The charge of bribery did not make sense to me, so I asked the archivist to bring me all the files relating to the Villa Schindler, including from before and after this period. Half an hour later, they arrived. From these legal proceedings, I gradually pieced together what had happened. Much of the information I gleaned was from papers produced by Hugo and Erich's lawyer, Dr Albin Steinbrecher.

It was these documents that taught me about the building of the villa in the 1920s. According to Steinbrecher, it had cost Hugo 250,000 Schillings to build. Also recorded is Erich's purchase of the adjoining plot – the one he might have built on, but which instead he allowed Hugo to use as an extra garden. Erich maintained his ownership of the land, which Steinbrecher asserted was worth at least 50,000 Schillings. I mulled over Erich's change of heart about building his dream house: possibly it was because of his ill-health, or maybe he was unhappy in his marriage to Grete and so the dream had lost its allure.

According to Steinbrecher, the Nazis authorities arrested Hugo in the spring of 1938 and accused him of tax evasion. I was surprised by this, since the charge book had referred to bribery. It seems that the public prosecutor changed the charge after it was recorded. Steinbrecher pointed out that the charge of tax evasion was odd in itself, because no audit had been carried out on the books of the S. Schindler company before the arrest – and when one was done retrospectively (alongside a review of the previous ten years' transactions), the auditors could not identify any serious irregularities.

I read the evidence put forward by the prosecutor in 1938,

which referred to matters such as the private use of the company car, the private use of heating and lighting in the villa and in the Andreas-Hofer-Strasse, and the personal use of food items by Erich and Hugo taken from the café. Presents paid for by the business and given to people unrelated to the business were also cited. What sounded initially like a serious charge emerged as fairly standard practices for two businessmen running a large hospitality concern – perhaps borderline infractions, at most.

I was also curious as to why Hugo was arrested and not Erich. One possible reason was that Erich was ill and confined to bed with his heart condition. Another might have been Hugo's more robust attitude towards the pressure tactics being applied over the fate of the Villa Schindler.

As I ploughed my way through the files, the picture became clearer. According to Steinbrecher, as his client Hugo sat in prison, he was telephoned by Dr Ulm, the head of the Innsbruck branch of the National Socialist Association of Lawyers. This was no social call. Dr Ulm was seeking to open a negotiation with Dr Steinbrecher. On behalf of Innsbruck's Sparkasse bank, Ulm offered to buy Hugo's villa and Erich's adjoining piece of land for the sum of 60,000 Reichsmarks. The Reichsmark had replaced the Schilling as Austria's currency a few days after the *Anschluss*, and this offer equated to only about 90,000 Schillings.

Steinbrecher dismissed the ludicrously low price and told Ulm that if the Sparkasse really wanted to buy these two properties, then it should put forward an appropriate figure. Ulm now revealed that it was really *Gauleiter* Hofer who wanted the villa and its garden, but he did not want to buy them *directly* from two Jews. He needed intermediaries. As Ulm explained, 'The Sparkasse is acting as the middleman for Hofer, and he has determined the price for the deal.'

Haggling ensued. Steinbrecher countered that if it was really Hofer who wanted to buy the villa, then he should improve his derisory price. Ulm reminded him that Hugo was already in custody and made his position perfectly clear by way of a threat combined with an ultimatum: 'If Hugo does not agree to the sale, then not only will he continue to be in custody, but he will be sent off to a camp. If, however, Hugo agrees to the sale, then he can be released immediately.' For good measure, Ulm warned Steinbrecher, 'It is open to Hofer to expropriate the property anyway, so the Schindler brothers would do well to agree to the deal that is on the table.'

It was plain to Dr Steinbrecher that this was no idle threat and that he needed to speak to both his clients at once. Ulm then arranged for him to visit Hugo in prison. When Steinbrecher informed Hugo of Ulm's threat, Hugo was furious and rejected the offer immediately, describing it as 'shameless blackmail'. Hugo would not allow himself to be subjected to extortion, even if it meant he would have to carry on sitting in prison. A perturbed Steinbrecher now sought out Erich, whose view was uncompromising: Hugo should not be allowed to stay in prison, even if it cost them their 'entire fortune'. He begged Steinbrecher to persuade Hugo to sell the villa and garden as stipulated by Ulm.

And so – according to Hugo's later witness statement – although he was still deeply unhappy about the deal, he and Erich both signed sales contracts, on 9 and 15 July 1938 respectively, selling the villa and adjoining land for the prices stipulated by Hofer. Both properties now passed into the ownership of the Sparkasse bank.

Dr Ulm had clearly been in no doubt that he would get his way. Even before receiving Hugo and Erich's consent, he had obtained in June the various permissions needed from the State Police and Eichmann's Property Office in Vienna for the transfer. Steinbrecher later stated that he never knew for sure whether *Gauleiter* Hofer ever paid the money across, but he considered it unlikely; more probably, Hofer got the Sparkasse bank to loan him the money. What is certain is that Hugo and Erich never saw a penny of the 60,000 Reichsmark purchase price. It was an expropriation in all but name.

Hofer himself – as I discovered in other 1940s documents from the Villa Schindler files – saw things in quite a different way. He insisted that he paid cash for the property to Ulm and instructed him to pay the money across to the Sparkasse. He claimed not to know how much of the purchase price Hugo and Erich had received, as it was the bank's responsibility to pay over the money. In reality, he would have known full well that any money paid by him (if it was paid at all) was paid into a frozen account, and that Hugo and Erich never received it.

Hofer furthermore insisted he complied with all the rules of 'normal honest commerce' in the acquisition of the villa and garden, offering 'evidence'. He claimed that although he was appointed *Gauleiter* in May 1938, on arriving back in Innsbruck he and his family were not provided with any accommodation, so he had to live for some time in a room in the Hotel Maria Theresia, which was located between the Café Schindler and the Bauer & Schwarz department store. Sitting in the archives, I smiled to myself at the thought of Hofer living wedged between these two Jewish-owned businesses as he went about his official duties. It must have irked him considerably.

According to Hofer, he sent his wife, his mother and Dr Ulm out flat-hunting. In the meantime, the Ministry of the Interior in Berlin offered Hofer accommodation in the old Imperial Palace, which Hofer claimed he rejected as being 'too ostentatious'. I was amused by Hofer's false modesty. I suspected that the truth was simpler: he had taken a shine to the Villa Schindler after his private tour by Kurt.

Hofer asserted that Ulm had told him the Sparkasse had purchased the villa and that Hofer could therefore rent it, where- upon he instructed Ulm to negotiate a rental contract with the bank. Hofer alleged that he entered into a rental agreement with the Sparkasse for a ten-month period at a monthly rent of 300 Reichsmarks, and that the idea of buying the house did not come up until the following year.

From the Villa Schindler legal files, I would find out a great deal more about the 'sale' of the villa and garden, including much more contradiction, claim and counter-claim, not least from

Hofer himself, but also from the Sparkasse bank's own evidence – very different to the *Gauleiter*'s. In July 1938, though, one fact was very clear. My grandfather and my father had lost their home. It was not even their first loss.

Wapping, London, 2019

From the Innsbruck County Archives, I have ordered copies of all the files relating to the Café Schindler. They arrive in London in a heavy cardboard box. I am astonished there are so many of them. As I sift through them, one puzzle is soon solved.

After my father's death, the last four remaining cups from the café found their way onto a shelf in my study. At first, they lay there gathering dust, largely ignored by me – until I embarked on this project. When I came to write this book, I took them down and looked at them properly for the first time as an adult. Although, as a child, I knew that they were precious and full of meaning, they were also in everyday use, taken for granted, unexamined.

Now, looking at the surviving ones with new and adult eyes, I was surprised to find that I had two cups emblazoned with an 'S' and 'Konditorei Café Schindler' and two with an 'H' and 'Konditorei Café Hiebl'. The design was identical, but the café's name had changed. How had I not noticed this before?

My box of papers from Innsbruck provides the answer. With these papers I can now trace the story of Franz Hiebl – a man handpicked by *Gauleiter* Hofer to run the Café Schindler, and a man who bends and contorts his way out of scrapes, Houdini-like, with political regimes of all descriptions.

Franz Hiebl was born in Innsbruck on 1 December 1911 to parents who ran the 'Zum Saggen', a traditional wood-panelled Tyrolean pub selling coffee, tea, wine, beer and food. If Hiebl's self-serving

An original Café Schindler coffee cup

A Café Hiebl lookalike cup

'autobiography' is to be believed, written in a prison cell on 29 October 1942, his mother and father lost their entire fortune through the ravages of inflation and had to start all over again by leasing hotels. Hiebl decided to follow in their footsteps.

After completing school, including two years at the *Handelsschule* (business school) in Innsbruck, from which he graduated with success – or so he wrote – Hiebl set off for Paris to gain some international experience. His sister was working as a hotel secretary, and Hiebl managed to obtain a two-month placement with her employer.

From Paris, he moved to England to work for six months as a tutor in a family. He returned to Innsbruck before setting off again, this time to Hamburg, where he worked as a waiter, before taking a junior position on the *Eberstein*, a cargo ship travelling between Hamburg and the United States. However, having worked his way up to First Steward, he then left the ship after a year, unable to see any further promotion prospects.

Then, according to his own testimony, Hiebl returned to the hospitality business by working as a volunteer in some of the biggest hotels in New York and Chicago, until plagued by homesickness 'for Germany', he returned to Innsbruck – and to a new passion: the National Socialists. Shortly after his arrival on 12 October 1930, he became party member No. 360,197. In his locality, he was in the vanguard; as Martin Achrainer has pointed out, the NSDAP had fewer than 350 members in the whole of the Tyrol at the time Hiebl joined it.

The same year, he was arrested for the first time, for tearing down posters belonging to another political party during the autumn elections. On that occasion, he was released immediately, because his parents were well known in Innsbruck. Unable to find a position in a hotel, he took a job as a waiter, but it did not last long. Although these were also the hard Depression years, his affiliation with the NSDAP was proving an additional factor in his inability to hold down a job. Instead, he threw his energies into promoting the Nazi SA, including putting up posters and painting or burning swastikas onto mountainsides 'almost every evening' – or so he later bragged. By 1933, he was also a member of the SS for good measure.

When, in June 1933, Chancellor Dollfuss outlawed the Nazis, Hiebl claimed responsibility (with others) for painting the 100-metre-high swastika on the rock-face of the Nordkette. It could, he later boasted, be seen from as far away as the Brenner Pass. I thought about this claim. The Brenner Pass is more than 30 miles (50 km) from the Nordkette. It was another flight of fancy.

As a Nazi 'illegal', Hiebl was engaged in distributing leaflets and came to the attention of the police again, who searched his flat to find chalk (presumably for graffiti), torches and pamphlets there. But when charges were drawn up, Hiebl went into hiding and then fled to Germany – stopping, he alleged, only to freshen up the paintwork on the Nordkette's swastika. Under party orders, Hiebl then trained with a newly set-up 'Austrian Legion' stationed at Lechfeld, in Germany.

After completing his training in October 1933, he became involved in smuggling propaganda and explosives for attacks planned by the NSDAP in Austria. He claimed, in 1942, participation in a prolific career of sabotage: blowing up electricity works on the Achensee and water-pipe installations in the Achen Valley, as well as organising explosions at further electricity works in the border village of Scharnitz, and other smaller actions.

Hiebl also claimed to have repainted that Nordkette swastika several times by crossing the border at Scharnitz under cover of darkness, carrying paint and brushes with him through the mountains. In these raids, Hiebl alleged – again probably untruthfully – that he and his colleagues had a number of encounters with Austrian police and security services, which left several people dead. These were dangerous activities, in Hiebl's view, because not only was there a warrant out for his arrest, but anyone caught with explosives could be sentenced to death.

That was why, he explained, he adopted the false name 'Heel' to escape detection.

Things went wrong for him in 1934, the year in which Dollfuss was assassinated. As Hiebl asserted, he was 'betrayed', arrested and nearly shot, before being sentenced to life imprisonment and incarcerated in the County Prison. Found in his shoe was a piece of paper that provided proof to the authorities that a putsch was being planned and directed from Germany. Despite being offered financial inducements, according to him, he never betrayed the names of the Nazis who had given him the plans. He also did not admit to being Hiebl. When the police threatened to bring his mother from Innsbruck to identify him, he arranged through a sympathetic warder for his mother to be transferred out of reach, to Germany.

After serving nearly two years in prison, Hiebl was released in July 1936, whereupon he fled again to Germany, and in Munich spent his time trying to assist his fellow Austrians to find work. He claimed to have done this for up to three thousand comrades. I concluded this was likely to be more Hiebl hyperbole. He put his flat at the disposal of Nazi colleagues, and it became a collection point for Nazi propaganda to be smuggled into Austria. At the same time, he attended evening classes at the local administrative school.

In February 1938, the month before the *Anschluss*, Hiebl was lying in hospital with severe concussion, following a serious car accident. There, he heard on the radio Chancellor Schuschnigg's rallying speech for his referendum, made from Innsbruck. He knew, so he said, that now was the time to 'liberate' the Tyrol. Against the advice of his doctors, he got out of his hospital bed and headed to Innsbruck, arriving in April before the German army marched into the city.

Now, in accordance with the instructions of *Gauleiter* Edmund Christoph, he threw himself into working 'day and night' to prepare Innsbruck for Nazi rule. He appeared to be much in demand. He was initially asked to run the *Landesarbeitsamt*

(County Employment Office) as well as the *Gau* Office for *alte Kämpfer* (old Nazi fighters), managing to find work for three thousand of them. Again, I didn't believe these figures. He also set about righting various perceived wrongs that he and his old Nazi comrades had suffered during the period when the NSDAP was illegal.

Hiebl was, it seems, highly esteemed in Nazi echelons. He attained the rank of *Sturmführer* (Assault Leader) in the SS and was awarded the *Blutorden* (Blood Order), a relatively rare award given to fewer than 6,000 Nazis in total. He earned it for his incarceration during the Schuschnigg era.

It was at the end of May 1938 that Hiebl was approached by *Gauleiter* Hofer and asked to take over the Café Schindler, as Hiebl's background had given him some knowledge of the hospitality trade. Turning to a police report dated 1947, I also found Hiebl described as a 'particular favourite' of Hofer and specially selected by him to transform the Café Schindler into a drinking club for high-ranking Nazi officials. Hiebl and Hofer went back a long way, and Hiebl was even at the station to welcome his friend back to Innsbruck on 25 May 1938, to take over as *Gauleiter* from Edmund Christoph.

Perhaps surprisingly, Hiebl said that he refused the offer. However, according to later evidence from the man who directed the local chamber of commerce in 1938, Dr Amann, *Gauleiter* Hofer intervened personally with Eichmann's Aryanisation department in Vienna to stop the sale of the café to a third party – something that Erich and Hugo were trying to organise.

Dr Amann – a prisoner himself in 1947, at the time of his evidence – commented somewhat bitterly that he was always concerned to check that recipients of Aryan assets had the money to pay for them and the relevant professional qualifications to run the business; and he was constantly at loggerheads with Hofer, who regarded the distribution of Jewish assets as more a matter of personal political reward.

In May 1938, other possible purchasers of the Café Schindler also emerged. Via his lawyer, one Oswald Blüml offered 500,000 Schillings in cash. His lawyer assured the relevant Nazi office that Blüml was an appropriate buyer, given he was also an Old Fighter who had risked his life smuggling numerous Nazis over the border after the events of July 1934. Yet another potential buyer valued the café at 600,000–700,000 Schillings and had arranged a loan of 300,000 to cover some of the cost.

None of these offers were of any interest to Hofer. He wanted to install Hiebl in the café. Dr Amann described himself as astonished by the speed with which the café was transferred to Hiebl, a man who seemed to have no money to buy it, albeit he did have relevant professional knowledge. Yet it appeared that Hiebl was still reluctant and, according to Hiebl, had to be asked several more times before he agreed.

With a further 100,000 Reichsmarks knocked off the sale price, to get the deal over the line, Hiebl eventually picked up the Café Schindler for a mere 400,000 Reichsmarks, well under the price that other parties were prepared to pay for it. Hiebl maintained that he paid for it using some of his own and his wife's money as well as a loan from the Sparkasse bank.

Completion of the transaction was complicated by the fact that Siegfried Salzer, Martha's husband and Hugo and Erich's brother-in-law, had invested money in the café and was owed 31,940 Reichsmarks. This loan needed to be repaid and the purchase money divided between various frozen accounts. For several reasons, I was surprised by the pedantic care taken by the Nazis to ensure that this debt was paid and the books were in order. It would, in the end, benefit Siegfried very little.

Franz Hiebl was now at the centre of Nazi life in Innsbruck and soon, he claimed, overwhelmed with his Nazi Party duties, which he had to fulfil alongside running what was to become the most important Nazi watering hole in town. He held roles as adjutant to Hofer and as city councillor, though he gave up the former because of pressure of work; he also took on some responsibility for the coffee-house sector within the overall administration of the *Gau* for the Tyrol. His personal life prospered, too. He married Berta Gruber in June 1938. As a holder of the *Blutorden*, Hiebl was entitled to a marriage grant of 2,000 Reichsmarks. He used it to buy a house.

I reflected on Franz Hiebl's trajectory, at least as he portrayed it in 1942. Within a few years, he had gone from illegal, itinerant agitator to high-ranking Nazi official in his native city. Once a drifter between various dead-end jobs, he was now respectable, married and the Aryan owner of the Café Schindler – my grandfather's café.

Café Patisserie Hiebl, Innsbruck, 1938

On his first day as owner of the former Café Schindler, Franz Hiebl calls the staff together. He tells them that they will all need to support National Socialism. With his encouragement, the employees sign up to the *Deutsche Arbeitsfront* (German Labour Front): since independent trade unions are banned in the German Reich, workers are inducted into this umbrella organisation, which is yet another instrument of Nazi control.

On 4 June 1938, Hiebl places a large advertisement in the *Innsbrucker Nachrichten*:

> *Café Patisserie Hiebl Opens!*
> *I want to inform my guests that the enterprise Schindler,*
> *previously owned by Jews, in the Maria-Theresien-Strasse,*
> *has come into my hands. The German population has now*
> *reacquired the ability to visit these centrally located,*
> *comfortable rooms.*

Hiebl also tells his customers that the band will play daily from 4.30 p.m. until 6.30 p.m., to accompany tea served at 5 p.m. The new owner appears keen to carry on the tradition of the café as the place to dance in Innsbruck, for he tells the town that 'there will also be dance music from 8.30 p.m. until 2 a.m.'

The Café Hiebl ballroom

The café quickly becomes the main haunt for Nazi officers who are on leave or recovering from injuries. Proper German music is played: waltzes during the day, Tyrolean drinking songs and Nazi songs in the evening. American music, and in particular jazz, are off the menu; Nazi ideology decrees that they are degenerate art forms. Much else, though, continues. The strudel remains the best in town, and Hugo's head pastry chef, Josef Mosna, who joined the business as a shareholder in 1937, adapts seamlessly to his new boss.

Hiebl is quick to rebrand the café. He takes down the Schindler lettering on the exterior and replaces the name with 'Fr. Hiebl' – but using exactly the same font and the same style of neon lighting. Hiebl banishes the crockery bearing the Schindler logo to the back of the cupboards and has his new crockery produced. He retains the same colour scheme: cream with red and yellow tram lines and, of course, an eagle; but this time with an 'H' emblazoned across the breast of the bird and the words 'Konditorei Café Hiebl' underneath.

Hiebl is canny and has enough business sense to know that the café's value lies in the goodwill it has garnered over the years, and in its many familiar attractions, including the distinctive branding, but minus the 'degenerate' music. In its way, the Café Hiebl is a tribute to the Café Schindler, even as this once Jewish venue is repurposed as a Nazi hangout.

Hugo Schindler is in no frame of mind, in his prison cell, to appreciate this unacknowledged tribute. Hiebl has the impertinence to talk about 'my guests' as he reopens the café, words that can only provoke indignation in Hugo, now that he is dispossessed. One month later, the Villa Schindler is gone too, effectively stolen. Both have been snapped up through the machinations of the Nazi *Gauleiter*, and both for insulting prices.

Eighty years later, I think again about that old antisemitic cartoon of Maria-Theresien-Strasse, with the successful Jewish enterprises crowding out the little 'German' ones. Locals like *Gauleiter* Hofer and his creature Franz Hiebl have had their revenge within a few months of the *Anschluss*. Nazis will now live in the house of my father's childhood; and Nazis will socialise in the café my grandfather and great-uncle founded and then made successful.

Now, when I pick up the Hiebl cups from the shelf in my study, I wonder who has drunk from them and what they did during the Third Reich.

13

The Jewish Nazi

Innsbruck, Summer 2019

There is a photograph I have seen of Hugo's cousin Egon Dubsky, the only son of Sofie's brother Leopold. I found it in a history of Jews in the Tyrol, and it is from the First World War. It shows a young, round-faced, short-sighted man with a bit of a squint. Egon, in uniform, looks shy and nervous; he certainly does not have Hugo's swagger and easy good looks. He is more fragile and ill at ease than his cousins. I assume he is less suited to rugged expeditions across mountains, for I never see Egon in any of the pictures of his father hiking with Hugo and Erich, the three of them members of the Alpine Club.

Egon Dubsky in First World War *Kaiserschützen* uniform

Leopold was the driving force behind the Dubsky family move to Innsbruck from Bohemia in the 1870s and had taught the Schindlers their distilling skills in his factory in the Heilig-geiststrasse. His son seems a very different character. I find some references to him elsewhere: one historian describes him as suffer-ing from nervous shaking, with a tendency to be easily influenced; a witness in later cases for restitution of property asserts he is *nicht als vollwertig zu nehmen* – that he 'lacks full mental capa-city'. I build an impression of an anxious man in poor health for much of the time.

I am curious to know more about him, but also to compare the fate of the Dubskys and their company during the darkening years of the 1930s with that of the Schindlers. I am therefore again at the Innsbruck County Archives. This time I ask to see all the files relating to the Dubsky business.

When I start to look through them, I uncover an entire slice of my family history that my father never told us anything about; and I soon discover why Kurt's Uncle Egon was never mentioned. Like my great-uncle Erich and his son Peter, Egon Dubsky converted from Judaism to Christianity in 1933. It was possibly an effort to protect himself against a rising tide of antisemitism. But he then chose a much more radical path, travelling even further from his roots – and straight into the arms of the National Socialists.

It was from the Innsbruck County Archives that I learned how Egon Dubsky became close to his Aryan bookkeeper Aloisia Bertoldi – known as 'Luise'. She had worked for the Dubsky company for many years. Through Luise, Egon got to know her brothers Johann and Karl Bertoldi, and it seems that this associa-tion sucked Egon into the world of underground Nazi politics.

After the Nazi Party in Austria was banned in 1933, the 'ille-gals' needed money, plausible front men, and vehicles to smuggle their pamphlets across the border from Germany. From December 1936, as I discovered, Egon was part of this apparatus, secretly bringing Nazi propaganda into the Tyrol. Did he really believe in this cause, or did a misguided survival instinct send him down this path?

There were clues in his dealings with a Dubsky company driver. Although Egon did not take to the mountains, he was a member of an Innsbruck sports club, where he met the known pro-Nazi Gottfried Auckenthaler. When Auckenthaler lost his job in 1936, Egon took the opportunity to employ him as a driver. According to one prosecutor's report in the County Archives, dated 25 August 1937, Egon intimated to Auckenthaler that if the Nazis should come to power, his Jewish heritage might harm him; and therefore in employing the pro-Nazi Auckenthaler, Egon could insure himself against such harm.

In fact, Auckenthaler later testified that Egon only agreed to employ him *on condition* that he was a member of the illegal Nazi Party. Auckenthaler boasted to his new Jewish boss that he was not only a fully paid-up party member, but also an Innsbruck SA man. This last detail was untrue, but the lie was sufficient to secure Auckenthaler the job.

According to prosecution evidence in 1937, Egon constantly tried to join the *Frontmiliz* (Front Militia), which was one of the Austrian paramilitary organisations that sprang up after the First World War to support the army. It is not clear from the Archives whether he succeeded. The Front Militia had a transport division, in which Egon may have served.

What is clear, though, is that Egon offered to look after two of the Front Militia's cars for which they needed garage space. One vehicle had some sentimental value to the Nazis, namely the Steyr car, in which none other than Franz Hofer had made his escape from Austria in 1933. Once Egon had the two cars in his garage, according to the prosecution file he tried to persuade Auckenthaler to steal them from the Front Militia and present them to the Nazi Party in Germany. Egon's harebrained plan envisaged that when Auckenthaler handed over the vehicles to the Nazis, he would point out that this gift was 'courtesy of Egon Dubsky'. Auckenthaler asserted that he pretended to agree to this scheme, but never took any steps to fulfil Egon's instructions.

As well as trying to ingratiate himself with the German Nazis, Egon made what he thought were further self-protective moves. On 22 January 1937, he and Luise entered into a *Gütergemeinshaft Vertrag*, a joint ownership contract. This meant that they both owned each other's assets (and were liable for each other's debts). Five days later, on 27 January 1937, Egon and Luise were married at a local Catholic church. Luise's brothers Johann and Karl Bertoldi were witnesses; and Egon stated his religion as Roman Catholic on the marriage certificate.

A few months later, on 17 July 1937, Egon's world came crashing around him when he was arrested by the Front Militia for illegal pro-Nazi activities. According to one witness, speaking later in 1949, Egon was mainly acting as a Nazi courier; according to Auckenthaler, Egon was passing information about the location and contents of the Front Militia's weapons dumps to the German Nazis. Egon was eventually charged with the attempted theft of the Front Militia's cars and running an illegal news service.

After his arrest, he spent time in custody until 21 August 1937: a lapsed Jew, locked up in Innsbruck with other illegal Nazis. His case was dropped in February 1938 as part of the amnesty for imprisoned Austrian Nazis wrung out of Chancellor Schuschnigg by Hitler. If Egon thought that his complicity in underground Nazi activity would confer privileges following the *Anschluss* in March, his expectations were to be shattered. The Dubsky company's commercial activities were now drastically reduced.

Luise, though, had been thinking ahead as to how to protect the business. Barely a month after the *Anschluss*, she applied – with Egon's consent – for the whole business to be transferred to a third brother, Friedrich Bertoldi, for the price of 35,400 Schillings. Friedrich only needed to find 15,000 Schillings, as Luise was deducting a sum of 20,400 Schillings, which she had already received from her father, Ferdinand.

In the local county museum, I found Friedrich Bertoldi's announcement of the transfer, which appeared on 13 June 1938 in the *Innsbrucker Nachrichten*, declaring that the 'Brüder Dubsky' business had passed into Aryan ownership and that Friedrich Bertoldi had purchased it. Honoured clients were politely asked to deal with the new firm. However, Friedrich was jumping the gun; they had not yet managed to get the business legally registered in his name at the Land Registry.

The very next day, 14 June 1938, the *Innsbrucker Nachrichten* took it all back by announcing 'Public Misled' – the Aryanisation of the firm Brüder Dubsky was declared invalid. The detail explained that any transfer of Jewish property could only happen with permission from the authorities, and that such announcements were to be made by the press office of the *Gau*. Therefore, as this announcement made clear, the company remained under the control of an appointed *kommissarische Verwalter* (temporary administrator).

In addition, it pointed to the family connection by naming Friedrich Bertoldi as Egon's brother-in-law. In Vienna, the *Vermögensverkehrsstelle* (Property Transfer Office) promptly withdrew its permission for the transfer to go ahead, and the Dubsky business ground to a halt.

The truth was that Egon, Luise and Friedrich had all fallen foul of *Gauleiter* Hofer, who was livid at this attempt to circumvent his control. As far as he was concerned, no transfer of property in Tyrol was to happen without his express consent, so he could dictate who benefited from the Aryanisation of Jewish businesses. Egon was in no better a position than his cousins Hugo and Erich.

On 18 July 1938, in another attempt to avoid a hostile Aryanisation of the business, Egon transferred the remaining half of it to Luise, so that at least on paper she was sole owner of all of Egon's property. However, she still needed to jump through some administrative hoops, which included getting herself registered at the Land Registry before she had full legal ownership. Her joy at making some progress in the bureaucratic nightmare proved short-lived, for the public prosecutor raised charges that the Bertoldis were seeking to camouflage the Jewish nature of the business.

Looking through the paperwork in the Innsbruck County Archives, I found I had mixed feelings about Luise. Was she doing her best to protect Egon and their business, out of love – or was she a gold-digger taking advantage of a weak-willed and unwell man, who found himself in an increasingly desperate situation? By the summer of 1938, all the Jewish businessmen in Innsbruck, including my grandfather, were scrambling to try and sell their businesses to trusted Aryan friends and acquaintances, if they could. I put aside my cynicism and started to believe that Luise and her brothers really were trying to protect and help Egon.

The Bertoldis were not the sort of people to give up easily. Friedrich complained to the *Reichswirtschaftsministerium* (Reich's Ministry for Economic Affairs), pointing out that he had been a loyal member of the Nazi Party when it was still illegal in Austria and listing all the many services he had provided to the party. Luise took even more drastic action.

Innsbruck, 6 August 1938

On this day, Luise Dubsky – on her brother's and her lawyer's advice – applied for a divorce from her husband. It was not acrimonious. Indeed, Egon had already given his approval for this application. Somehow, the Dubsky assets had to be completely separated from the Jewish Dubsky name if they were not going to fall into hostile Aryan hands. The reason for the divorce given in the application was that the marriage was undertaken in 'error'. Luise 'did not know that the respondent's Jewish roots would lead to enduring tensions in all areas of life'.

Twenty days later, Luise made an application to the Innsbruck

County Court for the registration of Egon's gift to her – of his half of the business – to be formally recorded at the Land Registry. The request was initially rejected, on the basis that all such transfers from Jews needed to be authorised by the Asset Transfer Office in Vienna.

She did not give up. Later in the year, Luise's lawyer appealed this decision, arguing that since 1 October 1938, only commercially *active* Jewish assets – rather than mere real estate – needed such permission. The Dubsky business had been mothballed for several months, so therefore, the argument went, the permission of the Asset Transfer Office was immaterial.

Egon and Luise had continued to pay staff salaries since June, despite having no income coming in. As the year dragged on, the pressures upon them only increased. On 17 October, Gestapo officers arrested Egon and he was told, in no uncertain terms, to leave Innsbruck. Instead, the next day, Egon attempted suicide. At least Luise was able to check him into the psychiatric clinic in Innsbruck while he convalesced.

As regards the business, there was a whisper of good news. Luise's lawyer succeeded in his argument in the Upper County Court of Innsbruck. By November 1938, Luise was registered as the legal owner of half the Dubsky business; she owned the other half contractually, even if that had not yet been legally transferred to her.

However, November 1938 brought something else, too: a visceral demonstration by the Nazi Party faithful of their hatred and contempt for Jews living among them. Neither the Schindlers nor the Dubskys, not even the Blochs, could remain immune to its effects.

14

The Toboggan

Wapping, London, 2019

I have grown up knowing that out of all my father's memories from the *Anschluss* year of 1938, there was one that was so vivid, and so traumatic, that it became pivotal to his life. It concerned the events of one night, which he always described to me with pinpoint accuracy. The night in question was 9–10 November 1938, but the world came to know it better as *Kristallnacht*, 'crystal night'. It is an oddly poetic name for a pogrom of organised violence, death and destruction meted out against synagogues, Jewish properties and Jewish people, across the German Reich. Hugo was one of its many victims – and my father used to describe how he was forced to witness it.

In order to understand exactly what happened and what he saw, I applied to the Innsbruck County Archives for the witness evidence from 1945–6, when the perpetrators finally faced justice. That was many weeks ago. Now it has arrived in London, in a large white envelope.

I open it with a mix of curiosity and fear. I wonder how these men will justify their actions; I also hope to find the voice of my grandfather here. But after I clear the table and spread out the contents of the package, I soon realise that the one voice entirely absent is Hugo's. I have to content myself instead with the words of others, including the accused, whose first witness statements are dated 1, 2 and 13 August 1945.

This was a mere six weeks after American occupying forces left the Tyrol and the local police started investigating crimes during the Nazi years. I am surprised at the alacrity with which the machinery of criminal justice appeared to swing into action to gather evidence in my grandfather's case, when there must surely have been so many more important and serious cases. But perhaps this focus on the bit players allowed the bigger targets to slip away.

The files I scoured revealed that three men were prosecuted for their part in the assault on Hugo. I saw that all of them were members of the *Nationalsozialistisches Kraftfahrkorps* (NSKK), the National Socialist Motor Corps, a paramilitary organisation that trained men in the use and maintenance of vehicles, as well as engaging in the transportation of vehicles and materials wherever the army needed them. After the war, NSKK members were keen to encourage the Allies to think of them as little more than motoring enthusiasts, the equivalent of Britain's Royal Automobile Club.

Their hierarchy suggested otherwise. With further research, I discovered that there were no fewer than nineteen different NSKK ranks, several of them sounding rather similar. I had no idea that there was such an elaborate system within this relatively unglamorous transport division; it broadly mirrored the ranks in the German army itself, albeit using slightly different titles.

Gauleiter Hofer himself was an NSKK *Obergruppenführer* – Senior Group Leader. Further down the hierarchy were the three accused: Josef Ebner was an *Obertruppführer* (Senior Troop Leader), August Hörhager a *Scharführer* (Squad Leader) and Hans Ruedl a *Truppführer* (Troop Leader). Ebner, the most senior of the three, was seven ranks up from the bottom. It was clear to me that all three defendants were relatively junior players – something they were subsequently keen to emphasise.

Immediately, I noticed an ostensible connection between Ebner and Ruedl on the one hand, and my grandfather on the other: all had served their emperor in the *Kaiserschützen*, on the Southern Front, in the previous war. Hörhager, too, had served on the Southern Front but in a different regiment – it appears with some distinction, as he won the Silver and Bronze Medals of Bravery in 1915 and a further Kaiser Karl Troop Cross in 1916.

For a moment, I conjured up an image of these four military veterans, including Hugo, reminiscing over a beer in the café about the extraordinary battles waged high up in the mountains. Except that in 1938, whatever bonds of camaraderie might once have existed among old soldiers had long since been corroded by the acid of National Socialism.

As I leafed through the closely typed pages of the descriptions these men gave of their own backgrounds, I got a glimpse of how the Nazis were able to appeal to the disaffected and the disadvantaged in Austria. Both Josef Ebner and August Hörhager described themselves as poor and out of work in the 1930s, while Ruedl also complained of his 'poor economic position'. Ebner and Hörhager, it turns out, had once been Social Democrats until they lost confidence in the party's ability to improve their lives. Hörhager stated that he had joined the Nazi Party in 1930 after seeing nothing but poverty and misery all around him; at Nazi meetings, he found clarity and companionship.

Ebner had trained as a house painter before the First World War. After the war, he returned to house painting, but was dismissed when the work ran out in 1934, the year in which he joined the Nazi Party. Thereafter, he was able to find only sporadic employment – life had been tough, he explained, but the party and the NSKK were good to him and lived up to their promises. For his minimal party dues of 50 *Groschen* per month, he had received financial help when times were bad. They had given him groceries and even done his washing. Until *Kristallnacht*, not much had been asked of him in return; he had attended inspections and occasionally been asked to work at checkpoints in Pradl, a district of Innsbruck.

Then I came to the events of that night in 1938. As a lawyer, I am used to drafting and analysing witness statements in civil cases. I am also quite familiar with the way in which witness recollections of the same events can differ. The more I read about

Josef Ebner

the night of 9–10 November 1938, though, the more shocked I was by the gaps in the accounts and the differences between their statements. All three men were even vague about the date of *Kristallnacht* itself; none of them could apparently remember with any certainty the names of those who had been part of their group. It sounded to me like self-imposed amnesia.

Nevertheless, I was broadly able to piece together what happened. I learned from the statements that the men who made up the NSKK unit known as *Sturm 5 (Pradl)*, led by Ebner, usually met in the Café Hammerle on the Museumstrasse, diagonally opposite Innsbruck's main museum, where I had already spent hours looking at back editions of the local newspaper.

Ebner described how on 9 November 1938, after their usual inspection, they were ordered to gather at the café by their company leader, *Sturmführer* Hochrainer. But having turned up

in uniform, they were told by Hochrainer to 'go home immediately, put on civilian clothes without any insignia and then assemble at the Boznerplatz'. It was, Hochrainer explained, going to be
a surprise reception for *Gauleiter* Hofer, who was returning from
celebrations in Munich. Ebner recollected no talk in the café
about attacking Jews.

Ebner returned to his wife Luisa and their three children in
their flat nearby, said nothing, changed his clothes, and left around
midnight for the Boznerplatz, west of Innsbruck's main railway
station. On arrival, he saw others from his *Sturm*, including
Hörhager, who counted about forty to fifty men gathered in the
dark, chatting quietly. Ebner could remember no speeches being
given; rather, Hochrainer moved among the groups, giving individual orders.

To Ebner, Hochrainer was uncompromising: 'Tonight, in the
entire *Reich*, all Jews are going to be beaten up simultaneously.
The groups are doing this as revenge for the murder of the German
diplomat.'

Ebner had already read in the local paper about the assassination of Ernst vom Rath, the German consul in Paris, by a young
Jew named Herschel Grynszpan. The Nazi regime would go on to
claim that the events of *Kristallnacht* were a spontaneous and
uncoordinated outpouring of patriotic and legitimate anger from
the German people. It was nothing of the sort.

Hochrainer now instructed Ebner to take a few men with him
who would be happy to volunteer – and he gave Ebner my grandfather's address in the Andreas-Hofer-Strasse. 'Thrash the
Saujuden' – 'Jewish pigs' – and 'smash the place up' was
Hochrainer's exhortation, according to Ebner; Hochrainer also
assured him that the police would not intervene.

Hörhager himself remembered Hochrainer saying: 'You are to
go to Schindler's place in the Andreas-Hofer-Strasse to beat that
Jew up so that he needs to be hospitalised. If you kill him, that is
fine too. You are covered. The police know to stay away.'

'Which of you would like to go thrash that Jew, Schindler?'

Ebner asked his men, including Ruedl, who, being a big man, he knew would be useful. In Ebner's statements, Hörhager was enthusiastic. According to his own statement, Hörhager could not remember volunteering. In any event, Hochrainer saw the three of them off with a wave, warning them to complete their mission properly, because checks would be carried out afterwards.

Unusually, Ebner was given only one address to target. I assume that he knew the Schindlers; everyone in Innsbruck did. Ebner marched in loose formation with his men the short distance from the Boznerplatz to the Andreas-Hofer-Strasse. The accounts vary as to how many men were with him, but it is clear that the group numbered between seven and nine. 'On the way,' asserted Hörhager later, 'I thought to myself that we should not be doing this and was not happy to undertake the task we had been set.' By contrast, Ebner remembered that an enthusiastic Hörhager insisted that Schindler be 'left to him' to be beaten up.

As they walked towards Hugo's flat, they must have heard screaming and the smashing of windows on some of the otherwise quiet streets that they crossed. *Kristallnacht* – named for all the shattered glass strewn in its aftermath – was already in full swing, and other roaming bands were hard at work on their tour of destruction. Groups from the SS were also out that night. They had been given orders to kill three prominent Jews and destroy the Jewish prayer room.

Ebner's group seem to have arrived outside the four-storey S. Schindler building in the early hours, though the exact time is unclear, varying between statements. All the windows were shuttered and dark. Ebner told Ruedl to keep watch and to whistle if anyone came, before going through the archway that led to the entrance to the flats above the shop, motioning to the others to follow him. The heavy wooden door was firmly locked, so he rang the doorbell for the first-floor flat, with its neat label *Fa. Schindler* (Family Schindler).

Like everyone else in Innsbruck, Ebner would have known that *Gauleiter* Hofer had taken over the Villa Schindler that summer and that Hugo was forced to move back into this flat above the company's headquarters.

No one answered from the first floor, which remained dark, but a light was switched on in the second-floor flat. I imagined Hugo, waking up immediately, hearing the bell and the men's voices directly below his window, and patting his beloved chocolate-coloured hunting dog to keep him calm. Hugo was no coward, and I suspect he would have got out of bed and walked quietly over to the window to sneak a look below, through a crack in the slatted wooden shutters; wondering what these men were up to, so late on a Wednesday night.

He must have known that a night-time visit did not bode well; and he would also have realised, with a growing horror, that if they gained entry to the building he was trapped. As I could tell from my own visits to the Andreas-Hofer-Strasse, even if Hugo had crept down into the back courtyard behind the flat, there was no rear exit.

The visitors were persistent, except that this time they rang the bell belonging to Hugo's upstairs neighbour. Hugo would have been able to hear Frau Freiger getting up and moving around. According to Sophie Freiger's later statement, when she looked out of the window she did not recognise any of the men despite the street lighting; with her poor night vision, she was certainly not keen to let strangers into the house.

Ebner demanded, 'We have to see Herr Schindler. Let us in immediately,' but Frau Freiger demurred. 'Herr Schindler lives on the first floor. Now go away. I am going back to bed.'

She resisted further pleas from Ebner that he had to travel that night and had 'urgent business with Schindler', forcing Ebner, according to his statement, to try other doorbells. 'Open up, Leo!' shouted another of the men, as they rang the doorbell of Leo Lischka on the third floor. He was a work colleague of Josef Schneider, one of the men in *Sturm 5*.

Lischka sent his sister to open the window and defuse the situation, but Schneider demanded to speak to Leo, who, after much hesitation, started to descend the stairwell. On the second floor he met Frau Freiger, with whom he conferred in whispers.

In his own witness statement, Lischka reported that he told her, 'Look, Frau Freiger, I don't want to let them in either, but we cannot really refuse entry to them. They are not in uniform, but I recognise them. They are NSKK men. Maybe they just want to ask Herr Schindler some questions.'

I shuddered, thinking that Hugo must have heard Lischka make his way down the wide stone stairs to unlock the front door.

Facing the men, Lischka asked, 'So, what is this all about?' before Schneider shoved him to one side and three of the men, led by Ebner, stormed past him up to the first floor. Lischka retreated to his flat on the third floor. Frau Freiger stood on the second-floor landing with her two children, who had woken up and were now with her, wide-eyed, looking over the banister; Lischka's sister stood beside her. They watched from above as Ebner rang the bell outside Hugo's apartment repeatedly, until Ebner shouted at them to get back into their flats.

'Help! Murderers! Open the door!' yelled Ebner, in an effort to lure Hugo out. Inside, Hugo lit a candle. He was probably shaking with fear now, but still he did not open the door, forcing Ebner to throw his weight at it. The door held. 'August. Josef. Help me!' shouted Ebner, and the three of them tried to force it, shaking the whole wall and dislodging clouds of dust and pieces of plaster. But still the door would not give way.

Innsbruck, 10 November 1938

Inside the first-floor flat of No. 13 Andreas-Hofer-Strasse, a bewildered Hugo Schindler wonders what will happen next. He knows he does not stand a chance against these thugs. He is now fifty years old, balding, slightly overweight – and fearful. In his younger days, he did some boxing; there are photographs to prove it, but that was more than twenty years earlier. His days as a fit soldier on manoeuvres in the mountains are now far behind him.

'Ruedl, come up here and help me. You're strong,' shouts Josef Ebner from the landing down to the street. More footsteps on the stairs. There is a further onslaught against the door of the flat, this time by four men, until it finally gives way.

Three men of *Sturm 5* topple into the cold, unlit hallway of the flat. August Hörhager is later careful to say that Josef Ebner and Hans Ruedl are ahead of him. There is a moment of surprise as they take in the slightly stooping figure of Hugo, in striped pyjamas, holding a candle in one hand and the collar of his hunting-dog in the other.

'We have done nothing to harm anyone,' Hugo pleads. 'Why are you doing this? I don't understand.' His voice shakes as he tries to summon the words to stop what he guesses is about to happen. He recognises the men: they are all local Innsbruckers.

Then, they find a weapon. Hörhager picks up Kurt's toboggan, which is propped up against a wall in the hall. He holds the woven seat as he lifts it high, before bringing it crashing down hard on Hugo's head. The iron strip nailed to a hooped runner, to protect the wood, cuts a deep vertical gash down Hugo's forehead; blood drips down his face and into his eyes.

For a moment, Hugo stands completely still. Then, he staggers backwards, moaning. The pain is excruciating. He drops the candle, which goes out, and loses his grip on the dog, who runs out of the open door of the flat and is caught on the landing by another of Ebner's men, Karl Tautermann. Later, Tautermann says he does not enter Hugo's flat; but he can hear Hugo screaming and a woman crying; he can also hear two women above him complaining loudly that it is a *Schweinerei* – a 'pig's mess', a scandal – and that it is outrageous that such a commotion is taking place in the middle of the night.

It was with the actual events inside the flat that the participants' versions began to diverge most sharply. In his own witness testimony, Hörhager made light of his involvement while saying that they each slapped Hugo, being careful to make the point that he only hit Hugo with his hand. Given the extent of Hugo's injuries, it seems more likely to me that he did indeed smash the toboggan over Hugo's head, just as my father recalled. Hörhager blamed Hugo's injuries on his fall following the slaps.

By contrast, Ebner described how Hörhager threw Hugo into the bedroom and carried on hitting him. Ebner denied that he himself hit Hugo, being preoccupied with taking a woman he presumed to be 'Frau Schindler' out of the room, who was standing there in her nightdress, crying. Ebner declared that as far as he knew, only Hörhager attacked Hugo. When Ebner checked back in the bedroom, he saw that it had been turned upside down, and that Hugo sat bleeding and crying on the bed. When Ebner was asked why he did not also hit Hugo, he said that the sight of the bleeding Hugo took away his desire to hit him.

Not content with causing injury, the men indulged in vandalism. Having already sold the villa (as well as the café and even the distillery), Hugo had filled the sitting room with packing cases of Schindler valuables while trying to arrange their onward passage to the new life he hoped for. Hörhager admitted only to breaking into a cupboard, and that he did so because there was so much confusion. In fact, the men forced open the crates and, in an orgy of destruction, smashed all the china and glass they could find.

In the opinion of historian Michael Guggenberger, Hörhager, seeing all the trappings of middle-class wealth around him – the nice lamps, a large clock and a piano – was seized with rage. He picked up the piano stool and started to smash the piano with it. Discordant notes mixed with his grunts, as he systematically worked his way up and down the keyboard. Returning to the bedroom with the remains of the piano stool, he calmly smashed Hugo so hard over the head with it that my grandfather was thrown to the floor, his arm rendered useless. Not content with this attack, another of the gang then moved in, raised his hobnailed boot and stamped on Hugo's face, knocking him unconscious.

The woman identified by most of the witnesses as Mrs Schindler screamed as Hugo passed out; shaking off Ebner's arm, she escaped the apartment and ran up to Lischka's flat, while somehow dodging the other men on the landing. She shouted, 'Please, you have to help! They are killing Hugo!'

'I can't,' Lischka is said to have replied through a crack in the door. 'There is nothing I can do. There are too many of them.'

Distraught, she returned to the flat, to find Hugo still unconscious, and everything turned upside down. All the furniture was knocked over; a lamp was torn from its socket; only one clock remained in place – because it was screwed to the wall. The kitchen had been emptied, and all the crockery and glasses smashed. Ruedl later claimed that none of this was his own doing, that he did not break any furniture, nor hit Hugo, and that he told the others to stop beating a defenceless man.

The whole episode lasted no more than twenty minutes. As the NSKK men left, one of them shouted at Hugo, 'You had no mercy on us, when we were unemployed for years!' Three of the group went home, while Hörhager, Schneider and Ebner walked to the railway-station's bar to report to Squadron Leader Mayerbrucker, who was waiting for them. Ebner described carefully what they had done, noting by name who had been cooperative and who less than helpful.

When questioned eight years later, Ebner conceded that their actions had lacked humanity and were not right, but he had 'received an order, it was happening all over the Reich, the others were all doing it and all of us felt a degree of hatred towards the Jews.' He added, 'I didn't really fancy the whole escapade, but as an older Stormtrooper, I would not have dared to say no. I was never one to get into fights.'

Hugo was not the only Jewish victim in the Andreas-Hofer-Strasse on *Kristallnacht*. Mr and Mrs Steiner at No. 3, Arthur

Goldenberg and his son Fritz at No. 29, and the Bauer family at No. 40 were also attacked. Flora Bauer's son Wilhelm, elsewhere in Innsbruck, was killed by the SS – one of three murders in Innsbruck and more than a hundred across the Reich that night.

Neither was Hugo the only member of my family facing threats on *Kristallnacht*. In the flat above the Dubsky shop at No. 2a Heiliggeiststrasse, Luise was at home with her 91-year-old father-in-law, Leopold. Egon was still in the clinic following his suicide attempt. When SA men burst into the flat in the middle of the night, Luise covered Leopold with a blanket in the hope that they would leave him alone. Mercifully, it worked, and the SA left Leopold unharmed, although they still demolished the flat in a destructive frenzy and with great thoroughness.

Given the beatings that the SA and NSKK handed out to other frail, elderly Jews in Innsbruck, Leopold himself had a very lucky escape. The Dubsky retail shop and production facilities on the ground floor of the Heiliggeiststrasse did not. These they smashed up, tipping bottles of *Schnapps*, brandy, vinegar and fruit juice onto the stone floor, sweeping typewriters and papers off the desks, and generally causing as much damage as they could. One SA man joked the following morning to colleagues that on his return home with his trousers stained red up to his knees, his wife had been mortified, assuming it to be blood; he was able to reassure her that it was merely raspberry juice from the Heiliggeiststrasse and other addresses.

In Linz by contrast, Eduard Bloch was spared the violence and vandalism meted out to others. However, he was distraught to see the Linz synagogue, where he prayed every day for his patients – including in 1907 for Hitler's mother – burned to the ground. In his later summation on *Kristallnacht*, he wrote: 'Everywhere temples were torched, monuments in cemeteries desecrated, and numerous murders and horrible acts were perpetrated on Jews.'

It was, as he described, carefully calculated:

. . . the fires were described in the newspapers as 'accidental'.
It is certainly curious though that the 'boiling anger of the

Volk' erupted simultaneously in all locations. Even more curious is the fact that the fire-fighting equipment was already in place nearby to prevent the fire [from the Synagogue] spreading to other [non-Jewish] buildings.

'Thus,' as he put it, 'the beautiful temple in Linz fell victim to modern barbarism.' To add insult to injury, 'the substantial fire insurance was confiscated by the Gestapo.'

In the days that followed, Eduard, Hitler's *Edeljude*, had to stand by and watch the struggles of his increasingly desperate co-religionists to leave Linz. On 17 November, 'the Gestapo suddenly decreed: "All Jews of Upper Austria have to sell their possessions, settle their affairs, and be prepared to leave the country within 48 hours".'

The order prompted another visit by Eduard to Dr Rasch at Gestapo headquarters, to plead on their behalf. Eduard was careful to point out that his intervention did not signify opposition to the order itself, but was rather a request for more time, 'unless of course the Jews of Linz were to leave the town as beggars.'

Rasch's response, as written by Eduard, spoke volumes, not only about his own indifference to the Jews in general, but about Bloch's unique status in Nazi eyes:

> Dr R. to whom I talked for quite a while, listened quietly and then interrupted saying, 'Tell me Herr Doctor, why are you taking care of the other Jews? Why do you care about their fate? The order to leave the country does not affect you nor the family of your son-in-law, Dr Kren. You may stay as long as you like.

Eduard's unequivocal response was that 'the suffering and the fate of my co-religionists affect me as if they were my own.' Rasch patted Eduard on the shoulder and said, 'Go home and don't worry; I'll think about what you said.' The next day, the Jews of Linz were given a temporary reprieve and the 48-hour evacuation order was cancelled.

But within the next few months, all the Jews of Linz were ordered to move to Vienna. Of the 650 members of the Linz Jewish community in 1938, Eduard could now count only seven other elderly Jews left in the city. Since he was only allowed to treat Jews, his career was effectively over.

Like Eduard Bloch, my great-uncle Erich seems to have escaped the mayhem of 10 November – though in his case through the most unlikely of flukes. In the albums I found photographs, dated October 1938, of beautiful clinic grounds in Bad Nauheim, near Frankfurt, accompanied by pictures of Hugo posing alongside a car on a new German *Reichsautobahn*. From statements by Erich's wife Grete, I knew that the Gestapo had allowed the family to keep one car belonging to Erich, on account of his deteriorating heart condition.

To me it seems highly risky, even foolhardy, but in October 1938, Hugo drove his brother more than 300 miles (500 km) from Innsbruck into the middle of Nazi Germany to put Erich in the clinic's care. I can only assume that Erich had been there before for treatment, when times were less fraught. In the end, being a patient at the clinic saved Erich, just as Egon Dubsky's continued stay in the Innsbruck clinic protected him. Some places were still – for the moment – beyond the Nazi mobs.

Hugo, of course, had been unable to escape the Nazi mob that targeted him. After the attack by Ebner and his crew, Hugo lay unconscious on the floor of his bedroom. Frau Freiger was trying to wake up Dr Biendl, who lived on the third floor, but he was out at his mother's house. He returned a short while later, when, according to his witness statement, he entered the Schindler flat to find the bedroom in chaos. Furniture was broken and there were splashes of blood everywhere. Biendl described himself shocked at Hugo's state: a 10-centimetre gash in Hugo's head was bleeding heavily and was deep enough to reveal his skull; his arm and leg were also injured.

Just as Dr Biendl was bandaging Hugo up, three members of the Gestapo arrived and screamed at him, 'What are you doing here?!'

Biendl insisted, 'As a doctor, I am obliged to provide medical help.'

After a few minutes spent looking around the room and noting the broken furniture, the Gestapo left, seemingly satisfied. According to Biendl, Hugo was 'utterly deranged' by his experience. He was also very lucky indeed to have this doctor as a neighbour, not only because of the medical treatment he received, but because the Gestapo might otherwise have arrested him and taken him into the uncertain fate of 'protective custody' – as they did with many other Jews that evening.

After the Gestapo left, Dr Biendl moved Hugo to a local sanatorium, where he used cold compresses to bring down the swelling. The next morning, Biendl discreetly stitched up Hugo's wound himself, under a local anaesthetic, before applying bandages. In his witness statement, the doctor did not recall any fractures, but his options were limited. He decided against getting Hugo X-rayed, because a trip to the X-ray room would have revealed Hugo's presence and led to awkward questions. Hugo remained only four days in the sanatorium before discharging himself on 14 November 1938.

Wapping, London, 2019

In order to work through the many statements and sometimes conflicting testimony about that night in Innsbruck, I write down the key points, creating a chronology. I try to reconstruct as accurately as I can what actually happened. I have been so engrossed in the facts that I do not realise how much time has passed. Exhausted and stiff from sitting for too long, I put the papers down and stand up to stretch.

I am trying to reconcile what I have been told in the past by Kurt with what I have on the table in front of me. Two remaining puzzles loom large – not about the precise details of who hit Hugo when; they are much more basic than that – about a presence and an absence. Who is the 'Mrs Schindler' who witnesses remember screaming in the flat? So far as I know, my grandmother Edith was hundreds of miles away, in London. Did she take a risk and return to Austria? And none of the witnesses – neither the attackers nor the neighbours – mention a child in the flat. Where is Kurt, whose memories of the attack were so vivid?

I re-read my notes to check I haven't missed something. Definitely, 'Mrs Schindler' is there, but there is no mention of Kurt. Perplexed, I do not sleep at all well that night. The next day, I recheck all the photo albums and paperwork for clues.

On a half-forgotten Nazi form dated before June 1938, detailing Edith's assets, I find her address given as '3 Lamaster Road, London NW3'. It must have been filled in by Hugo in her absence – which accounts for the lack of my grandmother's signature. It is one of the many bits of Nazi bureaucracy that I have found amongst Kurt's papers. There is no 'Lamaster Road' in London; but there is a Lancaster Road NW3, an address that Kurt mentioned to me. Hugo must have transcribed the address incorrectly when he had to present a complete set of forms for his family, including Edith, before being able to make any plans to join her in England.

I've not taken much note of this form before, because, up until this point, I've been far more interested in Hugo's own listing of assets, which he signed and submitted at the very last moment, on the deadline of 30 June 1938. A substantial document, it amounts to a summary of all he possessed, including the villa, the café, the jam factory and the building on Andreas-Hofer-Strasse, as well as the loans outstanding on them, their recent Aryanisation sales to third parties and the money he was expecting from those sales. It also lists such valuables as carpets, watches, jewellery and household silver, down to the very last silver teaspoon. I'm intrigued to see that he even owned specialist silver cutlery for eating asparagus.

I conclude that there is nothing, therefore, to suggest that Edith left the safety of England for the dangers of Austria; and that if she had done, I feel sure Edith would have made something of it in later life and told her grandchildren about *Kristallnacht*. She was not one to duck portraying herself as a heroine.

There were, of course, two other Mrs Schindlers: Hugo's mother Sofie, and Erich's wife Grete. I think that if the neighbours saw the 81-year-old Sofie there while her son was being beaten up, they would have made that clear. I suspect that Sofie was out of the way up in Igls, at Siegfried's house. Instead, I come to the conclusion that 'Mrs Schindler' has to be Grete, living in the flat while Erich is still closeted in the German clinic. The flat was, after all, spacious enough, with its six bedrooms, and Erich and Hugo owned it jointly. Grete and Erich had continued to live there when Hugo moved his family out to the villa in the late 1920s.

That still leaves the question about my father. He always told me that he witnessed his father being beaten up with his toboggan. Is it possible that he was asleep in the flat during the assault on Hugo? That seems unlikely, given the commotion. But there is not a single mention of him in the witness statements in front of me. Why does no one remember him? If the neighbours saw him – people who knew him – they would surely have mentioned him by name. Did Hugo hide his thirteen-year-old son somewhere in the flat, perhaps in a cupboard, and command him to stay quiet – somewhere where Kurt was able to hear and observe the brutality unfold? That also seems unlikely as the men turned the whole flat upside down.

I phone my sister Sophie to check what she remembers, and she surprises me: in her recollection, Kurt said that on *Kristallnacht* he was in Innsbruck, but not in the flat. Yet that does not make sense to me either: how, then, could he remember the details of the attack?

I return to the photo albums to search for more clues, and I find one small, shabby album that I have not looked at properly before. It was clearly put together by the young Kurt himself, and includes pictures of the villa in Innsbruck and of their family dog. But there are other pictures, too – not of Innsbruck, but of a ferry. In one of these tiny photographs, I convince myself that I can see Edith's parents, Albert and Hermine Roth, as they shelter from the wind in coats and hats on deck. But in truth, I cannot be sure.

Some of the pictures are labelled in rounded childish writing, in English: 'The view to the English coast'. Then, on one page I see more writing: 'The first day with Mumy'; and in the corner of another page, in faint but unmistakeable writing, is a date: 'September 1938' – two months before *Kristallnacht*.

I have my answer and it is, to me, a shocking one. I have to conclude that Kurt was not in the flat, nor in Innsbruck – nor even in Austria. By 10 November 1938, he was already safely with his mother in England. My father misled everyone all through his life. He could not have witnessed any of the violence of *Kristallnacht*.

He simply wasn't there.

Part Five

15

Brighton Beach

Wapping, London, 2019

I have not yet pieced it all together. However, I know that by September 1938, my father was reunited with his mother, in London. I should feel relief that he, as a thirteen-year-old boy, was spared the horrors of witnessing *Kristallnacht* first-hand. Instead I am shell-shocked.

In later life, every time Kurt was in trouble he sought the help of psychiatrists, telling them how he was forced to watch his father being attacked and beaten with his toboggan on *Kristallnacht*. It was a way of explaining his poor mental health and the reason why he had run up debts all over the world. Did he lie deliberately, or is it possible that he was suffering from a form of post-traumatic stress disorder from hearing what had happened to his father? If so, why did none of the many eminent psychiatrists who examined him over the years ever spot this?

I find one medical report amongst Kurt's papers from a Dr Crombach of the University Clinic at Innsbruck University, dated 21 February 1989. He records that Kurt told him that his father had been severely beaten up by the Nazis and that he was 'forced to watch'. Dr Crombach does not question Kurt's story. Perhaps understandably, he takes it at face value and faithfully notes that one origin of the 'severe neurotic disturbance' from which Kurt was suffering was the fact that he 'had to look on while his father was being tortured'.

I know from my own work with witnesses how fallible people's memories are. In my experience, the very first retelling of an event

253

that a witness gives me is often the most accurate. Sometimes, the more I probe and the more documents and pictures I show witnesses, the less their memory reflects what actually happened: the recollection gets rewritten and distorted over continuous re-telling. Is this what happened in my father's case?

I am also familiar with the self-justification and exaggeration of some witnesses. It is not uncommon for them to describe themselves in more glowing and heroic terms than is really warranted. However, it is rare to come across outright untruths in which someone inserts themselves into a set of violent events when they were nowhere near them.

Yet I know it does very occasionally happen. There have been some high-profile, notorious cases of 'survivors' who have made up detailed accounts of their sufferings at Nazi camps, sometimes even published them, and who have convinced historians and real Holocaust survivors of their authenticity, yet who were never inmates – and sometimes not even Jewish. Did Kurt believe what he was saying? In one way, I hope so; it lessens the offence, but I still feel very disturbed by Kurt's lie. I cannot help feeling embarrassed and disappointed that he chose to exploit for his own ends one of the worst pogroms of the twentieth century.

I turn to one of the experts in the area, my cousin John Kafka, who, in his book *Psychoanalysis*, has a whole chapter on false memories. He points out that 'if all memories are not exact reproductions, all memories are false memories'. I do some more reading and find that there is a recognised psychological phenomenon known as 'flashbulb memories', namely memories of very traumatic events that are both intense *and* sometimes inaccurate. The phenomenon seems a paradox. Yet it has been studied since the 1970s, particularly in the context of public traumas such as the *Challenger* disaster in 1986 and the 9/11 terrorist attacks in 2001. Occasionally, people who were nowhere near such events do insert themselves into them, in their memories.

This happened in the case of the NBC broadcaster Brian Williams during the Second Gulf War. Over a twelve-year period from 2003, he recounted repeatedly that a military helicopter in which he was travelling was forced down in the desert after being hit by a rocket-propelled grenade. In fact, he was not in that particular helicopter at all; in 2015 he was forced to apologise and recant, and was widely decried as a self-aggrandising liar. But some commentators, such as Malcolm Gladwell, were kinder; warning that we should not see memory as 'date-stamped video tape', but instead as something a great deal more fallible. He thought that we would be wise not to see such memory lapses in terms of character flaws.

Was Kurt's false memory a genuine mistake brought about by his undoubted trauma of hearing from his father, first-hand, about the horror of that night? Perhaps he felt guilty that it was *his* toboggan that was used to bludgeon Hugo, or that he was not there to protect his father. Did he feel, somehow, responsible?

I wonder if Dr Crombach is still alive. I find a website for him; his friendly face with its shock of white hair stares back at me. I make a scan of his thirty-year-old report and compose a careful email asking him if he is prepared to speak to me. I send it off. When there is no response to my chasing emails, I summon up the courage to telephone him.

Dr Crombach is initially reluctant to speak to me, explaining that he has been retired for twelve years and has disposed of all his professional papers. Sensing this reticence, I wonder if I have called at an inconvenient time, or whether he really does not want me digging around in the past – maybe he considers it inappropriate to breach patient confidentiality by speaking to me.

I do my best to reassure him and ask him to name a time that is more convenient. I explain that I am trying to piece together my family history and that I am puzzled as to where Kurt was on the night of 9–10 November 1938. Dr Crombach finally agrees to talk to me a few days later.

Nervously, I dial Dr Crombach at the appointed time, and he is ready to speak. I ask him whether he remembers Kurt, and after a pause he says he remembers him well. I ask if he has read the copy of his report I emailed him a few weeks earlier and he confirms that he has. I explain that I appear to have uncovered evidence that Kurt was safely in London on *Kristallnacht* and did not, after all, witness his father being attacked. I get the impression that Dr Crombach is not entirely surprised.

He makes clear, though, that it was not his job to probe the facts, but rather to examine the effect that these recollections had on Kurt. In any event, he says, at that time he would have accepted a Holocaust survivor's testimony at face value and would not have dissected it.

I then ask him whether it was possibly a false memory. Dr Crombach replies that it is quite possible that Kurt himself believed that he was there, or came, over time, to believe that he was.

In the end, I am left with two choices: To believe that my father sought to perpetuate a known untruth, in order to deceive and gain sympathy; or that, somehow, those events as relayed to him by his much-loved father impinged so deeply that he absorbed them into his own autobiography.

Kurt is not here to defend himself. I decide – for the moment – to give him the benefit of the doubt.

It took a few false trails before I was finally able to verify Kurt's passage to England. I thought I was onto it with a slim cardboard folder of correspondence between Edith, her parents Albert and Hermine, and Edith's uncle Otto Langer in Prague. My sister and I found these letters in Kurt's house after his death. Otto was one of Hermine Roth's younger brothers, and from the letters I could see that they were clearly very close. He remained in Prague during the war and wrote to Albert, Hermine and Edith of events as they unfolded.

I look at the letters, which were written in cramped handwriting on thin, tissue-like paper. My understanding of them was not helped by the fact that they were partly in Czech and partly in

German; however, I understood enough to gather that Albert and Hermine were in London by September 1938. Tucked into the back of the file, I then found definitive evidence: Albert Roth's Czech passport, date-stamped 17 September 1938 on his arrival in England. He was given three months' leave to remain, but, as the situation in Europe deteriorated, his permission to stay was extended.

Based on those documents, my working theory – and it seemed so obvious – was that Edith arranged for her parents to collect Kurt and bring him with them. After all, the dates seemed to match up. More-over, looking at the little photographs in Kurt's album of his ferry journey across the channel, I had identified two figures who plausibly could be Albert and Hermine on the deck of the ferry. It all chimed with other pictures in the album, of Albert and Hermine at London's tourist sites – keeping their grandson entertained by showing him Buckingham Palace, the Changing of the Guard and Hyde Park.

However, it then became clear from letters between Hermine and Otto that she and Albert fled first from Plauen in Germany (where they had a house) to Prague, and from there took a plane to England. They were not on the ferry with Kurt after all. I remained puzzled as to how Kurt got to England on his own from Austria, until I found the answer in Kurt's interview with an historian, Gerda Hofreiter, in 2011, when he was eighty-six.

Gerda had been researching children of the Holocaust and had made contact with various members of my family in that context. In the interview, Kurt described how his mother had arranged for an English officer to travel to Innsbruck to pick him up and accompany him, on a combination of trains and ships, to England in September 1938, so that he would arrive in time for the beginning of a new school year in England.

I read Gerda's interview notes carefully and saw that on this occasion Kurt was clear that Hugo had been on his own in the Andreas-Hofer-Strasse on *Kristallnacht*. Yet again, I was forced to re-evaluate Kurt's conscious recollection of what happened.

Finally, I had to conclude that he may well have used the assault on Hugo when it suited him to deflect his own problems.

In the small, battered and stained photo album, which I inherited, the thirteen-year-old Kurt stuck in his favourite pictures of the Tyrol, including of his dog outside the Villa Schindler and of his parents. It must have been a precious keepsake – small, portable and poignant. He must have known he might never see the Tyrol again. He added to this album the pictures that documented his journey, via Calais and Dover.

On arrival in England, Kurt stuck in more photographs. One shows him standing next to his mother; he is an anxious-looking and slightly chubby teenager, in a belted camel-hair coat. He was safe now, but he appears worried in this strange new country. He was about to restart his education, which had been interrupted in Innsbruck by the Nazis, who had excluded him from his school the previous summer. This time he was to attend a prep school in Kent. In any normal circumstances, a new school can make a child anxious. Now, Kurt faced a new school and new faces, in an unfamiliar country, where all his lessons would be in English. It was a daunting prospect, even if it was one that other children in his family had already faced.

Kurt's Linz cousin John Kafka was one of the earliest to leave Austria in 1933, aged twelve. As he was able to tell me himself, one day in 1932 his best friend at school suddenly told him, at break time, that his father had forbidden him to play with John because he was Jewish. In fact, he was the only Jewish boy in his class. His widowed mother, Claire Kafka, a Swiss national, began to consider a move out of Austria. She was entrepreneurial and had a more international outlook than the other Kafkas.

Claire consulted her brother-in-law in Strasbourg, who was pessimistic about Austria's future – given that the Nazis had just won 33 per cent of the votes in the German *Reichstag* – and he advised sending John to be educated in France, where some additional language skills would help to equip him for the future. Accordingly, in 1933, John was shipped off to a French boarding school.

When I visited John in Washington, in 2018, he was delighted that I spoke French, as he did not get much of an opportunity to practise it. We chatted away, switching between French, German and English, as John described the different phases of his life to me in the language he used at the time.

John hated the French school. Three years later, in 1936, his mother moved to Nancy and rented a small house there, so that he could attend a day school instead, which proved to be a much happier arrangement. By the crisis year of 1938, Claire had become desperate to get her older child, Gretl, out of Austria. By now, Gretl was married to Karl Gruber, and had a young daughter. After much wrangling, Claire managed to get hold of three French visas for them, and they arrived in France in August 1938. They were not able to remain settled in France for long, as war loomed, but they had at least got beyond the borders of the German *Reich*.

Martha and Siegfried's son Erwin managed to reach the United States by 1938, along with his daughter Marianne and his new wife, Joanna. When I met Marianne in Connecticut in 2018, she told me how she remembered saying goodbye to her grandparents at Vienna's main station, before setting off by train across Austria on her own, aged ten, to meet her father and Joanna in Italy. She recalled how excited she had been about the journey, and how oblivious she had been about the dangers facing those family members she left behind.

My grandmother's efforts to extricate her family did not end with Kurt. She was also able to arrange the escape of her sister Irene and Irene's future husband, Axel. My father told me that Irene arrived on a domestic servant visa. Assuming that is true, then she was one of 20,000 Jewish women who escaped Nazi Germany this way. These visas were not so much a humanitarian exercise by the British government, as an attempt to plug the shortage of home-grown domestic staff. After the First World War, there had been a historic shift, with many working-class women now preferring factory and office work to 'going into service', and middle-class households found it difficult to employ 'help'.

As Irene barely knew how to boil an egg and always had

servants herself, I doubt her professional engagement lasted very long. But at least she, too, was out of danger.

That left the rest of my Schindler family. According to court papers lodged at the Restitution Commission after the war, from July 1938 Hugo held a visa for Britain. He was in no position to travel, of course, being in prison as well as being embroiled in the negotiations and wranglings over all the unfinished business concerning the Schindler company and assets.

I found in one book a reproduction of the Gestapo list of Jewish commercial assets in Innsbruck, as of 8 September 1938. The name of each business appeared on the left-hand side, with its fate on the right: either liquidation or Aryan ownership. In this list, I saw the Schindler businesses make three appearances. The café was recorded as having already been sold to Franz Hiebl. The other two Schindler entries – the distillery and the jam factory and workshops at the Karmelitergasse – had a note indicating that while their sale had been pre-approved, it had not yet gone through. The *Schnapps* factory was to pass to one Ewald Jäger and the Karmelitergasse property to one Franz Brugger.

Furthermore, I discovered late in my research that it was this unfinished business that again put my grandfather at loggerheads with the regime and with the *Gauleiter*. Hofer was anxious to ingratiate himself with his *Führer* by accelerating the Aryanisation of Jewish businesses and then becoming, if possible, the first *Gauleiter* to rid his *Gau* completely of Jews through their emigration. The Nazis announced a deadline of 19 September for passport applications.

Hugo was not ready. The villa and café had gone, but the sale of the rest of the S. Schindler empire was not yet concluded. What now happened was described by a well-known Innsbruck businessman named Rudolf Brüll, whose furniture business also appeared on that Gestapo business list. On 21 September, thirteen days after the Gestapo compiled their list, Brüll along with Hugo and eighteen other local Jewish businessmen were arrested in a dawn raid at 6.30 a.m., shoved into cars and taken to the Gestapo headquarters.

There, they were forced to stand to attention facing a wall, while Gestapo men walked up and down the line insulting and hitting them, causing one 78-year-old to faint. SS *Obersturmführer* Werner Hilliges, the head of the Innsbruck Gestapo, informed them that they had to leave Innsbruck as soon as possible; furthermore, he presented an ultimatum: they had to sell any remaining businesses they owned to the buyers named on scraps of paper handed out to them by the local Commissioner for Aryanisation, Herman Duxneuner – or they would be sent to a concentration camp.

With that, the Schindler distillery business at 13 Andreas-Hofer-Strasse passed into the hands of Jäger. Hugo, worried about the fate of his employees, managed to get a clause inserted in the contract stipulating that Jäger had to continue employing the Schindler staff: Jäger agreed, provided that they were Aryan.

Having found out that Hugo had not one, but two run-ins with the Gestapo, involving police stations and prison cells, it seemed to me that by *Kristallnacht* he was a marked man. In the eyes of local Nazis, he had long outstayed his welcome – like the other remaining Jews. The *Innsbrucker Nachrichten*, reporting on *Kristallnacht*, referred to *das brennende Problem dieser unerwünschten Gäste* – 'the burning problem of these unwanted guests'. The newspaper celebrated the fact that the *Gau* would soon be finally free of 'the Jewish burden'.

The same newspaper also published an article focused specifically on Hugo and the café entitled, *Das Märchen vom anständigen Juden* ('The Myth of the Decent Jew'), in which it pointed out that those seemingly reputable and civilised Jews like my grandfather were particularly dangerous. In barely eight months, Hugo had sunk from being a well-to-do, born-and-bred Tyrolean and respected local businessman to a pariah.

Finally, it was made official on 19 September 1938: the remaining Jews in the *Gau* had to pack up and leave for Vienna within fourteen days. I found Hugo listed as the first entry on a short list of remaining Jews who did not yet have complete emigration papers, but who were nevertheless to be ordered to Vienna, there to become the responsibility of the Viennese Jewish community.[1] It would be two more months, though, before Hugo made that journey.

Innsbruck, 14 November 1938

Four days after *Kristallnacht*, Hugo leaves the sanatorium where Dr Biendl has treated him for his injuries, but there is now no time for convalescence. *Gauleiter* Hofer is stepping up moves to empty the Tyrol of its remaining Jewish inhabitants, and even Sofie, aged eighty-one but still a formidable force, can see that there is no future in trying to stay in Innsbruck. *Kristallnacht* has convinced many Austrian Jews that matters are only likely to get worse for them if they stay in the *Reich*. Not all, though, have the means, connections and necessary paperwork to leave the country.

Hugo now accompanies his mother to Vienna. Initially, they stay in the vacant flat belonging to Marguerite, Martha's daughter, who has already fled from Vienna to Paris. Shortly afterwards, they move to be with Martha and Siegfried at their house at 22 Maria-Theresien-Strasse. For Hugo the familiar and common street name can only have reminded him of the café he has lost. Martha's home is in an imposing building in an upmarket part of town, a short stroll from the Danube; but that is probably not much comfort to Hugo in those last frantic months as he scrabbles to organise his affairs.

As court papers at the Innsbruck County Archives show, Erich, too, arrives in Vienna in November, probably direct from his German clinic. At any rate, soon Grete and Peter are with him in the capital.

Once Hugo and Erich are both in Vienna, they try to finalise their paperwork and their last obligations. Even now, Hugo is trying to help out his ex-employees: in one letter from Vienna he asks his lawyer, Steinbrecher, to look into the fact that two of them have been dismissed, but have not received their termination payments. It is touching to me that this man, who is fleeing the Tyrol, still seeks to intervene on behalf of staff.

On 12 December 1938, Hugo and Erich file closely typed thirteen-page supplemental notifications of their assets. Much has changed since they put in their first lists of assets together, on 27 April. At that point, they were estimating the values of their shared assets. In the intervening seven months, the values have crystallised, as they have been forced to sell at prices dictated by others.

They have also incurred legal fees and other costs; and the Nazis' *Reichsfluchtsteuer* (emigration tax) – calculated at 25 per cent of their net worth as it stood on 1 January 1938 – must also be deducted. Needless to say, the emigration tax is not adjusted downwards in the light of the actual figures agreed for the sale of their property. Not that it makes much difference, as the sums have all been paid into blocked accounts.

The supplemental notifications demonstrate the way in which Erich and Hugo have been systematically stripped of their assets, at bargain-basement prices. The villa and adjoining garden have gone to the Sparkasse bank, which has sold it on to *Gauleiter* Hofer: now he, his wife Friederike and their seven children live in its fourteen rooms. The flat and the distillery business at the Andreas-Hofer-Strasse have been sold to Erwin Jäger; and the café has been transferred to Franz Hiebl. Other assets such as a building plot in Pradl and the factory at the Karmelitergasse have also been sold to third parties, again at substantially lower values than Hugo and Erich set out in their April lists.

Once Hugo's emigration tax of 69,258 Reichsmarks has been deducted from his net capital, he is left with 6,544 Reichsmarks, which is roughly equivalent in that year to US $3,000.

Hugo then has to obtain an *Unbedenklichkeitsbescheinigung*, a certificate of good standing, from the tax office, which indicates that all sums have been appropriately paid. It is only after this is all done that Hugo is allowed to leave Austria. Despite some pleading from his lawyer that he be allowed to transfer a larger sum abroad than standard, to cover his expenses until he can find work, Hugo – like almost every other emigrating Jew from the Reich – is allowed to take only ten Reichsmarks with him.

In December 1938, Hugo travels first to France, before landing at Dover. A photograph survives of him on his arrival, dressed in a suit, standing on Brighton beach. In material terms, Hugo has lost everything. He will never even see the contents of the Villa Schindler and the flat at the Andreas-Hofer-Strasse – the remaining accoutrements of a middle-class life that escaped destruction by the *Kristallnacht* raiders. They have been packed up and sent on to Hamburg, awaiting onward shipment. War will intervene, the goods will be seized in April 1941 and auctioned off, and the proceeds will disappear. In later years, this loss will become just one of Kurt's many restitution claims.

Hugo on Brighton Beach

Much later, as an adult, Kurt will entertain his own children with a favourite joke, asking them to define the term 'refugee'. 'It's simple!' he will gleefully explain. 'It is someone who has lost everything but his accent.' In December 1938, that man is Hugo, as he stands on a Brighton beach. But he has his life, his son and his wife; and they are all safe. A few months later, Erich secures his own family's visas: armed with his ten Reichsmarks, he leaves for England with Grete and Peter in May 1939.

They are, of course, among the luckier ones. Hugo now

watches, with rising anxiety, as in March 1939 Czechoslovakia – Sofie's old homeland – ceases to exist as an independent state. It is effectively the Third Reich's first foreign conquest, rather than an absorption of an ethnically German part of Europe. At this point, British and French politicians lose any lingering trust in Hitler's word; they know that their policy of appeasement has failed, and now they accelerate preparations for war.

And trapped in Austria – as it was once called – are family: the Dubskys in Innsbruck, the Blochs and Kafkas in Linz, and Hugo's mother, sister and brother-in-law in Vienna.

16

Viennese Letters

Austrian Consulate, London, 2017

As I stand here, applying for my first ever Austrian passport, I think about my grandparents and what they would have made of my reaching for closer connections to the country they had to flee.

I am not the only one here today. A young orthodox Jew in long black coat and a kippah speaks softly to the official behind the glass screen, explaining patiently why he has little in the way of documents to support his own application. He rocks slightly on his heels, giving his application process more of a religious quality than he perhaps intended.

When he turns round, we smile apologetically at each other. We both know that our grandparents once queued in Vienna for exit visas to England. Now, English Jews of Austrian descent have been applying in droves for Austrian passports; two generations ago – even one generation ago – that would have been unthinkable. This is the landscape after Brexit, in which the idea that borders might close has induced a collective panic, reawakening slumbering ancestral memories. While Austria, like much of Europe, has its fair share of right-wing extremists, it is a country at the heart of Europe, and that is where we both feel we belong.

It is a luxury now to have choices. When, in 1938–9, the flood was in the other direction, it was a choice denied to many; by lack of resources and contacts, by fear of separation, by bad timing and ill fortune, and by the tardiness and reluctance of nations to offer visas and sanctuary.

My grandmother Edith used to boast to me of having saved my family, and with good reason: her settling in London in February 1938 provided both an outside perspective and an anchor in a foreign country, which enabled her to hook both Hugo and Kurt out of Austria. The Kafkas in Linz were helped by having a perceptive brother-in-law in Strasbourg. The Blochs had Eduard's hotline to Hitler himself, a connection that shielded both him and his immediate family. Those without such help faced almost insurmountable obstacles.

When Hugo and Sofie were ordered to move to Vienna in November 1938, the Dubskys stayed behind. It must have been a difficult moment for both families. While Luise Dubsky, as an Aryan, was not in immediate danger, both her Jewish husband and father-in-law clearly were, but they were in no state to move: Leopold, at ninety-one, was old and ill and Egon was in the psychiatric clinic. For my great-grandmother Sofie in particular, it must have been traumatic to leave behind her older brother and the Tyrol, where she had spent her entire adult life, knowing that she was unlikely to see either again.

The Dubskys were also still trapped in the entanglements of their business and the battle with *Gauleiter* Hofer over its Aryanisation. On 10 September, Dr Egon Brozek was appointed by the Nazi regime *kommissarische Verwalter* (temporary administrator) with the task of Aryanising all of Egon's moveable and immovable assets. Like other business people who suffered damages during *Kristallnacht*, the Dubskys were charged a 'sin penalty', of 18,000 Reichsmarks, and the Aryanisation office ensured that any creditors of the business did not bother to pay them.

By 12 December, Brozek's temporary appointment became permanent when he was appointed *Treuhänder* (trustee) over all of Egon's assets. Two days later, Luise withdrew the divorce application she had started. To me this felt like a brave act of resistance: Luise continued to care for her father-in-law, while making it plain that she would be happy to have Egon back on his release from hospital. After five months in the psychiatric clinic, Egon, still unwell, was transferred to the sanatorium in Hall, just outside Innsbruck. I suspect that both Luise and Egon thought it would be the safest refuge for him.

It appeared that, together, the Bertoldis and Dubskys had managed to outwit Hofer and sidestep his control; but the furious *Gauleiter* had not given up. He was now trying to annul the two contracts that transferred both halves of the business to Luise. Hofer's lawyers in Innsbruck and Vienna got to work. According to the papers I read in the County Archives, the case turned on when exactly Luise had applied to be registered as the legal owner at the Land Registry.

Hofer wanted the transfers to be declared null and void, thereby forcing her to seek permission from the Asset Transfer Office; something which, in the light of the pressure applied by Hofer's lawyers, would be denied. If Hofer's lawyers could show that there was no valid permission, both halves of the property would revert to Egon's ownership. The business would be Jewish again – and available for transfer to one of Hofer's favoured recipients.

Hofer succeeded. There was only one more hurdle he had to jump: he still needed Egon's permission for a transfer. The Minister for the Economy had issued a clear diktat that no Jewish property of a non-commercial nature should be sold without the express permission of the Jewish seller. Rather than argue about whether Egon's property was commercial or not, Hofer's lawyer decided to obtain a 'voluntary' sale from Egon. He calculated that it was the safest way to ensure that all property transfers were legal, a matter of extreme importance to the regime in order to legitimise its plunder of Jewish businesses.

Luise and Egon were, therefore, put under ever increasing pressure to agree a 'voluntary' sale. All this time, the distillery and shop were still not trading and their debts were growing. Dr Brozek then stepped in and started selling assets and stock as part of a fire sale. He also racked up fees of some 30,000 Reichsmarks, which he recharged to the business.

On 19 July 1939, the trustee forced through the sale of the Dubsky retail shop in the Seilergasse, in the old part of Innsbruck, to Georg Strickner, an approved purchaser. The proceeds of 49,000 Reichsmarks were largely used to pay off debts. The Dubsky business was in trouble, but Luise had not given up yet. Even if no one else in Innsbruck was prepared to stand up to Hofer, Luise was determined to hold out against him.

Meanwhile in Linz, Eduard Bloch had concluded that he had to close his surgery. *Kristallnacht* and the forced removal of Jews to Vienna had ended his medical career. As he later wrote, 'After thirty-seven years of active work, my practice was at an end. I was permitted to treat only Jews. After the evacuation order, there were but seven members of this race left in Linz. All were over eighty years of age.'

Although he was assured protection for himself and Lilli, he fretted in particular about his grandchildren, Georg and Johanna, then twelve and nine years old. Their parents, Trude and Franz Kren, were applying for US visas, but were fearful that time was running out.

Bloch took matters into his own hands and travelled to Vienna to seek emigration permits for Georg and Johanna, so that they could take advantage of the British *Kinderstransport* scheme for sending endangered children, between the ages of four and seventeen, to stay with relatives, friends or foster parents. No adults were allowed to accompany them, as England was already suffering from high unemployment. Visas were waived and even Eichmann in his 'Central Office for Jewish Emigration' played ball, as he was prepared to issue all necessary permits for the children to join the *Kindertransport*.

On 24 April 1939, Trude, Franz and the two children travelled to Vienna, where they stayed the night with Martha and Siegfried at their house on the Maria-Theresien-Strasse. I can see from Martha's diary and letters that the relationship between cousins

Trude and Martha was exceptionally warm; indeed, Trude later described Martha as a woman of 'brilliant intellectual ability and many talents whose self-sacrificing love knew no limits.' This was to be a last gathering of my wider family. My great-grandmother Sofie was there, as was my great-uncle Erich (with Grete and Peter).

The next day, Trude and Franz took the children to Vienna's Westbahnhof, where they entrusted them to the care of some nuns. As Johanna would later recall, their parents did not tell them they were going to England, but tearfully reassured them that they would see each other again in three weeks' time. As the *Kindertransport* ships were not allowed to leave from German ports, the overcrowded train took them to Holland for the onwards sea passage to Harwich, where they landed on 27 April 1939; becoming two of the nearly 10,000 children – three-quarters of them Jewish – brought over on the scheme.

Johanna landed on her feet, living with two caring English families, but Georg embarked on a more difficult transition. After a brief and difficult stay with a relative, he was sent to a boarding school in Brighton, where he would feel neglected and unloved. On the rare occasions that he met up with his sister, she noticed that he was very hungry. His cousin, John Kafka, with his professional training as a psychiatrist and behavioural scientist, later identified this time in England as an important, formative period for Georg. He felt rejected by his parents – and blamed his grandfather both for arranging his separation from his parents and for the connection to Hitler, which Bloch so treasured. For Georg, it was shameful that Bloch did not hate Hitler.

Wapping, London, 2019

I go back to my father's papers, hoping to learn more about those Hugo left behind in Vienna. In a ragged brown folder, I come across a series of letters addressed to Kurt from his Aunt Martha and Uncle Siegfried, and from his grandmother, Sofie. I am amazed that they have survived and as I turn the yellowed pages, written on Siegfried Salzer's personal notepaper, I look fearfully at the dates.

On 8 March 1939, Sofie writes from Vienna to her darling, beloved grandson 'Kurterl' – diminutive for Kurt. She tells him how overjoyed she is at receiving his letter and how she had longed for news from him. She suspects some of his letters have gone astray as she has received only one long letter – which she answered immediately – and a joint card with Edith and Hugo. I have only one side of this affectionate conversation, but Sofie's slightly uneven inky words radiate love for 'her little Kurt' and a hunger for news of his new life in England.

Sofie thanks Kurt for his birthday wishes and tells him that she has spent a most delightful birthday with Erich, Grete and Peter. Sofie's everyday light-hearted news then betrays a chink of fear, as she describes Erich being 'very impatient' that his passport is not yet ready, as he is so desperate to 'bid adieu to beautiful Vienna'. Sofie says that Erich has gone, with Siegfried, to Frankfurt – to try and settle the remaining affairs of Siegfried and Martha's son Erwin, who is already in the United States.

Interestingly, in her letters, she makes no mention of her own daughter, Marguerite, who I know – from a book I found on Kurt's shelves in the cottage – had fled in early 1939 on one of the last trains leaving from Vienna to Paris. Marguerite was a successful artist, who had graduated with honours from Vienna's *Kunstgewerbeschule* (School of Arts and Crafts), before pursuing a career in ceramics and sculpture, including with the Vienna *Werkstätte*, an organisation inspired by William Morris and Charles Albert Ashbee's Guild of Handicrafts. Once Marguerite was in Paris in 1939, a lack of materials forced her to reduce the size of her projects; she created exquisite ceramic buttons and pins, but these led her to commissions with *haute couture* houses such as Lanvin, Balenciaga, Patou and Schiaparelli.

On the back of one letter, Martha writes in beautiful flowing script how wonderful it is to hear good news, particularly when it is from Kurt. Martha confides how heavy her heart is with the thought of leaving Sofie behind in Vienna, when she and Siegfried emigrate. Martha has clearly realised that while she and her husband might have a chance of escaping to join Erwin, it will be difficult to arrange for Sofie's passage to America. None of them is young, I reflect, especially by the standards of the time: Sofie is eighty-two, Siegfried is seventy-two and Martha is sixty-one.

Martha urges Kurt to intercede on Sofie's behalf in England: 'You are often invited as a guest to people, please please ask your friendly hosts whether they can help with your grandmother's immigration.' It strikes me that this desperate plea placed an enormous responsibility on Kurt's thirteen-year-old shoulders. What if he does not meet the right people or his hosts are not interested, or his requests are not effective? Martha offers to send Kurt small things that he might need such as toothpaste, toothbrushes, a book and colouring pencils. She tells him that she has recently sent paints and crayons to Marianne, who is now using them to decorate her letters to them.

I know from a letter from Erwin that he has been working flat out on an exit route for them, trying to secure visas for Cuba, for onward passage to the United States, and offering to put up the money required. On 13 June 1939, Sofie and Martha write again, apologising for missing Kurt's birthday (on 9 June) and saying that Martha and Siegfried's attempts to get to Cuba look 'questionable' and have run into 'great difficulties'.

Their focus has now switched and instead, this letter says, they are all trying to get to London and are looking forward to seeing the family again. Sofie comments that this is better for her as they can then all stay together. Sofie declares herself delighted that Kurt is greatly enjoying school and interprets it as a sign that he likes learning. She implores him to make good use of this never-to-be-repeated *schöne, goldene Jugendzeit* – 'beautiful, golden time of youth'. Sofie regrets that Kurt and Peter are not in the same school, but like Jewish grandmothers the world over, she comforts herself with the idea that both Peter and Kurt are attending 'good schools'.

She worries, though, about the weather in England and whether

Kurt and his parents have acclimatised. I smile at this. The Austrian belief that the weather in London is terrible was still prevalent when I went to school in Austria in the 1980s, and I was constantly forced to reassure people that Londoners did not live in perpetual fog.

In an undated letter, I think from early summer 1939, Sofie writes again to her beloved 'Kurterl' – to thank him for a card he has sent her from his summer holidays, which she considers are well-deserved after his tiring school year. She asks about his school report, and is sad that he has not yet had the opportunity to meet up with Georg, with whom she believes Kurt will get on well. Sofie says they don't yet have any certainty about their exit plans and have been held up by an eye operation that Siegfried needs to have. Uncle Siegfried is still in the sanatorium, and Aunt Martha is spending her whole time at his side. She asks Kurt to write back to her in detail about his life, as everything about it interests her.

On the back of Sofie's letter, Martha has typed her news. Her words are selfless, as she passes on upbeat tidbits to try and keep the next generation together. She, too, wants Kurt and Georg to meet up; she wonders whether Kurt's new interest in sport has replaced his love of postage stamps, but she still includes some stamps in her letter. They are old pre-*Anschluss* stamps, and she asks Kurt to let her know if they are useful because she can send more, which he can use to swap with other collectors. She offers to put together a packet of stamps for him. Unfortunately, she says, she cannot send food because it is not allowed.

Martha lets Kurt know that Georg's sister Joanna, whom she calls 'Hannerl', has already learnt English; and that Marianne is now in Lexington in the United States, in a large house belonging to a Reverend, and is going to go to scouts camp. It is marvellous, comments Martha, that Marianne learnt how to roast potatoes over a camp fire with Kurt in Igls, during the many summers when they played there together in the garden – skills that she is now putting to good use in America.

I am struck by the care Martha and Sofie take over their joint letters. And Martha's reference to postage stamps jogs my memory that Kurt carried on collecting as an adult. I telephone my sister Sophie to see if she knows what happened to his stamp collection; she tells me that she has it in two carrier bags and will bring it to London when she is next over from Paris.

On 6 July 1939, Sofie writes again – about how glad she is to receive a letter from Kurt, and about Martha, too, being so delighted to hear from Kurt that she had 'a happy feeling in her heart all day'. Sofie urges him, 'Please darling Kurterl, write to me again, tell me how you all are, what grades you got at school and where you will spend the holidays. Everything about you interests me, every detail.' Martha writes again her own news at the bottom of Sofie's letter and tells Kurt that she has sent him a tin of Nivea; if that arrives safely, she will send him another little packet.

Sofie says that on the emigration front, everything is in limbo and they are striving to get to England, but this is bound up with 'great difficulties'. According to Sofie, 'Erwin is pulling every string he can in order to be helpful.' Sofie comments that 'naturally he would prefer to have his parents with him as soon as possible. But he is also trying to obtain an affidavit for me and hopes that he will be successful shortly.' I sense some tension here between Hugo and Edith in London, and Erwin in the United States, over Sofie, who is the oldest of the three left behind in Vienna, and the least likely to obtain a visa.

I looked in the shabby cardboard folder for more letters. But there were none. The voices from Vienna appear to have fallen silent. Kurt's link to the grandmother and aunt he clearly adored was severed.

On the same day that Sofie wrote her letter of 6 July, a US-sponsored conference was opening in the French resort of Évian, which would play a large part in deciding the fate of the German Reich's remaining Jews. Representatives of thirty-two countries attended. Each delegation, in turn, stood up and offered hand-wringing sympathy for those clamouring to be let in, but no concrete proposals, often pleading their own economic troubles or unemployment rates.

The British had recently restricted Jewish immigration to Palestine as a result of Arab unrest there, so one significant door had closed – except for those Jews who were prepared to risk illegal entry. In the United States, President Roosevelt had deplored *Kristallnacht*, but was under domestic pressure to resist immigration, lest it take jobs and overwhelm the existing social programmes for a country still living in the Depression's shadow.

Roosevelt's representative, the businessman Myron C. Taylor, assured the assembled countries that the current (but often unfulfilled) US annual immigration quota of 30,000 for Germany and Austria would still apply. It was also imperative that all immigrants could support themselves. Australia agreed to a maximum of 15,000 Jewish immigrants, pointing out that Australia did not have a race problem and did not want to import one.

Only one of the thirty-two countries at the conference offered to take significant numbers: the small Caribbean nation of the Dominican Republic. But there were conditions. Refugees going there would have to be self-financing and become pioneer farmers, clearing and developing the land.

The Évian conference represented both a failure of international resolve and a propaganda coup for the Nazi regime, which could point to the hypocrisy of nations all too keen to criticise the *Reich*'s antisemitism, but ultimately unwilling to let in the *Reich*'s Jews. Those nations bore their share of responsibility in missing this opportunity to agree worldwide sanctuary for an increasingly threatened people.

An 'Intergovernmental Committee on Refugees' was set up to continue the work begun at Évian. In the end, though, the numbers able to emigrate were dwindling, not only because of the unavailability of visas – for all concerned, it boiled down to money. As the German observer at Évian reported, with a degree of calculated cynicism, to SS *Gruppenführer* Heydrich on 27 July 1939:

The future of the present emigration policy will therefore depend to a great extent on the decisions of the Inter-governmental Committee. However, as the German Foreign Office has already issued a statement rejecting any interference in the measures against the Jews in Germany and stating that the government of the Reich refused to permit the emigrating Jews to take larger shares of their capital with them, it has to be assumed that the emigration of Jews from Germany will steadily decline.

Siegfried and Martha were scrambling to liquidate their assets. As far as I could tell from the Land Registry in Innsbruck, the forced sale of their house at Igls had taken place on 17 March 1939. Siegfried's interest in the Café Schindler had already been refunded and spent, partly to pay his exit taxes and to pay Sofie's income tax bill as well as various lawyers' bills. Looking at Erwin Salzer's 1939 letters from America, I discern a rising panic on his part. He, too, mentions the Dominican Republic as a possible destination for Sofie – but I could not see this 82-year-old woman reinventing herself as a farmer. The options were running out.

Then, what peace remained was ruptured. On 1 September 1939, Hitler sent tanks, armies and aircraft into Poland. Two days later, Britain and France declared war on the German Reich: the Second World War had begun, and with it the door to England slammed shut. Martha, Siegfried and Sofie would have to consider other possibilities.

The Kafkas in France were also having to rethink. France was no longer safe, and although they were refugees themselves, war now cast them as enemy aliens. Claire's brother-in-law stepped in again and rented for them a small flat in Brive-la-Gaillarde, south of Limoges. Claire moved there, trying to put as much distance as possible between herself and the Germans, and she set up home with her daughter Gretl and her grand-daughter.

Her son-in-law Karl and John Kafka arrived separately. Karl

bought a car, taught himself to drive, and with John in the passenger seat, revising for his final school exams, they headed south to meet up with Claire. Even before German forces launched their *Blitzkrieg* on Belgium and France, French roads were clogged with the traffic of people wanting to get away from the most likely war zone in north-eastern France. The journey took Karl and John many days.

Eighteen-year-old John passed his baccalaureate and then found work as a teacher in a Catholic boarding school. His situation exposed the confused tangle of identities that war created. The family, as citizens of the enemy German Reich, had to report weekly to the police. At the same time, John was a Jew teaching in a Catholic school. Father Renaud, who employed him, warned him to keep his Jewish identity secret. When John asked what he should do when the others crossed themselves, Father Renaud advised him to make a Star of David instead, as no one would notice.

Their sojourn in Brive ended in March 1940. By this time, Claire and John had received papers allowing them to cross to the United States. Travelling north again, they embarked from Le Havre to sail to New York, and from there carried on to Chicago. Once in the United States, Claire managed to get visas for her daughter Gretl and Karl, and their daughter too. Eventually, the whole family were reunited in American safety.

Eduard and Lilli Bloch's daughter Trude had by then already managed to get papers for the United States. War had removed the possibility of them joining their children in England. Instead, on 3 October 1939, in the opening weeks of war as Germany and soon the Soviet Union carved up Poland between them, Trude and her husband Franz boarded a ship in Genoa, bound also for New York.

The rupture of the family was felt by Eduard; he later wrote that he

... felt as if a part of my heart was being ripped out; this physical pain manifested itself organically; I felt the pain for weeks in my heart, however I pulled myself together at the departure; only a small amount of the stream of tears that flowed internally reached my eyes. What more could I hope for as a sixty-nine year old?

Now that their children and grandchildren were all abroad, Lilli and Eduard began working on their own exit strategy. Their desire to leave seemed to surprise the head of the Linz police who, according to Bloch, sought to reassure him: 'No one here is going to do the slightest thing to harm you. If you have material worries about the future, you can be reassured, you will be well provided for.'

Eduard was unimpressed; he expressed thanks for his concerns but insisted that he could not stay in a city in which his fellow Jews had been so terribly treated, and that he would rather stand on a street corner in New York 'begging for alms with a hat in my hand than stay in Linz'. The policeman understood; he even said that in Bloch's position, he would feel the same. Linz was no longer a home. The Blochs were now determined to leave what had become, to Eduard, 'this city of horrors'.

He did, though, have some unfinished business. Eduard made one last attempt to retrieve his two postcards from Hitler. He asked a contact who had worked as a cook in Hitler's household to make a personal plea to Hitler's adjutant, the naval officer Alwin-Broder Albrecht, on the basis that the cards were 'the most valuable souvenir of his medical activity'. He also asked Hitler for permission to transfer a modest sum of extra money abroad to give him enough time to take additional exams in the United States. Albrecht wrote back that Hitler had rejected this request. Eduard never did find out for sure what happened to his postcards, though he believed they ended up in Heinrich Himmler's possession.

For the next year, the Blochs made preparations – a year in which the Reich, lately supported by Mussolini's Italy, vanquished France and was triumphant across the continent. As bombs fell on Britain, the Blochs were terrified that their grandchildren would be injured. In the summer of 1940, Britain's fate was unclear, as the Royal Air Force struggled to keep control of the skies against *Luftwaffe* bombers and impending invasion.

Now even Eduard Bloch, with his protected status, was becoming increasingly anxious: his and Lilli's passports were due to run out that month.

They managed to obtain a six-month extension on their passports, and on 19 November 1940 Eduard and Lilli left the country, clutching visas allowing them to travel via France and Lisbon. Of all the Jews leaving Austria, Eduard probably had the most unusual combination of documents with him: a letter of recommendation from the Nazi *Gau* administration of Linz, as well as a Torah scroll, retrieved from the local Gestapo after they had taken it from the Linz synagogue. He also managed to obtain from the Gestapo a copy of a decree dated 14 September 1938, which required that 'all feasible easing of restrictions, including those affecting foreign currencies, are to be granted to *Obermedizinalrat* Dr Ed Bloch Linz.'

By November 1940, when Eduard went to cash in this favour, he was told that no foreign currency was available and he had to leave with only sixteen Reichsmarks. Still, that was more than the regulation ten Reichsmarks, which was all the likes of Hugo and Erich were allowed to take with them. Eduard wrote later of how, as news spread of his imminent departure, many Catholics had prayers said for him in the churches of Linz and old patients came to say 'goodbye'. Sometimes they even stopped him in the street and instead of the customary 'Heil Hitler', they greeted him with a rather comical, 'Heil Dr Bloch.'

Eduard was required to make his own grateful acknowledgement. As the Blochs arrived in Vienna, on the first leg of their journey, he was advised to write a thank-you letter to the *Führer* for all the privileges that he had enjoyed. So, on 25 November 1940, Bloch acceded, with these words:

Before I cross the frontier in order to take a ship to New York, where my only child is working hard to look after the whole family, I feel duty bound, your Excellency to express my deepest gratitude for the protection given to me during the last two years. Although I leave Linz in poverty, I am clear that I have always and selflessly done my duty. Please accept your Excellency this expression of my permanent gratitude and deepest humility.

On a gloomy November night, the Blochs left Vienna on a crowded train for Berlin. There they stayed twenty-four hours before boarding another packed, filthy train for Occupied Belgium. The Blochs became anxious when they were told of a last-minute change of itinerary: the train would now cross the German border near Aachen. When it stopped at the border, members of the SS swarmed aboard and ordered all Jews off the train, along with their luggage (which the porters were not allowed to carry).

As they descended the train, Jews were abused and kicked; some fell into puddles and others fainted. The normally mild-mannered Bloch, enraged by this behaviour, strode up to an SS man, demanding to speak to the commander. Astonished that a Jew should dare to speak to him in this way, the SS man merely pointed at a young colleague, to whom Eduard now showed a copy of Hitler's decree of 1938. It turned out to be invaluable after all.

As if by magic, the young man told the Blochs to get back in the train and he would have their luggage brought to them. The porters were suddenly allowed to help the other Jews, everyone got back on the train, and only light spot-checks were carried out on the luggage, while the Blochs' was not checked at all.

In fact, by being equipped with the *Führer*'s decree, Eduard had averted disaster, since the intention (revealed by the accompanying Aryan travel guide) had been to exploit a long search of the Jews' luggage on the platform to cover the decoupling of the carriages, so that everyone would miss their various onward connections.

From Belgium, the Blochs headed south through France to the Spanish border, and after an exhausting and uncomfortable journey finally arrived in Lisbon. Lilli and Eduard were delighted to find Martha's glamorous daughter Marguerite there. She, too, was waiting for a ship to New York and explained to the Blochs that in May 1940, feigning pregnancy, she had fled south from Paris through enemy lines, to try and meet up with her compatriot and sometime collaborator (as well as distant relative), the potter Lucie Rie.

According to Richard McLanathan's book *The Art of Marguerite Stix*, she was caught by the authorities of the new Vichy regime, which had been set up to govern southern France semi-independently under the watchful eye of Berlin, and she was placed into an internment camp at Gurs, in the Pyrenees. There, Marguerite carried on drawing using the few materials she had at her disposal – ink and lipstick – to create detailed pictures of camp life, some of which she smuggled out and would survive.

In July 1940, Marguerite was released; but she had no papers. With the help of some Czech Protestant ministers, she was able to acquire a Czech passport and then make her way to Lisbon, where she obtained an American visa. Marguerite was tough and resourceful; though I imagine that her brother Erwin must also have helped her from the United States. Eventually, in one of the bars on the Lisbon waterfront, she met the captain of a Cork transport ship, the SS *Melo*, and persuaded him to take her on his ship. In March 1941, she became the only passenger with a crew of thirty-seven men as they set sail for Baltimore.

By then, the Blochs had already set off on their own ocean voyage, on 15 December 1940, aboard the *Marques de Comillas*. On the third day and still suffering from terrible sea sickness, they were told to assemble with the other passengers in the dining room with their papers, because some English officers wished to inspect them. When Eduard handed over his passport, the officer commented to another, 'Dr Bloch – a well-known name.'

'Doctor,' declared the Englishman, 'you are the former Jewish physician of Hitler.' Bloch confirmed it was true, but his fear that he might be arrested was unfounded. The English officer merely wished him goodnight. Apparently, Bloch's story had been written up in the English press, under the title, 'The only Jew whom Hitler recognises'.

After this wholly unexpected encounter, the Blochs' sea passage to the New World continued uneventfully. On 8 January 1941, they arrived safely in New York.

Wapping, London, 2019

Today, Richard McLanathan's beautiful book *The Art of Marguerite Stix* is lodged on my bookshelves; but throughout my childhood, it sat in my father's bookcase. I am not sure that Kurt ever explained properly who this cousin was, or maybe I never heard what he said. He was maddeningly vague in his assertions that various people were related to us, so I stopped listening. However, I always loved this particular book, full of its beautiful illustrations of shells, jewellery and ceramics.

It was not until I picked it up after Kurt's death and began to delve into the family's story that I realised how extraordinary Marguerite's life and career had been as a New York artist, until her death in 1975, or where she fitted in with the rest of my family. Now, I am keen to tell my sister Sophie about this newly worked-out connection.

When Sophie arrives in London the next weekend, she brings with her Kurt's stamp collection, as promised, in two large carrier bags. Typically, little has been pasted into albums; Kurt lacked the patience and attention to detail that define a true stamp collector. The collection amounts to piles of empty envelopes, and postcards sent to us and to Kurt, along with first-day covers and scores of stamps ripped off the edges of envelopes. We tip it all onto the dining-room table and start trying to sort it out.

There among the stamps, we come across an unopened envelope addressed to Siegfried Salzer, but not at the usual address in Vienna. It bears the postmarked date of 6 August 1942 and an 8 Reichspfennig red stamp with the words *Deutsches Reich* and a profile picture of Hitler.

We open it carefully. It still has a slip of paper in it. I am nervous as to what it might say. I recognise the name of the sender: it is Hermann Schneeweiss, the family accountant who acted for Erich and Hugo and assisted in the calculation of their exit and other taxes. I look at the slip of paper. It is a bill for Schneeweiss's services in paying the *Reichsfluchtsteuer* – flight or exit tax – for Siegfried and Martha.

But payment of a flight tax is useless if you have nowhere to go.

17

Rock Cakes

The Wiener Library, London, 2019

I am in Russell Square at what is, to give its full name, the 'Wiener Holocaust Library'. It describes itself as 'one of the world's leading and most extensive archives on the Holocaust and Nazi era'.

One of its many contents is a small blue booklet, which before the Second World War was handed by police to all Jewish refugees on their arrival in London. Entitled *Whilst you are in England, Helpful Information and Guidance for Every Refugee*, it is printed in English on the left-hand pages, and in German on the right-hand ones. Given the refugees' likely experiences at the hands of the Gestapo, this booklet is careful to remind its readers that in England, 'the police are your friends and are ready to help you wherever you are'.

Other expectations, though, are moderated. The booklet warns that refugee organisations are overwhelmed, so new arrivals should be patient and not complain, because the organisations are dealing with 'a large number of others whose plight is as tragic as your own.' The publication also sets out a code of conduct. It urges refugees to spend their spare time learning English and its correct pronunciation, warning them 'not to speak German in the streets and in public conveyances and in public places such as restaurants.' Indeed, it is better to 'talk halting English rather than fluent German.'

'Do not,' insists the booklet, 'make yourself conspicuous by speaking loudly, nor by your manner or dress,' because 'the

Englishman greatly dislikes ostentation, loudness of dress or manner, or unconventionality of dress or manner.'

This is nothing new for my family. They are arch-assimilationists and have practised melting into the background for decades. Now, following their flight from Austria, a whole new effort of fitting-in is required. The words in this booklet betray a fear of unsettling the status quo: Britain's existing Jewish community is concerned that the new arrivals will show them up and jeopardise their own hard-won place in English society.

Above all, the new arrivals are warned to avoid being harbingers of fascist doom and 'not to spread the poison of "it's bound to come in your country",' because 'the British Jew greatly objects to the planting of this craven thought.' The booklet makes it clear that the British Jewish community has promised the Home Office that it will be responsible for the upkeep and care of the refugees out of its own pocket and that they 'may not take work without permission from the Home Office, lest it take away work from British people.'

British Jews do not need to worry about the Schindlers. This family is keen to mould itself to its new surroundings.

When Kurt arrived in England in September 1938, Edith already had six months of networking and acclimatisation and she lost no time in showing Kurt the ropes. Immediately, she told her son that they should not speak German outside the house. He remembered how she told him off on one occasion, when he talked to her in German on a bus. So, in laboured, heavily-accented English, they made conversation with each other as they visited London's tourist sites. It must have felt unsettling and alienating to this sheltered, thirteen-year-old boy.

In late December 1938, Kurt was reunited with his father. All the photographs of Hugo in England show him beaming; joy and relief are written all over his face. In some of them, I think I can detect a faint vertical scar on the right-hand side of his face, which I presume to be his *Kristallnacht* souvenir. It did not seem to bother him. He wrote to his Austrian lawyer, Steinbrecher, that he was completely recovered, which he attributed to having 'the constitution of a horse'.

Kurt's education was an immediate priority. One section of the little blue refugee booklet dealt with the training of young people, and seemed to dash the middle-class expectations that the Schindlers had for Kurt. According to the booklet, the new arrivals should not expect to be trained as 'doctors, dentists, lawyers, professors, etc., as there are already far too many professional men amongst the refugees for the needs of today.' Instead the boys could be trained in agriculture and handicrafts. I can well imagine Edith bridling at the idea of a manual occupation for Kurt. She was determined to pull every string she could.

Through the Jewish Refugee Committee at Woburn House, and with the help of its founder Otto Schiff and his colleague Philip Magnus, Edith managed to arrange a school place for Kurt at a prep school called Quernmore in Bromley, Kent, from 1938 until the end of 1939. He was entering this school at an age when most of its pupils would have been leaving. My father later complained about the terrible food there – he developed a hatred of custard – and said he had wasted more than a year catching up on his schooling.

Hugo had to think about earning a living. He was at least in a more fortunate position than Erich, who following his arrival in England in May 1939, was severely ill and unfit for work. Erich, Grete and Peter therefore lived in more humble circumstances in North London. They would have received limited handouts from the Jewish Refugee Committee, which was responsible for looking after all the refugees in London, though its resources were overstretched.

As Peter remembered, Hugo had picked them up from the station on their arrival in London and taken them to their accommodation. But something in the relationship between the brothers seemed to crack in London. It baffled me, as they had been so close as young men, playing at soldiers in Igls; later working well together as successful business partners all their adult lives, right up until December 1938, when they were negotiating their exits from Vienna.

From this time, I did find in the Innsbruck County Archives letters from Erich in London to Erwin Jäger, the purchaser of the Aryanised S. Schindler distillery business, which suggest some form of brotherly collaboration. In the first, Erich requested copies of recipes for Schindler liqueurs, and in the second one he asked Jäger to send him some cake recipes. I imagined that the latter were for Hugo, who harboured ambitions to recreate the Café Schindler in London. Maybe the plan was to combine the new venture with a distillery.

Initially, Jäger was reluctant to part with the Schindler family recipes, claiming they were his as part of the purchase price he paid for the business. Erich contacted their family lawyer, Steinbrecher, who established that Jäger feared Erich might sell the distillery recipes to a competitor in Germany. Once it became clear that this was not Erich's intention, Jäger sent over four of the five recipe books.

Edith must have ached for the glamorous and moneyed life she remembered from the good years in Innsbruck. It is no wonder that she and Hugo set about planning to open a London café. I'm sure they did their research. The obvious competition was the chain of J. Lyons Corner Houses, though the ambience in them was quite different to the Café Schindler. At Lyons, the service was hurried, and the atmosphere more utilitarian – a democratic café open to everyone. Edith would have observed that people often sat in their coats and hats, and ordered tea and buns brought to them by the waitress or 'Nippy'.

By contrast, it was unthinkable in the old Café Schindler for people to keep their coats on. Coats were whisked away by the maître d' before the guest was shown to a comfortable banquette. Worse still was the selection of dry cakes on offer at Lyons: rock cakes, Eccles cakes, scones and bath buns. No cream, no strudel and no proper coffee. I suspect that Edith would have made little allowances for the privations of wartime as she and Hugo planned a much more upmarket venture.

War from September 1939 altered everything. Britain enacted its own policies and procedures with regard to 'enemy aliens', and nationality overrode Jewish or political identity. On 6 November 1939, Hugo and Edith were called for interview by the Alien Tribunal. There is no transcript of the interview, but I could imagine them sitting beforehand in the waiting room in their best clothes: Hugo in the smart black suit and white shirt he wore in the Brighton beach picture, and Edith in her black overcoat with its astrakhan fur collar.

I felt certain that they brought with them the photograph album they had put together of the Café Schindler, to attest to their good name and to their ambitions to open a café. To compile the album, Hugo had commissioned a professional photographer to take photos of the café, the headquarters in the Andreas-Hofer-Strasse, and the jam factory. He had pasted them onto the thick black pages of the album and, using contrasting white ink, written out explanations in both English and German under each photograph.

He had also glued in his precious letters of recommendation. One was from an Englishman who had sampled S. Schindler cherry brandy in 1937; he was so impressed that he had written from an address in Bermondsey, London, to praise it as the finest he had ever tasted and to enquire whether it was available in England. There was also a letter from an Austrian who had worked for a year for Hugo in his confectionary business, before moving to England in the 1930s. He vouched for Hugo's integrity, that his business was of the highest standard, and his treatment of staff was a 'first rate example to the trade'.

The third, even more valuable letter, was from the renowned (but now sadly no more) travel company Thomas Cook. Dated 4 November 1939, it arrived two days before the interview, and confirmed that Thomas Cook had regularly recommended the Café Schindler to their guests – and crucially that the Schindlers were good employers.

I doubt, despite all this effort, that the members of the Alien Tribunal were much interested in Hugo and Edith's business plans. The questioning would have been perfunctory. The 120 tribunals had many cases to process: in total, they heard evidence from all 73,800 'enemy aliens' living in Britain. The tribunal would have been more interested in their reasons for moving to England and their political affiliations. I can well imagine the panel commenting drily that a café selling 'enemy food' with Germanic-sounding names was unlikely to be popular in the circumstances.

At the end of the hearing, the tribunal classed Hugo as a 'Category B alien', meaning he would not be interned but was subject to some restrictions, while Edith was classed as 'Category C', allowing her to remain at liberty. To achieve the latter status, the refugee needed character references and to demonstrate that he or she had thrown in their lot with Britain. It's possible that Edith's gender and her longer residence in the country worked in her favour. Both avoided Category A status, reserved for the most dangerous people who could be expected to assist the enemy or hinder the defence of the United Kingdom, and therefore had to be interned immediately.

In January 1940, Kurt moved to a new school, and one more to his taste than the Kent prep school. He was enrolled at Harrow, in north-west London, one of England's most prestigious boys' public schools. It also happened to be local, for the whole family – Hugo, Edith, and her parents – were now living in Harrow at No. 96 High Street, in a flat that had been offered to them as refugees, according to the *Old Harrovian* newspaper.

Once Kurt had transferred to Harrow, he was much happier. Certainly, the photographs show a contented fourteen-year-old, whether beaming broadly in his Harrow uniform of top hat and tails – his proud mother's arm entwined with his – or dressed up in cricket whites, or enjoying picnics with his parents and his Roth grandparents. To judge by these images, this Tyrolean, German-speaking Jewish boy had become an English public schoolboy, even if the rules of cricket remained impenetrable to him. The authors of the little blue booklet would surely have approved.

Edith with Kurt in Harrow school uniform (1940)

Edith was very status conscious, in a period when secondary education was not freely provided by the state. Apart from Harrow's convenience, she no doubt chose the famous school for the connections that she thought Kurt would make there. Kurt would operate on much the same principle when he chose schools for my sister Sophie and me. In Kurt's case, though, the expensive schooling was not to last. After only one term at Harrow, Edith took him out of school.

Kurt later claimed that the reason for his quick departure was Edith's fear that Harrow School might be bombed. He was her precious only child, so on one level that rings true; and the school was in a potentially exposed position, on top of a hill. But the timing is curious. This was still the period of the 'phoney war', before the Nazis launched their *Blitzkrieg* in the west, and several months before British civilians had experience of aerial bombing.

In fact, by March 1940, many of the children and mothers who had evacuated London in 1939 had gradually returned to their homes.

According to the Harrow archivist, there is nothing in the archives about why Kurt left. Yet I know from letters Edith sent to her Uncle Otto in Prague, that she and Hugo were short of money. I concluded that they simply could not afford the fees. If money was a factor, or the deciding factor, Edith might well have hidden that fact from Kurt. Either way, the result was the same. On looking at the dates of his Harrow schooling, I realised for the first time that my father's interrupted secondary school education, across two countries, finished at the age of fourteen. It seemed so young to me.

Kurt later described his new destination as agricultural training. In reality, I think this was a labouring job on a farm, a position that he obtained thanks again to the Jewish Refugee Committee. My father learned nothing from working on a farm, but acquired a life-long dislike of physical labour. At least he was safe from the bombs that were starting to fall on London.

July 1940 was the beginning of a sustained crisis for Britain, following the fall of France and the beginning of the long phase of bombing and aerial conflict that formed the Battle of Britain and then the Blitz. With fear of invasion high and tensions over homeland security increasing, the War Office and the Home Office disagreed on how to handle the 'enemy aliens'. No one was keen to repeat the wholesale internment adopted in the First World War; but there were suspicions of a Fifth Column of Germans and Austrians in England, ready to help the would-be invaders.

Early one morning, there was a knock at the door. For the third time in his life, Hugo was arrested. Edith hurriedly packed a bag for him before he was led away. It must have been terrifying, as she was not told where they were taking him. Hugo was put on a train to Liverpool, and only when he arrived at Liverpool Docks did he realise that he was being shipped across to the Isle of Man.

It was a fate shared by many in his position, and on their arrival at Port Douglas the procedure was always the same: the men were marched to a row of boarding houses on the sea-front. From the photographs I have seen, they look worried and uncertain as they clutch their small suitcases, and are being escorted by soldiers. The seaside boarding houses that accommodated them were requisitioned specially for the purpose. Their transition from holiday lodging to prison was achieved by means of a high barbed-wire fence, which separated them from the sea.

I can imagine Hugo feeling particularly vulnerable at this moment. He was stateless and now an enemy of the state in which he had sought sanctuary. As some small compensation, he was joining a large and vibrant community, with some of the best and brightest of European Jewry now concentrated on this small island. However, in one of the government's more insensitive decisions, all known fascists and Nazi sympathisers arrested were also interned on the island and lodged nearby.

Boredom and fear about what might be happening on the mainland, because of the initial news blackout, were the main problems for the internees. I can't know for sure what Hugo did on the Isle of Man, but I would be prepared to bet that he helped run the Austrian-style café. Perhaps Hugo turned out his trademark *Apfelstrudel* to homesick fellow internees, as he chatted about the café he had lost.

There was no rationing in force at the camp, and it had access to plentiful local ingredients; so the camp café was able to conjure up better food than was available on the mainland. Indeed, the hearty fare on the island became a source of tension for the local mainland population after newspapers ran stories on it. The *Daily Mail* led the way, also criticising the entertainment available to the internees, which apparently included golf, sea-bathing and cinema shows.

In the end, Hugo's internment was only a matter of weeks. By September 1940, fears of invasion were receding, as the RAF had managed to keep control of the skies, and the *Luftwaffe* had switched to bombing cities. The authorities must also have recognised they had nothing to fear from a Jewish ex-café owner in his fifties. Hugo was released on 12 September 1940. I never heard from my father that Hugo ever complained about his time on the Isle of Man. I suspect that, as with most other refugees, he accepted that the authorities had to err on the side of caution. Ironically, the place from which he was released was relatively safe from the bombs – but he now returned to a London in the maelstrom of the Blitz.

In suburban North London, my great-uncle Erich was spared the experience of internment. However, the reason for that – his failing health – brought its own consequences. In 1941 he suffered a fatal heart attack, though Grete put his death down to something more poetic: broken-heartedness at the separation from his beloved homeland and the Tyrol.

Erich's funeral was an occasion for a Schindler gathering, and I was astonished to learn from Peter's interview with Gerda Hofreiter, in 2011, that this was the first time he had seen Hugo since his arrival in England in May 1939. What had occurred between the brothers to cause such a rupture? Grete's 94-year-old friend in Innsbruck, Gerti Mayer, also described to me in 2019 a falling-out between the brothers, but she did not know any details.

As far as I could tell, looking at the evidence, there seemed to be two possible inter-connected explanations: arguments about money and arguments about Sofie, Martha and Siegfried, who remained trapped in Vienna. Perhaps Hugo blamed Erich for leaving their mother, sister and brother-in-law behind. As one of Sofie's letters to Kurt had said, Erich had been itching to leave. But it would have been an unfair accusation, as Hugo had done the same thing five months previously.

I doubt whether it would have made any difference if Erich had stayed. Visas were granted on an individual basis, and it was not uncommon for some family members to get visas and others to be refused; and even if Erich had contemplated staying, I suspect that Sofie would have insisted that he should go. That leaves money as the explanation for the falling out between the brothers. If Hugo was earning some money (or possibly had been able to transfer money to Edith before leaving Austria) and Edith was busy socialising and bragging about it, that may well have been a source of friction.

Grete – so much younger than Erich, and with her life ahead of her – remarried almost immediately after Erich's death, taking her British husband's surname, Tray, a further shaking-off of her Austrian identity. Peter, her son, did likewise. As soon as he turned sixteen, Kurt's cousin was sent out to work as a clerk.

Kurt took a different path. With the help of a Pitman correspondence course, he was able to pass the examinations for the School Certificate in 1942. Despite all the dislocations of his last few years, my father's achievements were sufficient for him to be accepted by Jesus College, Oxford, in October 1942 to read chemistry. This must especially have delighted Edith, given that Oxbridge was – and still is – such a marker of social status in Britain. It was only in researching this history that I discovered that Kurt left Oxford after only a year, 'sent down' in 1943 without a degree. I don't really know why.

In various documents I found among his papers after he died, Kurt claimed he had left because he was opposed to being 'asked to do war work'. The Oxford archivist I consulted mentioned that 'hush hush' war work was indeed done by chemists at Oxford, but it seems unlikely that a first-year undergraduate would have been invited to get involved; and anyway, most refugees were desperate to help Britain defeat the Nazis – they knew only too well what awaited them if Germany were victorious.

Once, when pressed, Kurt admitted to me that he simply could not keep up with his academic work. This seems the most likely explanation. He was still only eighteen and his interrupted schooling gave him little formal preparation for undertaking a degree. It did not stop Kurt, in later life, bragging about 'his time at Harrow' and the 'fun he had at Oxford', without ever letting on how brief that time was at both institutions. Perhaps his awareness of the truth helped explain why he became intensely proud of his children's academic achievements. They went some way towards completing his own unfinished business.

In June 1943, when Kurt turned eighteen, he was old enough to join the armed forces. Many young Jewish refugees of his age were desperate to help the Allied war effort and defeat the Germans. The usual path they took was to join the Pioneer Corps, which had been the only unit at the outset of the war to accept 'enemy aliens'. By the end of the war, one in seven Jewish refugees had joined up, but Kurt never did.

As for his parents, as far as I can tell, after the Isle of Man episode they had a quiet war while living on a modest income, and keeping an anxious eye on what was happening in Europe. Hugo worked, within the constraints that war permitted and the blue booklet described. I learnt later that he was employed as a baker and patissier's assistant in London. I imagine my stoical grandfather taking this in his stride, and my grandmother bristling at the collapse in social status it represented.

Occasionally, news about Innsbruck filtered through. On 20 December 1943, with what must have been mixed emotions, Kurt spotted a report in the *Oxford Mail* of bombs being dropped in day raids on the city. Hugo pasted a copy of the article into the photo album he had prepared to showcase the café. They might well have guessed that their old jam factory, lying near the important transport intersection of the railway station, was at risk. In fact, it took a direct hit. They could not have known it, but the café was damaged too, as was the Andreas-Hofer-Strasse property. Only the villa, lying as it did slightly outside the centre of Innsbruck and still occupied by the *Gauleiter*, was spared.

But the café did not just suffer damage to its bricks and mortar. Its reputation, under its new Nazi proprietor, had also taken a battering.

The jam factory before the bombing, Hugo
standing with his car in front of it

The bombed jam factory

18

Jellied Eels

Innsbruck, Austria, 2019

I am in the County Archives again, digging through the files on
the café. I want to find out how it fared during the war years, after
it was Aryanised under the control of the *Gauleiter* Hofer's crony,
Franz Hiebl.

From a photograph in the Archives, I see that in order to provide
extra drinking space for his new clientele of Nazi officers, Hiebl
has turned the café's ground-floor shop, which in Hugo's day had
sold chocolates and candied fruit, into a new venue. So, the Hiebl
Café now has a 'Hiebl Bar'. It opens on 24 December 1938, in the
same month that the dispossessed former owner lands as a refugee in England.

Given that so many Jewish businesses were pushed into liquidation in 1938, at least in Hiebl the café has a manager who
understands the hospitality business and is committed to running
Innsbruck's premier venue. In Hiebl's own 1942 'autobiography',
he resorts to hyperbole to describe his dedication to the café and
claims that 'in the true sense of the word, he worked day and
night, as he had such a burden of debt on the business, that he
needed every penny to pay it down.'

Hiebl, keen to show slavish devotion to the Nazi regime, also
presents himself as a man of many parts beyond running the café,
who frequently volunteers his services to the SS and has asked
repeatedly to be sent to the front to fight. As I read the Archive
papers, however, something more intriguing starts to emerge.

By 1942, rumours start to circulate in Berlin that the Hiebl Café has become a centre for black marketeering. An anti-corruption commission is dispatched to investigate, and it confirms that there is a lively trade in the café in restricted goods and other hard-to-find items. Behind the façade of the perfect, loyal Nazi, Hiebl has been running an illicit operation procuring luxuries for his war-fatigued guests. Hiebl is arrested for racketeering and black marketeering. In wartime, these are capital offences.

As a lawyer, I like evidence. So I began my investigation into the case against Hiebl by trying to weigh the credibility of his claims that he was keen to put his life at risk, at the front, against what I knew of his activities and what they suggested about his character.

While he was assiduous in ingratiating himself with the Nazi regime, I found little evidence of his risking his life for it. In his role in transport logistics, Hiebl turned up in various parts of Nazi Europe, including in places whose names would become notorious – in Krakow, Berlin, Oranienburg, Buchenwald and Holland – but spent his army time mainly delivering vehicles. As well as contributing to Hitler's war, Hiebl's deployments provided him with extensive opportunities to source black-market goods in areas where rationing had not yet bitten as deeply as in Innsbruck.

With Hiebl regularly on the move, the day-to-day running of the café fell to his wife, Bertha. However, with nearly half of the café staff already called up, and a young child to look after, Bertha herself was overstretched. Pleading the pressure they were under, Hiebl asked the *Gau* authorities whether he could close part of the café – a request, he asserted, that was turned down. I assume this was because the café remained such an important morale-boosting institution in Innsbruck.

In his autobiography, Hiebl claimed he had to resort to using 'foreign workers' in the café, something he considered less than desirable. He described how his café clients keep coming to him demanding items that he could no longer offer them in Innsbruck. They allegedly told Hiebl that they could get these 'elsewhere'; at the same time, customers were beginning to complain about the quality of what was on sale in the café. Hiebl portrayed himself as obliged to satisfy these clients. As he put it, 'This became about my reputation as a Nazi and whether I could run my business properly.'

According to Hiebl, many of those versed in the hospitality trade thought it a miracle that he could run the business at such a high level, while still discharging his commitments as an SS officer; a miracle that could only be achieved, he said, by throwing himself into his work and neglecting his family.

In February 1942, Hiebl was asked to transfer to Berlin, to another part of the Army Transport Department. He claimed that once more he asked, without success, to be sent to the front. Instead, he carried on being exposed to temptation in various corners of the Reich. On 19 September 1942, Hiebl was arrested. That day, too, his wife gave birth prematurely to their second son.

The charge sheet against Hiebl was grave and varied. It included embezzlement, going AWOL from the army, document forgery, tax evasion, and currency and customs offences. The most serious charges, given wartime conditions, included buying 14,750 bottles of Scotch whisky and 200 bottles of Sauternes in Holland, which he transported to Cologne and from there to Innsbruck. In addition, he was accused of purchasing tinned peaches, plums, anchovies, ham, and pickled onions, as well as almonds, which he transported himself in his own army lorry to Lublin, and sent onwards from there by train to Innsbruck.

In another expedition to Holland, he bought soap, silk stockings, cigarettes, rum, cognac, liver pâté, egg-nog, chocolate, tinned pineapple, tinned ham, a hoover, 36 gramophone records, a piano, tinned milk, and 96 jars of jellied eels at a price of between 1 and 2.5 Guilders per jar.

This last item caught my eye. I have never seen jellied eels on a Tyrolean menu. They are made by simmering freshwater eels in stock, with herbs, and then letting them cool, before being eaten cold, once the gelatinous broth has set. Eels being nutritious, cheap and plentiful, the dish is much more at home in London, where it was traditionally eaten by the poor of the East End – though versions also exist in Holland, France, Germany and Italy.

Perhaps Hiebl thought he would try something new, simply because it was available and he could sell it as a delicacy from Holland; or maybe it was an indication of how international his clientele had become, given the mix of people now passing through Innsbruck. Hiebl bragged about looking after officers, armaments workers, convalescing soldiers and holiday makers.

Hiebl, according to the charges, then compounded his black-market crimes by falsely accounting for his goods in his books. He invented travel costs where none had been incurred, and he fabricated falsely high prices for his purchases. He created a trail of false invoices to document these fictitious prices, with the intention of deceiving his bookkeeper – except that Hiebl was not terribly good at fraud. His staff noticed that many of the invoices to Hiebl were filled out in his own handwriting, even where deliveries were apparently from a third-party supplier.

On page 27 of the charge sheet, the prosecutor got into his stride. Given the particularly despicable nature of Hiebl's activities, the prosecutor calls Hiebl a *Volksschädling*, an 'enemy of the people'. First and foremost, Hiebl is a man from whom *persönliche Sauberkeit* – literally, 'personal cleanliness', but meaning 'integrity' – should be expected, for Hiebl, with his medals, stands at the very pinnacle of the Nazi movement. He has breached the trust of the *Führer*. The court might consider prohibiting Hiebl from working and indeed shutting down the café; more threateningly, though, he must now be 'eradicated from the people'. This last injunction from the prosecutor was a call for the death penalty.

Reading over these charges, I was fascinated by the reference to *persönliche Sauberkeit*. I looked up the piece of law under which Hiebl was charged. Paragraph 4 of the *Volksschädlingsverordnung* – the 'Enemy of the People Regulation' (5 September 1939) – stated that 'any person who exploits the extraordinary conditions caused by the war to commit a crime, shall receive the death penalty, if this is required by healthy national feeling due to the particularly reprehensible nature of the crime.'

Like much Nazi-era legislation, it was carefully thought through, designed to protect a German war economy against the black market. Dark and morally corrupt though the Nazis were, it was critically important to the regime's self-perception to foster its own image of upright, clean honesty, in the national cause.

Among the papers in the archive, I found Hiebl's own detailed instructions to his lawyer on how to approach his defence. He went through the 33-page charge sheet paragraph by paragraph and commented indignantly that he simply could not be a '100% Nazi for 12 years and then suddenly an enemy of the people'.

He complained that:

> ... if I had been given the opportunity, in response to my many pleas, to be sent to the front, none of this would have happened. I saw how everyone without exception purchased stuff for themselves and that there was a plentiful supply of goods, so I purchased goods for the business, so that I could offer my guests (soldiers and holiday makers – the wounded) more and better items.

Hiebl claimed he had made no profit – quite the contrary – that it would have been more profitable to use cheaper substitute products, whereby he would have earned more money. This struck me as a bad argument to make, given that Hiebl was blaming his motivation for racketeering on his guests' complaints about poor-quality food and drink in the café.

Hiebl's wife did not escape the net. Bertha was accused of fewer crimes, but again, in the context of the legislation, they were serious. They included acquiring 1,504 eggs from her father's farm and moving them without authorisation to Innsbruck and receiving 230 pairs of silk stockings, of which she sold 96 and retained the rest for herself.

The prosecutor noted that Bertha ran the café when Hiebl was away, and that she lived in fear that her remaining staff, especially her pastry chef Josef Mosna, would be called up. She was alleged to have inveigled an army official into sending over a doctor, who detected a barely noticeable facial tick on Mosna; it was sufficient to have his call-up papers revoked. The official's reward from the Hiebls was a box of chocolates.

Hiebl's defence rested on his argument that he was only ever trying to supply good luxury products to his guests at the café. He claimed never to have considered benefiting himself, although he conceded that some of the facts, especially the bottles of whisky, 'look somewhat different'. In the conclusion to his October 1942 autobiography, Hiebl begged for frontline duties – in order to escape the firing squad that otherwise awaited him:

> Now that it has been explained to me how serious my misdemeanours are, I only have one wish, to demonstrate at the front, that it was not only earlier that I was prepared to put my life on the line for the *Führer* and the movement, but even more so now, when the Reich's very existence [*Sein oder Nichtsein des Reichs*] is at risk.

It is a sign of Hiebl's desperation that he risked, at this time, voicing any doubt at all about the eventual victory of the Nazi Reich.

Among the court files, I found an extraordinary exchange of correspondence between the Hiebls and their criminal lawyers. In the UK, such correspondence is 'subject to legal professional privilege' and is therefore private; it would never end up in a court file. The letters provided me with real insight into the tensions behind the case.

On 18 December 1942, Bertha's lawyer, Dr Markl, wrote to Hiebl in prison to explain that he was very troubled by one of Hiebl's letters, and that Hiebl misunderstood the situation. I could tell that Hiebl had lost trust in his own lawyer, Dr Mann, and wanted his old friend Markl to represent him as well as his wife. But as Markl explained, this would almost certainly create a conflict of interest. He counselled Hiebl against switching lawyers: it could give the impression that Dr Mann had lost confidence in winning the case, and such psychological considerations should not be ignored. Instead, Markl reassured Hiebl that he was in good hands – and promised to work behind the scenes with Mann.

At Hiebl's request, Dr Markl agreed to approach *Gauleiter* Hofer, to ask for him to intervene in the case, though Markl doubted Hofer would be prepared to do so. Finally, Markl reassured Hiebl that the delay in the proceedings over Christmas 1942 would be a good thing: the case was difficult, the papers extensive, and so the defence lawyers needed time to get fully up to speed.

Dr Mann, meanwhile, was encouraging Hiebl to sell the café so as to secure the future of Hiebl's wife and children. He also argued that this would improve his standing in the eyes of Hofer, who, according to Mann, was keen for it to be sold. Markl agreed with Mann and pointed out that Hiebl had few friends. Having spoken to Hofer, he believed Hofer would do everything he could to help Hiebl but that, as *Gauleiter*, he had to take account of the difficult circumstances in which Hiebl found himself. Markl also pointed out that Hiebl would need to stay in Hofer's good books if he wanted to buy property in the future. He concluded that Hiebl had only one friend – the *Gauleiter* – and, bitter though that might be, Hiebl needed to hear the truth.

The lawyers conferred behind the scenes. Mann told Markl that Hiebl still could not believe that he had fallen from grace and had lost all political clout, and furthermore that Hiebl was bringing unfortunate attention to himself by continually demanding personal favours while sitting in prison. Hiebl looked only to his own comfort – not very appropriate for an SS man, particularly given the seriousness of his situation. Hiebl was even asking Mann to smuggle cigarettes and letters in and out of prison, which he refused to do. According to Mann, it was this refusal that turned his client against him.

This all rang true to me. Dr Mann's letters describe a not uncommon cause of tension between lawyers and their clients: yes, lawyers are required to follow their clients' instructions, but they are also there to uphold the rule of law of the regime in which they operate. With some clients, these two requirements come into conflict.

Dr Mann tried to disabuse Hiebl of the idea that his case was trivial, as Hiebl continued to insist he was the victim of political intrigue. But Hiebl accused Mann of not defending his interests robustly enough and was furious when the trial was postponed to the end of January 1943. Mann confided in Markl that he had to restrain himself from asking Hiebl why he was so keen to have a quick verdict, given that it was likely to be the death penalty. In short, Dr Mann was feeling he could no longer represent his client.

Meanwhile, as news got out that Hiebl was in severe trouble, two potential buyers for the café appeared. One, a south Tyrolean hotelier, offered 600,000 Reichsmarks for it – significantly more than Hiebl had paid the Schindlers five years previously, though of course his own purchase had been an Aryanisation. I assumed that this larger figure represented something nearer its true value, and perhaps it is just as well my grandfather did not know this particular detail at the time.

In May 1943, in Salzburg, Hiebl's fate was decided. The judge finally handed down a seventy-page judgement. It was, he wrote, a difficult case and finely balanced. He recognised that Hiebl had misused his position in the SS, the army's vehicles, and his military deployment to hide his activities. But was he really an 'an enemy of the people', who had exploited the exceptional circumstances caused by the war to commit offences, namely the purchase abroad of items and import of those items into the Reich without the necessary documents?

The judge concluded he was not. The reason for this was that through Hiebl's own undoubted commercial ability and healthy ambition, he had managed to make a success of 'the Jewish Café

Schindler', which was frequented by the most senior members of the Nazi Party as well as by every foreigner who came to Innsbruck; above all, it was visited by wounded soldiers who were recuperating in the city. The judge found it understandable that Hiebl had hit upon the idea of offering these guests something special, even though there was a war going on.

In this light, Hiebl's foreign purchases were comprehensible, especially if one took into account that such goods were still available elsewhere in Nazi Europe and that the populations of Holland and the Protectorate of Bohemia and Moravia – Nazi Czechoslovakia – were faring better than the Tyrol.

Although, in his view, the court could not in any way sanction Hiebl's behaviour – and Hiebl deserved a severe punishment for breaching the rules of the wartime economy – his actions were not so reprehensible that the 'healthy sensibilities of the people' absolutely required him to be named 'an enemy of the people'. By a whisker, Hiebl sidestepped the death penalty.

I found descriptions of 'the Jewish Café Schindler' as the haunt of the most senior Nazis interesting. Despite a name change, despite a new owner and the expulsion of the Schindlers from the country, the heritage of the café patently lived on in the judge's mind as somewhere exceptional; somewhere worth saving and a refuge for those who sought it out. And ultimately, its reputation and utility were enough to save Hiebl's life.

Instead of putting Hiebl in front of a firing squad, the judge handed down a fifteen-year sentence and a 123,000-Reichsmark fine; Bertha received a four-year sentence and an 11,200-Reichsmark fine. If unable to pay the fines, they faced the prospect of a longer prison term. Mosna did not escape either – the pastry chef incurred seven months in prison and a fine of 500 Reichsmarks. In addition, Hiebl was thrown out of the SS and stripped of his medals for ten years. The state also seized a very long list of contraband. I could not help noticing that in the list of seizures only one jar of jellied eels remained. Clearly, they had been an astute purchase.

Photo of Hiebl's black-market haul seized by the Nazis as part
of the investigation into his illegal, black-market activities

Although Hiebl had escaped the death penalty, the verdicts
seemed to spell the end for the café itself, with the owner, his wife
and his head pastry chef all in gaol. Hiebl was now determined to
pull every string he had left to get his and Bertha's sentences
reduced. On 13 September 1943, he wrote triumphantly to Mann,
his lawyer, that whilst on a brief leave before starting his sentence,
he had visited *Reichsführer* Heinrich Himmler, no less, in his
army quarters. It was, Hiebl trumpeted, Himmler's 'personal
wish' that Bertha should continue to run the café. To achieve this,
her sentence would be commuted to a one-year suspended prison
term, meaning she could start back at the café immediately.

I was astonished that Heinrich Himmler, head of the SS (whose
codes of 'honour' Hiebl had transgressed) and one of the most
senior Nazis in the entire Reich, troubled himself with Hiebl and the
management of a provincial café. After all, looking at his diary in
the autumn of 1943, he was busy formulating key Nazi extermina-
tion policy. On 6 October, he attended a conference for the Reich's

most senior leaders in Posen. *Gauleiter* Hofer was also present at the conference. In his speech, Himmler posed the question, 'What shall we do with the women and children?' before delivering his answer:

> I have decided even here to have a very clear solution. I do not find it justified to destroy the men – that is to say kill them or have them killed – and allow revenge in the form of children to grow up for our sons and grandsons. It was necessary to come to the difficult decision to have these people disappear from the earth.

I wondered whether, in the interval between speeches about the murder of women and children, Hofer and Himmler chatted amiably about the café and the difficulties in which Hiebl found himself. Certainly, Hiebl got his way as regards his own sentence, too. His fifteen years were reduced to seven, and these were commuted to a period of immediate service at the front; before setting off, he was given seven days' holiday to spend with his wife. Hiebl reported that Himmler would speak directly to Hofer about the café, when he next came to Innsbruck; he also expressed the hope that his service at the front would be over by Christmas 1943, allowing him to return to Innsbruck.

During his 'holiday', he asked his lawyer to set in motion the repurchasing of those assets seized by the state, and expressed concern about the future ownership of the café, clearly nervous about what Himmler would order Hofer to do with it. In the meantime, Hiebl instructed his lawyer not to discuss the café with anyone, anywhere, in case something were to happen to him at the front: 'We have to fight this battle alone, but I hope that we will win it just as we have won the past ones.'

What Hiebl intended was to keep the café for his children, but, as he told his lawyer, much would depend on Hofer. On 16 September 1943, Hiebl wrote to the Munich court asking for the release of certain seized items he regarded as essential to running the café, including gramophone records, a piano and three radios

– all of them purchased on the black market. Clearly, music was still going to play a big part at the Café Hiebl.

The next month, Hiebl transferred half of his house to his wife and a further quarter to each of his two under-age sons, Peter and Dieter, in advance of carrying out his duties at the front. He was a survivor, but needed to plan ahead.

Hiebl did return safely from the front – and he continued to operate the Café Hiebl until shortly before the end of the war, when more Allied bombs brought about its closure.

Wapping, London, 2020

I have two picture postcards in front of me, which Hugo pasted into his photo album of the café. They are from a few months before the war. The first is dated 8 February 1939, and it shows South Tyrolean hunters, in *Lederhosen* and feathered hats, and was posted from Italy. I imagine it was chosen to remind Hugo fondly of the time he spent there.

It has been sent to Hugo in London by one of his former employees at the Café Schindler, whose name is Adolf Werner. Adolf is, he says, inconsolable that he will never again have such a good boss. I check the 50th Anniversary tribute poster produced in 1931 by the Schindler employees, but I cannot see Adolf's name among the list of signatures, so I presume he must have joined afterwards.

Three weeks later, on 24 February, Adolf writes again, this time in a postcard showing a night-time view of the Rhine. He is in Germany, in Cologne, and he is evidently carrying out a task at Hugo's behest. From the message I can tell that he is there to collect money from a loan that Hugo has made. Adolf describes the city as a 'house of horrors' – a reference, I assume, to what he sees around him on the streets of Cologne, within the heart of the Nazi state.

I dare say that, in 1939, Hugo needs that money – although I am not sure that it ever reaches him. In gaining sanctuary in London, Edith and Hugo have traded their status as big fish in the small pond that was Innsbruck for a modest life, partially dependent on refugee aid, on the suburban periphery of a large foreign city.

I know that the London incarnation of the Café Schindler remains a pipe dream. Edith and Hugo simply lack the necessary capital and connections to get it off the ground, and anyway this war is hardly propitious for such a venture. The focus now is on keeping a low profile; surviving rather than thriving.

Although I suspect that Hugo was unaware of Hiebl's narrow escape from the death penalty in Innsbruck, I wonder what his reaction might have been, knowing of Himmler's intervention. Would he have been a little proud that his café was deemed so important to the life of Innsbruck, and to the functioning of the Nazi regime there, that its continued survival warranted the intervention of the *Reichsführer* himself?

19

Return to Sender

Innsbruck, Austria, 21 September 1941

Egon Dubsky is, for the moment, still safely closeted in the sanatorium in Hall, just outside Innsbruck. On this day, Dr Egon Brozek – the regime-appointed trustee of Egon Dubsky's assets – writes to Luise Dubsky's lawyer.

Brozek wants to know whether Egon and Luise are prepared to sell the Dubsky shop and distillery facilities at Nos. 2 and 2a, Heiliggeiststrasse. For some time, a wine merchant down the road, by the name of Franz Gutmann, has wanted to buy the properties, and now Dr Brozek wishes to pursue the matter.

Brozek explains that he does not in any way recognise Luise's ownership claims over the properties; nevertheless, Gutmann would prefer to have Luise's agreement. In closing, he points out that if she does not agree to the sale for 160,000 Reichsmarks, including the inventory, then he will take steps to force through the sale; which is supported by the Commissioner for Aryanisation, Herman Duxneuner.

The next month, Duxneuner, Brozek and Gutmann – along with a member of the Gestapo – pay a visit to Luise in the flat above the shop in the Heiliggeiststrasse, where she lives with her father-in-law Leopold. At this meeting, Luise refuses to sell to Gutmann, prompting fury from Commissioner Duxneuner, who issues a threat: 'We will sell this property without the right signature . . . Frau Dubsky, if you help us, we will leave your husband in peace in Hall, otherwise we will ship him to Poland today.'

Brozek later asserts that he cannot remember details of the

encounter – except for the fact that he said nothing during it, and that he was 'upset' at Duxneuner's words. By now everyone knows what a mention of Poland means for a Jew. It is a place of no return.

I found the post-war report describing the meeting at the Dubsky flat in the Innsbruck County Archives. The archivist handed it over with strict instructions to keep the loosening papers, which were coming away from their binding, all in the same order. When I picked up the pale green folder, threaded with thin cord, and examined its fragile yellowed sheets, torn and barely legible in parts, I realised that it was central to understanding what happened to the Dubskys. The file formed part of restitution proceedings after the war, and its first page, a 'political announcement', left no ambiguity: it condemned the activities of Brozek, Duxneuner, Guttman and one Dr Bilgeri as particularly terrible.

After that encounter in the flat, Luise hurried to her lawyer, Dr Wolfhartstätter, who was clear in his advice: sell now and don't haggle too much over the price if you want to save your husband. Luise confessed that to keep her husband in Innsbruck she would even give away the property, though Wolfhartstätter did not think that necessary, and they would try for the best possible price. By now, I had completely abandoned my suspicions that Luise had only married Egon to get her hands on his business for her brothers.

Dr Wolfhartstätter describes how he later attended a negotiation at the flat with Luise, Brozek, Duxneuner and a tall Gestapo officer from Berlin who, he was told, was there to make sure everything 'ran smoothly'. The inventory was an immediate problem: it belonged jointly to Leopold and Egon, and so as Wolfhartstätter only represented Luise, he was reluctant to negotiate over it.

Luise offered a sale price of 200,000 Reichsmarks before quickly coming down to 175,000, and Wolfhartstätter tried to support Luise's price by pointing out that he had previously had two offers from third parties for 320,000 and 300,000 Reichsmarks. With the price agreed, the question of the flat over the shop remained. Gutmann wanted it for his cellar manager, but Luise wanted to remain in her home with her father-in-law Leopold. The meeting concluded without agreement.

As the finalisation of the sale dragged on, Duxneuner harassed Wolfhartstätter by phone, accusing him of sabotaging the negotiations. Duxneuner then cranked up the pressure, and on 3 November 1941 he wrote to Dr Prantl, the managing director of the Sparkasse bank with whom Egon had his business loans. Duxneuner ordered the bank to cancel Egon's loans 'in order to Aryanise the Dubsky firm in favour of a South Tyrolean returnee', before signing off with the customary 'Heil Hitler'.

Obediently, two days later, Prantl informed Egon at the sanatorium that the Sparkasse was calling in both loans by 15 November 1941, plus interest, which amounted to a demand of just over 36,352 Reichsmarks to be paid within a mere ten days. If the money were not paid, he threatened, the bank would foreclose. Given what I had already seen of the Sparkasse's role as middleman in the sale of the Villa Schindler to *Gauleiter* Hofer, I was not surprised by the bank's behaviour.

At a further meeting in his office, Duxneuner gave an ultimatum: the sale had to be completed by 22 November 1941. When Luise's lawyer explained that there were still differences between the parties in respect of certain conditions, Duxneuner lost his temper, saying that he'd had enough, that *Gauleiter* Hofer was waiting for the contract, and it was scandalous that the business had not already been Aryanised. Once more, the threat of Poland was made. By now, Dr Wolfhartstätter was also furious. He refused to negotiate under such pressure and threatened to step back and put the finalisation of the discussions back into Luise's hands. They telephoned Luise – but she caved in to the pressure and agreed to the rest of Duxneuner's demands.

Brozek now produced a contract for the building and the inventory for a combined price of 175,000 Reichsmarks. A sale contract was finally signed on 10 December 1941 for the sums of 163,000 Reichsmarks for the building and 12,000 Reichsmarks for the inventory. The only saving grace was that Luise was allowed to stay in the flat, with Leopold. The money was paid over in June 1942 and was placed straight into a blocked account. The balance on the account was used to pay creditors and settle another tax on Jews.

Down but not out, Luise and Egon complained about the way they were treated to the *Reichswirtschaftsministerium* – the Economics Ministry. This had the effect of forcing Hofer to explain what had happened, and to reassure the authorities that Aryanisation of the Dubsky business was entirely lawful and the Dubskys had voluntarily agreed to the sale. He followed up by commenting it was clear that Luise, with the agreement of her family, had 'thrown herself away' on 'this Jew', was still not divorced, and that there was no evidence of the various political services that Egon had rendered to the party.

Egon remained in Hall, but he must have known that it was not really a place of safety. Hitler's euthanasia programme, code-named mysteriously 'T4' to muddy its purpose, had been operating since 1939 to remove and murder patients from psychiatric clinics. Some were given lethal injections, others were taken away and gassed in early experiments, which paved the way for the more widespread use of another gas in death camps. Three hundred and sixty patients were plucked from the Hall clinic in this way. Yet Egon was never taken.

Dr Czermak, who was in charge of compiling the lists of those who were sent to the T4 killing camps, removed his name multiple times from the lists of those who were to be killed. In fact, it was the very haggling over the Dubsky properties that kept him safe, for if anything happened to him before the sale were completed, his estate would pass to Luise. If Eichmann's poster was to be believed – the one showing the steps Jews needed to take before emigrating – there were only six Jews left in the Tyrol by 31 March 1941. Egon was one of them. But those men who had threatened him with Poland had lied: it was not the hold-up in the sale that put him in danger, but the end of that process, because Egon was now superfluous to their requirements.

In the spring of 1943, the Head of the Gestapo for Tyrol and Vorarlberg, Werner Hilliges – the man who had threatened my grandfather and other Jewish businessmen in September 1938 – ordered the arrest of those Jews in mixed Jewish-Aryan marriages. They were to be transported to the labour camp of Reichenau, on the north-eastern edge of Innsbruck. It lay in a working-class, semi-industrial, semi-agricultural area; even today, farmhouses selling fresh milk sit cheek by jowl with light industrial units and blocks of flats.

There is one book on the camp by Johannes Breit, published in 2017. It explains that the Reichenau camp was used to 're-educate' workers, particularly Italian workers who had been dispatched by Mussolini to work in the Reich in return for raw materials from the *Führer*. Poorly treated in their workplaces, they had some-times absconded, were intercepted on their way back to Italy via Innsbruck, and thus ended up at Reichenau. Other forced labour-ers also arrived there from conquered lands in the east.

They were hardly invisible to Innsbruckers, for groups of pris-oners were deployed in town on construction sites and to clear rubble. Inside the camp, punishments – sometimes fatal ones – were common: in winter prisoners were stripped naked and had ice-cold water poured over them.

In May 1943, Egon was picked up from the sanatorium and removed to the camp. Less than a month later, on the evening of 2 June 1943, Hilliges ordered Egon to be brought before him. What happened next, according to the official report three days later, was that 'Egon Israel Dubsky, unemployed, Catholic, previously Jewish, resident in Innsbruck, Heiliggeiststrasse 2 died on 2 June 1943 at 19.30.' The cause of death was given as 'death through shooting (headshot)'.

Hilliges, whom the camp commandant Mott later described as reeking of drink – but in full possession of his faculties – shot

Egon in the head at close range. Egon collapsed immediately and died shortly afterwards. Some testimony after the war pointed to an attempted escape. Certainly, Luise believed that it was the practice of the camp to stage escape attempts to give a pretext for executions. A ladder was brought out and placed near the execution wall; prisoners were told to walk towards it, and then shot. But as Egon was shot at the front of his head, Luise's explanation seems unlikely.

Hilliges later claimed that Egon had attacked him with a tool, and that he killed Egon in self-defence. However, that also seems far-fetched. I suspect that Hilliges simply decided that this was the day on which to kill my cousin, Egon Dubsky.

Kurt had never, to my recollection, spoken to me about Egon's murder, despite mentioning the Dubsky shop a number of times as being yet another lost family asset. Looking at the official verdict on his death, I was overwhelmed with pity for Egon. Stripped of his profession, his middle name altered from Anton to Israel, he died at the feet of the local Gestapo chief. He and Luise had worked so hard to keep him safe. Neither his Nazi friends, nor his marriage to an Aryan, nor his Catholicism had protected him. Desperate to keep out of the regime's crosshairs, in the end he was simply another one of its Jewish victims.

The Reichenau camp carried on, although later in 1943 its purpose changed. By September, Italy had been invaded by the Allies and was on the verge of falling – indeed, changing sides – and German troops had occupied South Tyrol. Reichenau then became a transit camp for Italian Jews, political prisoners and other opponents of the Third Reich – a first stop, often *en route* to the death camps in the east.

Wapping, London, 2019

I am holding the small, rectangular blue envelope addressed to Siegfried Salzer, which I found in my father's stamp collection. I am curious about the address. It reads, 'Wien 2, Haasgasse 8/13'.

I later visit the address and find it is in the heart of Leopoldstadt, the Jewish quarter of Vienna. I am puzzled as to why Siegfried, Martha and Sofie have moved there.

Then it dawns on me. It was in 1941 that the Nazi authorities ordered Vienna's remaining Jewish residents to be crammed into *Sammelwohnungen*, 'collection flats'.

It was not a permanent arrangement. The flats were a staging post for their occupants' ultimate destination: the camps. Haasgasse 8/13 was one of these flats; they were usually grossly overcrowded with limited cooking and washing facilities.

I look at the envelope more closely and see that someone has written on the front 'return to sender' with the date, '28/8', and on the back, faintly in pencil, *Empf. abgewandert Polen* – 'Recipient has emigrated to Poland.'

It is one of the most chilling euphemisms that the Nazi state employed. 'Emigrated', with its suggestion of agency and choice and positivity, of a flowering of a new life somewhere else. Instead, this sad little blue envelope holds in its four corners the last traces of Sofie, Siegfried and Martha in Vienna.

Siegfried Salzer did not get to open his blue letter enclosing the latest bill from Herman Schneeweiss. I found out that it missed him by one day. Instead, for more than 75 years it remained unopened, buried in Kurt's carrier bags of stamps. I have no idea how it got there.

From the Czech database of Holocaust victims, I discovered that Sofie, Martha and Siegfried were deported from Vienna on 27 August 1942 with Transport No. 38. Their destination was the Theresienstadt Ghetto, in Northern Bohemia (now the Czech Republic) just near the small fortress in which Gavrilo Princip was incarcerated and later died, after assassinating Archduke Franz Ferdinand and his wife Sophie.

I spent a long time imagining what those last days in Vienna must have been like in the stifling heat of August, the three of them confined to one room, possibly crammed in with strangers, and fearful of what the future might hold. Martha's diary includes a short entry for Summer 1942, and a letter she wrote the day before their forced evacuation. Her voice is clear and brave. I was struck by the depth of her love for her family and the lack of recrimination; she was fully aware of the danger the three of them were in:

> With giant steps we appear to be rushing towards the abyss into which we shall fall. Feeling as if my heart were caught in a vice, I have just one wish, that is to use that very brief span of time that I presumably have left to let all the love flow out.

Martha then sent her diary for safekeeping to her cousin Lilli, Eduard's wife, now in New York. To read her covering letter was unbearably painful:

> My darling Liliechen,
>
> Unexpectedly today we received the order for departure tomorrow morning, although it had been intended only for the coming month. Imagine what that means and in view of Mammerle's [Sofie's] deplorable state of health. But I prefer to take her along rather than abandon her here, and my very dear, cherished, generous mother prefers to be together with us even though she fears the journey. I am writing this in bed, what will our next resting place be? But supposedly Theresienstadt, where we are going, is relatively bearable, and supposedly people are allowed to go about freely in the town . . .
>
> I would have liked to record the recent past in this journal, although all feelings have been dismal.
>
> I know, you have thought about us with anxiety and sadness, but no sign of your love has reached us. Like a miner

buried alive, I have been sending out signals. Were they not heard, not understood, unanswered?

I am sending you old journal notes. I place them in your hands, my dearest Lilli, since they are not intended for my children. After all, they illuminate only a very brief portion of my life, plunging me into the deepest of grief as a result of the loss of my father and brother, and tell nothing about the happiness I received from the children in their tender youth, my best years of life, the memory of which continues to resound in me. [These events] occurred before that time when their development and unique characteristics, their gifts of intellect and heart moved me and filled me with pride.

My darling Lilli, I must close. An immeasurably difficult day is ahead of me. It will call for strength and composure and a great deal of work, with which I must begin in the early dawn if I want to manage it at all. I have not yet given up all hope to be able to survive this difficult time. But if that which will be inflicted on us on the coming day should prove to be unbearable, I have the means to bring about a painless end. When you see how cruel a natural end can be and mostly is, the freely chosen one does not frighten. But it must be really physically unbearable before I would choose to make use of this means.

So stay well my dearest beloved Liliechen, be happy in the midst of your loved ones, to whom I send my most heartfelt greetings especially to Trudinderl. Embracing you full of faithful love, I remain, your Martha.

After the overcrowding in the Haasgasse, I can well imagine Martha pinning her hopes on better conditions in Theresienstadt. Established in late 1941, Theresienstadt was the poster child of Nazi camps, portrayed as the model ghetto, a place of well-ordered life. Those Jews sent there in 1942 were often the elderly and well-to-do, and included notable figures in the Jewish community.

The veneer of respectability hid the reality of a concentration camp where death was meted out, if not through gas chambers, then through disease, malnutrition, maltreatment and overcrowding; especially in the late summer of 1942, shortly after Sofie, Martha and Siegfried arrived, when the number of inhabitants peaked at nearly 60,000. Thousands died each month through deliberate neglect. But Theresienstadt was also, for many, a temporary camp. Thousands more died later when they were shipped onwards to places with names about which there could be no ambiguity, like Auschwitz.

My great-grandmother, in her eighties, fell victim almost immediately. Her death on 4 September 1942, only days after arriving, was put down to pneumonia, according to the certificate. I am struck by the irony that Sofie ended up back where she began, in Bohemia. She left Bohemia voluntarily as a young bride, for a new life and new opportunities; she was dragged back as an octogenarian on a train of deportees. Eleven days later, on 15 September, Siegfried's death followed, attributed to a bowel infection. I found both these death certificates in Theresienstadt's online archives. In under two weeks, Martha had lost her mother and her husband. She had to face the world alone and I wondered whether she still had with her the 'means to bring about a painless end'.

During the war, neither the Schindlers in England nor Martha's children Erwin and Marguerite in the United States had any news about Sofie, Martha and Siegfried. I've imagined Kurt sitting anxiously in London, worrying that he had not managed to fulfil Martha's request for help. In my father's papers I found a letter from Erwin, dated 8 June 1946. The family were trying to piece together what had happened. Erwin wrote that he had tracked down the doctor who had worked at Theresienstadt, and been told by him that Siegfried and Sofie had both died there. Erwin had also spoken to another witness, who had seen his mother in Auschwitz.

The records I dug out showed that Martha was dispatched to Auschwitz on 16 May 1944. Her departure – a month before an inspection by the Red Cross in June 1944 – was part of a hasty programme to reduce numbers in the Theresienstadt camp in order to make it presentable as a spa town for elderly Jews, where they could live out their lives in peace. Buildings were painted, gardens planted, and cinemas and cafés opened. The Red Cross inspectors were taken in by this hoax – according to the Holocaust Memorial Museum in Washington – partly because they had expected to see ghetto conditions like those in occupied Poland, with people starving in the streets.

Erwin wrote in his 1946 letter that while he had no definitive proof, he was forced to conclude that his mother was gassed in Auschwitz. Perhaps by that point, she no longer had the means to bring about her own death, or despite everything she knew and had experienced, she had clung onto the hope that she might survive 'these difficult times'.

In the death camp there were no neat death certificates; dying there was a mass, anonymous affair. Despite all the research done on Auschwitz and the Holocaust since then, I was unable to improve on Erwin's findings and give this kind, talented woman the dignity of an exact date of death.

Innsbruck, Austria, 2019

At Innsbruck's main cemetery I can find no trace of Egon Dubsky's grave. I assumed that after his execution his body would have been returned to Luise for burial, but although both his parents' graves are here in the Jewish cemetery, there is nothing for Egon. I track down the cemetery administrator and he types Egon's name into his database. Egon was not in the Catholic cemetery either. Puzzled, I conclude that he must have been buried at the Reichenau camp.

The site of the camp is a forty-minute walk from the railway station. I set out with my husband Jeremy on a hot summer's day. There is no signposting for it until you get to the corner of its street. Nearby is the Langer Weg, a busy main road. Jeremy spots a swastika daubed on the pavement here. Someone has tried unsuccessfully to scrub it off the cement, but it is still clearly visible. We are both unsettled.

The site is oddly industrial. The land where it once stood lies behind locked gates and is now used by the City of Innsbruck as a car pound; there is also a furniture manufacturer there. The only clue to the former use of this site sits behind a pretty, well-kept flower bed. It is a large, rectangular stone plaque erected in 1972. I have to read the words on it several times, but they still make no sense:

> *Here stood in the years 1941–1945 the Gestapo collection camp Reichenau, in which patriots from all of the countries which had been occupied by the Nazis were imprisoned and tortured. Many of them found their death here.*

'Patriots?' Who were these patriots? Surely you choose to be a patriot, but by definition you do not choose to be a forced labourer, a Jew, or homosexual or mentally ill. Why were those who commissioned this memorial so coy about the real reasons these inmates were imprisoned and tortured here? Why are there no names of the 200-odd people who died here? The 1972 memorial said more about the time of denial in which it was erected than about what actually happened here.

From Breit's book, I learn that there were, in fact, three camps here, taking up a space larger than two football fields. They operated from the end of 1941 until 1945 and were hidden in plain sight. Reichenau lay close to a well-known tavern, the 'Sandwirt', and it is impossible that people were unaware of its existence at the time. Yet when I ask my Innsbruck friends, few have heard of the camp, and none of them have ever been to see the site. It is a forgotten corner of Innsbruck's history.

I find this especially strange because, in its last days, Reichenau was an overnight stop for 139 celebrity prisoners. As voices (including Hofer's) whispered in Hitler's ear, in April 1945, that he could still hold the Tyrol as a mountain redoubt and carry on the fight from there, these high-value prisoners of seventeen different nationalities were bussed into Innsbruck. They might have proved to be useful hostages, who could be traded against concessions from the Allies.

Their numbers included the pre-*Anschluss* Chancellor Kurt Schuschnigg and his wife Vera, the former French Prime Minister (and President) Léon Blum and his wife Jeanne, Prince Xavier of Bourbon-Parma, and a dozen or so members of the family of Claus Schenk, Graf von Stauffenberg, the man whose briefcase full of explosives had nearly assassinated Hitler on 20 July 1944. The last had been rounded up under the Nazi principle of collective family guilt. There were also thirteen members of the British army.

These VIPs were then moved to a hotel in the South Tyrol, from where – after a tense few days in May 1945 during which they had no idea whether they would be shot by their nervous, trigger-happy guards or liberated – they were eventually handed over to American forces.

Reichenau's sparse and evasive memorial makes me angry. I ask historians in Innsbruck whether something, anything can be done to make it better. Everyone I speak to agrees it is inadequate, but no one seems to have a clear idea how to go about improving it. This is not a priority for anyone. I feel that I am being fobbed off.

While the Reichenau camp may be largely forgotten, I become determined that Egon, Martha, Siegfried and Sofie should not be allowed to slip through the cracks. I know that I need to find a way to ensure they do not disappear.

Most of all, though, I think of those selfless letters that Sofie and Martha exchanged in 1939 with Kurt, their grandson and nephew; an emotional bond maintained across generations and across borders. And I contemplate the fears and worry that Kurt must have felt when he continued to write to them, but received no reply. When Erwin confirmed their fates, in 1946, I wonder about the effect on the 21-year-old Kurt of hearing that his indulgent grandmother and aunt have been murdered.

I now understand why Kurt kept that photograph near his bed of Sofie, sitting on the bench in Igls, and why his voice always betrayed sadness as he explained who she was – but not what happened to her. Did he feel responsible? Did their deaths warp his relationship with the truth and shape his character: so that it no longer mattered whether what he told us was true or not?

When I am back in London, I return to family photographs – the ones given to me by Tom Salzer. There is the formal portrait of the seven of them, taken before the First World War. But there is also a later one, showing a middle-aged Martha, a slight smile on her lips, as she now looks straight out at the camera – and now at me. She wears a simple, black velvet dress, and holds what looks like a dark fur muff. The clothes are understated, unlike the elaborate beaded dress she wore in the earlier portrait. I imagine her choosing the velvet carefully from amongst Siegfried's stock and commissioning a local needlewoman to sew the dress for her.

Martha Salzer

Can you form bonds with those you have never met though the medium of old photographs? I certainly have. In this portrait, Martha has kind, thoughtful eyes. I keep this photograph on my desk in London, and whenever I am daunted by the enormity of the task I have taken on, I look at it.

Having Martha there provides gentle encouragement to tell her story.

20

The Gauleiter's Guest

The skies above Innsbruck, 25 February 1945

Tonight, after two abortive attempts, an Allied plane carries three men from Italy over the Brenner Pass to the mountains above Innsbruck. They are an unlikely trio. One is a German Jew, another is a Dutch Jew, and the third, whose contacts will be vital to the success of their mission, is a deserter from the Austrian army. If they are discovered, they will be shot as spies.

Nearing their drop zone, they parachute down, with their equipment, onto the edge of a 2,913-metre-high glacier. They land in deep, soft snow. The plane passes over them a second time and drops their kit: ski equipment, a radio set, a hand-operated generator, batteries, a Eureka machine for short-range radar, and an 'S Phone'. This last is a radio telephone, which has been specially developed for agents working behind enemy lines so that they can communicate with aircraft and co-ordinate landings. They also have food, tobacco, maps, condoms and pistols, as well as US $3,100 in cash and gold – a sizeable sum.

The three of them manage to locate all the equipment save for one container with two pairs of skis. However, in the darkness they are not exactly sure where they are. They bury some of the equipment so as lighten their load. The Austrian puts on their only pair of skis, while the German and the Dutchman have to walk and crawl in order to make their way downhill, through shoulder-high snow. It is an exhausting trek, but at the end of it there is welcome relief on reaching an alpine hut, the Amberger

Hut. It is closed, given the time of year, but they break in. Here they rest for a few days, before retrieving their buried supplies and equipment.

Then, the three men move down to the next village, Gries, where they pretend to be German soldiers who have got themselves lost. They borrow a sled from a local and proceed down to Längenfeld. After staying the night, they go by truck and train to Innsbruck and from there to the village of Oberperfuss, which will be their base. It is the Austrian deserter's native village, and where his fiancée and her mother also live, whose confidentiality will be vital.

Why are they here? In essence, to gather intelligence to shorten the war – or at least prevent its unnecessary prolongation. Now that battle rages over Italy, and the Nazi Reich is beset on all sides, there is a constant traffic of troops, raw materials and armaments passing through Innsbruck, between Germany and Italy. If the Allies can get good intelligence on this critical route, with a view to knocking it out, it will put enormous pressure on the Germans.

There are other matters that the Allies would like to know more about. Half-buried underground outside Innsbruck is a facility manufacturing the Messerschmitt Me262, the world's first jet-propelled fighter bomber. It has only recently been deployed, and it is one of the new 'wonder weapons' that Hitler boasts to his entourage can yet win the war.

Furthermore, the Allies have seen blueprints and construction plans for an enormous lozenge-shaped Tyrolean fortress area, bolstering reports that Hitler will use the Tyrol as a last, impregnable bastion. This development is a worrying one, suggesting that the Third Reich will fight to the last man. Instrumental in fostering this idea is *Gauleiter* Hofer. Having eliminated the Jews from his *Gau* – the Schindlers, Dubskys and many others have emigrated, are in camps or are dead – he would now like to think he has the *Führer*'s very fate in his hands and he can offer him sanctuary.

And if it all goes wrong, there is always the escape tunnel the *Gauleiter* has built beneath the Villa Schindler. That is, if he gets the chance to use it.

Everything I discovered during my research after my father's death suggested that Franz Hofer was my family's nemesis during the Nazi years – from commandeering their home to forcing the sale of the café to his friend Hiebl, to ensuring that Egon Dubsky lost his business and ultimately his life. *Gauleiter* Hofer's baleful influence spread deep and wide throughout western Austria. Invariably his name turned up in whichever strand of my family's story I followed.

I noticed the careful way in which he operated, as he found ways to align his own interests with that of the Nazi Party, never quite getting his hands dirty but letting his wishes be known. So often, his underlings claimed to be implementing Hofer's agenda, or made excuses that they could not do this or that because Hofer would be furious. It seemed to me that in the Tyrol and Vorarlberg he carved out his own fiefdom, his power ultimately resting on his carefully fostered relationship with the *Führer*.

It was in 2016, in a footnote to an article I was reading about Hofer, where I first discovered a reference to what has been described as 'the most successful spy operation of the entire Second World War'. It was only then that I realised the way in which the small provincial town of Innsbruck, my family's home town, became important to both sides in the final stage of the war.

Innsbruck's strategic position as a centuries-old European crossroads was emphasised by the battle over Italy, but another reason was more intimately connected with Hofer. By late 1944, he was lobbying for the creation of a Tyrolean *Alpenfestung* (Alpine Redoubt) for Hitler. I suspected, on one level, this simply appealed to Hofer's vanity – the idea of playing host to Hitler in a much larger way than he had done hitherto during Hitler's occasional visits to Innsbruck.

Hofer sent a memo with his idea in November 1944, but Hitler's private secretary, Martin Bormann, failed to put it in front of the *Führer* until the following year as he was worried that it might look defeatist. In the meantime, Joseph Goebbels grasped the propaganda value of the idea, 'leaking' blueprints and plans to fool the Allies into thinking that the construction of the fortress was already well under way.

The Allies badly wanted eyes and ears on the ground, and it was this desire that motivated the elaborate piece of espionage called 'Operation Greenup'. Even now, it is a little-known story. It does feature in the Quentin Tarantino action movie *Inglourious Basterds*, though in a highly distorted and fictionalised form. Then I discovered that a Canadian film maker, Min Sook Lee, made a documentary film about Greenup in 2012 – *The Real Inglorious Bastards* – and I contacted her. She sent me the web link to her film and told me that even though she had made it in Innsbruck, the local people had not been particularly interested.

The film was moderately successful at various Jewish Film festivals in the United States, but did not have wide exposure. Seven years later, in 2019, the historian Peter Pirker brought out a book about Greenup, written in German, called *Codename Brooklyn*. I was delighted that the story was finally in circulation, although it was still far from mainstream. For me, Greenup – occurring in my family's home town and involving Hofer – was bound up with both my family's history and that of Innsbruck. It cast light on the way Innsbruck treated this period of its history more generally.

The spies chosen for the operation shared a hatred of the Nazi regime and were in their twenties, but that was about all they had in common. Nevertheless, they became a tight-knit group. Frederick 'Fred' Mayer was a German Jew, who had escaped to the United States as a teenager, and joined the US Army when he turned sixteen. As he put it in Min's documentary, 'It felt like I had my chance to do what I set out to do: kill Nazis.' In December 1942, he was recruited by the recently established Office of Strategic Services, modelled on Britain's MI6, for intelligence training.

He teamed up with a Dutch Jew, Hans Wijnberg. In June 1944, they were shipped across to Algiers, where Allied forces were preparing invasions of southern France. Anxious to see active service, they were eventually transferred to the OSS office in the Italian city of Bari – an office dealing with German and Austrian spy operations.

It was at Bari where they met the pivotal member of their threesome, Franz Weber. He was a disillusioned Wehrmacht officer, who had deserted before being picked up by Italian partisans and handed over to the Americans. Both the Americans and the British were highly interested in the fact that this prisoner of war came from Oberperfuss, knew Innsbruck and its surrounding area, and could provide key local information and contacts. Although Weber had no insights about the Alpine Redoubt, nor about the Messerschmitt factory, he was keen to help where he could.

After Mayer sounded out Weber, to affirm his trustworthiness, the plan for the mission evolved. Its main objective would be to gather intelligence about the railway network and the Messerschmitt factory. Their safety would depend on Franz's local knowledge, and his ability to find accommodation for the other two spies and make some reliable local contacts.

Days after their parachute drop, when the trio had made their way to Oberperfuss, Franz's fiancée Anni was initially furious; the whole village knew Franz was a deserter, and thus risked a firing squad, and she had hoped he was sitting out the war safely in an Italian POW camp. Nevertheless she and her mother Anna, who ran the local guesthouse, the 'Zur Krone', agreed to help. Fred and Franz moved into the attic of an annex of the 'Zur Krone'; Hans was installed, with his radio, in the attic of a neighbouring farmhouse. On 8 March he sent out his first message, which ran:

'All well. Be patient until 13 March.' The OSS had assumed its agents had been captured and shot, as it was eleven days since the drop, so the message brought huge relief.

Franz's role was now essentially over, and he needed to stay hidden lest he be recognised, jeopardising the entire operation – and the lives of his whole family, who risked being killed in retribution. By contrast, it was Fred's role to be out and about, incognito, to learn what he could. Luckily for him, Oberperfuss in wartime contained many more foreigners than previously, some of them seeking refuge from bombing in Innsbruck itself.

In the days and weeks that followed, Fred gathered intelligence, which Hans relayed. The Messerschmitt factory was staffed by around 2,000 locals and an assortment of prisoners-of-war and forced labourers from all over Europe. Several workers lived at the 'Zur Krone', and through them and other means, he learned that part of its production was already shut down, because of shortages of materials.

Franz's family and friends were then able to put together a Wehrmacht officer's uniform and some documents for Fred, so he could take on the role of a soldier wounded by Italian partisans, now convalescing in Innsbruck. Having secured new accommodation in Innsbruck, Fred now infiltrated the local officers' mess and the Nazi drinking spots to learn as much as he could about railway movements. I assume these haunts included the Café Hiebl, especially as it was only five minutes' walk from where he was lodging.

Fred gleaned information about freight and troop movements, as well as the number and type of trains heading for the Brenner Pass from Innsbruck's main railway station. He also collected information on arms dumps and military facilities, along with details of a house south of Berlin, to which Hitler was planning to move. All this was relayed back to Hans via a network of largely female collaborators. It became obvious, from its absence in any conversations heard by Fred, that Hitler's Alpine Redoubt was thus far a myth.

With information from Fred Mayer's reports, on the night of 10 April 1945, thirty-five B-24 bombers and eight Liberators of the US Army Air Force dropped 150 tons of bombs on Innsbruck – the fourth attack on the city. By bombing at night – at Fred's urging – they struck when more trains were gathered at the station: during daylight hours they were shunted to different locations for protection. The aircrews had express instructions to target only the station, though collateral damage nearby included – once again – the ex-Schindler factory and garage at 21 Karmelitergasse. The attack was enough to put the main station out of action, and it seems that 174 prisoners from the Reichenau camp were forced to clear the rubble.[1]

Fred Mayer's next incarnation, improbably, was as a French collaborationist electrician – a role made possible only because of his knowledge of French. He was also able to acquire real identity papers by mingling with some French workers who had fled from Vienna as the Russians advanced on the capital. With these, he was able to gain entry to the Messerschmitt factory itself and report, first-hand, on the shortages of components there.

Two days after the Innsbruck air raid, *Gauleiter* Hofer was in Berlin, itself under siege from the Russians. He was summoned to Hitler's bunker in the Reich's Chancellery, the place where an increasingly agitated *Führer* was see-sawing from wild fantasies about German victory to abject gloom at defeat. Now, at this eleventh hour, he finally authorised Hofer to begin preparations for the *Alpenfestung*, for which Hofer would be given the honorary and grandiose title of 'Reich Defence Commissar of the Alpine Redoubt'.

Meanwhile, Fred and Hans were doing their utmost to bring forward the liberation of the Tyrol. Since 2 April, Hans had been sending messages to the OSS office in Bari, asking for weapons and explosives to be dropped, with which a burgeoning group of local resistance fighters were promising they would be able to secure Innsbruck. But in Bari their handlers were wary and ordered business as usual, unless they received a 'top-notch plan' with full details. In the end, events were taken out of their hands.

With the *Reich* collapsing, numerous different resistance groups and cells were emerging in Austria – some in the army, others in the police and in the civilian population – and Fred saw his task as trying to link up with them and coordinate them: a difficult challenge. For reasons that are not entirely clear, one of these putative groups detonated a bomb on the Maria-Theresien-Strasse during a parade for Hitler's birthday, 20 April 1945. It exploded opposite the Café Hiebl, as photographs testify, and the Maria-Theresien-Strasse in front was strewn with rubble – after which the Austrian red-white-red flag was unfurled and resistance leaflets were distributed.

This precipitate action was a disaster for the spies. The Gestapo arrested eighty police officers, and the network began to unravel as new information led to more arrests. At 11 p.m. that evening, Fred Mayer himself was arrested, as was Franz's sister Eva Weber; another sister, Margarete Kelderer, was given twenty-four hours to say goodbye to her two young children in Oberperfuss. Up in the village, the deeply Catholic inhabitants sat up in an overnight vigil to pray for the safety of Fred and Eva.

What followed for Fred, in the basement of the Gestapo head-quarters at 1 Herrengasse, was interrogation and torture – though it was more problematic than the Gestapo would have liked. Trained to resist interrogation, for four long hours Fred stuck to his cover story and insisted he was a French electrician. At one point, the Gestapo brought in the already bruised and bloodied Robert Moser, one of Fred's helpers and the owner of the radio shop that notionally 'employed' Fred, to say that he had already confessed to Fred being a US spy. Moser did not survive his own interrogation.

Fred was keen to slow things down as much as possible. He knew that Margarete was heading for Oberperfuss to warn the others, and wanted to gain time for Hans and Franz to make their escape. Once he thought enough time had passed, Fred abandoned his French identity, admitting to being an American, but claimed he had arrived in Innsbruck from Switzerland. His two interrogators were augmented by another two, who intensified the beatings. They wondered if he might be Jewish – but his resilience did not correspond to their notions of Jewish weakness, and, since so many Americans were circumcised, especially among the military, a physical examination proved nothing.

The torture became more varied. He was beaten with a whip, but the officer trying to immobilise him sometimes ended up receiving a lashing instead. The Gestapo decided to force Fred into a kneeling position, with his handcuffed hands around his knees; then they stuck the barrel of a rifle under his knees so as to suspend him between two tables. As they beat him, his body swung. They poured soapy water into his mouth and nose. Still, he refused to identify other members of his team.

Throughout Fred's interrogation, arrests continued; so many of them that the Gestapo ran out of space at their headquarters and resorted to using the Reichenau camp instead. Gestapo officers also followed Margarete to Oberperfuss, but the villagers stayed silent – and Hans and Franz were already in a designated safe house outside the village.

Despite themselves, the Gestapo were impressed at Fred's fortitude. With information from another arrestee, they now believed him to be an American colonel, prompting them to interrupt their interrogation to inform *Gauleiter* Hofer. In their eyes, 'Colonel Mayer' suddenly became a potentially useful figure. After all, the American forces were getting ever nearer. Only the most fanatical and delusional Nazis believed that they could outface defeat. The question for Hofer now became, how could he gain the most advantageous terms?

Volders, Innsbruck, 26 April 1945

Six days after his arrest, and showing signs of the torture he had received, the US spy Fred Mayer was invited to take lunch with

Gauleiter Hofer. The venue was Hofer's country residence, the Lachhof, near Volders just outside Innsbruck; it was now safer there for his family than the Villa Schindler.

The spy sat down to eat with the *Gauleiter*, his wife and several other officials. Franz Hofer enquired of his guest as to how he thought the war was going. The American replied that he believed it would be over shortly, and therefore it would be advisable for Hofer to surrender. Hofer was trying to gauge the situation; his eyes were firmly on the future – his own.

Four days previously, on 22 April, Hofer had been in Bolzano. There, he had told Dr Rudolf Rahn, the German ambassador to Mussolini's rump fascist state in North Italy, that 'the war is lost . . . every further battle is useless slaughter, and when the *Führer* comes here, to organise a last stand at the alpine fortress, then I will intern him in a sanatorium.' He voiced his own plan: the South Tyrol should remain in Austrian hands, thereby right-ing the historic wrong done to Austria after the First World War, when it was forfeited to Italy. And he himself should be installed as Governor of North and South Tyrol.

Now there was an unexpected player in the drama: the man before him. The *Gauleiter* quizzed his guest. Would the Allies be interested in making common cause with the Germans against the communist partisans in Yugoslavia? Shrewdly, and aware of the unfolding tensions between the Western Allies and the Soviet Union, he had calculated that the best way to advance his own agenda was by offering to join forces with the Americans to help them combat communists.

Fred demurred, responding that the Allies wanted an end to the war, and anyway Hitler was not known for abiding by treaties that he signed. They discussed whether Hofer would surrender the Tyrol to the Allies. Hofer was undecided – he was still trying to work out what scenario would be of best advantage to him. But events moved fast.

Eight days after Fred Mayer's arrest, on 28 April 1945, *Gauleiter* Hofer received the order from Hitler to build the *Alpenfesten*. It demonstrated the sheer delusion of the collapsing *Reich*. Two days later, on 30 April, Hitler committed suicide in his Berlin bunker. That day, before hearing this news, Hofer was still defiant – in public at least – calling on all Tyroleans to defend the Tyrol. By 2 May, his instructions were more nuanced: 'Peace in honour, freedom and justice is only possible if, until peace is achieved, we keep our weapons in our hands and that in all unoccupied areas there is total peace and order.'

It was not quite a call to surrender, but his mealy-mouthed formula was clearly not a call to fight to the last.

Hofer's discussions with Fred Mayer continued. The exact dates of them are unclear from the OSS debriefing report, but what does emerge is that Hofer's conversion to a peaceful surrender hinged on Fred's promises, as an officer, to offer Hofer house arrest, and that Hofer and his staff would be treated respectfully as officers when the Americans arrived. In reality, Fred had no authority to make such promises; it was pure bluff. The *Gauleiter* then asked Fred to go and meet the approaching Americans in order to convey this arrangement.

On 3 May, American forces crossed the Italian border into Austria. Fred picked up Hans from Oberperfuss, they donned their US uniforms and returned to Innsbruck, where they installed Hofer and other senior Nazis in Hofer's country house, in order to keep them safe from revenge-seeking resistance fighters. Leaving Hans in charge of the compliant Nazi prisoners, Fred attached a white flag to his car and drove out to meet the approaching Americans, who were duly astonished to see this battered young compatriot declare that he had all the senior Nazis under lock and key.

Innsbruck was handed over with barely a shot being fired. Rather, to their surprise, the Americans were showered with flowers and offered cognac as they arrived. One soldier commented that the population was behaving towards them more as if the troops were liberators than conquerors. Suddenly, it was red-white-red Austrian flags and red and white Tyrolean flags appearing everywhere, rather than the swastikas of the last seven years. The Nazi administration evaporated. Two of the Gestapo officers who interrogated Fred hastily cobbled together false identities and fled.

Dyno Lowenstein, the three spies' commanding officer, arrived in Oberperfuss and congratulated his young team, who had achieved more than he could possibly have imagined. Fred went on to praise the women of Oberperfuss who looked after them; in his view, 'the only people one could really trust were the women, they were as obstinate as iron.' Shortly afterwards, Franz married one of these iron maidens, his fiancée Anni. He wore a suit made out of cloth given to him by the OSS; she wore a wedding dress made from the parachutes the spies had used, which Franz had retrieved from their hiding place under the snows of the glacier.

Fred Mayer, Hans Wijnberg, Franz Weber with
two of their helpers from Oberperfuss

Innsbruck, Austria, 2019

Min has put me in touch with Fred Mayer's daughter, who confirms that during his life, Fred had a fair amount of recognition in the United States for his exploits in the Tyrol. I ask some of my Austrian friends whether they have heard of him. None of them has. One friend shrugs his shoulders sadly and explains that as one of the three agents was a deserter from the German army, I could hardly expect most people to celebrate these spies.

It confirms to me that in Austria, perhaps more than in many other countries, memory, truth and responsibility have been contentious. I wonder how many of those Innsbruckers cheering the arriving Americans in 1945 also rapturously welcomed the *Anschluss* seven years earlier. When putting together their account of the episode, Hans and Fred wrote that:

> . . . in the first few years of the war, the Tyroleans were generally pro-Nazi as they profited from this and the Nazi army was victorious. The support for the Nazi regime only hesitantly reduced, and until the last weeks of the war there was practically no resistance movement.

Almost as soon as the Nazi administration fell, the rewriting of the recent past began. In the power vacuum, Hofer's successor – now as *Landeshauptmann* (Country Governor) of the Tyrol rather than *Gauleiter* – was Karl Gruber, an Austrian electrical engineer. His credentials for the post were unusual, for he had spent the war working in a Berlin factory, until his return to take over the leadership of the disparate elements of the resistance.

Later, he became Austria's foreign minister and did everything he could to ensure that Austria was seen not as a willing collaborator, but as the Nazis' first victim. He also kicked into the long grass the claims by Austrian Jews to reparations and damages payments. They were simply not a priority for him.

As for the Nazis, later in 1945 the CIA captured Walter Güttner, the Gestapo officer who had been primarily responsible for Fred's torture. Fred was offered the opportunity to visit him in his cell. Güttner, too, had been beaten.

According to Fred (in Min's later film), Güttner told him, 'Do anything you want with me, but please don't hurt my family.'

Fred replied, 'Who do you think we are? Nazis?'

Güttner, though, had no need to fear. Although he was primarily responsible for Moser's death too, he did not face punishment. According to the judge, Güttner was only carrying out orders, and Fred Mayer was, after all, an enemy who contributed to the bombing of Innsbruck.

Franz Hofer was interrogated by the Seventh Army in Augsburg, Germany. The former *Gauleiter* was keen to emphasise how helpful he had been in shortening the war and demanded that he be given the legal immunity that he considered was promised to him by Fred Mayer. The Americans could not identify any specific crimes committed by Hofer against US citizens. The question then arose as to whether Hofer should be dealt with by the post-war Austrian authorities or by the German ones.

Hofer would exploit this jurisdictional confusion to his own advantage and he became a master of evasion; as my family would discover only too well.

Part Six

21

Old Labels, New Liquor

Innsbruck, Austria, 5 May 1945

Hostilities in the Tyrol are officially over. On this day, American forces move in to make use of the ex-*Gauleiter*'s residence at the Villa Schindler: it remains one of the nicest houses in town, undamaged by Allied bombs. Three days later, the Wehrmacht surrenders unconditionally at a signing ceremony in Berlin. A few hours before that event, a Provisional Government in Austria – in existence for less than two weeks in Vienna – passes a Prohibition Act making the Nazi Party illegal, as it was in 1933.

Will it be enough to overturn cultural and political belief systems so carefully cultivated by the Nazis over the previous twelve years?

A game of musical chairs ensues, as it seems the whole world is once more on the move. Those who have sat in positions of power for years, like Franz Hofer, and those who have grown rich on Nazi Party connections, like Franz Hiebl, are under arrest, in detention or on the run; some try to get abroad. Those who fled the Nazis, like the Schindlers, contemplate their futures and whether they dare return to reclaim what was theirs. In some places, there is barely anyone left to return. As many as 65,000 Austrian Jews – including my great-grandmother Sofie, my great-aunt Martha and great-uncle Siegfried, and my cousin Egon – have perished.

Everywhere now, there are men and women in uniform, in armies of occupation, or heading home for demobilisation. Soviet troops occupy Eastern Austria and will remain there for another decade. The last months of the war in Europe have not solely been about defeating Germany. They have also been about jockeying for territory between the Western Allies and the Soviet Union. Austria is split between them, its future uncertain.

Wherever they can do so, German and Austrian troops have tried to go west, to surrender to the Americans and British rather than the Russians. In later years, my father, who feared communists almost more than Nazis, will recall how Austrians wondered whether they would ever be able to get the Russians to leave their capital.

Across much of the old Reich a sullen, hungry population begins to count the cost of its embrace of the Nazi Party. Revelations about the death camps prompt shame and widespread denial and disbelief. But people find it easier to see themselves as casualties of a disastrous war, who have suffered bombing, starvation and, in some cases, systematic rape, murder and pillaging by Soviet troops. The framed portraits of the *Führer*, which were hung in so many sitting rooms, are quietly put away in attics, alongside old uniforms, helmets and medals; some will re-emerge decades later in flea markets and on specialist websites.

Compared to the horrors elsewhere, the war's end in the Tyrol is relatively civilised. By 5 May, Franz Hofer has already negotiated his own surrender under what he hopes will be gentlemanly terms, befitting his status. He asserts that Fred Mayer has promised him a genteel house arrest; it is not quite that. In a reversal of fortunes, for months to come Hofer will be held – like many other Nazis whose fates are to be decided – in the Dachau concentration camp, over the border in Bavaria.

Today also, Franz Hiebl abandons the café and tries to flee. Twelve days later, he is arrested by the Americans. His destination, for the time being, is also Dachau. Both are held under considerably better conditions than the previous inmates endured.

As a new Austrian republic takes shape, the battered civil and criminal justice systems have to recalibrate. What was so recently lawful is now unlawful. What was unlawful is lawful. What had been 'purchased' by Aryan families from fleeing and dead Jews is now under threat.

In London and in Innsbruck, Hugo Schindler and Luise Dubsky begin to look for justice.

In 1945, ten years of Allied occupation began in Austria, during which time the country was divided into British, French, US and Russian zones; and Vienna – like Berlin – was itself divided between the four powers. The Tyrol and Vorarlberg were in the French zone. Yet very quickly too, a broad-based Second Austrian Republican government was formed. 'We were Hitler's first victim,' became the mantra. It was a perspective accepted by the Allies – as a means to Austria achieving national unity and moving on. After all, the argument went, Austrian sovereignty had ceased to exist with the *Anschluss*, so responsibility for wrongs done during the Nazi period could not be laid at the door of post-war Austria.

This urge to amputate the Nazi era created distinct challenges for Austria's dispossessed and dispersed Jews, as I discovered from wading through the post-war court files in the Innsbruck County Archives. From London, Hugo and his nephew Peter re-engaged their pre-war lawyer in Austria, Dr Albin Steinbrecher, to launch restitution claims for the villa and its garden along with the Schindler businesses, including the café.

These claims were under way by 1947. However, such restitution proceedings were, in many Austrians' eyes, unwelcome reminders of the Nazi era and obstructions to the country's acceleration away from its recent past. They dominated relations between Jewish and non-Jewish communities for decades, their momentum sapped by the lack of political will. As I found, it was not uncommon for cases to last ten or even fifteen years – by which time the parties were dead, exhausted or had run out of funds to litigate.

I learned from one historian in Innsbruck that there were only three judges without Nazi connections who were able to hear the cases, and so delays were endemic. These judges had a difficult job, and had to consider conflicting arguments. If they restituted a business in its entirety, it might leave Aryan owners who had invested large sums in it (and paid for bomb-damage repairs) out of pocket. In fact, the law allowed judges to refuse restitution altogether in cases where the Aryan owner had invested substantial sums or had significantly changed the nature of the business.

Many Jews did not get their property back at all. Sometimes cases were settled out of court, with the Aryan owners retaining possession, but topping up the derisory payments made at the time of the forced sales. Where restitution was ordered, the Jewish family then had to repay the sums that they may, or may not, have received from the original forced sale. It would be another half-century before the Austrian government created a National Fund for victims of National Socialism, following considerable public pressure.

Restitution proceedings reinvigorated strains of antisemitism. For some, these claims betrayed Jewish greed and constituted an unpatriotic burden on the new Austrian Republic, when really blame should have been laid at the door of Germany. The cases ground on, getting bogged down in sometimes bizarre counter-claims. I was astonished to discover that even Nazis on the run from the authorities were able, simultaneously, to have their lawyers argue their counter-claims in the courts.

In Innsbruck in 1946, one of the clear victims of the war, the widowed Luise Dubsky, was already experiencing the system's vicissitudes. She applied for a war victim pass, entitling her to a small pension and perks such as cigarettes and alcohol. Luise set out everything that had happened to her and Egon, but the authorities were sceptical of her claims and unsympathetic about the choices she had been forced to make.

Like so many Aryans married to Jews, Luise had launched – but never completed – a divorce petition; it had seemed the best way of saving the business. She then thought better of it and made it clear she wanted Egon back when he returned from the sanatorium. Now, referring to it, the judge caustically wrote on her file: 'During the NS [Nazi] time, she wanted rid of the Jew. Today she wants to obtain an advantage out of his death!!'

The judge ordered an investigation. In examining the Dubskys' background, the investigator noted that Luise was always cited as an opponent of the Nazis, both before and after 1938, in contrast to her husband's considerable involvement with the illegal Nazi Party before the *Anschluss*. However, those questioned commented that Egon was not seen as *vollwertig*, having 'full mental capacity'. Egon may not have understood what he was doing. It was, the investigator noted, difficult to gather information, and witnesses were very reticent.

On 15 June 1946, though, the tables were turned on Franz Gutmann, who had bought the Dubsky business. The state prosecutor thought the case had enormous public interest: Gutmann was perceived to be someone who had personally profited greatly from the Nazi regime, but was now trying to hide his past. For the prosecution case, Luise submitted a long statement, in which she described parties in Gutmann's cellar, attended by *Gauleiter* Hofer and other senior Nazis. She noted that Gutmann also supplied large amounts of wine to senior Nazis, including to those who were present when Egon was shot. She did not say it, but she implied a link between the wine supplies and the reasons for Egon's death.

Gutmann tried to resist. He argued that restitution was entirely inappropriate given Egon's previous attempts to curry favour with the Nazis; but the judgement found this irrelevant to the restitution process. According to the judge, while Egon's dalliance with the Nazis may have been tasteless or a character flaw, it hardly benefited either Egon or Luise.

Egon's murderer, Werner Hilliges, was now a wanted man. The Gestapo chief was arrested in 1946 and tried by the French military authorities in 1948 for this crime. He was sentenced to life imprisonment with hard labour. By the mid-1950s, however, the thirst for justice had apparently been slaked, and to my enormous surprise, Hilliges received a presidential pardon in December 1955. One month later, he committed suicide.

Innsbruck, Summer 2019

I have walked off the beaten track to a forgotten corner of the city, which does not see many tourists, nor indeed much footfall generally, despite being only a short distance from the centre of town. The road I stand in is named, very aptly, Heiliggeiststrasse: Holy Spirit Street. I am looking up towards where Leopold Dubsky's old shop would have been, and I am amazed to find that it is still here – or a version of it.

Of course, this place no longer has the Dubsky name over the door, but nevertheless, it is a distillery and it still sells brandy and *Schnapps*. The exterior is painted dark red, and the shop window displays fruit presses, bottles and a few wooden crates, cultivating a shabby-chic look. I peer in through the door. Inside it looks much like a traditional pharmacy, with bottles of clear alcohol on polished dark-wood shelves.

I try the door and find it locked. The shop is closed for lunch, but a woman at the back interrupts her sandwich-eating to open up for me. I suspect I am her one and only customer of the day and that she is anxious not to miss me. I go inside and explain that my great-great-uncle Leopold founded the business.

She looks slightly bemused, confessing that she knows little of the history; but when she catches my name, she points to a dusty bottle of vanilla liquor on a shelf. The glass relic has an original 'S. Schindler' label. This bottle, watching over the shop, must be more than eighty years old. I fancy it might be the only survivor in the Tyrol of all the thousands of bottles of alcohol produced by the Schindlers. I wonder who was responsible for saving it, and why they did so. I ask whether I can see the cellar and distillery – but am told they are not open to the public.

The name above the old Dubksy shop in 2019 was 'Lauda' – and it rang bells. This was a name I'd seen among my father's papers, printed in slanted black type over the white 'S. Schindler' name on a beautiful red, gold and black label for *Himbeergeist*, raspberry liquor. The image of the raspberries was as detailed as any plate from a nature book, the veins in the leaves and the tiny thorns on the branches forming a backdrop to the luscious raspberries, which hung temptingly over the lettering.

Yet I was puzzled why the Lauda name was on the labels, a partial typographical erasure of my family name. Kurt had spoken in dark terms about the Lauda family, but never explained who they were. Or maybe again, I did not listen. It was only when I was in the Archives in Innsbruck that I pieced the story together.

The Lauda family had moved to Innsbruck from South Tyrol during the Nazi period, and *Gauleiter* Hofer had insisted on a sale to the Laudas of the nearby Hermann family distillery business, around the corner from the Dubsky shop on the Leopoldstrasse. The Hermanns were forced to move to Vienna. From there, they were transported to the Lodz Ghetto in Poland in 1941, from whence they never returned. It was a fate that could so easily have been Hugo and Erich's.

After winning back the Dubsky business from Franz Gutmann after the war, Luise came to an arrangement with the Laudas, leasing to them the Heiliggeiststrasse distillery, from which they carried on trading. It was clearly a pragmatic arrangement for Luise, who neither had the capital nor the desire, or skill, to run a distillery herself. In a post-war act of thrift, the Laudas rescued and repurposed the Schindler labels they had found in the Dubsky cellar.

Luise stayed on, though, living in the flat above the shop, as she had done during the Nazi period. She lived there until her death in 1964; and after Egon, she never remarried.

Dachau detention camp, Bavaria, Occupied Germany, 1948

Franz Hofer, the former *Gauleiter*, is still a prisoner, awaiting his fate in the Dachau camp complex, which now lies in the US-controlled zone of Occupied Germany. From London, Hugo Schindler and his nephew Peter have launched restitution proceedings against both him and the Sparkasse bank to reclaim the Villa Schindler and its garden. More seriously, Hofer faces charges of war crimes. It is hardly surprising, given his immense influence in western Austria and his direct relationship with Hitler.

The Innsbruck prosecutor has issued an arrest warrant against Hofer for high treason and for offences under the war crimes laws, and he requests Hofer's extradition from Germany. Hofer is specifically accused of responsibility for the local murders on *Kristallnacht* and the exile of Jews from the Tyrol. If convicted, he will face a penalty of anything between ten years' imprisonment and death.

The Americans agree to extradite Hofer to Austria, but he is determined to fight his corner. In one statement, Hofer claims he is innocent of any crimes and that the Austrians cannot prosecute him, because the Americans have decided not to do so. This is a very poor legal argument indeed; he is grasping at straws. But just as it looks as if Hofer will be extradited, he slips through the fingers of his captors.

On 22 October 1948, Hofer escapes. He is in transit from Dachau to a Munich court hearing, and it is unclear what happens. Has he simply got lucky with an inattentive guard, or has an old Nazi comrade sprung him from a prison van? Maybe his escape was enabled by the CIA or MI6 – many Nazis have been proffering their services to the Americans in the newly emerging struggle against the shared enemy of communism. The CIA and MI6 are possibly also reluctant to have the details of their recent spy operations come out in court. The historian Peter Pirker will take this last view, but the mystery is never resolved.

Hofer is not the only Dachau escapee. In the course of being transferred from Dachau to Regensburg camp, Franz Hiebl, too, has already managed to evade his guards. The County Court in Innsbruck has started criminal proceedings against him for war crimes, but in 1948 these are suspended. The authorities profess not to know where he is, and all proceedings to seize Hiebl's assets run into the sand. It does not seem to occur to them to try and reverse Hiebl's wartime transfer of his house to his wife and children.

In 1949, the Munich court convicts the absentee Hofer to ten years in a work camp. Since no one appears to know where he is, either, he does not actually serve this time. Somewhere, he remains at liberty.

The footsoldiers of *Kristallnacht* are not as lucky as the man at the top who gave the orders. Witness statements have already proved crucial, in 1947, in gaining convictions for the men who beat up Hugo Schindler in November 1938. Josef Ebner, August Hörhager and Hans Ruedl are given sentences of between fourteen months and two years; Ebner and Hörhager also have their assets confiscated. Hochrainer, the man who passed on the orders, and who participated in five other attacks that night, has also been sentenced to two years' imprisonment and seizure of his assets. No charges are pressed against the other men in the group who converged on Hugo's apartment, as they did not touch him.

In Innsbruck, Bertha Hiebl – Franz's wife – claims she is now destitute, responsible for two small boys, and has no idea whether her husband is alive or whether he will ever return to Austria. As Kurt remembers it, Hugo sends her some money to tide her over. The dispossessed Jew subsidises the Nazi wife.

In the event, as I discovered, the proceedings to reclaim the Café Schindler were speedier than many other restitution cases. In 1949, it was once more the property of my family. It was quite a different story as regards Hugo and Edith's villa and the adjoining land inherited by Peter and his mother Grete.

The application, in Hugo and Peter's names, was made in January 1947 and then submitted by the lawyer Steinbrecher. Since Hugo was still living in London, I assumed that he felt he could not move back until he had secured the return of his assets. But the case was more complicated than either Hugo or his lawyer anticipated.

At the Innsbruck County Archives, I pored over the application, presented to the court in 1948, which set out the background to what had happened in 1938. The document was on yellowed paper, with beautiful green, blue and purple eagle stamps on it to show that the relevant court fee of 48 Schillings had been paid. It was a relief to see the pre-1938 Austrian currency back and the re-emergence of the Tyrolean eagle after the unremitting piles of swastika-emblazoned documents I had slogged through.

In the document, Steinbrecher explained that he was Peter and Hugo's representative to pursue claims against Franz Hofer, who was described, euphemistically, as 'the ex-*Gauleiter* of Tyrol and Vorarlberg of presently unknown address', with the Sparkasse bank as the second defendant.

In addition to the demand for the return of the villa and adjoining garden, damages were also claimed for the use of their respective properties and garden, from the day that Hofer moved in (15 July 1938) until the day the US forces took over the villa and garden (5 May 1945), as well as costs. In respect of the Sparkasse, Steinbrecher claimed that the bank was jointly liable for damages, as it had become the dishonest owner of the properties that it sold on to Hofer.

When I read the submissions made by Steinbrecher and Hugo, I concluded that of all the complex post-war restitution cases, this one felt like an open-and-shut case; the villa and garden would surely be turned over quickly to their rightful owners. As I turned the remaining pages in the court file, though, I was astonished to find another thick wad of correspondence, including a defence submission from Hofer himself, dated 23 February 1948.

How is it that a man in Dachau at the time, battling extradition to Austria, was able to give detailed instructions to his court-appointed lawyer? As a lawyer myself, I fully understand and subscribe to the concept that all accused parties are entitled to a defence in their *criminal* cases. However, it seemed extraordinary that Hofer was both allowed, and took the trouble, to submit a statement to the Innsbruck court in a civil restitution case, let alone one where the sale had been forced through on pain of Hugo being sent to a camp.

Hofer claimed that the idea of buying the villa from the Sparkasse only came up in 1939, when it needed repairs. He asserted that if he had intended to buy the villa from the outset, then he would not have needed to enter into a rental agreement. This, I could see, was Hofer's attempt to camouflage the real reason for using the Sparkasse as intermediary – his distaste at buying directly from two Jews.

Hofer further argued that with Hugo no longer in the Tyrol, he had acted for the sake of the property. He failed to mention his own role in driving Hugo and Erich out of the Tyrol. He suggested his wife and mother as witnesses to support his testimony, as well as the former Minister for the Interior, Wölke, although he too was a fugitive from justice.

Hofer vehemently denied that he blackmailed Hugo and Erich into selling the property. He asserted that Hugo's arrest and the seizure of his property occurred at a time when Hofer was not even in the Tyrol. He did concede that someone in the Nazi Party might have given his lawyer Ulm direction to acquire the house, for the party, but said it was nothing to do with him.

If he had wanted to buy it, why would he have entered into a rental contract with the Sparkasse and applied for a rental allowance from the Ministry of the Interior? He insisted the Sparkasse would have lent him the money to buy, if he had wanted to do so immediately. Indeed, Hofer's audacity stretched to claiming to know nothing whatsoever about the negotiations between the Sparkasse and Hugo and Erich.

The restitution case lacked credibility, Hofer argued. He did not believe that Ulm would have engaged in the crime of black-mail, and the situation would have allowed the property to be expropriated anyway. He also maintained that Hugo did not object to the sale, only to the low price that was on offer; and that Ulm would surely not have broken the law and engaged in black-mail simply about a price difference that was being paid by the Sparkasse and not by him personally – in any event, the difference of 20,000 Reichsmarks was neither here nor there.

Hofer's 'killer point' was that he did not believe Ulm threatened Hugo with dispatch to a concentration camp, demonstrated by the fact that Hugo refused the contract: 'It is generally the case and one's experience that people do not put their freedom and life at risk over a relatively small price difference.'

Pointing out that he had made certain changes, such as laying two floors and replacing blinds, Hofer claimed it was now *he* who should be compensated. He insisted that he was entitled to assume Hugo and Erich had received all the money paid for the villa – even though he would have known it went into a frozen account. To add insult to injury, Hofer complained that although the villa looked handsome from the outside, it was impracticable on the inside, as it had relatively few usable rooms. While he admitted that he had no documents to support his position, he directed the court to Austria's Ministry of Finance and tax office.

I turned to the next document in the file and found a defence from the Sparkasse. It contradicted most of Hofer's statement. The Sparkasse held that it was only the straw man in the arrangement, that from the beginning Hofer was to be the ultimate purchaser but he did not want to appear to be the *first* purchaser; that Ulm told them the price and the conditions of sale were already set, and that the Sparkasse had nothing to worry about in that regard.

The Sparkasse was, it said, obliged to confirm that it would sell the villa on to Hofer in whatever timescale Hofer determined, and at the same price for which the Sparkasse had purchased it. Before buying it, Hofer would use the villa and pay rent by way of adding interest to the capital spent by the Sparkasse in the purchase.

Without a trace of irony, the Sparkasse described itself as the 'conscientious guardian of the assets of its clients' (and especially the smaller savers), and diametrically opposed to the ethos of the Third Reich, which sought to use the Sparkasse as a tool to exercise its power. The Sparkasse claimed that it did what it could for people, but it was clear that in this case what amounted to an express order of the *Gauleiter* could not be ignored. To do so risked consequences for the institution's financial wellbeing. Moreover, the bank's board of local businessmen were concerned that they would suffer personally.

In short, they folded in the face of the pressure exerted by the *Gauleiter*, in an involuntary venture for which there was no commercial justification. The Sparkasse conceded that the purchase price (over which they had no control) was certainly too low, but that Hofer's 'rent' was about right for the time. The bank rejected most of Hugo's claims against them, insisting that, according to the restitution law, only Hofer was responsible for payment of damages, not the bank.

Helpfully for Hugo, the statement closed by saying that the transaction was completed under duress and in justifiable fear of the consequences if the Sparkasse refused to comply. In a final plea, the Sparkasse pointed to its critical role in the rebuilding of Austria after the war. Any payment in this case would be damaging for those efforts – and for that reason alone, the application should be denied.

Hugo and Peter won the first round of litigation; but I can well imagine their outrage on finding that Hofer appealed on the basis of procedural impropriety – specifically that his suggested witnesses had not been interviewed. Hugo's submission in response dripped with irony. He pointed out that it was pointless for Hofer to protest that the then-omnipotent *Gauleiter* knew nothing of the machinations that led to him acquiring the villa: Ulm would never have dared to engage in such extortion without Hofer's knowledge.

Hugo asserted that his case was proven by the fact that Hofer purchased the house a year or so later at exactly the same undervalued price as the Sparkasse had paid for it; indeed, Hofer's statement that he acquired the villa in an honest transaction was so monstrous that it did not even deserve further debate.

The restitution cases ground on and eventually the villa was delivered up to the family, to join the café and the distillery, which had been returned to Hugo and Peter. Erich's widow Grete came back to Innsbruck, moved into the Andreas-Hofer-Strasse flat and, on Peter's behalf, busied herself with the distillery and the café.

Wapping, London, 2019

I am working my way through yet more papers rescued from my father's Hampshire cottage, trying to track the movements of my family after the war. I know that on 8 July 1948, my grandparents and my father Kurt were granted the status of naturalised British subjects. During the war years, they had been rendered stateless. Now, they had a new identity, a new country. Yet it is unclear to me where they now call home.

I look at the passenger records available online at the National Archives at Kew. They confirm that on 16 November 1949, Edith and Hugo set sail to the United States on a ship belonging to the Cunard-White Star line. I note that Kurt is not with them. I see too that in the column marked 'profession' in the passenger lists, Hugo has written 'none'. I am sad to see that this proud entrepreneur is no longer confident enough to put 'businessman', 'distiller' or 'patissier' as his profession. His country of future residence is listed as the UK. Perhaps this really is his intention as they board the ship, or everything is in flux.

My father claimed that Erich's widow, Grete, spooked my grandmother about returning to Austria lest it 'fall to the communists'. Grete had pointed to the fact that Czechoslovakia was now behind the Iron Curtain and the east of Austria was still in the hands of Soviet troops. At Edith's suggestion, therefore, Hugo had raised some money to travel with Edith across the Atlantic. According to his correspondence, Hugo was looking into buying American confectionary machinery.

I can track Hugo's movements from his letters. He is staying with John Kafka's mother Claire, in New York, in December 1949. It is from there that he writes to Dr Steinbrecher in Innsbruck. There has been something to celebrate. Hugo expresses his delight at the success of another set of restitution proceedings – against the Jägers, for the distillery business and premises on Andreas-Hofer-Strasse. But there is a fly in the ointment. He is very upset by the installation of 'Fr Gr' – Grete – as trustee over the business, as he has concerns over her competence to run a distillery business.

Above all, in his view, Grete must be prevented from hiring or dismissing staff, and he is particularly concerned about a Mr Smyth, who is in her company and always looking to cheat the business. Hugo instructs Steinbrecher to ensure that Grete should not be allowed any bank-signing rights. Hugo wants his lawyers to make it clear to Grete that she cannot take out any more money than is justified by the trusteeship. For good measure, he points out that other than small travel expenses, he has taken nothing out of the business but rather has invested in it.

He will, he tells Steinbrecher, jump on the next good ship to Europe and hopes to be back in Innsbruck by mid-January 1950. He has, he says, learned a lot in the United States and does not regret the trip at all. Now, though, he hopes to bring in various innovations in Austria.

He has made his decision. He will return. As it happens, his son is ahead of him.

22

Schlutzkrapfen with the Gauleiter

Innsbruck, Austria, 2019

The City of Innsbruck Archives hold all sorts of surprises. One of them is an application by my father, dated June 1949, for 'assistance'. I am astonished to find him, aged twenty-four, in a displaced persons' camp near Salzburg.

I don't remember Kurt ever telling us about this. These camps were set up primarily for those who were liberated from the concentration camps, as well as for refugees from Eastern Europe who did not want to return to the Soviet-controlled areas. Kurt is obviously in neither category. Why is he here?

I study the application carefully for clues. In the rubric for 'citizenship', Kurt gives his status as 'stateless-Jew'. This is not true. I know from the archives in Kew that he and his parents became British subjects the previous year. Moreover, in the National Archives there is a later naturalisation certificate for Kurt, dated November 1949, a process that must already have been in train by the time he left England. He fails to disclose this on the form. One entry on the form is correct: he gives the date he left Innsbruck as September 1938 – more confirmation that he was not in Innsbruck on *Kristallnacht*, whatever he told us and his psychiatrists (and possibly himself) later on.

More mysteries follow. On the second page of the form, Kurt states: 'I have come to Austria to find out exactly whether in fact anyone in my family is still alive. Unfortunately, they were all victims of the Nazi murder campaign 1942–3, as was explained to me by witnesses in Innsbruck. I now want to emigrate to Israel.' In

Section 15, he declares he has no relatives. The handwriting is not Kurt's, but his signature is at the bottom, so I assume that he was interviewed, and his details jotted down. Perhaps error crept in as a result of miscommunication. Yet it all seems too bizarre for that.

Why does Kurt declare all his family are dead? At that very moment, his parents are in London, as are his Aunt Grete and his cousin, Peter. His Linz cousin, John Kafka, and his favourite Viennese cousin, Marianne Salzer, are in the United States. Is Kurt thinking of Sofie, Martha and Siegfried? But that doesn't make sense either, for Erwin Salzer confirmed, in his letter of 1946, that they had died. Did Kurt need to prove it to himself?

It was not until I found the letters Kurt received from Sofie, Martha and Siegfried that I realised how close he was to them. Is it possible that Hugo never told Kurt about Erwin's letter? I have to acknowledge that it is – or perhaps I want to believe that he did not really know their fates. I hate the idea that in order to get financial assistance, he was portraying himself as alone, abandoned in the world.

The form has one more surprise. Kurt apparently now wants to emigrate to Israel. Never, to my knowledge, did my father even visit Israel during his life; he was always staunchly assimilationist and anti-Zionist. Is this what he has to say to receive whatever travel funding is on offer in the camp?

I don't know what to think. Nothing accords with the father I knew – except for the troubling absence of truth. But then again, these were such times of dislocation for millions, and of trading old identities for new ones in the post-war world. Was Kurt genuinely confused about who he was, or who he wanted to be? He seemed to be in Austria on his own, as Hugo and Edith were still in London, before their winter trip to the United States.

Perhaps Kurt agreed to go on ahead to Austria, to reconnoitre prospects for restarting life there, or maybe somehow to help with Steinbrecher's pursuit of the restitution claims. Perhaps he had discovered the truth for himself about Sofie, Martha and Siegfried, and then he experienced a crisis of some sort. He was suddenly inspired by the idea of Israel as a possible homeland, a way of wiping the slate clean and becoming one of the young Jews now working to make this new state work. Did Hugo and Edith have any inkling of this?

Or am I just making excuses for him?

All I do know is that before very long, Kurt is no longer alone in Austria. And though he has a travel plan, it does not involve Israel. Rather, it will involve an old adversary.

I can only imagine that in 1950, when my grandfather and grandmother joined Kurt in Austria, their joy at being reunited sat alongside more mixed emotions at returning to a place from which they'd sought refuge. They were not part of a flood; very few of Innsbruck's pre-war Jews chose to return. Those that did so met with incomprehension from those that stayed away. Why on earth go back to a country that had treated you so badly, to a population that had disowned you, and very probably to meet continuing resentment or hostility from locals, particularly when they were defendants in restitution proceedings?

But this was the Tyrol. Here were the mountains and land-scapes and culture so important to Hugo, if not so much to Edith. I have a lovely portrait of the three of them, taken on a mountain walk above Innsbruck. It is not a rugged hike, as Hugo and Kurt wear suits and ties, and Edith is decked out in a skirt and jacket, with a smart white shirt. In particular, I love that the pose they adopt exactly mirrors the triangle of Hugo and two companions photographed atop the mountains in the First World War. Now, Kurt is on the left, strikingly handsome; Edith is in the middle, beaming, with Hugo on the right.

Hugo was clearly delighted to be back in the Tyrol. There was now a place for the family to live in Innsbruck, in the flat at the Andreas-Hofer-Strasse, even if the legal tussle continued over the Villa Schindler, where French occupation authorities were currently

Kurt, Edith and Hugo, 1950s, after their return to Austria

Kaufhaus Kraus (previously the Jewish-owned department store Bauer & Schwarz) suffers severe bomb damage and closes. Café Hiebl (previously Café Schindler) suffers some bomb damage too.

ensconced. If things became tough, the Schindlers knew they would not be trapped again: they now had their British-subject status as a way out. And with the restitution of the Schindler businesses, Hugo was once more a man of responsibilities – for one thing, he had a café to run.

Hugo set about repairing the damage caused by the resistance and Allied bombs, and the Café Schindler was reborn in 1950. Once again, despite the fragile economic times of a country recovering from war, Hugo rolled out the red carpet to a battered post-war generation wanting to forget the trauma of another self-destructive war. Edith, though, remained restless and took off again on long trips, often to the United States.

In the meantime, the Munich courts had made another effort to track down the café's wartime owner, not to please the Schindlers, but because of suspicions that Hiebl was involved in the deaths of Jews. Eventually, with the help of Austrian police, the court concluded there was no evidence to support the allegation; but they did uncover evidence to suggest Hiebl's involvement in the 1940 murder of Dr Richard Steidle, the ex-head of the Austrian *Heimwehr* paramilitary.

The anti-Nazi Steidle and his son Othmar had been interned as political prisoners in Buchenwald concentration camp. From a conversation with Hiebl, in which the Nazi allegedly told Othmar that 'one of you pigs will not make it home alive, I am here to ensure that', Hiebl seemed to be implicated in what followed. Othmar was transferred to another camp and survived the war to deliver his testimony; but his father, according to witnesses, was ordered to walk towards the fence and was shot in the back. However, given that Othmar was not present, and the other witnesses seemed not fully sure of their evidence, the proceedings were eventually dropped.

Looking through the witness statements, I had to admit that the evidence against Hiebl was not strong. Also, to me it did not sound like his style. A wily, shifty and corrupt opportunist, yes; but a cold-blooded murderer?

In the event, on 24 March 1950, Hiebl did materialise, to turn himself in to the Munich police. For some Nazis on the run, the climate had improved. Hiebl knew that the West German *Straffreiheitsgesetz* (Immunity Act) had come into force on 1 January 1950, which provided amnesties – under certain conditions – to those who had committed crimes normally punishable with six- to twelve-month prison sentences. For Hiebl, this was his Get Out of Jail Free card, at least in Germany. The Bavarian state prosecutor now terminated all criminal proceedings against him.

As Hiebl shook off the spectre of German criminal charges, his friend Franz Hofer was still under a death sentence *in absentia*, as well as a defendant in the restitution proceedings for the Villa Schindler – and if the Austrian authorities were to be believed, still nowhere to be found. However, they were not looking very hard. At least one person had discovered where he was: my father. And so, he set off for his second-ever encounter with the *Gauleiter*, one that would be even more bizarre than the first, when he was a twelve-year-old boy.

Kurt used to relish telling us this story. In his version, he decided to take matters into his own hands and track down the fugitive – I have no idea whether Hugo and Edith knew what he was up to. I suspect not. There was unfinished business between the ex-*Gauleiter* and the Schindlers. I imagine Kurt leaving Innsbruck early, given the long car journey ahead. Petrol rationing was still in force, and it would have been difficult for him to obtain enough for the 500 miles (750 km) he needed to cover the drive there, not to mention his return journey.

I don't know how Kurt got hold of Hofer's address. I suspect that he had a tip-off from someone in Innsbruck: there were plenty of people locally who still had their discreet contacts with Nazis in hiding. By whatever means, Kurt found out that Hofer was living in Mülheim-an-der-Ruhr, in northern Germany.

This time, in a reversal of their roles in 1938, it was Kurt who was the uninvited visitor, knocking unannounced on the door. It is possible that my father made this story up, but I think not. By now, I have learned to distinguish better between Kurt's fiction and his facts: his habit was to tell stories with a kernel of truth, but embellished to fit whatever objective he had in mind. Here, though, his only motive lay in the sheer joy of recounting the episode for his children. There was never a written record of that encounter, but details remained lodged in my head from Kurt's frequent retellings – and I can fill in the rest.

The Hofer residence, Mülheim-an-der-Ruhr, Germany, 1950

Since their last encounter, when *Gauleiter* Hofer ruffled the hair of an adolescent Kurt Schindler, Kurt has grown into a tall, handsome young man. Hofer does not recognise the stranger on his doorstep; but Kurt recognises Hofer immediately; to him, Hofer seems unchanged, and Kurt is always good with faces. They converse:

> *Hofer:* Who are you?
> *Kurt:* Kurt Schindler.

Hofer's face clouds over, and he steps back as if to close the door. He might not recognise the young man, but he knows the name. Kurt has anticipated this response.

> *Kurt:* Please don't do that. I just want to talk.
> *Hofer (suspiciously):* Are you on your own?
> *Kurt:* Yes.
> *Hofer:* Does anyone know you are here?
> *Kurt:* No.

Hofer makes a quick mental calculation. If he closes the door, the young man might make a scene and that will bring him unwanted attention. It is easier to let Kurt inside and deal with him there. Kurt does not look as if he will be physically dangerous, and anyway Hofer is a crack shot – the winner of pre-war shooting competitions – and still has a gun in the house.

Thus, Kurt Schindler gains entry to the house of the ex-*Gauleiter* of the Tyrol and Vorarlberg, a fugitive from justice. It is, for the young man, an act of audacity and sheer chutzpah.

Hofer invites Kurt into the sitting room, where they sit down and talk. Initially, Hofer tries small talk, all the time wondering precisely why his visitor is here. He cannot conceal his curiosity.

Hofer: So how did you find me?
Kurt: A contact in Innsbruck told me you were living here.

Hofer has been trying, quietly, to get on with his life. He does a bit of buying and selling to make ends meet. But things are tricky. After all, the Austrians wish to extradite him – or at least they say that they do. Kurt is slightly nervous. He leans forward, and puts his elbows on his long legs, trying to appear calm. He smiles and runs his hand through his hair, as he tries to work the conversation around to the reason for his visit. His gambit takes his host rather by surprise.

Kurt: We have your books and a set of encyclopaedias. There must be about twenty volumes. You left them in the study in the villa. Some of the nature plates are really beautiful.

Hofer (laughs incredulously): You drove all this way to tell me that?

Kurt: Well, it was one of the things.

Hofer (sighs and becomes reflective): We left in a bit of a hurry, it is true. There was no time to pack properly. I needed to get Friedi, my wife, and the children to safety. *(He pauses.)* Those were terrible times.

Kurt: Yes, we've still not got the villa back. The French occupation troops are now using it.

Hofer (looks curiously at Kurt): Well, that is hardly my fault.

Kurt: I am not here to talk about the encyclopaedias.

Hofer: So why *are* you here?

Kurt (finally gets to the point): I think it would be a nice gesture if you paid rent for the seven years that you lived in our house with your family.

At first, Hofer is taken aback. Then, he is relieved. Here, at least, is something that fits his worldview: a Jew who wants money. Nevertheless, Hofer is keen to change the subject, though he remains intrigued with his visitor – and hungry for news of Innsbruck.

Hofer: How is the café?

Kurt: We are reopening. As you know it was closed due to the bomb damage in 1943. It has been hard to raise capital, though, and reparations are slow to come through.

Hofer: Yes, I was in Innsbruck when the bomb fell on the store next door. It was lucky that it was not a direct hit. It was a shame. Hiebl was very upset. But then he had his own issues to deal with. Such a good café. I went there when I was a student before the war. Best strudel in town.

Kurt (despite himself, is flattered and smiles): Not just strudel, of course; we serve the whole range of cakes. But about the other matter.

Hofer: Ah yes! Let's talk over a glass of wine. I have a fine Austrian white a friend has given me.

Hofer calls over to his wife to bring out an expensive Austrian white wine from the cellar. They adjourn to the dining room, where Hofer uncorks the bottle and pours two glasses from it. Together, they taste it – and agree that Austria produces some of the finest white wines in the world.

The conversation continues, until Hofer invites Kurt to stay for dinner. He accepts. Together, they sit down with Hofer's family to a taste of home: spinach *Schultzkrapfen* – a type of spinach ravioli, originally from South Tyrol. Friedi brings them in from the kitchen and places them on the table before announcing *Maultaschen!* – the name of a similar German dish. Kurt will later remember, with devilish delight, how Hofer turns on his wife and yells at her for using a North German name rather than the South Tyrolean one.

Hofer turns to Kurt and declares, 'That's Germans for you. They never get our food right!'

On this point, Kurt Schindler and Franz Hofer are united: Austrians against Germans. Germans never understand Austrians.

And so began the most unlikely of dining clubs. For several years after the war, Kurt would make the long drive from Innsbruck, collect back rent from Hofer, eat dinner, drink wine and leave again. They steered clear of contentious subjects.

My father did not feel the need to help the Innsbruck court find Hofer. Why would he, when he had arranged this extra-judicial form of restitution from him? In 1953, Hofer's sentence, *in absentia*, was reduced to five years; in 1955, he was categorised merely as a *Belasteter*. This was one of the five categories of Nazi offender in the post-war denazification process, and it represented someone who – in theory – was subject to immediate arrest and imprisonment for up to ten years, but whose crimes could not warrant a death sentence.

Gradually Hofer started to use his real name, as he resumed his old occupation as a freelance salesman. His whereabouts were increasingly an open secret, too; he even gave the occasional interview to the press, in which he always declared his continuing devotion to the *Führer*. In the 1960s, the Austrian authorities had one more crack at bringing him to justice, but it faltered in 1974, when the prosecutor refused to reopen the case, believing Hofer's assertion that he had not been involved in a critical conversation about planning *Kristallnacht*.

Hofer's one-time friend Hiebl was, by 1951, living under the name 'Peter Huber' in Altötting, Bavaria, but still wanted by the Austrian authorities. The Schindlers were still on his trail, since they were not satisfied with the outcome of the proceedings against him, and they now tried to issue further restitution proceedings in Bavaria – I assume because of the significant profits he made out of the café in the seven years that he had run it.

In 1951, the Innsbruck court investigated Hiebl's various old boasts about his pro-Nazi acts of heroism. Under this investigation, Hiebl the chameleon seemed to undergo yet another transformation.

Now, he asserted he had never held office for the Nazi Party or SA, and was never active in either of them; neither did he ever bring Nazi propaganda into Austria. He could not, he said, remember whether he himself had distributed propaganda material. He never brought weapons into Austria, nor participated in any acts of violence. He certainly never blew anything up, he said, whether on his own or with others; categorically denying involvement in the explosions at the electricity works at the Achensee and the electricity lines at Scharnitz, which he noted were, in fact, never damaged.

Even the shameless Hiebl recognised what an audacious volte-face this was. He justified it on the basis that his previous evidence, during his wartime arrest in 1942, was in the context of an SS court process in which he was trying to show himself 'in a better light' and create an impression of being 'active in the service of the movement'. He had, he claimed, gambled on those statements in the expectation that they would not be checked.

The court concluded that he had probably exaggerated his actions before, that he did not participate in *Kristallnacht*, and that he did not help blow up the Achensee power station nor the water network in the Achen valley. But it decided that he *had* imported pre-*Anschluss* Nazi propaganda and been involved in various Nazi fights and igniting flaming swastikas on the mountainsides.

Still, Hiebl was out of Austrian clutches. One day, Hugo spotted a van he recognised as Hiebl's in the Maria-Theresien-Strasse, outside the café. He immediately notified the police, who seized it and passed the information on to the public prosecutor.

It emerged that it was not Hiebl in Innsbruck, but his wife Bertha. She had been driven there by Josef Schneele, a butcher at the well-known Munich restaurant the 'Donisl', which was managed by Hiebl under lease from a German brewing company. At 8 a.m. the next morning, Hiebl himself rang up, alleging that the van had been sold to a third party (but the paperwork had not yet come through), so it had to be returned, otherwise the Austrian authorities would be interfering with the property of a German national. He could not yet travel to Austria himself, although his lawyers were 'working on it'.

Schneele explained that he had driven several times to Innsbruck, accompanied by Frau Hiebl, but had never driven Hiebl there, as Hiebl 'has his own car, a Porsche sports car'. He could not confirm nor deny whether Hiebl himself had ever driven to Innsbruck. For this particular trip, Schneele's girlfriend had come along, and they visited the 'the former Café Hiebl'. I wondered why Schneele chose to visit a café with which he had no personal connection. Perhaps it was curiosity about a place that Hiebl had spoken about; but I suspected Hiebl had instructed him to visit, as he was curious to know what Hugo was up to with the place he had run for seven years.

The police refused to return the van, because it was still in Hiebl's name. It was a small victory for Hugo.

Innsbruck, 1952

On 13 June 1952, in the office of the Schindler business on the Andreas-Hofer-Strasse, Hugo Schindler died at his desk. He was sixty-four years old. He had fought through one world war, survived another one – equally dangerous, although in quite different ways – and built up, then lost, and then mostly regained a local business empire in Innsbruck. He was the only one of Sofie and Samuel's five children to have made it through the Second World War.

Hugo never returned to live in the Villa Schindler. The French authorities were still using it. He had made the odd visit to the house, accompanied by Edith – a visit recorded for posterity in photographs that show relief visible on their faces. At least, by the end, he knew it would be only a matter of time before the family were able to resume their lives at the villa.

He never saw Franz Hiebl brought to justice, although the case rumbled on. In June 1955, Hiebl appealed for a right of free passage in and out of Innsbruck, in order to visit his 80-year-old mother. The court said he was welcome to submit to the proceedings at any time – but he was denied any guaranteed free passage in and out of Austria; and it was confirmed that the warrant for his arrest was still in force. On 13 April 1956, the Innsbruck court ruled that the seizure of Hiebl's van was legal and rejected an appeal by Hiebl's lawyer.

In 1957, Germany and Austria announced an amnesty for certain Nazis. Hiebl applied to the court for the criminal proceedings to be dropped and for the costs of those proceedings to be waived, as he wanted urgently to be able to get into Austria. His wishes were granted two days later. One small silver lining of Hugo's premature death was that there was no danger of him spotting Hiebl in his Porsche, speeding along the Maria-Theresien-Strasse, past the café that once – as a police report observed in 1947 – made Hiebl 'unusually high profits'.

In Mülheim, the former *Gauleiter* continued his quiet civilian life. The only official retribution the Hofer family suffered was that, in 1964, the Austrian courts turned down an application for the return of the Hofer country residence, outside Innsbruck. Franz Hofer died of natural causes in 1975, at the age of seventy-two. He was buried in an unmarked grave in Mülheim.

A decade later, on occasions in the Tyrol during the 1980s, my sister Sophie and I leafed through the ornate twenty-volume set of encyclopaedias inherited – involuntarily – from the *Gauleiter*. The text was difficult to read, but the pictures were as beautiful as ever. There were other books, too, that were once in Hofer's possession and have since passed to us. They include Hofer's personal guide to German army uniforms.

Today, I keep it in the bottom of an old trunk with my other Nazi-era documents.

23

Das Schindler

Innsbruck, Austria, 2019

Newspapers have helped me a lot in my research. In searching through the enormous bound volumes of old newspapers at the Innsbruck City Museum, I have been able to track the highs and lows in my family's fortunes in the city. Now I find a glowing obituary of my grandfather. It emphasises how long-established his roots were in Austria. I think he would have liked that.

I wonder, though, about his sense of identity in his last two years back in Innsbruck, a time inevitably complicated by war. Once I could say he was Austrian, then Tyrolean, then Jewish. Was it the same at the end? I do not think he clutched his Jewish identity any closer to his heart than he did before the war; and given Austria's political turmoil and fragmented post-war state, being a patriot in any national sense was now harder. I have little doubt, though, that he still felt Tyrolean to his core. It was an allegiance sufficient to make the Schindler business one of the very few pre-war Jewish businesses in Innsbruck to survive. But with his death, who else in the family shared that allegiance?

I roll forward to the mid-1970s. Much has changed. I see from the newspapers that on the Maria-Theresien-Strasse there are still New Year celebration parties. There is even what the newspapers call 'Schindler dancing', as if it were a style, like Tango. But Schindler dancing does not take place at the Café Schindler. The venue has a new name, the Café Maria Theresia. An era has come to an end.

Edith and Kurt were both in the United States when Hugo had his fatal stroke, and so they hurried back to Innsbruck. Bereaved though they were, they also faced new obligations and challenges, as they now inherited fifty per cent of the ownership and running of the Café Schindler, shared with Peter – who remained in London – and Grete, who lived in Innsbruck, acting as her son's proxy.

This combination of personalities, ambitions and interests was not a recipe for success.

Everyone had different ideas; none of them had any real training in day-to-day management, and all of them lacked the ability to compromise or delegate. My father had the intelligence and charm to be the perfect ambassador and salesman for the business, but no patience with the tedious matters of costs, revenue and cashflow. He was unfocused. Kurt's dreams of installing an espresso bar came to nought, because there was no money to invest, and perhaps because Peter – a more grounded and practical businessman, suspicious of Kurt's flights of fancy – was unconvinced.

Kurt also wanted to launch a Schindler twist on a traditional drink served to thirsty skiers, but his idea for *Skiwasser* – lemonade and raspberry juice – also bit the dust. It was not all downhill: in 1956, the Café Schindler won the gold medal for its patisserie at an international exhibition in Vienna. I think, though, that was probably its last moment of glory.

Two years after Hugo's death, in 1954, Edith and Kurt finally reacquired the Villa Schindler. At the same time, Peter received the adjoining garden – the plot on which his father had originally planned to build his own house. Despite the long restitution battle, according to Kurt, Edith then sold the villa without consulting him. With Hugo gone, my grandmother had even less interest in living in Austria and was still looking to the United States as a new home.

Kurt now moved back to the flat at the Andreas-Hofer-Strasse, but he, too, was torn about where he wanted to be and remained so all his life; he loved Austria and specifically the Tyrol, but he was restless. He also had, as he told me, broader ambitions than being the owner of a provincial café. In addition, he was distracted by his obsession with getting back every last Schilling in restitution claims – something else that endured all his life, and which seeped, damagingly, into family relations. Just as Hugo and Erich seem to have fallen out during Erich's last years in London, so the cousins Kurt and Peter fell out in their adult lives.

As family rows intensified, and even tipped into litigation, the inheritors of the Café Schindler concluded the time had come to sell up. In the autumn of 1959, the café that Hugo and Erich had launched in 1922 passed into new ownership. For another fifteen years or so, it continued as the Café Schindler under new management, before changing its name and then vanishing altogether.

After selling up, Kurt and Edith moved back to England, and Kurt married my mother, Mary. Blonde, beautiful, intelligent and enormously loyal, she stuck with my father when others would have left. I have no doubt that they loved each other deeply.

Much less life-enhancing was Kurt's addiction to litigation in pursuit of what, he felt, he and the family were still owed because of the disruptions of war. His life was consumed by it. He continued to chase ever more far-fetched and remote restitution claims, sometimes as self-appointed agent for others in the family. His costs in so doing always exceeded any financial gain, and he usually fell out with others, as he tried to pocket any proceeds to cover those costs.

Among Kurt's papers, I came across several despairing letters from his cousins Erwin Salzer and Peter, saying that they did not wish to have anything further to do with him and his restitution efforts. In one, Erwin rebuked Kurt for going beyond the terms of the power of attorney that Erwin had given him. This looked to me like a plausible reason for the argument that Kurt and Erwin had in the 1950s, and which Tom Salzer remembered so well. Kurt and Peter had already fallen out badly over the café, and Peter came to regard Kurt as a 'thief' – according to Peter's son Richard. Although my father's aim was always to rebuild the Schindler businesses, too often his actions alienated his family and tarnished his name.

Kurt's ability to sabotage his own goals was one manifestation of his complexity. He had a taste for luxury, but lacked the ability to earn the money to finance it. He had intelligence, charm and good looks, yet the way he chose to live his life was often corrosive to relations with others. Sadly, he never had the insight to see this. He cast himself as the victim and remained in that role all his life.

Even in his late eighties, Kurt was still trying to go to law. He talked about claims relating to stolen art; claims relating to Edith's father's match factory in Plauen; and claims relating to a tobacco shop concession, granted in 1945, which took up space on the ground floor of the Café Schindler.

As I was the only lawyer in the family, Kurt usually wanted to discuss them when we saw each other. I would arrive at his Hampshire cottage to be faced with reams of paper to read. However, he never wanted to hear any advice that contradicted what he already wanted to do. Tired of his obsessions and unconvinced by the merits of his various claims, I stopped listening. When he died, the endless piles of papers in his house were evidence of a lifetime of litigation and an inability to move on to a more fruitful life.

Three years after his death, I have ploughed through those papers as never before. I have connected with unfamiliar relatives, read history, immersed myself in archives from Innsbruck to Washington; developed a whole parallel life of exploration and note-taking and writing. The irony of it all is that had my father not been the frustrating and inexplicable man he was, had he not been the hoarder of documents and letters and artefacts from the past, or told maddeningly elusive tales of people and places – of a past that was both glittering and traumatic – I might not have had the motivation to start this journey in the first place.

The truth was, he left too many loose ends, and I could not resist them. I wanted to find out why he was the way he was; but in trying to follow him, he led me into something larger: a whole world of Schindlers, Dubskys and Kafkas, of nineteenth-century Bohemia and twentieth-century Austria, of two world wars, a fallen empire, the poison of antisemitsm and a Nazi dictator, and throughout it all a pervading family tradition devoted to good food, good drink, good music and good dancing. I have to thank my father for that.

I am left with some difficult questions, too.

Would Kurt's life have been different if he had not been uprooted so brutally in 1938; and did the murder of his much-loved grandmother, aunt and uncle throw his young life off course? Would he have acquired the skill and aptitude to run the Schindler businesses had Hugo lived a little longer? Did he, in some way, want to emulate Hugo – pillar of society, war hero, successful and benevolent entrepreneur, a man of steady integrity – but knew he was simply made of different stuff?

Most importantly of all, did he deliberately lie or was his memory warped by his experiences?

On this last question, I have come to believe that some of his untruths were false memories that became embedded in his mind and polished through endless retelling. Sometimes he told the truth, sometimes he did not. He was unreliable, but charming and fascinating. And perhaps I have accepted too that one response to the hard reality of the world as he found it was to create a more malleable alternative reality – where debts never needed paying, where every last bit of the old Schindler assets could be gathered in, and the music and the dancing still went on.

It was while Kurt was still living that I first made my own return to Innsbruck in 2015, with my family. Enough years had passed to soften the more difficult memories of living there, when I was wrenched unexpectedly from England. So now I was keen to show off the highlights – I was tourist guide and amateur family historian. As we strolled through the old part of town, I told my children that their great-grandfather had once had a shop there selling *Schnapps* and that he had also run the most glamorous café in town. My children knew the story well, but humoured me in the way that teenagers do when a parent starts on a favourite hobby horse.

As we turned into the Maria-Theresien-Strasse, I was in full swing extolling the virtues of Austrian coffee and cake and how important the coffee house culture was to the Enlightenment, when I looked up to my left and broke off my lecture. There, on the first floor of the building that had housed our old café, were the words 'Das Schindler' – 'The Schindler'.

I was shocked. After decades of absence, our name had suddenly reappeared on Innsbruck's main street on the exact same building that had once housed the café.

Without hesitation, I strode over to the building, pushed open the heavy door on the ground floor and followed signs up to the first-floor café. My family followed slightly nervously after me. Was I going to make a scene and embarrass them? In the stairwell, there was a large if somewhat grainy picture of the original café in the 1930s. On the landing were various awards won by the restaurant. I walked into the main room, which I knew so well from photos, but had never visited before. It was like stepping into a film set. I half expected Hugo to come forward and greet me.

In my head, questions chased each other as I tried to gather my German to formulate a polite but firm approach to the owner.

'Can I speak to the boss please?'

'He is away. How can I help?'

'My name is Schindler,' I said, expecting that somehow that simple statement would make everything clear.

The waiter looked at me blankly. I was not sure myself what I wanted. I felt deflated and slightly foolish. In the meantime, my children, excited to see their name everywhere, were busy collecting souvenirs: business cards, napkins and pens were quickly lifted from the table near the entrance and stowed in pockets and bags.

'Can I have the boss's email address?' I asked, before we left again.

When I got back to London, I looked up the owner, Bernhard Baumann, online and duly emailed him. We met the following year. Initially, Bernhard was somewhat nervous; no doubt the lawyer sign-off on my email concerned him. Perhaps he had, somehow, got wind of my father's litigious nature, and was worried that I would kick up a fuss about his unauthorised use of the Schindler name.

However, in the intervening year I had come to terms with the idea that someone else had brought 'our' café back to life. After all, apart from the revived name, it was no different to the situation in the 1960s and early 1970s after Kurt had sold the café. It was not as if I or my sister had either the training or the ambition to run it; indeed, I felt delighted that Bernhard had, in the twenty-first century, brought the Schindler name back to life on the Maria-Theresien-Strasse. It is, today, the sole surviving name out of all the Jewish-owned shops and businesses that existed in 1938, before their erasure by *Gauleiter* Hofer.

The good-looking Bernhard was the perfect host, enthusiastic and hospitable. I was curious as to how he had come to be running the place. Bernhard told me that he had been born into a farming family near Salzburg. He had then completed an apprenticeship in hospitality, and trained in Miami Beach and northern Germany, before opening a golf-themed restaurant in Salzburg. Bernhard had fallen in love with a young woman from Innsbruck, so he moved to the city and looked for a site on which to open a restaurant, before spotting the building that had once held the Café Schindler.

Bernhard explained that he had mentioned his plans to a number of locals and to the Innsbruck licensing authority, and they had all insisted his venture should be called the 'Café

Schindler'. He had been nonplussed by the idea. He had never heard of the Schindlers or their business and was surprised by the vehemence with which people advocated the name. It was only when, in the City Archives, he came upon all the photographs of the café, from the 1920s onwards, that he became convinced that adopting the name 'Schindler' would bring his new business a proper heritage. Moreover, he chose a 1930s-style decor to reflect the café's history.

Rather than the full German name, 'Konditorei Café Schindler', Bernhard used just 'Das Schindler'. He wanted to signal that Schindler's was open all day, serving breakfast, lunch and dinner, and was thus a restaurant rather than traditional café. For good measure, he registered the trademarks 'Das Schindler', 'Schindlerei', 'Schindlers' and 'Schindler'; indeed, I was impressed to find that he had already seen off a usurper in Switzerland, who had tried to open a copycat restaurant. I was also amused by the thought that if I now wished to open a café in my own name in Innsbruck, I would need a licence from him.

According to Bernhard, even before he opened Das Schindler in March 2010, there was enormous excitement about it. He explained that opening a restaurant in a first-floor venue is usually tricky, as you have to convince people that it is worth making the effort to walk up the stairs. But he had no such difficulty. Customers flocked to the place, and Bernhard could not believe his luck. He had hit upon the perfect formula: an upmarket venue with a genuine history and one that lived on in the hearts of the people of Innsbruck.

Just as in Hugo's day, there was music, too. Bernhard even hired August Rokas – a pianist then in his eighties, who had played at the Café Schindler in the 1950s – to entertain guests at the 2010 opening. Das Schindler was booked out in the first few months, often with table reservations from people who wanted to bring four generations of their family to experience a slice of Innsbruck's history.

The modern-day 'Das Schindler'

Das Schindler, Innsbruck, 2019

Bernhard Baumann is a worthy successor to Hugo Schindler.
He is warm; he greets every guest personally and knows many
of them by name. He has also chosen an excellent chef, who
sources fresh local ingredients for his dishes and makes a fabu-
lously good *Sachertorte*-style cake – and of course, *Strudel*. In
its first decade of existence, Das Schindler has won numerous
awards.

This evening, my husband and children are here in Das
Schindler, for dinner. It is the end of my sabbatical – I have
more or less completed my research. Thoughts about three
previous generations, about Kurt, Hugo and Sofie, flit through
my mind, jostling with family chat and anticipation for the
food to come.

I now know that some of the claims Kurt made about the
people to whom we were related were exaggerated or simply
wrong. We were related to Franz Kafka, Adele Bloch Bauer and
even Alma Schindler, but so distantly that it was not something to

brag about. I could find no link to Oskar Schindler: while Samuel Schindler had come from the same part of Prussia, it seems unlikely that Oskar was himself Jewish.

Then again, some of Kurt's most interesting tales, about his uncle, Dr Bloch, and *Gauleiter* Hofer, have turned out to be true. Now I have discovered the detail of them. I have also derived enormous joy from identifying most of the people in the photograph albums that I inherited from Kurt. And now, too, I understand more clearly what happened in Austria during the last century and how the reverberations of a dark chapter affected my family and shaped people's thinking today.

For much of the last three years I have, necessarily, been living in the past. And yet, here I am, in a thriving twenty-first-century restaurant called Schindler. It is as if an old ghost has reasserted itself and demanded its place back among the living. Perhaps the best thing is that all my looking backwards has enriched the present and the future. I have made a host of new friends in Austria. Most importantly, a family that had been scattered by feuding, litigation and war has been reunited and is now in regular contact.

The first course arrives: modern Austrian fare – pasta with truffle oil and fresh mushrooms for the vegetarians; steak for the meat-eaters. But I am more interested in pudding. There is no debate. We all order *Apfelstrudel*.

We gaze out of the window onto the Maria-Theresien-Strasse and, as the sun sets on the Nordkette, we raise a toast to the café and to Kurt, in all his complexity.

The Schindlers have come home.

Epilogue: Memory and Memorials

Wapping, London, 2020

I have come up, time and time again, against the issue of conflicting memories. Never more starkly than with my father. Today, he is both clearer and more perplexing to me. I know more about the shape and contours of his outer life, while his inner life and his thought processes remain to a great extent inexplicable.

Hardest to deal with are the obvious mistruths, or the very likely mistruths, of which his absence on *Kristallnacht* was the one that disturbed me most. I also think that in 1948, in contrast to what he told the authorities in the displaced persons' camp, he had not the slightest intention of emigrating to Israel. In those cash-strapped times, I think he was simply interested in receiving whatever financial assistance was on offer.

Even accepting the utter fallibility of memory, or the phenomenon of 'flashbulb memories', did not entirely remove a taint. It was not until my sister arrived in London, in 2019, with Kurt's stamp collection, that I was brought face to face with the fallibility of my own memory.

In those two bulging carrier bags, we found a cache of postcards sent by him during his time in prison – first-day covers, posted from Brixton, Wandsworth, Maidstone and Ford Open prisons. They were always accompanied by the order to keep them safe. I had entirely forgotten that he had done this. It was his way of reaching out to his two young daughters. It reminded me of the love he had shown us, even when locked away from us. It diluted my instinct to judge him. It encouraged me to recalibrate some of my feelings of estrangement and anger towards him.

Those postcards and hundreds of empty envelopes also spoke a certain truth about my father: his rootlessness. He had lived in many countries, at so many different addresses, never settling. But his childhood and a large part of his adult life were in Austria and, after his death, I felt he needed to be there too.

When I visited the Schindler family grave in Innsbruck, I realised that many names were missing from it. As I stood in front of the stained marble, with its faded old lettering, I knew it was my responsibility to make up for this omission. I contacted a local stone mason and he agreed to add not only Martha, Siegfried and Sofie's names, but also those of our parents. I consulted my sisters about the inscription.

The male Schindlers who were already on the grave all had their professions carved in gold. Sophie and I struggled to come up with anything to encapsulate Kurt's life. We decided simply to put the dates under his name. That seemed kindest. Kurt and Mary's ashes will be interred there, in the beautiful little Jewish cemetery in Innsbruck.

In the course of my research and revisitings, the landscapes of my Innsbruck adolescence have changed. Today, I see them with fresh eyes.

The Bozner Platz with the tiny shop where I used to buy *Vanillekipferl*, those crescent-shaped, almond-and-vanilla biscuits, is now in my mind also a place where the Nazis of the NSKK gathered before beating up my grandfather. The Sillgasse, on which I played basketball as a teenager, is the site of the Jewish prayer room destroyed by the SS on *Kristallnacht*. The Maria-Theresien-Strasse, which I walked through twice a day on my way to and from school, is not only the location for my grandfather's glittering café, but also a place of National Socialist parades, once bedecked with swastikas. Retracing my teenage steps has been difficult. I have re-inked my own memories in darker colours.

Austria, too, has had to see itself afresh. During my sabbatical, I borrowed a history textbook from one historian friend in Innsbruck. It is now used throughout the country to teach the *Matura* – the Austrian equivalent of A-levels. I see it is quite different to what I was using in history lessons of the late 1980s.

In my old book, the coverage of the Second World War was crammed into two pages – an afterthought, at the end of the syllabus. They began with the comment that while concentration camps existed, they were invented by the British in the Anglo–Boer War in South Africa. Though factually correct, this was also a shockingly misleading way to frame what was anyway a cursory reading of the events of 1939–45. Turning to the new textbook, I was relieved to see that the subject is now covered in forty-four pages and has moved away from the mantra that 'Austria was Hitler's first victim'. This book opens with a gentle but clear comment:

> Even today there are people – often one-time Nazis or their children and grandchildren who have been influenced by their homes' environments – who speak of the 'positive sides' of the National Socialist Dictatorship in Austria. Obviously for these people their own positive personal memories or interpretations take precedence so that even the reports by victims of their suffering and the academic facts about the crimes of the National Socialists do not alter them.

Ever more imaginative ways of communicating history are emerging. Over the last ten years, Michael Guggenberger has gone through the evidence of what happened on *Kristallnacht*, written up a short piece on each of the dozens of incidents and included the subsequent history of each person affected. Günter Lieder, president of the Jewish Community in Innsbruck, recorded the German-language version. I was able to play my part when in 2019 I recorded the English-language version. These readings, online and accessible by an app, mean that anyone can walk an Innsbruck street and download a description of what happened there on 9–10 November 1938.

I have spent so much time thinking about the connection between memory and memorials, beyond the deeply personal questions of what to inscribe on family gravestones. What makes a good memorial? Do they serve a point, and if so, what point?

The generation of perpetrators, victims and bystanders of the Holocaust has all but died out. The children of the Second World War have had their own children, grandchildren and great-grand-children. Yes, the echoes of the Holocaust reverberate through the generations, but with each successive generation the sounds are fainter. There is less emotional connection. New generations have to forge new ways to understand and remember, and art, symbols and structures play an important role.

In design, all memorials inescapably reveal much of the mindset of those who erect them. In Britain, the war memorials fit easily into a comfortable national story – heroic sacrifice in a decent, democratic cause. In Germany and Austria, war memorials are also self-examinations: confrontations with responsibility and guilt.

Germany has an extraordinary number of Holocaust memorials – 243 in Berlin alone at the turn of the twentieth century, according to one report.[1] Austria, in denial or semi-denial, is – or was – different. Memorials were slow to arrive, and when they did appear, the inscriptions could border on the bizarre. In some Austrian towns, memorials are only now just being commissioned.

The Reichenau camp in Innsbruck, where my cousin Egon Dubsky was shot in cold blood, betrays little of what went on there. Its reference to 'patriots' being incarcerated and dying there lends it a heroism that is spectacularly absent from its bloody history. Some may have been patriots, but most were there for other reasons – certainly, Egon was. Egon and Luise had no children to remember them. I would very much like to improve the Reichenau memorial, so that the camp, and what happened there, are properly remembered – and so that the Dubsky name does not slip through the cracks of memory.

I would also love to see a celebration of the extraordinary bravery of Fred Mayer, Hans Wijnberg and Franz Weber – and their band of female helpers – in convincing *Gauleiter* Hofer to hand over Innsbruck without bloodshed and further damage to the city's beautiful architecture. Their names are currently invisible in Innsbruck's public realm. I think they should be as well-known there as the Tyrolean hero Andreas Hofer. This does not need to take the form of a monument, but maybe a street name or a day of celebration in their honour would be appropriate. That may be a bigger challenge.

In Linz, I was astounded not to see a Holocaust memorial in the centre of Hitler's favourite city. I could find only one memorial to the Jews of Linz, in the deserted, locked graveyard on the edge of town. I asked a local historian, Verena Wagner, whether I had somehow missed the local memorial. She told me that various schools, including hers, had plaques to commemorate former Jewish pupils who were victims. She told me, too, that the City of Linz had recently – eighty years after the events themselves – launched an artists' competition to design a memorial.

Wandering the pretty baroque streets of the old town, it was clear to me how all traces of the Third Reich had been scrubbed from the buildings and pavements. Linz largely appeared, until recently, to have collective amnesia about the past. Now, however, the city authorities have announced that they will erect small posts with facsimile doorbells and names on them outside homes where Jews once lived. I contacted John Kafka in America to let him know. He was delighted – and he got in touch with a local historian to ensure his family's names would appear on one of these posts.

At least Vienna has one really good memorial: Rachel Whiteread's brutal tribute on the Judenplatz to the 65,000 Austrian Jews killed by the Nazis. The bunker-like block takes the form of a library of concrete closed books, lined up and turned in on themselves, the spines no longer visible and the knowledge in them confined, inaccessible. Even the doors to the library are closed – there is no doorknob. It is a powerful and painful memorial to forgetting.

How the public interacts with a memorial determines its

success. Rachel Whiteread refused to have an anti-graffiti coating applied to the concrete surface of her library. Her view was: 'If someone sprays a swastika on it we can try to scrub it off, but a few daubed swastikas would really make people think about what's happening in their society.'

Her comments echoed my own feelings on seeing the swastika graffiti on the pavement near Reichenau. It was ugly, but in a way it was more informative than the Reichenau memorial itself. It told me something about the dangerous allure of Nazism to those in society – like the disaffected veterans who gathered at the Bozner Platz on *Kristallnacht* – who feel, in a popular twenty-first-century phrase, 'left behind'.

In Innsbruck, right in the centre of town, there is now a memorial to the Jews murdered on *Kristallnacht*. In 1995 the Provincial Youth Government proposed erecting one. A design competition followed, among school pupils, and in 1997 a tall, slender Menorah (Jewish candelabra), bearing the names of the victims, was unveiled on the Landhausplatz. This is a square in which public concerts are staged in summer, and which has been landscaped to encourage skateboarding. I feel it is entirely appropriate, and uplifting, that this memorial – designed and called for by the young – sits in a place whose purpose is to attract the young, a place where they hang out, dance and listen to music – and now absorb some of the past.

Memorials to victims are usually public expressions of personal remembrance. But they can also be more personal and intimate. Somewhat like the blue plaques in Britain, celebrating the residences of notable figures from the past, Vienna has its *Steine der Erinnerung* – memorial stones – especially in the Jewish quarter of Leopoldstadt.

These 10 cm by 10 cm brass plaques have simple messages: 'Here lived X', with their dates and fates. These *Steine* are intended as little memorials you come across accidentally, embedded in the pavement outside the person's last known home. The *Steine* commemorate anyone who fell victim to the Nazis, whether murdered, forced to flee, or driven to suicide – and they are not restricted to Jewish victims. The *Steine*, sitting flush with other cobblestones or paving, are an eloquent representation of the way in which, until 1938, Jews and other victims of the Nazis lived side by side with their neighbours.

Vienna, 24 September 2020

We have travelled to Vienna to install *Steine* for my great-grand-mother, my great-aunt and my great-uncle, outside Martha and Siegfried's home in Vienna's own Maria-Theresien-Strasse. Sofie lived here too, in her last years after *Kristallnacht*. Innsbruck has no tradition of laying such stones, so I opted to include her on the ones I commissioned for Martha and Siegfried.

I have approved the template in advance: a square metal sheet subdivided in four. The top-left stone reads simply *Hier wohnten*, 'Here lived'. Sofie, Martha and Siegfried each have their own stone, in German, which reads in English:

SOFIE SCHINDLER
27.2.1857
On 27.8.1942 Deported to Theresienstadt
Murdered on 4.9.1942

MARTHA SALZER, born Schindler
23.6.1878
On 16.5.1944 Deported to Auschwitz
Murdered in the Holocaust

SIEGFRIED SALZER
9.4.1867
On 27.8.1942 Deported to Theresienstadt
Murdered on 15.9.1942

A small crowd turned out and I invited twenty-one others from around the world to attend by Zoom. We had a short ceremony during which Marianne's voice was relayed on a portable loud-speaker from the US and she described how her grandparents had provided her with a loving home for seven years, before she fled to the US. Marianne's daughter, Alison read a blessing and I read Martha's last letter.

My cousin Richard read Kaddish in English from London and my husband Jeremy read it in Hebrew, dedicating his reading not only to the Schindlers and the Salzers, but all those who did not make it out.

Steine der Erinnerung for Martha, Sofie and Siegfried

Acknowledgements

After clearing out the cottage in which Kurt had lived, I was left with piles of papers, thirteen extraordinary photo albums and a lot of unanswered questions. I returned repeatedly to the album that was dedicated to the Café Schindler. As I mulled over the story of the café during the New Year holidays of 2017/18, I envisaged writing a private account for my children, complete with recipes.

It was my husband, Jeremy Taylor, who convinced me that I should write 'a proper book'. It felt like a fitting thing to do after the death of my father and as a way of laying to rest some of my more troubled feelings about him. And so it is to Jeremy and our three grown-up children that this book is dedicated. Jeremy has been unstinting in his support for this project. He and our children, Sepha, Georgia and Zac, have put up with me living for months at a time in 1938, as well as my tendency to combine our summer holidays with obscure pieces of research and long treks up mountains.

I also have a second dedication to the lost and unremembered. To those like Egon Dubsky, Sofie Schindler, and Martha and Siegfried Salzer, whose names would otherwise disappear without trace.

My sisters Sophie Letellier and Caroline Bucknall have been generous with their memories of our family life. Sophie – a talented graphic designer – captured our complicated family tree on paper. I am also more grateful than I can say to Caroline for looking after Kurt, her stepfather, when I was too angry with him and alienated from him to do so.

My daughter Georgia tested and wrote up our recipes and we had a lot of fun together deciding which of them should be included. My other daughter Sepha helped with proofreading and the final selection of photos.

I also owe an enormous debt of gratitude to my partners at Withers, who allowed me to take a three-month sabbatical in 2019 to travel, research and write. My wonderful team of employment lawyers held the fort and ensured that clients were looked after impeccably in my absence. My secretary Bev Marshall deserves a special mention. She coped patiently with my literary double-life – lawyer during the week and writer at weekends – as well as the avalanche of German-language emails that poured into my work inbox.

I am a trustee of an inspirational creative-writing charity called the Arvon Foundation. To improve my advocacy for the trust, I booked myself onto a family memoir course in April 2018. It was taught by Ian Marchant and Lois Pryce. Before the course, I was required to deliver 3,000 words. It was the stimulus I needed to crack on and get some writing done. Both Ian and Lois were kind and encouraging, and I enjoyed the week enormously: the incredible staff at the Hurst, the collective cooking, the tutorials, and above all the time and space to learn the craft of writing. My fellow writers were good company and we kept in touch as a mutually supportive group and met sporadically to discuss our progress on our highly varied and interesting projects.

Then I met the wonderful Ben Dunn, who was just launching his career as a literary agent and, on day one of his new life, agreed to take me on as a novice author. I could not have got this project off the ground without his wise and patient counsel. I had no idea when I embarked on it how much work went into a book like this. Ben introduced me to Rupert Lancaster, my editor at Hodder & Stoughton, and his brilliant team, who encouraged and guided me throughout. Thanks in particular to everyone at Hodder who has worked on the book, and in particular Anna Baty, Cameron Myers, Rebecca Folland, Sarah Christie and Kate

Brunt as well as Barry Johnston who proofread the manuscript and Mouse Vickers who took many of the beautiful photos that appear in the book..

As I finalised my research and wrote up the various aspects of my family's life, I realised how many strands there were to it. I was in danger of becoming overwhelmed by the complexity of what I had taken on. My friend, Mark Hawkins-Dady, debated every chapter with me and helped me over several months to weave those strands together into a more coherent whole. I owe him an enormous debt of gratitude.

And then there is a whole host of other people who have given generously of their time, ideas and considerable erudition. These include Jeffrey Ohrenstein of the Memorial Scrolls Trust in London, who explained to me the history of the scrolls that the trust looks after, as well as Adam Hanus at the Municipal Muzeum in Horažďovice. The staff at the Wiener Library in London, and at the archives I visited in Vienna, Linz and Innsbruck, not only answered questions, but suggested new sources that I had not previously considered.

I had been cautious about talking about my project in Innsbruck. I was worried that my digging around in the past would alienate old friends and that new friends would be dismissive about an amateur historian writing up her family history. I could not have been more wrong. In 2018, I visited the Innsbruck City Archives for the first time and chatted to Lukas Morasch and his team. Lukas was helpful and encouraging, and his team showed me pictures I had never seen of the Café Schindler.

My friends Claudia and Josef were very supportive, even going so far as to drive us all the way to the Zillertal so that I could write about Philippe Halsman. I also received warm and generous help on sources, and answers to my almost unlimited questions. First and foremost here, historian Niko Hofinger deserves a special mention. He had contacted me fifteen or so years ago, as he wanted to interview my father. I deflected him at the time: Kurt was ill, and I could not imagine that much good would come of such an interview. I regret that decision now. But out of that initial and rather unfruitful encounter we developed a strong bond, and Niko answered questions and suggested sources. His knowledge of the Jews of Innsbruck and their fate seemingly knows no limits. To crown it all, he also discovered that we were distantly related.

Niko introduced me in 2017 to Michael Guggenberger, who had written an essay on my grandfather and *Kristallnacht*, and wanted me to comment on it. Michael too became a friend and helped me decipher handwriting and original documents when I could not make head nor tail of them. Michael had a long-term project writing up the fate of all the Jews affected by *Kristallnacht*. In 2019, I was honoured to be asked by him to record the English-language version of his completed script, so that it could be downloaded as a tour guide and teaching aid.

Both Michael and Niko read drafts of this book, and it has benefited enormously from their comments. They helped iron out inconsistencies and mistakes that had crept in. Any that remain are, of course, entirely my responsibility.

I also met Gerda Hofreiter, another local historian who had interviewed both my father and Peter Tray towards the end of their lives. Gerda kindly shared with me her interview notes and her impressions of both men. Through long afternoons in the archives, and through friends, I made contact with other historians and teachers in Innsbruck and Linz, who were all very helpful along the way. They include: Horst Schreiber, Irmgard Bibermann, Sabine Pitscheider, Regina Knitel and Verena Wagner.

In October 2018, I flew to the United States to meet a whole branch of the family I had not met before: the Kafkas. I loved meeting John Kafka and his wife Marian, their sons Alex and Paul, and their families. John sadly died in 2020 and I am so very glad that I did meet him. Paul Kafka Gibbons has become a firm friend, and I relish our sporadic FaceTime calls.

I also met Marianne Cornish and her brothers Tom and Ronald Salzer. Tom was the first family member I contacted, at the suggestion of my son Zac, who introduced me to the world of online genealogy. Tom was generous. He dug out family photos I had never seen before and sent me a CD of them. Marianne, meanwhile, was kind and gentle: a soothing balm for some of the anger I felt towards my father. Marianne's daughter Alison pulled out Martha Salzer's diary and sent it to me. I also tracked down Susan Lovell, great-granddaughter of Lilli and Eduard Bloch, who was herself fascinated by the era I was researching, and was delighted to find she had cousins in England and France. With the help of all these people, I put together our collective family tree.

Coincidence also played a considerable role. I was writing part of the original proposal one evening when I received an email, out of the blue, from a Jeremy Shindler. He was researching his family history and thought we might be related. We met up and he helped me piece together our shared roots in Upper Silesia, as descendants of the Schindler tribe.

My cousin Richard Tray also reacted with enormous warmth when I approached him. Given how badly our fathers had fallen out, it was a tremendous relief to find that we had so much in common. Curiously, the week before I contacted him, also out of the blue, he himself had just been approached by Gabrielle Müller, granddaughter of Richard Müller, Innsbruck's best photographer of the era. Gabrielle and I struck up a warm friendship that culminated in our meeting her incredible parents, Herbert and Margot. Herbert had played jazz in the café in the 1950s. Herbert chatted to my son Zac about jazz. He and Zac (himself an aspiring jazz musician) are now firm friends. Gabrielle later gave me the original glass plate of a Richard Müller photo of the café – a very generous gesture.

The Jewish community in Innsbruck was kind enough to open its doors to me, too. Thomas Lipschütz showed us around the beautiful synagogue and presented me with a 6-kilo, three-volume history of the Jews of the Tyrol. It was great for research, although I did wonder what EasyJet would make of the additional weight. Dr Esther Fritsch, the honorary president of the Jewish community in Innsbruck, was also welcoming and happy to debate various aspects of community life and memorials with me. Stefan Gritsch, secretary of the Jewish community, was always on hand with helpful suggestions and explanations.

As I sat alone with my laptop in countless cafés in London, Innsbruck, Vienna and Linz writing up and editing this book, I also developed an enormous gratitude to the baristas in those cafés who kept me caffeinated over those many, many months. I like to think I was doing my bit to keep alive the coffee-house tradition: somewhere to think, read and write.

Recipes

Kaiserschmarrn

Kurt's signature dish. Essentially a light pancake batter made with beaten egg white and chopped into bite-sized chunks in the pan, and sprinkled with sugar so that it caramelises.

Ingredients
200g plain flour
20g sugar
Pinch of salt
3 eggs
300ml milk
Butter for frying

Method
Separate the eggs and whisk the whites until stiff. Mix together the flour, most of sugar, salt, egg yolks and milk until you have a smooth batter. Fold in the egg whites. Melt the butter in a pan and fry a ladle or two of the mixture at a time. As soon as it has set, chop the pancake into rough strips and sprinkle with the remaining sugar while still in the pan, cooking it further until the strips have caramelised. Turn them out onto a plate, dust with icing sugar and serve with stewed fruit: apples or plums work best.

Karl Santol's Cheesecake V

From his 1914 book *Der Praktische Konditor*, p. 113, author's own translation.

Ingredients
500g cream cheese
1 egg yolk
100g sugar
70g plain flour
Pinch of salt
Juice of half a lemon
4 dessert spoons milk or sour cream
6 stiffly beaten egg whites
Handful of raisins

Method
For the sponge base, mix 100g unsalted butter, 100g sugar, 1 egg, 100g self-raising flour, ½ teaspoon baking powder, 1 tablespoon milk and blind bake (or alternatively use crushed digestive-style biscuits with butter pressed in the baking tin).

Mix the first seven ingredients together to a smooth filling. Fold the egg whites into the cream cheese. Put half of the mixture on top of the blind-baked sponge base. Add a handful of raisins and then add the rest of the cream cheese. Bake in a hot oven at 180°/gas mark 4 until golden brown and the surface is beginning to crack.

Apfelstrudel (Apple Strudel)

Traditional strudel is made with a *gezogener Teig* – a pulled dough, made from plain flour, oil, salt and water. It needs a skilled hand. It has to be rolled out so thinly, on clean cloth, that the patissier can read the local newspaper through its pale floured surface, then slicked with a little melted butter. If you are not ready for the full Austrian experience, a good frozen or chilled puff pastry works well.

Ingredients

1 roll of puff pastry (or 300g plain flour, 120–130ml water and 3 dessert spoons of sunflower oil, kneaded into a smooth dough and allowed to rest)

Soft, fresh white breadcrumbs

A generous handful of any of pine nuts, walnuts, almonds, currants, raisins

A mix of 2–3 peeled and roughly chopped cooking and eating apples

1 tsp cinnamon

2–4 tbsp sugar

25g butter

Method

Melt the butter in a frying pan, add the breadcrumbs and cook until golden. Add nuts and apples. Season with cinnamon and as little sugar as you think you can get away with. Cook gently until they begin to soften. Allow to cool (or the mixture will melt the pastry). Roll out the pastry into a 3–4mm-thick oblong. Without overfilling, add the cooled apple/breadcrumb/nut mixture in a strip down the middle. Carefully pull the sides up and together around the mixture and seal them down the middle, by pinching the pastry together. Fold up the two ends of the pastry and seal, forming a neat parcel.

Prick to allow steam to escape, and then brush with a lightly beaten egg before baking in a 200° oven (gas mark 6) for 10–15 minutes until golden. Allow to cool and dust with icing sugar. Serve with whipped cream, custard or ice cream.

Linzertorte

Linzertorte is a particularly lovely cake. Whilst *Apfelstrudel* has made its way into the rest of the world, this cake – native to Linz and allegedly one of the oldest cakes in the world – is relatively unknown outside Austria.

The pastry base incorporates freshly ground hazelnuts or almonds, making it crumbly, nutty and light. This is layered with raspberry or redcurrant jam and topped off with a plaited pastry lattice, which allows the molten jam to bubble through the gaps. Some sort of culinary alchemy occurs when baked sweet jam and nutty pastry are combined with whipped cream, creating a contrast between the sharpness of the caramelised jam, the nutty pastry and the sweet cream.

Ingredients
For the pastry:
250g plain flour
250g cold butter
50g icing sugar
185g ground hazelnuts (or ground almonds if easier to find)
¾ tsp ground cinnamon (+ more to taste)
¼ tsp ground cloves (+ more to taste)
Pinch of salt
Zest of a lemon
For the filling/topping:
3–4 tbsp redcurrant jam
Zest of a lemon
Flaked almonds or hazelnuts to taste

Method
Pour the flour into a large bowl. Chop up the butter into small cubes and rub it into the flour until the mixture resembles breadcrumbs. Add in the ground nuts, icing sugar, spices and a pinch of salt. Grate in the lemon zest. Without overworking the dough, bring it together using a teaspoon or two of water to form a pastry. Split the dough in half and form two balls of pastry. Wrap them in cling film and leave them to rest in the fridge for 30 minutes.

Set the oven to 180° (gas mark 4). Grease the bottom and sides of a round 8-inch (20cm) cake tin. If desired, dust with polenta flour or breadcrumbs to help prevent sticking. Press 2/3 of the dough into the base of the tin to a depth of about 1cm: use your knuckles to flatten it down. Blind bake for 20 minutes. Meanwhile, roll the remaining dough into several small sausages for the lattice. After 20 minutes, take the pastry base out of the oven. Spread the jam on the base and add the lattice. Put this back in the oven for 25 minutes. Once cooled, dust with icing sugar and flaked almonds and serve.

Das Schindler *Sacher Torte*

Bernhard Baumann, the owner of 'Das Schindler' on the site of the old Café Schindler, has kindly allowed me to reproduce his chef's version of *Sachertorte*.

Ingredients
For the cake base:
180g dark chocolate
180g butter
150g icing sugar
150g granulated sugar
6 egg yolks
6 egg whites
180g flour
200g apricot jam
For the icing:
220g dark chocolate
250g granulated sugar
180ml water

Method
Beat room-temperature butter with the icing sugar until fluffy. Add the egg yolks one at a time and then the melted chocolate. Beat the egg whites with the granulated sugar until stiff and fold gently into the chocolate mix. Sieve the flour into the mixture and

fold in gently. Pour into a 25cm cake tin and bake at 180°/gas mark 4 for 40–50 minutes. Allow to cool to 50°, put on a flat surface and cut into three layers. Spread the apricot jam on each layer and place one layer on top of another. For the icing, melt all the ingredients together and stir well. Ice the cake and serve with whipped cream.

Selected Bibliography

General History

Albrich, Thomas (Ed.), *Jüdisches Leben im Historischen Tirol*, Vols 2 and 3, (Haymon Verlag, Innsbruck-Wien, 2013).

Capková, Katerina, *Czechs, Germans, Jews? National Identity and the Jews of Bohemia*, (Berghahn, New York, 2015).

Davies, Norman, *God's Playground, A History of Poland, Vol. 11, 1795–to the Present*, (Oxford University Press, Oxford, 2005).

Iggers, Wilma, *Die Juden in Böhmen und Mähren – ein historisches Lesebuch*, (C.H. Beck, Munich, 1986).

Okey, Robin, *The Habsburg Monarchy, c. 1765–1918: From Enlightenment to Eclipse*, (European studies, Palgrave Macmillan, 2001).

Schama, Simon, *Belonging: The Story of the Jews 1492–1900*, (The Bodley Head, London, 2017).

Steinberg, Jonathan, *Bismarck, A Life*, (Oxford University Press, Oxford, 2011).

Wistrich, Robert, *The Jews of Vienna in the Age of Franz Joseph*, (Oxford University Press, Oxford, 1989).

Wodzinski, Marcin and Spyra, Janusz, *Jews in Silesia*, (University of Wroclaw, Cracow, 2001).

First World War

Butcher, Tim, *The Trigger*, (Vintage, London, 2014).

Keegan, John, *The First World War*, (The Bodley Head, London, 2014).

Keller, Tait, *Apostles of the Alps*, (University of North Carolina Press, Chapel Hill, 2016).

Lussu, Emilio, *A Soldier on the Southern Front*, (Rizzoli International Publications, New York, 2014).

Morscher, Lukas, *Tiroler Alltagsleben im Ersten Weltkrieg*, (Haymon Verlag, Innsbruck-Wien, 2014).

Murisi, Paoli, *Hell in the Trenches: Austro-Hungarian Stormtroopers and the Italian Arditi in the Great War*, (Helion & Company Ltd, Warwick, 2018).

Schindler, John, *Isonzo: The Forgotten Sacrifice of the Great War*, (Praeger, Westport, CT, 2001).

Smith, David James, *One Morning in Sarajevo: 28 June 1914*, (Weidenfeld & Nicholson, London, 2008).

Stephens, Philip, *The Great War Explained*, (Pen and Sword, Barnsley, 2012).

Thompson, Mark, *The White War: Life and Death on the Italian Front, 1915–1919*, (Faber and Faber, London, 2008).

Von Lichem, Heinz, *Spielhahnstoss und Edelweiss. Die Frieden und Kriegsgeschichte der Tiroler Hochgebirgstruppe 'Die Kaiserschützen' von ihren Anfängen bis 1918, K. k. Tiroler Llandesachützen-Kaiserschützen-Regimenter Nr. 1, Nr. II, Nr. III*, (Stocker, Graz, 1977).

The Halsman Trial

Hoffinger, Niko, *Man spricht nicht gerne von dem Prozess, es sind noch zu viele Fremde da. Die Halsman-Affaire in Innsbruck, 1928-1991*: https://www.academia.edu/22287960

Pollack, Martin, *Anklage Vatermord. Der Fall Philipp Halsman*, (Fischer, Frankfurt, 2004).

Ratner, Austin, *The Jump Artist*, (Penguin, London, 2013).

Second World War

Achrainer, Martin, 'Der Chef fährt Porsche. Aus dem Leben eines Hasardeurs', in *Gaismair-Jahrbuch 2004*, (StudienVerlag, Innsbruck, 2003).

Albrich, Thomas (Ed.), *Die Täter des Judenpogroms 1938 in Innsbruck*, (Haymon Verlag, Innsbruck-Wien, 2016).

Bendler Gebhard, 'Alpinismus . . . eine spezifisch deutsche Kunst?' Deutsch_nationalismus und Antisemitismus in den Innsbrucker Bergsteigervereinen 1869–1938, (Diplomarbeit 2009)

Bernard, Philippa, *Out of the Midst of the Fire*, (Westminster Synagogue, London, 2005).

Bishof, G., Pelinka, A., Lassner, A., et al., *The Dollfuss/Schuschnigg Era in Austria, a Reassessment*, (Transaction Publishers, New Brunswick and London, 2003).

Breit, Johannes, *Das Arbeitserziehungslager Innsbruck-Reichenau und die Nachkriegsjustiz*, (Maturafachbereichsarbeit Juni 2007, S 41, 48–50).

Breit, Johannes, *Das Auffang und Arbeitserziehungslager Innsbruck-Reichenau von 1941 bis 1945 von 2017*, extract: https://www.tyroliaverlag.at/leseproben/9783702235703/leseprobe.pdf

Brustein, William and King, Ryan, 'Anti-Semitism in Europe Before the Holocaust', in *International Political Science Review*, Vol. 25, No. 1, pp. 35–53, 2004: https://journals.sagepub.com/doi/pdf/10.1177/0192512104038166

Cesarani, David and Kushner, Tony, *The Internment of Aliens in Twentieth Century Britain*, (Routledge, Abingdon, Oxon, 1993).

Chappell, Connery, *Island of Barbed Wire*, (Robert Hale Ltd, London, 1984).

Clay Large, David, *Between Two Fires: Europe's Path in the 1930s*, (W.W. Norton & Company, New York, 1990).

Eppel, Peter (Ed.), *Widerstand und Verfolgung in Tirol, 1934–1945*, Dokumentationsarchiv des Oesterreichischen Widerstandes, (Österreichischer Bundesverlag, Vienna, 1984).

Festschrift: *Anlässlich des fünfzigjährigen Bestandes des Linzer Tempels, die Juden von Linz*, (Jüdischen Kultusgemiende, Linz, 1927).

Gillman, Peter and Leni, *Collar the Lot*, (Quartet Books, London, 1980).

Guggenberger, Michael, '"Wenn er kaputt geht, ist's auch gleich!" – Hugo Schindler als Opfer im Innsbrucker Novemberpogrom', in Gaismair-Jahrbuch 2018, (StudienVerlag, Innsbruck, 2017).

Hamann, Brigitte, *Hitler's Edeljude*, (Piper, Munich, 2008).

Kaltenegger, Roland, *Operation Alpenfestung*, (FA Herbig, Munich, 2000).

Kubizek, August, *The Young Hitler I Knew*, (Pen & Sword, Barnsley, 2011).

Macher, Flora, *The Austrian Banking Crisis of 1931: One Bad Apple Spoils the Whole Bunch*, London School of Economics: http://eprints.lse.ac.uk/87151/1/wp274.pdf

Maximilian, Oswald, 'SA-Standartenführer Johann Mathoi' in: Thomas Albrich (Ed.), *Die Täter des Judenpogroms 1938 in Innsbruck*, (Haymon Verlag, Innsbruck-Wien, 2016).

Mayrhofer, Fritz and Schuster, Walter, *Nationalsozialismus in Linz*, (Archiv der Stadt Linz, Linz, 2002).

Pirker, Peter, *Codename Brooklyn: Jüdische Agenten im Feindesland Die Operation Greenup 1945*, (Tyrolia Verlag, Innsbruck-Wien, 2019).

Schreiber, Horst, *Die Machtübernahme. Die Nationalsozialisten in Tirol 1938/39*, (Haymon Verlag, Innsbruck, 1994).

Schreiber, Horst, '"Nach marktmäßigen Grundsätzen" – Die "Arisierung" der Firma Dubsky' in: Thomas Albrich (Ed.), 'Wir lebten wie sie . . .', *Jüdische Lebengeschichten aus Tirol und Vorarlberg*, (Haymon Verlag, Innsbruck, 1999).

Schreiber, Horst, 'Die Essig und Spirituosenfabrik Dubsky' in: Gabriele Rath, Andrea Sommerauer, Martha Verdorfer (Eds.), *Bozen Innsbruck – Zeitgeschichtliche Stadtrundgänge*, (Folio Verlag, 2000).

Schreiber, Horst, 'Jüdische Geschäfte in Innsbruck – Eine Spurensuche', Projekt des Abendgymnasiums Innsbruck, Tiroler Studien zu Geschichte und Politik 1, Michael Gaismair Gesellschaft (Ed.), (StudienVerlag, 2001).

Schreiber, Horst, 'Werner Hilliges: Leiter der Gestapo Innsbruck' in: *Nationalsozialismus und Faschismus in Tirol und Südtirol: Opfer, Täter, Gegner*, Tiroler Studien zu Geschichte und Politik, Michael Gaismair Gesellschaft (Ed.), (StudienVerlag, 2008).

Schreiber, Horst, *1938*, (StudienVerlag, Innsbruck, 2018).

Silverman, Lisa, *Becoming Austrians, Jews and Culture Between the World Wars*, (Oxford University Press, Oxford, 2012).

Smith, Daniel, *The Lives of the Jews of Horažd'ovice*, (The Westminster Synagogue, London, undated): https://westminstersynagogue.org/sites/westminstersynagogue.org/files/images/The Jews of Horazd'ovice (2012).pdf

Staudinger, E., Scheucher, A., Ebenhoch, U., and Schneipl, J., *Zeitbilder 7&8 Geschichte und Sozialkunde Politische Bilding, Vom Ende des Ersten Weltkrieges bis in die Gegenwart*, (Österreichischer Bundesverlag Schulbuch GmbH & Co, KG, Wien, 2012).

Wagner, Verena, *Jüdischer Lebenswelten, Zehn Linzer Biographien*, (Archiv der Stadt, Linz).

Winter, Tobias: *Die deutsche Archivwissenschaft und das 'Dritte Reich': disziplinge-schichtliche Betrachtungen von den 1920ern bis in die 1950er Jahre*, (Duncker & Humblot, Berlin, 2018).

General

Allen, Stewart Lee, *The Devil's Cup*, (Cannongate, Edinburgh, 2000).

Bürgin, Dr Eugin, *Kaffee*, (Sigloch Edition, Würzburg, 1978).

Clare, George, *Last Waltz in Vienna*, (Macmillan, London, 1981).

De Waal, Edmund, *The Hair with the Amber Eyes*, (Chatto & Windus, London, 2010).

Dynner, Glenn, *Yankel's Tavern*, (Oxford University Press, Oxford, 2014).

Eckert, Anneliese and Gerhard, *Das Kaffee Brevier*, (Verlag Hölker, Münster, 1979).

Frie, Roger, *Not in my Family*, (Oxford University Press, Oxford, 2017).

Kafka, John S., *Psychoanalysis: Unveiling the Past – Discovering the New*, (IP Books, New York, 2016).

Mahler, Gustav, *Letters to his Wife*, (Faber and Faber, London, 2005).

Nieman, Susan, *Learning from the Germans*, (Penguin, London, 2019).

O'Connor, Anne Marie, *The Lady in Gold*, (First Vintage Books, US, 2015).

Santol, Carl, *Der Praktische Konditor*, (Verlag JJ Arndt, Leipzig, 1914).

Notes on Sources

Chapter 1: Sofie and Samuel
1. https://jewishreviewofbooks.com/articles/1132/polands-jewish-problem-vodka/

Chapter 2: Imperial Gherkins
1. August Kubizek, *The Young Hitler I Knew*, (Pen & Sword, Barnsley, 2011).

Chapter 3: Compote
1. Martha Salzer's diary, 19 October 1915.
2. Martha's diary, 27 July 1917.
3. Martha's diary, 8 August 1916.
4. Martha's diary, 26 October 1915.
5. Martha's diary, 23 August 1917.
6. Richard McLanathan, *The Art of Marguerite Stix*, (Harry N. Abrams, New York, 1977), p. 15.
7. Thomas Albrich, in *Jüdisches Leben im Historischen Tirol*, Vol. 2, p. 310.
8. Martin Achrainer, in *Jüdisches Leben im Historischen Tirol*, Vol. 2, p. 291.
9. Achrainer, in *Jüdisches Leben im Historishen Tirol*, p. 325; my translations.

Chapter 4: Rum on the Eastern Front
1. Martha's diary, 25 November 1915.
2. John Keegan, *The First World War*, (Pimlico edition, 1999), p. 174.
3. Richard McLanathan, *The Art of Marguerite Stix*, p. 15.
4. Lukas Morscher, *Tiroler Alltagsleben im Ersten Weltkrieg*, p. 69.
5. Martha's diary, 16 October 1915.

Chapter 5: Schnapps on the Southern Front

1. Quoted by Verena Wagner, *Linz 1918/1938*, Archiv der Stadt Linz, 2018, p. 81.
2. Mark Thompson, *The White War*, (Faber and Faber, 2008), p. 324.

Chapter 6: Food Riots

1. Eric Hobsbawm, *Interesting Times: A Twentieth-Century Life*, (Pantheon, New York, 2002), p. 8.
2. Lukas Morscher, *Tiroler Alltagsleben*, p. 131.
3. Morscher, p. 143.
4. Morscher, p. 188.
5. *Innsbrucker Nachrichten*, 2 August 1918, No. 147, p. 2, cited in Morscher, p. 117.
6. Horst Schreiber, *Die Machtübernahme*, in Innsbruck.
7. Gaismair-Jahrbuch, 2018, essay by Sabine Pitscheider, p. 164.
8. *Innsbrucker Nachrichten*, no. 280, 6 December 1919.
9. *Tiroler Anzeiger*, 6 December 1919.
10. *Deutsche Zeitung*, 7 December 1919.
11. Brustein, William and King, Ryan, 'Anti-Semitism in Europe Before the Holocaust', in *International Political Science Review*, Vol. 25, No. 1, 35–53, 2004.
12. Sabine Albrich-Falch, *Jüdisches Leben in Nord-und Südtirol von Herbst 1918 bis Frühjahr 1938* and https://www.uibk.ac.at/zeitgeschichte/zis/library/albrich.html
13. *Volkszeitung*, 2 October 1920.

Chapter 7: Apfelstrudel

1. William H. Ukers, *All About Coffee*, (The Tea and Coffee Trade Journal Company, 1922).
2. Kurt Drexel and Monika Fink, *Musikgeschichte Tirols*, Innsbruck, 2001, Vol. 3, p. 584.
3. 'Konditorei-Café Schindler täglich 5-Uhr–Tee mit Tanz unter der Leitung des Herrn Konstant der Tanzschule Schwott. Bis 2 Uhr früh geöffnet. Voranzeige: ab 15 Jänner Jazzband Kapelle Sar-Seidle', *Innsbrucker Nachrichten*, 8 January 1925, p. 10.

Chapter 8: The Matchmaker's Daughter

1. From a letter to John Kafka from Trude now in the Washingon Holocaust Museum.
2. John S. Kafka, M.S., M.D., *Psychoanalysis*, p. xviii.

Chapter 10: Anschluss

1. Thomas Albrich, *Jüdisches Leben im Historischem Tirol*, p. 86.
2. Brigitte Hamann, *Edeljude*, p. 221.
3. *Mander, s'isch Zeit!* – South Tyroler dialect for 'Männer es ist Zeit'.
4. Horst Schreiber, *Die Machtübernahme*.

Chapter 11: Postcards

1. In her own account of that time, which is in the US Holocaust Museum.
2. *Collier's* magazine.
3. *Collier's*. Bloch's actual words: 'What was he now to do to the people I loved?'
4. 'Mitteilungen des Deutschvölkischen Turnvereines Urfahr', March 1938, 'Adolf Hitler in Urfahr' interview with the postmaster's widow and one-time neighbour of the Hitler family.
5. Albert Speer, *Spandauer Tagebücher*, (Propyläen/Ullstein, Berlin and Frankfurt am Main, 1975), pp. 142 ff.
6. *Collier's*, 1941.
7. Horst Schreiber, *Die Machtübernahme*.
8. Thomas Albrich, *Jüdisches Leben im Historischen Tirol*, p. 193.
9. *Collier's*.
10. Hamann, *Hitler's Edeljude*, p. 286.

Chapter 15: Brighton Beach

1. Grete Köfler, *Widerstand und Verfolgung in Tirol 1934–1945*, Vol. 1, (Österreichischier Bundesverlag, Vienna, 1984), p. 445.
2. Horst Schreiber, in his article 'Innsbruck im Bombenkrieg'.

Chapter 20: The Gauleiter's Guest

1. Michael Kasper, 'Franz Hofer Jänner bis Mai 1945', Innsbruck, June 2002, from: 'Proseminar aus Zeitgeschichte: NS Herrschaftsapparat in der Provinz, Sommersemester 2002'.

Epilogue: Memory and Memorials

1. Quoted by Susan Nieman, from a 2000 report, in her book, *Learning from the Germans*, 2019.

Picture Research by Jane Smith Media

Cover: Project Archive, Niko Hofinger

Page xvi/16: Caroline Bucknall

Page xxi/21: Private Archive of Markus Wilhem

Page xxii/23: Sophie Schindler

Page 4: Hugo Schindler/ Elizabeth Vickers

Page 11: Samuel Schindler

Page 15: Stadtarchiv Innsbruck

Page 18: Jewish Museum in Prague

Page 21: Meriel Schindler

Page 27: United States Holocaust Museum/ courtesy of Dr John S. Kafka

Page 28: Meriel Schindler

Page 29: The History Collection / Alamy Stock Photo

Page 30: Keystone Press / Alamy Stock Photo/KEYSTONE Pictures USA

Page 39: Hugo Schindler/ Elizabeth Vickers

Page 40: Stadtarchiv Innsbruck

Page 41: Hugo Schindler/ Elizabeth Vickers

Page 42: Private archive of Tom Salzer

Page 45: Private Archive of Tom Salzer

Page 46: Hugo Schindler

Page 50 top: Private archive of Tom Salzer

Page 50 bottom: Private archive of Tom Salzer

Page 57: Bibliothek Ferdinandeum

Page 71 top: Otto Schindler/ Elizabeth Vickers

Page 71 bottom: Otto Schindler/ Elizabeth Vickers

Page 72: Stadtarchiv Innsbruck

Page 77: Private archive Tom Salzer

Page 78: Geni/ private archive Tom Salzer

Page 82 top: Photographer unknown/ Elizabeth Vickers

Page 82 bottom: Photographer unknown/ Elizabeth Vickers

Page 83: Photographer unknown/ Elizabeth Vickers

Page 91: private archive Tom Salzer

Page 98: Jeremy Taylor

Page 105: (Abendblatt, 28 May 1919, No.100 page 3) Project Archive, Niko Hofinger

Page 106: Mary Evans / Imagno

Page 120: Stadtarchiv Innsbruck

Page 123 top: Hugo Schindler/ Elizabeth Vickers

Page 123 bottom: Richard Muller/ Gabriele Müller

Page 130: Stadtarchiv Innsbruck

Page 134: Photographer unknown/ Elizabeth Vickers

Page 138: Private archive of Tom Salzer

Page 141 top: Hugo Schindler/ Elizabeth Vickers

Page 141 bottom: Private collection of Tom Salzer

Page 143: Erich Schindler

Page 146: Hugo Schindler/ Elizabeth Vickers

Page 149: Unknown artist/ Elizabeth vickers

Page 167: Stadtarchiv Innsbruck

Page 169: Stadtarchiv Innsbruck

Page 178: Stadtarchiv Innsbruck

Page 180: Bpk / Deutsches Historisches Museum / Arne Psille

Page 195: Stadtarchiv Innsbruck

Page 196: INTERFOTO / Alamy Stock Photo

Page 197: Stadtarchiv Innsbruck

Page 199: Project Archive, Niko Hofinger

Page 203: akg-images

Page 205: Jewish Museum Vienna

Page 210: Stadtarchiv Innsbruck

Page 217 top: Elizabeth Vickers

Page 217 bottom: Elizabeth Vickers

Page 224: Stadtarchiv Innsbruck

Page 226: Project Archive, Niko Hofinger

Page 236: Project Archive, Niko Hofinger

Page 264: Edith Schindler/ Elizabeth Vickers

Page 290: Hugo Schindler/Elizabeth Vickers

Page 296 top: Photographer unknown/ Elizabeth Vickers

Page 296 bottom: Photographer unknown/ Elizabeth Vickers

Page 306: Tiroler Landesarchiv

Page 323: Private collection of Tom Salzer

Page 336: National Archives and Records Administration, College Park, provided by Page Pirker

Page 359 top: Photographer unknown/ Elizabeth Vickers

Page 359 bottom: Stadtarchiv Innsbruck